PRAISE FOR *STRATEGIC RI* *CRISIS MANAGEMEN*

'This is the right book at the right time – imaginative, far sighted and relevant. I take great pleasure in recommending it for anyone interested in any aspect of strategic risk and crisis management.'

Ljiljana Markovic, Academic Director, European Center for Peace and Development

'Captivating. David Rubens has brought a lifetime of scholarship and practical work on risk and crisis management to a subject we spend too little time thinking or, more importantly, doing something about. His entertaining stories and practical lessons offer a useful handbook for everyone who confronts risks and crises in today's world – that's all of us.'

General Stanley McChrystal, author of *Team of Teams*

'David Rubens provides an incredibly timely and indispensable guide, equipping managers, policy makers, and all of us with the knowledge and insights for managing complex risks that we need if we are to find a safe course through the treacherous waters that lie before us.'

Stephen E Flynn, Founding Director, Global Resilience Institute, Northeastern University

'There is an ever-increasing need to look at strategic risk and crisis management from a meta-perspective, allowing both high level integration of multiple stakeholders and ensuring that there is meaningful engagement in the issues facing communities around the world. David Rubens' book offers both a deeply researched and highly detailed academic analysis combined with a practical approach that will have real value for practitioners, whatever area of risk management they are involved in.'

Nadine Sulkowski, Project Lead, Erasmus+ BUiLD programme (Building Universities for Leading in Disaster Resilience), University of Gloucestershire

'Crisis management practitioners have recognized for years that a definitive and detailed handbook that can help all levels of those involved in crisis management planning, policy or execution is needed. This is now available, and I strongly recommend anybody and everybody interested or engaged in crisis management have this book in quick and easy reach.'

David Horobin, Head of Crisis Management, Geneva Centre for Security Policy

'Extremely useful and timely – it fills the gap between academia and practitioner, providing vital insights to discuss complex risks while providing a framework for action.'

Xavier Castellanos Mosquera, Under Secretary General, International Federation of Red Cross and Red Crescent Societies

'In a world of chaos and instability, this book matches formal academic rigour with a deep understanding of the challenges that the world is throwing at us. It offers the reader a structure and methodology that is invaluable in developing frameworks that would support our own activities within the regional and global risk environment we are all operating in.'

Marqueza Cathalina L Reyes, Senior Technical Adviser for Climate and Disaster Resilience, Climate Change Commission, Philippines

Strategic Risk and Crisis Management

A handbook for modelling and managing complex risks

David Rubens

KoganPage

Publisher's note

Every possible effort has been made to ensure that the information contained in this book is accurate at the time of going to press, and the publishers and author cannot accept responsibility for any errors or omissions, however caused. No responsibility for loss or damage occasioned to any person acting, or refraining from action, as a result of the material in this publication can be accepted by the editor, the publisher or the author.

First published in Great Britain and the United States in 2023 by Kogan Page Limited

2nd Floor, 45 Gee Street
London
EC1V 3RS
United Kingdom

8 W 38th Street, Suite 902
New York, NY 10018
USA

4737/23 Ansari Road
Daryaganj
New Delhi 110002
India

www.koganpage.com

ISBNs

Hardback 978 1 3986 0977 8
Paperback 978 1 3986 0975 4
Ebook 978 1 3986 0976 1

British Library Cataloguing-in-Publication Data

A CIP record for this book is available from the British Library.

Library of Congress Control Number

2022949920

Typeset by Integra Software Services, Pondicherry
Print production managed by Jellyfish
Printed and bound by CPI Group (UK) Ltd, Croydon, CR0 4YY

CONTENTS

ABOUT THE AUTHOR

Dr David Rubens is a Professor at the United Nations University for Peace European Centre for Peace and Development (Belgrade), where he is Programme Director for the International Postgraduate Study Programme in Strategic Risk and Crisis Management.

Dr Rubens founded the Institute of Strategic Risk Management in 2018, which has established itself as a leading platform for academics, practitioners and policy makers across the range of security, risk and crisis management-related sectors.

PREFACE

Writing this preface in August 2022, it feels that the world is in a state of flux. It is unstable, chaotic and lacking cohesion. It seems that not only the world itself but the social structures and frameworks that have been developed to support human society and human development have reached the limits of their capabilities and are crumbling under the pressures that the modern world is throwing at them. For many people, the world is a dark place, one of unknowns, uncertainties and a feeling of ever-present anxiety.

At such a time, it would be hoped that our leaders, whether political, business or academic, or from any of the other myriad sectors that make up our multi-stranded support networks, would step forward with a vision and a sense of responsibility that would allow us to believe that we were in the hands of people who had both the technical skills and the moral authority to take hard decisions in uncertain times, and to do so in a way that would ensure, as much as reasonably possible, the safety, security and wellbeing of the billions of people whose lives are being impacted by the planetary-level changes that are affecting every one of us, directly or indirectly, and will continue to affect us for the foreseeable future

If this seems to be highly emotive language, it is because these are highly emotive issues. Getting things wrong in the 2020s (in the face of challenges which are often the result of getting things wrong in preceding decades, even though then, as now, it was known that failure to engage with and respond to those challenges would merely push the problems down the road to be dealt with by future generations) is an option that can only lead to increased suffering at the community, national and global levels. These are no longer theoretical constructs but affect the food we eat, the water we drink, the air we breathe, the cities we live in and the businesses we work at.

This book is the direct outcome of two significant strands in my life over the past few years. The first was the opportunity to do doctorate-level research from a pracademic perspective at the University of Portsmouth, initially under the Department of Criminology and latterly under the newly developed Doctorate in Security and Risk Management programme. My interest in strategic risk and crisis management was the foundation for five years' work developing a model of strategic risk and crisis management that would work within non-hierarchical crisis management environments. Having completed the doctorate in 2015, I then spent the following years teaching programmes around the world in both academic and practitioner settings.

It became clear from those experiences that the vast majority of people tasked with developing high-level strategic risk and crisis management frameworks and capabilities, whether within national, city, corporate, critical national infrastructure or any other sector, had little if any awareness of the unbelievably rich work that had been done in academia on all aspects of strategic risk and crisis management, and that without that knowledge, their attempts to create effective frameworks that were both sensitive enough and robust enough to deal with the challenges that they were tasked with facing were not only limited but not fit for purpose. There was, quite simply, a basic failure to understand many of the fundamental issues that would allow them to develop the capabilities needed to prepare for and respond to the increasingly complex global challenges that we were facing.

The other strand was the Institute of Strategic Risk Management which I founded in 2018. The ISRM was created with the express purpose of establishing a platform where academics, practitioners and policy makers could come together and explore the issues that we are collectively facing in a way that would have meaning from both a conceptual and a practitioner perspective. It is clear that this is something that resonated on a deeply meaningful level, as we now have more than 30 international chapters and have developed close and collaborative relationships with some of the world's major academic institutions and non-governmental (NGO) and other organizations.

A knowledge of the academic material that underpins the strategic risk and crisis management models that are being used by governments and other agencies does not solve all of your problems, but it does give a foundation and framework to discuss complex issues in a meaningful way. I realized early on in my doctoral studies that what was missing was not more theory or policy, but rather a structure and framework that would allow those aspirations to be translated into efforts that could have influence and impact in the real world, allowing decision-makers at whatever level to be able to make better decisions and to create better outcomes.

The world is undoubtedly complex, challenging and chaotic, but the issues we are facing are not random. An understanding of the principles and material covered in this book will allow decision-makers, whether in ministries, agencies or corporate organizations, to have a better understanding of how to create a structured model of the challenging risk environment that we are operating in and to create better responses that will have real impact on real lives.

It has been a privilege to have been part of this sector for the past 30 years, and I hope that this book helps those making decisions today, and those who will become the decision-makers of tomorrow, to understand our world a little better.

ACKNOWLEDGEMENTS

A book of this nature is the result of a lifetime's journey of study, experience and exploration. However, it is also the result of thousands of conversations, lectures, symposia and other interactions with academics, practitioner, policy makers and anyone else with a view that they want to share.

I have been lucky on that journey to have had the opportunity to spend time with, learn from and be influenced (and inspired) by multiple teachers, mentors and guides.

There are too many to mention here, but some of the most significant are those who have influenced my academic journey, which includes Dr Martin Gill (University of Leicester) and Dr Francis Pakes and Dr Alison Wakefield of the University of Portsmouth.

My thanks to Lord Toby Harris, Chair of the UK National Preparedness Commission and President of the Institute of Strategic Risk Management for his guidance, friendship and support, and to all of those involved in the ISRM, whose efforts and commitment have made it the organisation it is today.

My special thanks to Dr Gavriel Schneider, Chair of the ISRM Australia New Zealand Chapter, who as friend, colleague and confidant influenced this book through our long talks during Covid-19, and whose thoughts on his concept of Presilience influenced many of my own thoughts.

Simon Rüegger and Dr Jörg Greulich had input on a number of chapters.

Marcus Griener did the heavy lifting in terms of text preparation and fine-tuning the referencing.

Thanks to the team at Kogan Page who gave support throughout the process – Isabelle Cheng, Anne-Marie Heeney, Susi Lowndes and Viv Church.

Introduction

Three decades ago, there was not enough theoretical material or research work on response to social crises and disasters to have warranted more than a footnote attesting to that fact. A paragraph could have summarized all the relevant work and activity of two decades ago. Even ten years ago, several pages might have sufficed to summarize totally the burgeoning activities in the area. The growth of the area has been exponential, not linear, and today the research efforts and theoretical advances have reached such a level as to force us to be highly selective in our coverage in this paper.

QUARANTELLI & DYNES (1977:23)[1]

If you are reading this book, then the likelihood is that you are engaged in some form or other in security or risk management, business continuity, resilience, emergency response, crisis management or any of the other myriad labels that we use to describe our attempts to create a rational understanding of risk, and to prepare ourselves, our teams and our organizations to be able to respond to and engage with a wide range of possible events in the safest and most appropriate manner.

If that is the case, then the past couple of years have undoubtedly been challenging to the point of exhaustion and collapse. Although it is easy to concentrate on Covid-19, and the catastrophic impact that has had on every aspect of our local, national and global systems, the truth is that our understanding and modelling of strategic risks were being challenged by multiple scenarios even before coronavirus arrived at the end of 2019. At the beginning of 2020, we started to realize that this was not just another pandemic scare but was the nightmare scenario that many people had been discussing, predicting and modelling, though clearly in a way that failed to prepare us adequately for the challenges that an actual pandemic has brought.

Hyper-urbanization, resource depletion, climate change, global warming and adverse weather events, critical national infrastructures, flood, droughts, global supply chain management and water scarcity were all things that had already started to move beyond what we had considered as classical risk management issues. They were now in a realm where the word *unprecedented* was being increasingly used to describe events that were outside of the planning or management scenarios of standard risk registers, and in many cases went beyond the experience or capabilities of those tasked with modelling, preparing for and engaging with exactly those sorts of large-scale and high-impact events. Their urgency and criticality were only exacerbated by the additional challenges caused by overlaying a global pandemic on those pre-existing conditions.

If there is one thing that we have learned from these events – and there is probably no community in the world that can feel they are safe or immune from the possibility of such events happening to them – it is that the tools and methodologies that we have developed around risk management seem to have reached the limit of their applicability. The events that we are seeing now are transcending the capabilities of those frameworks to engage with and respond to those events to keep us safe and secure from harm.

Recent examples of such high-impact events include the blocking of the Suez Canal by the Ever Given cargo ship, immediately disrupting around one third of global shipping and impacting the flow of supplies to shops and restaurants on our high streets; major cloud-based IT failures that impacted our abilities to stay connected with the world; floods, storms and fire that seem to have come from another dimension in terms of their scale, scope and intensity; and the sight of major cities around the world losing control of the infrastructures that support their daily activities and those of their inhabitants.

It is easy, and perhaps understandable, to see that in the face of such stressful events, we try to see them as *unprecedented*, something that goes beyond anything we have seen before, and in the face of which we have few, if any, tools that would allow us to take control, to manage and guide rather than flounder in unstructured responses that seem to have minimal impact.

The role of risk management

If there is one theme that seems to run though all these events, it is that they are seen as being unexpected, beyond what we could have reasonably foreseen, outside of our normal planning structures. And yet, from another perspective, it is exactly these sorts of events that effective risk management should be able to identify, classify, analyse and engage with. If we are not able to do that, then what is the role, if any, of risk management in the present day? The truth is that the nature, scale and impacts of the events that we are likely to see in the coming years will only become more frequent and more intense and will have potentially exponentially larger impacts in multiple ways across every aspect of our hyper-connected world.

If the classic example of cascading consequences is the *butterfly effect* where the flapping of wings in one part of the world can lead to a storm somewhere seemingly entirely unconnected, then what will be the impacts when the global infrastructures that we have developed in recent decades, and which we have become increasingly dependent on, start to fail on a regular basis?

The truth is, we are already at that stage. The complexities of the modern world have gone beyond our abilities to have a complete understanding of the hyper-connected systems that we are dependent on. The 2008 global financial collapse was just one example of where the systems themselves were so complex that there was no one who understood how they truly worked. There was certainly no organization that had the ownership or oversight to ensure that effective management practices were put in place to prevent exactly the sort of collapse that happened then and has happened in multiple sectors, with multiple examples, since then.

For those of us who have an understanding of strategic risk management, and particularly those who are able to combine practitioner experience and insight with academic study – what has increasingly been recognized as the *pracademic* approach – what is surprising is not that these fundamental risk management failures are happening. Instead, the question is why the work that has been done over decades – and in many cases since the 1970s – has not been utilized to establish a framework where these issues can be discussed in a rational manner. A familiarity with the fundamental academic models of strategic risk and crisis management would undoubtedly allow decision-makers, whether national or local governments, global corporations, critical infrastructure suppliers or anyone else who has the responsibility of managing these risk issues, to benefit from the work that has been done, the models that have been developed and the understanding that has been created.

Knowledge of the standard works of strategic risk management will not solve all the problems, but it does provide a framework for complex issues to be discussed in a rational and progressive way, and in such a manner that would undoubtedly support the development of a structured understanding of the range of risks that we are facing and the challenges that creates. Above all, it would provide the foundation for the development of the sort of integrative multi-stakeholder approaches that will be fundamental to any risk management methodologies that would be robust enough to stand up to the challenges of the high-impact events that we will be facing in the coming years.

About this book

This book is not designed to be a *How to* guide to risk management. Although it discusses multiple frameworks and best practices that would undoubtedly be of value to anyone tasked with developing risk management frameworks appropriate to their own operating environment, that is not its primary aim. It is much more to give the reader, someone who has their own experiences, insights and capabilities, an awareness of the undoubted value that a familiarity with the academic work would bring.

It has been written with the experienced risk manager in mind. Whatever context you might be operating in, whether government, corporate, NGO, critical national infrastructure, community or any other area where these issues are increasingly critical, the likelihood is that you are being tasked with the development of complex risk and crisis management programmes, often for complex organizations operating in complex environments. As such, the objective is not so much to tell people what it is that they need to do, though that is undoubtedly important. A failure to ensure the basic capabilities at the individual, team, departmental and organizational levels will significantly impact any risk management operation you try to put in place, and will almost certainly become a critical failure point in the event that such capabilities are tested in the reality of a crisis situation. Rather, the objective is to create an overarching framework that will allow all the myriad pieces, both internal and external, to come together at a time of maximum stress and to be able to function as effectively and efficiently as possible in what is likely to be a maelstrom of chaos, confusion and the breakdown of the very structures that were presumed to be in place to support your response operation.

Crisis events, and particularly the ones that we are facing currently and will continue to face for the foreseeable future, are characteristically chaotic, with high levels of the phrase that has been used to describe the current risk environment VUCA: volatile, uncertain, complex and ambiguous. That is undoubtedly true, and the inability to engage with those issues is in itself a critical failing. But given that, we must also recognize that crises and the challenges that they cause are not random. Although each crisis event is unique (and that should be one of the characteristics of a genuine crisis – you shouldn't be having the same crisis for the second time), the challenges that they create are not unique. In fact, they are highly predictable and can be considered in some ways as inevitable. Beyond the individual incidents there is a class of events called *crises* that allows us to recognize patterns, shapes, trends – and it is that recognition that takes crisis from something that is unknowable, random and chaotic, and allows us to use our skills, capabilities and experience – combined with the insights that a familiarity of the academic work that is covered in this book – to develop a range of disciplines, methodologies and frameworks that will actually prepare us for the challenges to come.

One of the foundational concepts discussed in this book is that of *wicked problems*, something first discussed in a seminal paper in 1973 by Horst Rittel and Melvin Webber.[2] Given that it is almost 50 years since that paper was published, it is perhaps surprising that the ideas of wicked problems are not more known, and that there is so often a lack of understanding of what the true significance of those ideas is even among those who are trying to give them relevance within the 2020s' risk context.

The paper that introduced this concept to the world listed 10 principles of wicked problems. The first nine are technical and have immediate relevance to the nature of the threats we are facing today, but the tenth is both the shortest and simplest. It says, quite simply: 'The planner has no right to be wrong.' Given the impacts of the crisis events that we are seeing, and the significance these have for every aspect of our lives, wherever we live in the world, it is my hope that this book will become a tool in the armoury of risk managers everywhere to understand this chaotic world we are living in, to be able to develop more effective risk and crisis management frameworks and capabilities, and above all to live up to the responsibility that we, the risk management community, have taken on to ensure, as much as possible, the safety, security and wellbeing of the organizations and communities that we are responsible for.

Endnotes

1 Quarantelli, E L and Dynes, R R (1977) Response to social crisis and disaster, *Annual Review of Sociology*, 3, 23–49

2 Rittel, H W and Webber, M M (1973) Dilemmas in a general theory of planning. *Policy Sciences*, 4(2), 155–169

1

Setting the scene

An overview of historical crisis management research

As identified in the very first words of this book, the quotation from Quarantelli and Dynes (1977),[1] the amount of academic work associated with strategic risk and crisis management had grown exponentially even when they were reviewing the sector, more than 40 years ago. With the advances in academic publishing since then, and the growth of online journals, it is literally impossible to keep up with the full range of relevant publications, and that is not including non-academic reports, government documents, post-event reviews and the full plethora of information sources available to the modern student or researcher.

However, there is a body of work that can be considered as consisting of the classic risk management academic literature, which is built on recognized authorities and academic schools of thought. For anyone to claim to be a student of this subject without having at least a passing recognition of many of these writers, and a deeper knowledge of some of them, could leave that person open to challenge from other academics, as well as other audiences that they might wish to educate or influence.

The problems that current strategic risk and crisis management students, academics and practitioners are grappling with have undoubtedly developed over the past 25 years. It could even be said that in some ways that process can no longer be discussed in terms of evolutionary change, where there is a clear line of development between previous models of strategic risk and crisis management and the current situation, but can be considered as a mutation, where there is both a generation and a species jump. Under this understanding (which is the basis of much of the work of Patrick Lagadec, one of the leading conceptualists in this field), the scale, scope and intrinsic nature of current crises seem to have become a new species, rather than one that can be considered, in conceptual terms, to have developed from what appears, at least from the present perspective, to have been a kinder, gentler, more rational and even more forgiving crisis environment.

However, although the details and applications may have changed, many of the basic concepts that established the underlying foundations on which current risk and crisis management understanding is based were developed in what could be seen as the golden years of risk and crisis management academic development, running from the 1970s through to the first years of this century. This includes work from the immediate aftermath of the 9/11 World Trade Center attacks (2001) and responses to Hurricane Katrina in 2005. The former led to a rethinking of issues concerning high-level multi-agency integration and coordination, while the latter involved a radical reconsideration of the fundamentals of crisis management. In particular, there was an awareness of a need for a new model of crisis response that wasn't dependent on military-style, centralized, hierarchical command-and-control structures.

The likelihood is that when the next major risk and crisis management failure takes place, wherever in the world you are reading this, then the root causes of that failure will be linked to work that was developed in the founding years of academic development, and for reasons that were identified even then as being critical in the development of effective risk management frameworks and capabilities.

This chapter offers a speed-dating approach to the main strands of risk and crisis management literature. It includes all the main thinkers and theorists associated with the various aspects of the subject covered in this book and it has two main objectives. The first is to give you, both the academic student and the general reader, a chance to get up to speed with risk and crisis management literature, and to develop an understanding of some of the main issues associated with the subject, so that you can then have an educated discussion about many of the issues covered here. At the same time (and to continue the speed-dating analogy), it is designed to give you the opportunity to identify academic thinkers and writers that you might find interesting, which will then give you the opportunity to get to know and explore them in greater depth.

It starts with a background, introducing the main issues that will be addressed in the book, namely the nature of 21st-century threats, the dominant role of hierarchical, command-centred crisis management systems, and the inability of crisis management policy makers to learn lessons from repeated failures to develop more effective crisis management capabilities. It then sets out a taxonomy of crises, differentiating between those incidents that can be considered part of the normal activity continuum and those that fall into genuine crisis categories. The chapter goes on to review some of the main strands in crisis management academic research, identifying the main authorities in each sector, and then looks at the issues surrounding hyper-complexity in crisis events, discussing the dilemmas and challenges that are unique to such events. Finally, the chapter examines some of the causes of repeated crisis management failures, many, if not most, of which are seen to be rooted in basic management failures rather than technological or systems breakdowns, and thus to be due to internal organizational vulnerabilities (many of which are known and acknowledged) rather than the result of the external event itself.

The nature of crises

The crises of the 21st century are undoubtedly growing larger in scale and more destructive in their impact, and any model of crisis management that claims to offer solutions to 21st-century threats will need to demonstrate an ability to react and respond in an environment defined by catastrophic crises and hyper-complexity (Lagadec, 2007).[2] These incidents can no longer be predicted by extrapolating from previous incidents, as is the case in classical risk management. Rather than regular, reproducible and recurring events that can be predicted, modelled and managed on scientific principles, they are singular and unreproducible (Weinberg, 1985).[3] As well as affecting multiple jurisdictions, undermining various policy sectors and critical infrastructures, escalating rapidly, and changing and evolving as they do so (Ansell et al, 2010),[4] they are likely to be volatile with unpredictable outcomes, requiring the integration of large numbers of agencies that may not have faced such a situation before (Turoff et al, 2008).[5]

Crisis management command systems across the world, but most notably in the United States, are firmly grounded in a centralized, hierarchical model of command and control. These are often accepted as the *de facto* default setting for crisis management, especially following the development of the formal incident command system (ICS) (Irwin, 1989; Smith & Dowell, 2000; Lutz & Lindell, 2008; Ansell et al, 2010). Dynes (1994) went so far as to label it the dominant planning model, which was specifically modelled on military command-and-control structures. The US Department of Homeland Security (DHS)-mandated Federal Emergency Management Agency (FEMA) ICS follows this model, irrespective of the nature or scale of the incident, a requirement that was maintained even after the policy changes following Hurricane Katrina (FEMA, 2007, 2011; Moynihan, 2009a). Such centralized command systems are based on a military model of command and control, in which a strictly hierarchical command structure has unity of command as the guiding principle.[6] This system may well be the framework that is best suited to support the development of enhanced capabilities able to respond to the 'ambiguity and turbulence' (Tierney & Traynor, 2004:164) of what might be considered as known and routine scenarios (Bigley & Roberts, 2001).[7] In such circumstances (and under the specific conditions discussed in the chapter on Incident Command Systems), a formalized ICS may be able to adapt to the needs of a coordinated multi-agency network management approach rather than being stuck in a systems-led hierarchical command system (Moynihan, 2009a). However, its fundamentally hierarchical structure is precisely the weakness that makes it incapable of adapting and responding to the rapidly escalating 'vicious and unmanageable circles' (Boin et al, 2003:102) associated with disaster response. It is the attempt to extend the domain of rationality and bureaucratic organizing to the uncertainty of chaotic environments (Buck et al, 2006) that has been a critical factor in the repeated failures of crisis response programmes at exactly the time that they are most needed.

Although it is the unique nature of each crisis that underpins the failure to respond appropriately or effectively, the operational causes of those failures are often both simple and predictable (Lagadec, 2005; Comfort, 2007). It is notable that once an incident goes beyond normal operational status and escalates into a 'unique and unfamiliar' problem (Munns & Bjeirmi, 1996:81), the subsequent breakdown in response capability is almost inevitably identified as being due to a breakdown in fundamental incident management functionality (Dyne, 1970; Quarantelli, 1988). These can take place at the personal (micro), agency (intermediate) or community/multi-organizational (macro) levels (Bharosa et al, 2010). Official reviews into major crisis management failures (e.g. Hurricane Katrina (2005), Fukushima (2012), the BP Deepwater Horizon oil spill into the Gulf of Mexico (2006) and the Utroya Island massacre (Norway, 2012)) repeatedly identify the same five fundamental organizational weaknesses Mintzberg listed in 1980:

- lack of understanding of the nature of the crisis;
- lack of realistic modelling of required responses;
- lack of leadership;
- lack of effective communication; and
- lack of inter-agency capability.

These are in line with Quarantelli's (1988:375) observations in his review of crisis and disaster management research findings that there were likely to be critical problems concerning communication and information flow, authority and decision-making, and failures to manage increased coordination and a loosening of the command structure. As the 9/11 Congressional report unequivocally stated, aside from the specific operational issues, the underlying fault-lines in the government's failure to develop an effective crisis management capability were founded on its 'broader inability to adapt how it manages problems to the challenges of the twenty-first century' (US Congress, 2004:353).

Risk management at the level discussed in this book can be seen as a subbranch of futurology. It is not merely a matter of identifying the threats that exist, and will continue to exist, but rather determining what exactly the threats of the future might consist of. The work of leading authorities such as Patrick Lagadec and Louise Comfort, among others in the classical field, and Bruce Schneier in the emerging field of cyber-based crisis management, has been predicated on the fact that the models of risk and crisis management that have stood us in good stead (or at least have been accepted as the natural form of crisis management, given the lack of a better or more effective model) are no longer fit for purpose in facing up to the challenges of emerging threats. From this perspective, the inability to identify the fundamental requirements of a 21st-century crisis management capability, and to learn the lessons of previous failures, is a moral issue as much as a technical or managerial one (Jarman, 1998).

Taxonomy of crises

Although there are many definitions of crises, the underlying criteria were set by Hermann (1963), with a three-stage definition taking into account threat, time pressure and uncertainty. Despite the fact that many studies presume that both time pressure (urgency) (Grint, 2008) and uncertainty (surprise)

(Veil, 2001) are prerequisites for crisis, Hermann & Dayton (2009) found that in 50 per cent of the cases they investigated there was time for consideration in the run-up to the crisis situation, which were themselves anticipated scenarios (what Boin et al (2010:1) labelled 'predicted disasters'). Only 40 per cent of the situations were considered genuine surprises, where the policy makers were caught off guard and had no plan of action.

The generic use of the phrases 'crisis' and 'crisis management' in the literature covers a wide range of scenarios, though often with little clear relevance to genuine crisis situations (Gundel, 2005):

- Lalonde (2007)[8] describes crises including natural disasters, technological catastrophe, terrorist attack or management failure;
- Quarantelli (2008) analyses 'consensus-type' crises – natural and technological disasters – and conflict crises – riots, civil strife;
- Pearson and Clair (1998) list organizational crises that co-mingle potential crisis management problems (natural disasters, terrorist attack) with normal operating management procedures (copyright infringement, bribery);
- Veil (2011) analyses corporate and organizational crises;
- Roe (2009) analyses decision-making in financial crises; and
- Van Wart and Kapucu (2011) offer examples of crises developing from human error.

Further, there is a separate field of study concerning crises and international disputes ('t Hart, Rosenthal & Kouzmin, 1993[9]; Stern, 2000; EPC, 2005).

There is also a hierarchy of urgency and potential catastrophic consequences running from incidents, accidents, conflicts, rupture and crises (Pauchant & Mitroff, 1992), which in turn are classified as normal crises (Bigley & Roberts, 2001),[10] routine crises (Moynihan, 2008, 2009b), from creeping crises (Lalonde, 2007; Hermann & Dayton, 2009);[11] Hermann & Dayton, 2009) to unthinkable and inconceivable hypercomplex catastrophic crises (Dror, 1999; Lagadec, 2007).

Rittel and Webber's 'dilemmas in a general theory of planning'

A three-level crisis hierarchy was outlined in Rittel and Webber's seminal paper 'Dilemmas in a general theory of planning' (1973),[12] which allowed crises to be categorized by their inherent characteristics rather than specific properties. The three levels were labelled:

- 'tame problems' (those that could be solved through well-established response protocols);
- 'loosely structured problems' (which need to be managed by innovative solutions developed through the collaboration between a number of different agencies that share a common working culture); and
- 'wicked problems' (those that, due to their chaotic nature and overwhelming scale, cannot be considered 'rational problems' and therefore are not approachable from a traditional crisis management perspective of solutions delivery).

As well as in crisis management, the theoretical models of wicked problems have been used to explain issues of problem solving in the UK's National Health Service (Koh, Clegg and Deighan, 2010), military decision-making (Kalloniatis, Macleod & La, 2009), disaster relief (Tatham & Houghton, 2011) and public policy (Roberts, 2010; Roe, 2009).

At the extreme end of crisis modelling, crises are considered to be those 'landscape crisis' situations (Howitt & Leonard, 2006)[13] which are so impactful that they leave historical marks (Farazmand, 2014) and project a 'serious threat to the basic structures or the fundamental values and norms of a social system' (Rosenthal & Kouzmin, 1997:280). Weick (1993:633) described the extreme end of such situations as 'cosmology episodes', when the universe is no longer a rational, orderly place. They are likely to be characterized by a total breakdown in the normal operating environment, where management and presumed crisis management responses are no longer either applicable or accessible (Roux-Dufort, 2007). As well as facing the normal pressures of urgency and uncertainty, they are situations with trans-jurisdictional impacts and potential for catastrophic damage. Situations which can be anticipated, planned and practised for, and approached under the terms of standard operating procedures, should more correctly be considered 'routine emergencies' (Howitt & Leonard, 2006)[14] rather than true crisis situations.

Crisis management and critical decision-making

Literature concerning decision-making within crisis management environments falls broadly into two areas. First, there are theoretical studies into specific aspects of decision-making within a wider context of organizational dynamics (leadership, authority, group think, peer pressure, information sharing, networking, etc), which although pertinent to crisis management are not confined to that particular activity. The second aspect involves research into operational failures within crisis and emergency management responses, attempting to identify intrinsic faults, weaknesses or vulnerabilities that have led to those failures. This includes both academic papers and official reviews, which often allow an insight into the activities of a wide range of actors involved in all aspects of those operations, including a forensic analysis of the decision-making processes that otherwise would not be available.

High-reliability organizations

On the response side of the emergency management equation, there is a relatively well-developed body of theoretical literature concerning decision-making in high-stress environments. Perrow (1984),[15] Toft and Reynolds (1994) and Turner and Pidgeon (1997) all identified specific models of critical-pathway decision-making integral to crisis escalation and resolution. These ideas were used to develop a model of systems management and decision-making within what were labelled high-reliability organizations, which combined tightly bounded and highly interdependent organizational frameworks, highly complex operating environments and a high level of criticality of their continued functionality (Weick, 1987; Roberts, 1990; Schulman, 2004[16]). Examples of studies into HROs include US air traffic control (La Porte, 1988), naval air operations (Rochlin, La Porte & Roberts, 1987; Rochlin, 1989; La Porte & Consollini, 1991), nuclear power plants (La Porte & Thomas, 1990; Schulman, 1990) and critical national infrastructure in general (de Bruijne & Eeten, 2007;[17] Santella, Steinberg & Parks, 2009). The traditional HRO model was based on the presumption that the key to successful management of highly complex and interconnected systems was increased use of technology and automated systems management, and the removal of the single most likely cause of systems failure – human error (Pauchant & Mitroff, 1992; Flood & Carson 1993; Lagadec, 1997; Dror, 1989; Schulman, Roe, van Eeten & de Bruijne, 2004;[18] de Bruijne and van Eeten, 2007[19]).

The modelling of decision-making within HROs led to a belief that the appropriate management model for highly complex environments was an incident command system based on military-style, centrally directed hierarchical command systems ('t Hart et al, 1993). The concept of a multi-agency ICS was originally developed in response to failings to deal with forest fires in California in the 1970s, and ICS literature therefore often focused on those specific issues (Weick, 1993; Irwin, 1989; Smith & Dowell, 2000; Lutz & Lindell, 2008). The theoretical justification for the universal applicability of a single ICS model is based to a large extent on a widely cited paper, Bigley and Roberts (2001),[20] which made the case for the hierarchical ICS framework as a universal template for HROs within complex and volatile environments. Despite criticisms of both the system and its implementation (Wenger, Quarantelli & Dynes, 1990; Buck et al, 2006; Moynihan, 2009a) the ICS was nominated by FEMA in 2004 as the mandated crisis management system, as a central component of the post-9/11 National Incident Management System (NIMS) (US Department of Homeland Security, 2004), a move which was confirmed following the failures of the response to Hurricane Katrina in 2005 (US DHS, 2008).

New models in emergency and crisis management

The catastrophic failures of the US emergency and crisis management community in responding to the challenges set by Hurricane Katrina and the destruction of New Orleans (2005) set in chain a radical rethink of the requirements of a crisis management capability appropriate to the challenges of the 21st century. Hurricane Katrina proved beyond doubt that the emergency management frameworks put in place after 9/11 were not only failing but were not 'fit for purpose' on any level of conception or delivery (Comfort, 2007). There is an extremely rich source of literature from the post-Katrina period, including both government reports and academic papers. The official US government response was that the current system was ineffective (White House, 2006; US House of Representatives, 2006; Ink, 2006). However, the academic community was more condemnatory, with a realization that the centrally commanded, hierarchically managed system needed revolutionary rather than evolutionary change (Comfort, 2007; Farazmand, 2007).

The nature of the debate concerning future developments in emergency management and crisis management methodologies (and one which this book broadly supports) can be summed up in the title of a paper by one of the leading conceptualists of the 'new paradigm' movement: 'A new cosmology of risks and crisis: Time for a radical shift in paradigm and practice'[21] (Lagadec, 2009). A central aspect of the new paradigm of crisis management was a realization that 21st-century emergent crises could no longer be described through the language of 'routine emergencies' (Rubens, 2016:88)[22]. The realization of the need to move from static, centrally commanded, process-led decision-making to a much more fluid understanding of the realities of crisis response is at the heart of the debate on the future of emergency and crisis response frameworks (Rosenthal et al, 1989; Grint, 2008). Current thinking as to the best way to understand the realities of these largely unstructured groups is based around the concept of free-forming and fast-mutating networks of emergent multi-organizational networks (EMONs), consisting of national agencies, local response teams, ad hoc voluntary groups and the local community itself (Marcum, Bevc & Butts, 2012; Butts, Acton & Marcum, 2012; Stallings & Quarantelli, 1985). This concept was further developed by Lutz and Lindell (2008), into planned multi-organizational networks (PMONs) and mixed multi-organizational networks (MMONs).

The developments in the understanding of the limitations of bureaucratically managed and hierarchically controlled response frameworks were paralleled by a similar change in the understanding of critical decision-making within crisis environments. This was characterized by the recognition that rather than using a formal analysis of competing response options, decision-making in crisis environments is based more on intuitive responses to unstable situations. The realization that naturalistic decision making (NDM) allows responders to build a picture of the environment that they are operating in (Weick, 1988; Dynes, 1994; Klein, 1997; Klein & Cooper, 1982) led to a 'recognition-primed decision model' (RPDM) (Klein, 1997; Ross et al, 2004) and other models of 'time-stressed, information-poor decision-making' (Turoff et al, 2008; Waldenström, 2008;[23] Lipshitz, Klein, Orasanu & Salas, 2001; Lipshitz & Strauss, 1997; McAndrew & Gore, 2013).

Burns (1963) had already identified the need to develop a non-hierarchical model of leadership and decision-making, which was supported by Braybrooke & Lindblom (1970), and which Dyne (1970) developed further in his study of crisis management under pressure. Although there had been some studies of organizational failures in crisis environments, notably Three Mile Island (Shelanski, Sills, Wolf, 1982) and a seminal work by Weick (1993) on the Mann Gulch fire disaster, these theories and models were revisited post-9/11 (Kendra & Wachtendorf, 2002; Wachtendorf & Kendra, 2004; Boin, Lagadec, Michel-Kerjan & Overdijk, 2003; Boin & 't Hart 2003;

Kapucu, 2005; Butts et al, 2007) and again after Katrina (Comfort & Kapucu, 2006; Howitt & Leonard, 2006;[24] Comfort 2007; Marcum, Bevc & Butts, 2012). The dominant conclusion within all these works was that rather than specific failures of skills or technical capabilities, these failures were due to a misunderstanding of the nature of crises and the need for organizations to develop a radically new conceptualization of decision-making and hierarchical control. Organizations are seen as self-creating entities whose internal workings affect their decision-making, rather than neutral edifices which merely deliver a service (Landau, 1973; La Porte, 1982; Agnew & Brown, 1986; LaPorte & Consolini, 1991; Powell, 1989). A wide range of authors has examined the specifics of decision-making in crisis environments, including such issues as homogeneity of decision-making groups, peer group pressure, risk aversion, blame shifting and tendency to agree/disagree in crisis environments (Janis, 1972; Jarman & Kouzmin, 1990; Rosenthal & 't Hart, 1991; 't Hart, Rosenthal & Kouzmin, 1993;[25] Van Beuren et al, 2003; Lagadec, 2005; Comfort, 2007; Garnett & Kouzmin, 2007; Hermann & Dayton, 2009; Lodge, 2009;[26] Stark, 2010 and Boin, Hart, McConnell & Preston, 2010).

There is an understanding in the academic world, even if it has not yet made an impression among practitioners, that there is a need to change the basic concept of crisis leadership from one that is predicated on a hierarchically structured and procedurally driven management style to one that is inherently free-forming, self-managing and based on embodied knowledge of experienced practitioners (Dynes, 1994; Bresnen et al, 2003). One model for such an institutional change is the Revolution in Military Affairs (RMA) framework (US Department of Defense, 2001), introduced by the US military in order to transform itself from an organization based on highly prescriptive commands transmitted from distanced managers, requiring a high level of administrative support and process-driven bureaucracy, to one based on rapid reaction forces, where small ad hoc teams can be brought together and moved to the hot spot within a matter of hours or even minutes (Boin, 2009; Lagedec, 2009).

As well as the technical aspects associated with emergency response and crisis management, there is a whole section of crisis management literature dedicated to examining how the lessons learned from operational experience can be codified, so that they can be absorbed into organizations rather than depending on the embodied knowledge of experienced individuals. A wide range of authors has looked at ways in which organizations involved in crisis and emergency management can learn, and what the barriers are to learning that lead to repeated failures (Burns & Stalker, 1961; Schein, 1993; Daft & Weick, 1984; Pauchant & Mitroff, 1992; Smith & Dowell, 2000; Corbacioglu & Kapucu, 2006; Lagadec, 2006; Van Wart & Kapucu, 2011). Much of their work is based on the foundation set by Argyris and others (Argyris, 1976, 1993; Argyris & Schon, 1978) involving 'double loop learning', that is, a process that implies revolution in organizational thinking, as characterized by the US military acceptance of RMA, rather than minor and relatively insignificant incremental changes.

The nature of hypercomplex crises

If traditional crisis management modelling saw crises as little more than large-scale incidents, 'an event circumscribed to a specific area, within a global system that otherwise remained stable' (Lagadec, 2007:1), the nature of the threats that we now face is infinitely more complex, with cascading consequences that are literally incalculable. The transformational nature of modern threats has been described as comprising 'un-ness' –'unexpected, undesirable, unimaginable, unscheduled, unplanned, unprecedented and definitely unpleasant' (Hewitt, 1983:10),[27] to which Rosenthal et al (2001:5)[28] added 'unwanted and almost unmanageable, causing widespread unbelief and uncertainty'.

The 'hypercomplex' scenarios examined by Lagadec (2007) reflect the concerns first circulated in a paper setting out the parameters for 'wicked problems' (Rittel & Webber, 1973).[29] Hurricane Katrina was a classic example of a wicked problem, in that the original triggering event soon became relatively unimportant in describing and prioritizing the consequential crises. Secondary, and in themselves catastrophic, crisis dilemmas included the rescue of thousands of stranded citizens, the housing, feeding and caring of tens of thousands of people, the restoration of a city, the preservation of public safety in light of the impact on critical infrastructure, the impact on adjacent jurisdictions and, on another level, the political implications of the perceived failures of the government, the emergency management community, the homeland security agencies and the president himself, who was seen to embody those failures on the public stage (Waugh, 2006).[30]

In terms of impact and consequences, Hurricane Katrina was perhaps the first crisis event that transcended the traditional concept of crisis management frameworks or organizational jurisdictions. The failure to deal with the primary events and their secondary consequences effectively and in a timely manner could no longer be seen as simple management failures but are rather a challenge to the legitimacy of governments tasked with ensuring public safety (Boin & ’t Hart, 2003; Boin, 2009:367; Stark, 2010).

The 2011 Fukushima earthquake/tsunami is another example of a situation where the initial ‘triggering event’, although catastrophic in its own terms, was soon superseded by the impact of a nuclear reactor meltdown and the subsequent cascading effects on the food supply to Tokyo, the threat of a transnational nuclear cloud, and the impact on global supply chains of the disruption of Japanese component manufacturing (Escaith et al, 2011;[31] Norio et al, 2011[32]). This was no longer a matter of ‘incident response’, albeit on an unprecedented scale, but had potential implications for the social, political and economic continuity of a country (Boin et al, 2003; Guhar- Sapir et al, 2016)

In describing such fundamentally undefinable scenarios, Rittel & Webber (1973)[33] identified a new subset of crises that would not only fail to respond to classical risk management methodologies but had mutated into a completely different class of event. These crises are similar to a virus that mutates so much from its original form that it not only refuses to respond to traditional approaches but redefines the parameters of the threat. This was visible in the BSE ‘mad cow disease’ situation in the UK when the triggering virus jumped the species barrier (Lagadec, 2005), creating a situation where the new threat needed to be seen in terms of a completely new and distinct threat topology rather than merely being a subset of previously modelled problems, or anomalies that fell outside of the parameters of crisis response. Unbounded and hypercomplex events are not merely a higher, more dynamic form of accidents (Lagadec, 2009),[34] they are a central reality of the modern world. If classical risk management was the domain of the statistician, predicting future possibilities based on an analysis of an aggregate of the masses, the threat set by the new paradigm is predicated on the criticality of the singularity, the outlier – the unknowable and inconceivable (Weinberg, 1985; Lagadec, 2005).

The dilemmas that wicked problems pose to crisis managers, strategists and planners are twofold. First, by the nature of their scale, complexity and non-bounded nature, the choice of any particular response option can be made only in a context of ambiguity, information asymmetry and organizational fragmentation (Lodge, 2009).[35] It is this ambiguity created by lack of central locus combined with unbounded limitations (Howitt & Leonard, 2006)[36] that distinguishes the true wicked problem from, for example, the major fire that Bigley & Roberts (2001)[37] use in their critique of ICS within disaster management scenarios. The second problem that the wicked problem sets is that there are no categories of wicked problems that can act as a template for possible responses (Rittel & Weber, 1973;[38] Rittel, 1972[39]). There are no 'ready-made solutions' to such crises (Lagadec, 2009: 478).[40] Any response to a wicked problem is, by definition, going to be innovative, self-generating and based on *ad hoc* meetings of minds between a disparate range of knowledge-holders, who will develop situationally responsive solutions based on their own experience and insight (Weick et al, 1999;[41] 't Hart et al, 1993; Howitt & Leonard, 2006[42]).

As previously described, the polar opposite of such undefined, unbounded and ultimately unknowable situations are the tightly coupled, interdependent systems described by Perrow (1984),[43] labelled as HROs (Weick et al, 1999).[44] Such systems, often sitting within the national critical infrastructure, are characterized by the potential catastrophic effects of even minor systems failures, involving both fast-escalating (developing into fully blown crisis) and rapidly cascading (affecting multiple levels of society across a wide geographical spread) consequences. High Reliability Theory (HRT) is the theoretical modelling of decision-making which sets as its objective the creation of operation management programmes that are fail-safe ('systems that are not only foolproof, but *damned* foolproof', Schulman, 2004:23[45]), within the context of such highly complex, interconnected and dependent networks. HRT depends on granular modelling of systems dependencies, identifying potential vulnerabilities and creating safeguards to minimize the likelihood of malfunction, while simultaneously ensuring that any gestating problem will be identified at the earliest possible stage in order to allow early (and low-input) intervention.

Despite the fact that such HRO systems are designed and engineered to the final component, the eight defining characteristics of these organizations that were identified by Roberts and Rousseau (1989)[46] share qualities common to all crises events. They are:

- hyper-complexity;
- tight coupling in which all sections of the process are highly interdependent, with little if any room for divergence from protocols;
- extreme hierarchical differentiation, in which roles and responsibilities are both highly detailed and extremely distinct from each other;
- large numbers of decision-makers in complex communication networks;

- a uniquely high degree of accountability;
- high frequency of immediate feedback following decisions;
- compressed time factors in which cycles of major decisions and their cascading consequences occur within a few seconds; and
- multiple critical outcomes which must all be handled in parallel but which have a dependency relationship on the other simultaneous decisions (Roberts & Rousseau, 1989).

Roberts and Rousseau insisted on a strict interpretation for inclusion in HROs, excluding hospital surgery theatres and petroleum refineries, for example (Roberts & Rousseau, 1989).[47] There were also questions as to both its accuracy in portraying highly managed technical environments (Perrow, 1994)[48] and its relevance to smaller and less complex organizations (Lalonde, 2007).[49] This suggests that lessons may in fact be drawn from the highly designed environment of critical infrastructures that could have value and relevance within the unformed chaotic milieu of crisis management.

The limitations on the range and relevance of HROs to other organizations of a greater or lesser complexity as set out by Roberts and Rousseau were considered by a leading researcher of the second generation of HRO development, Weick. He gave an attitudinal perspective to the qualities of HROs that he coined 'mindfulness' (Weick and Sutcliffe, 2001:v). Mindful organizations could be identified by their adherence to five practices:

- they were preoccupied with failures rather than success; that is, determined to become zero-failure organizations;
- they had an understanding of (and to a certain extent an empathy with) complexity and therefore did not feel the need to simplify interpretations;
- they had a sensitivity to operations and understood their challenges and demands;
- they had a commitment to resilience, associated with a determination that they would not fail; and
- they had a deference to expertise, recognizing the insight that experts could give which was demonstrated by a fluid decision-making system rather than one that was based on hierarchy and job descriptions[50] (Hopkins, 2007:7).

It has generally been accepted that the highly interdependent and tightly bounded nature of high-reliability systems precludes the possibility of innovative solutions to potential or actual problems. However, even within the systems dependency and tight coupling of a major power management system or a nuclear submarine, it is precisely the ability of operators dealing with the immediate realities of emerging problems to create innovative solutions using their experience and improvisational abilities that allows them to deal with surprises and volatile events (Mintzberg & McHugh, 1985;[51] Schulman, 2004;[52] de Bruijne & van Eeten, 2007[53]). This critical capability was encapsulated in Ryle's description of 'a union of some Ad Hockery with some know-how... the pitting of an acquired competence or skill against unprogrammed opportunity, obstacle or hazard' (Ryle, 1976:129).[54] In fact, the undirected actions of self-asserting operators responding to the contingencies of a crisis situation are seen as critical in almost every crisis ('t Hart et al, 1993:33). Given the increasing likelihood of critical failures occurring in ever more organizations, and the increased risk this poses to the public both in terms of direct impacts and secondary consequences, the lessons learned from HROs could be usefully transposed into what have been seen as less critical organizations (Grabowski & Roberts, 1997; Roberts & Bea, 2001). As we enter what will undoubtedly be the highly disruptive events of the middle years of the 2020s, the challenge will be to develop a model of risk management that fits over the unprecedented events that we are facing, events which will change the world in ways that we can predict and hopefully mitigate, as well as in ways we cannot yet imagine.

An understanding of the fundamental themes of classical risk and crisis management as described by many of the authorities[55] covered in this section will not provide ready-made solutions, but will give practitioners and policy makers, whatever sectors they are working in, a framework to discuss and with which to engage with complex issues in ways that are supported by a structure and methodology that would not otherwise be available to them.

Endnotes

1 Quarantelli, E L & Dynes, R R (1977) Response to social crisis and disaster, *Annual Review of Sociology*, 3, 23–49

2 Lagadec, E (2007) Unconventional crises, unconventional responses: Reforming leadership in the age of catastrophic crises and hypercomplexity. Center for Transatlantic Relations, Paul H. Nitze School of Advanced International Studies, Johns Hopkins University

3 Weinberg, A M (1985) Science and its limits. In *De Minimis Risk*, Springer US, pp. 27–38

4 Ansell, C, Boin, A & Keller, A (2010) Managing transboundary crises: Identifying the building blocks of an effective response system. *Journal of Contingencies and Crisis Management*, 18, 195–207

5 Turoff M, White, C & Plotnick, L (2008) *Dynamic Emergency Response Management for Large Scale Decision Making in Extreme Events*, Springer

6 't Hart, P, Rosenthal, U & Kouzmin, A (1993) Crisis decision making: The centralization thesis revisited. *Administration & Society*, 25(1), 12–45

7 Bigley, G A & Roberts, K H (2001) The incident command system: High-reliability organizing for complex and volatile task environments. *Academy of Management Journal*, 44(6), 1281–1299

8 Lalonde, C (2007) Crisis management and organizational development: Towards the conception of a learning model in crisis management. *Organization Development Journal*, 25(1), 17

9 't Hart, P, Rosenthal, U & Kouzmin, A (1993) Crisis decision making: The centralization thesis revisited. *Administration & Society*, 25(1), 12–45

10 Bigley, G A & Roberts, K H (2001) The incident command system: High-reliability organizing for complex and volatile task environments. *Academy of Management Journal*, 44(6), 1281–1299

11 Lalonde, C (2007) Crisis management and organizational development: Towards the conception of a learning model in crisis management. *Organization Development Journal*, 25(1), 17

12 Rittel, H W & Webber, M M (1973) Dilemmas in a general theory of planning. *Policy Sciences*, 4(2), 155–169

13 Howitt, A M & Leonard, H B (2006) Katrina and the core challenges of disaster response. *Fletcher Forum of World Affairs*, 30(1), 215–221

14 Howitt, A M & Leonard, H B (2006) Katrina and the core challenges of disaster response. *Fletcher Forum of World Affairs*, 30(1), 215–221

15 Perrow, C (1984) *Normal accidents: Living with high risk technologies*. Princeton University Press

16 Schulman, P R (2004) General attributes of safe organisations. *Quality and Safety in Health Care*, 13(suppl 2), ii39–ii44

17 De Bruijne, M & Van Eeten, M (2007) Systems that should have failed: Critical infrastructure protection in an institutionally fragmented environment. *Journal of Contingencies and Crisis Management*, 15(1), 18–29

18 Schulman, P R (2004) General attributes of safe organisations. *Quality and Safety in Health Care*, 13(suppl 2), ii39–ii44

19 De Bruijne, M & Van Eeten, M (2007) Systems that should have failed: Critical infrastructure protection in an institutionally fragmented environment. *Journal of Contingencies and Crisis Management*, 15(1), 18–29

20 Bigley, G A & Roberts, K H (2001) The incident command system: High-reliability organizing for complex and volatile task environments. *Academy of Management Journal*, 44(6), 1281–1299

21 Lagadec, P (2009). A new cosmology of risks and crises: Time for a radical shift in paradigm and practice. Review of Policy Research, 26(4), 473–486

22 Rubens, D (2016) The topology of crises. *Crisis Response Journal*, 12(2), December

23 Waldenström, C (2008) What is difficult in naval sensemaking. In Proceedings of the 13th International Command and Control Research and Technology Symposium

24 Howitt, A M & Leonard, H B (2006) Katrina and the core challenges of disaster response. *Fletcher Forum of World Affairs*, 30(1), 215–221

25 't Hart, P, Rosenthal, U & Kouzmin, A (1993) Crisis decision making: The centralization thesis revisited. *Administration & Society*, 25(1), 12–45

26 Lodge, M (2009) The public management of risk: The case for deliberating among worldviews. *Review of Policy Research*, 26(4), 395–408

27 Hewitt, K (1983) The idea of calamity in a technocratic age. *Interpretations of Calamity from the Viewpoint of Human Ecology*, 1, 3–32

28 Rosenthal, U, Boin, A & Comfort, L K (2001) *Managing crises: Threats, dilemmas, opportunities*. Charles C Thomas Publisher

29 Rittel, H W & Webber, M M (1973) Dilemmas in a general theory of planning. *Policy Sciences*, 4(2), 155–169

30 Waugh, W L (2006) The political costs of failure in the Katrina and Rita disasters. *The Annals of the American Academy of Political and Social Science*, 604(1), 10–25

31 Escaith, H, Keck, A, Nee, C & Teh, R (2011) Japan's earthquake and tsunami: International trade and global supply chain impacts. *VOXEU*, April, 28

32 Norio, O, Ye, T, Kajitani, Y, Shi, P & Tatano, H (2011) The 2011 eastern Japan great earthquake disaster: Overview and comments. *International Journal of Disaster Risk Science*, 2(1), 34–42

33 Rittel, H W & Webber, M M (1973) Dilemmas in a general theory of planning. *Policy Sciences*, 4(2), 155–169

34 Lagadec, P (2009) A new cosmology of risks and crises: Time for a radical shift in paradigm and practice. *Review of Policy Research*, 26(4), 473–486

35 Lodge, M (2009) The public management of risk: The case for deliberating among worldviews. *Review of Policy Research*, 26(4), 395–408

36 Howitt, A M & Leonard, H B (2006) Katrina and the core challenges of disaster response. *Fletcher Forum of World Affairs*, 30(1), 215–221

37 Bigley, G A & Roberts, K H (2001) The incident command system: High-reliability organizing for complex and volatile task environments. *Academy of Management Journal*, 44(6), 1281–1299

38 Rittel, H W & Webber, M M (1973) Dilemmas in a general theory of planning. *Policy Sciences*, 4(2), 155–169

39 Rittel, H W (1972) *On the Planning Crisis: Systems analysis of the 'first and second generations'*. Institute of Urban and Regional Development, 390–396

40 Lagadec, P (2009) A new cosmology of risks and crises: Time for a radical shift in paradigm and practice. *Review of Policy Research*, 26(4), 473–486

41 Weick, K E, Sutcliffe, K M & Obstfeld, D (1999) Organizing for high reliability: Processes of collective mindfulness. *Crisis Management*, 3, 81–123

42 Howitt, A M & Leonard, H B (2006) Katrina and the core challenges of disaster response. *Fletcher Forum of World Affairs*, 30(1), 215–221

43 Perrow, C (1984) *Normal accidents: Living with high risk technologies*. Princeton University Press

44 Weick, K E, Sutcliffe, K M & Obstfeld, D (1999) Organizing for high reliability: Processes of collective mindfulness. *Crisis Management*, 3, 81–123

45 Schulman, P R (2004) General attributes of safe organisations. *Quality and Safety in Health Care*, 13(suppl 2), ii39–ii44

46 Roberts, K H & Rousseau, D M (1989) Research in nearly failure-free, high-reliability organizations: Having the bubble. *Engineering Management*, IEEE Transactions on, 36(2), 132–139

47 Roberts, K H & Rousseau, D M (1989) Research in nearly failure-free, high-reliability organizations: Having the bubble. *IEEE Transactions on Engineering Management*, 36(2), 132–139

48 Perrow, C (1994) The limits of safety: The enhancement of a theory of accidents. *Journal of Contingencies and Crisis Management*, 2(4), 212–220

49 Lalonde, C (2007) Crisis management and organizational development: Towards the conception of a learning model in crisis management. *Organization Development Journal*, 25(1), 17

50 Hopkins, A (2007) The problem of defining high reliability organisations. National Research Center for Occupational Safety and Health Regulation. January

51 Mintzberg, H & McHugh, A (1985) Strategy formation in an adhocracy. *Administrative Science Quarterly*, 160–197

52 Schulman, P R (2004) General attributes of safe organisations. *Quality and Safety in Health Care*, 13(suppl 2), ii39–ii44

53 De Bruijne, M & Van Eeten, M (2007) Systems that should have failed: Critical infrastructure protection in an institutionally fragmented environment. *Journal of Contingencies and Crisis Management*, 15(1), 18–29

54 Ryle, G (1976) Improvisation. *Mind*, 85(337), 69–83

55 Cabinet Office (2017) National Risk Register of Civil Emergencies, 2017 Edition. Available at: https://assets.publishing.service.gov.uk/government/uploads/system/uploads/attachment_data/file/644968/UK_National_Risk_Register_2017.pdf (archived at https://perma.cc/39QC-ALLD) (Accessed: 20 April 2022)

Further reading

Agnew, N M & Brown, J L (1986) Bounded rationality: Fallible decisions in unbounded decision space. *Behavioral Science*, 31(3), 148–161

Ansell, C, Boin, A & Keller, A (2010) Managing transboundary crises: Identifying the building blocks of an effective response system. *Journal of Contingencies and Crisis Management*, 18(4), 195–207

Argyris, C (1976) Single-loop and double-loop models in research on decision making. *Administrative Science Quarterly*, 363–375

Argyris, C (1993) *Knowledge for Action: A guide to overcoming barriers to organizational change*. San Francisco: Jossey-Bass Publishers

Argyris, C & Schon, D (1978) *Organizational Learning: A theory of action perspective*. Reading, MA: Addison-Wesley Publishing Co

Braybrooke, D & Lindblom, C E (1970) *A Strategy of Decision: Policy evaluation as a social process*. New York: The Free Press

Bharosa, N, Lee, J & Janssen, M (2010) Challenges and obstacles in sharing and coordinating information during multi-agency disaster response: Propositions from field exercises. *Information Systems Frontiers*, 12(1), 49–65

Bigley, G A & Roberts, K H (2001) The incident command system: High-reliability organizing for complex and volatile task environments. *Academy of Management Journal*, 44(6), 1281–1299

Boin, A (2009) The new world of crises and crisis management: Implications for policymaking and research. *Review of Policy Research*, 26(4), 367–377

Boin, A & Hart, P T (2003) Public leadership in times of crisis: Mission impossible? *Public Administration Review*, 63(5), 544–553

Boin, A, Lagadec, P, Michel-Kerjan, E & Overdijk, W (2003) Critical infrastructures under threat: Learning from the anthrax scare. *Journal of Contingencies and Crisis Management*, 11(3), 99–104

Boin, A, Hart P T, McConnell, A & Preston, T (2010) Leadership style, crisis response and blame management: The case of Hurricane Katrina. *Public Administration*, 88(3), 706–723

Bresnen, M, Edelman, L, Newell, S, Scarbrough, H & Swan, J (2003) Social practices and the management of knowledge in project environments. *International Journal of Project Management*, 21(3), 157–166

Buck, D A, Trainor, J E & Aguirre, B E (2006) A critical evaluation of the incident command system and NIMS. *Journal of Homeland Security and Emergency Management*, 3(3)

Burns, T (1963) Industry in a new age, *New Society* [18], 31 January. Reprinted in Pugh, D. S. (ed.) (2007) *Organization Theory: Selected readings* (3rd ed.). London: Penguin

Burns, T & Stalker, G M (1961) Mechanistic and organic systems. *Classics of Organizational Theory*, 209–214

Butts, C T, Petrescu-Prahova, M & Remy Cross, B (2007) Responder communication networks in the world trade center disaster: Implications for modeling of communication within emergency settings. *Mathematical Sociology*, 31(2), 121–147

Butts, C T, Acton, R M & Marcum, C S (2012) Interorganizational collaboration in the Hurricane Katrina response. *Journal of Social Structure*, 13

Cabinet Office (2017) National Risk Register of Civil Emergencies, 2017 Edition. Available at: https://assets.publishing.service.gov.uk/government/uploads/system/uploads/attachment_data/file/644968/UK_National_Risk_Register_2017.pdf (archived at https://perma.cc/B553-UDQX) (Accessed: 20 April 2022)

Comfort, L K (2007) Crisis management in hindsight: Cognition, communication, coordination, and control. *Public Administration Review*, 67, 189–197

Comfort, L K & Kapucu, N (2006) Inter-organizational coordination in extreme events: The World Trade Center attacks, September 11, 2001. *Natural Hazards*, 39(2), 309–327

Corbacioglu, S & Kapucu, N (2006) Organisational learning and selfadaptation in dynamic disaster environments. *Disasters*, 30(2), 212–233

Daft, R L & Weick, K E (1984) Toward a model of organizations as interpretation systems. *Academy of Management Review*, 9(2), 284–295

De Bruijne, M & Van Eeten, M. (2007) Systems that should have failed: Critical infrastructure protection in an institutionally fragmented environment. *Journal of Contingencies and Crisis Management*, 15(1), 18–29

Deepwater Horizon Report. Bly, M (ed.) (2011) *Deepwater Horizon accident investigation report*. Diane Publishing

Dror, Y (1999) Beyond uncertainty: Facing the inconceivable. *Technological Forecasting and Social Change*, 62(1), 151–153

Dynes, R R (1970) Organizational involvement and changes in community structure in disaster. *American Behavioral Scientist*, 13(3), 430–439

Dynes, R R (1994) Community emergency planning: False assumptions and inappropriate analogies. *International Journal of Mass Emergencies and Disasters*, 12(2), 141–158

EPC (2005) Lynch, D. EPC working paper no. 21. Communicating Europe to the world: What public diplomacy for the EU?

Escaith, H, Keck, A, Nee, C & Teh, R (2011) Japan's earthquake and tsunami: International trade and global supply chain impacts. *VOXEU*, April, 28

Farazmand, A (2007) World crisis in public service and administration. *Public Administration and Public Policy New York*, 129, 1137

Farazmand, A (2014) Learning from the Katrina crisis. *Crisis and Emergency Management: Theory and Practice*, 461

Flood, R L & Carson, E (1993) *Dealing with Complexity: An introduction to the theory and application of systems science*. Springer Science & Business Media

Fukushima Report. Kurokawa, K (Chair) July 2012. Kurokawa Investigation Report of the Nuclear Accident Investigation Commission of the Diet of Japan (commissioned October 7, 2011). For English readers: http://www.nytimes.com/2012/01/16/business/global/independent-panel-to-start-inquiry-into-japans-nuclear-crisis.html (archived at https://perma.cc/KYK3-VVXT)

Garnett, J L & Kouzmin, A (2007) Communicating throughout Katrina: Competing and complementary conceptual lenses on crisis communication. *Public Administration Review*, 67, 171–188

Grabowski, M & Roberts, K (1997) Risk mitigation in large-scale systems: Lessons from high reliability organizations. *California Management Review*, 39(4), 152–161

Grint, K (2008) Leadership, management and command: Rethinking D-Day. Basingstoke: Palgrave Macmillan

Guha-Sapir, D, Hoyois, P, Wallemacq, P & Below, R (2016) Annual Disaster Statistical Review, Centre for Research on the Epidemiology of Disasters (CRED). https://www.emdat.be/sites/default/files/adsr_2016.pdf (archived at https://perma.cc/ZS7R-G3B8)

Hermann, M G & Dayton, B W (2009) Transboundary crises through the eyes of policymakers: Sense making and crisis management. *Journal of Contingencies and Crisis Management*, 17(4), 233–241

Hewitt, K (1983) The idea of calamity in a technocratic age. *Interpretations of Calamity from the Viewpoint of Human Ecology*, 1, 3–32

Hopkins, A (2007) The problem of defining high reliability organisations. National Research Center for Occupational Safety and Health Regulation. January

Howitt, A M & Leonard, H B (2006a) Katrina and the core challenges of disaster response. *Fletcher Forum of World Affairs*, 30(1), 215–221

Howitt, A M & Leonard, H B (2006b) Beyond Katrina: Improving disaster response capabilities. https://www.hbs.edu/faculty/Pages/item.aspx?num=23549 (archived at https://perma.cc/5YWC-FYCE)

Howitt, A M, Leonard, H B & Giles, D (eds.) (2009) *Managing Crises*. Sage

Hurricane Katrina. United States. Congress. House. Select Bipartisan Committee to Investigate the Preparation for and Response to Hurricane Katrina, 2006. A failure of initiative: Final report of the select bipartisan committee to investigate the preparation for and response to Hurricane Katrina (Vol 109). Government Printing Office

Ink, D (2006) An analysis of the house select committee and White House reports on Hurricane Katrina. *Public Administration Review*, 66(6), 800–807

Irwin, R L (1989) The incident command system (ICS). *Disaster Response: Principles of preparation and coordination*, 1, 30

Janis, I L (1972) *Victims of groupthink*. Boston, MA: Houghton Mifflin

Jarman, A (1998) Futurizing risk management. *Journal of Contingencies and Crisis Management*, 6, 224–229

Jarman, A & Kouzmin, A (1990) Decision pathways from crisis. *Contemporary Crises*, 14(4), 399–433

Kalloniatis, A C, Macleod, I D G & La, P (2009) Process versus battle-rhythm: Modelling operational command and control. In 18th IMACS World Conference MODSIM09 Proceedings (pp. 1622–1628)

Kapucu, N (2005) Interorganizational coordination in dynamic context: Networks in emergency response management. *Connections*, 26(2), 33–48

Kean, T and Hamilton, L (2004) The 9/11 Commission Report: Final report of the national commission on terrorist attacks upon the United States (Vol. 3). Government Printing Office

Kendra, J M & Wachtendorf, T (2002) *Elements of community resilience in the World Trade Center attack*. Disaster Research Center, University of Delaware

Klein, G (1997) Developing expertise in decision making. *Thinking & Reasoning*, 3(4), 337–352

Klein, J H & Cooper, D F (1982) Cognitive maps of decision-makers in a complex game. *Journal of the Operational Research Society*, 33(1), 63–71

Koh, C S, Clegg, B & Deighan, D (2011) *Tackling NHS wicked problems – developing a novel methodology*, Birmingham: Powerful Organisations

LaPorte, T R & Consolini, P M (1991) Working in practice but not in theory: Theoretical challenges of 'high-reliability organizations'. *Journal of Public Administration Research and Theory: J-PART*, 1(1), 19–48

LaPorte, T R & Thomas, C W (1995) Regulatory compliance and the ethos of quality enhancement: Surprises in nuclear power plant operations1. *Journal of Public Administration Research and Theory*, 5(1), 109–138

LaPorte, T R, Roberts, K & Rochlin, G I (1988) Aircraft carrier operations at sea: The challenges of high reliability performance. California Univ Berkeley Inst of Governmental Studies

Lagadec, P (2005) Crisis management in the twenty-first century: 'unthinkable' events in 'inconceivable' contexts. *Handbook of Disaster Research*, Springer Nature, pp. 489–507

Lagadec, P (2006) The borderline of chaos. *Crisis Response*, 2(3), 62–63

Lagadec, E (2007) Unconventional crises, unconventional responses: Reforming leadership in the age of catastrophic crises and hypercomplexity. Center for Transatlantic Relations, Paul H Nitze School of Advanced International Studies, Johns Hopkins University

Lagadec, P (2009) A new cosmology of risks and crises: Time for a radical shift in paradigm and practice. *Review of Policy Research*, 26(4), 473–486

Lalonde, C (2007) Crisis management and organizational development: Towards the conception of a learning model in crisis management. *Organization Development Journal*, 25(1), 17

Landau, M (1973) On the concept of a self-correcting organization. *Public Administration Review*, 533–542

Lipshitz, R & Strauss, O (1997) Coping with uncertainty: A naturalistic decision-making analysis. *Organizational Behavior and Human Decision Processes*, 69(2), 149–163

Lipshitz, R, Klein, G, Orasanu, J & Salas, E (2001) Taking stock of naturalistic decision making. *Journal of Behavioral Decision Making*, 14(5), 331–352

Lodge, M (2009) The public management of risk: The case for deliberating among worldviews. *Review of Policy Research*, 26(4), 395–408

Lutz, L D & Lindell, M K (2008) Incident command system as a response model within emergency operation centers during Hurricane Rita. *Journal of Contingencies and Crisis Management*, 16(3), 122–134

Mannarelli, T, Roberts, K H & Bea, R G (1996) Learning how organizations mitigate risk. *Journal of Contingencies and Crisis Management*, 4(2), 83–92

Marcum, C S, Bevc, C A & Butts, C T (2012) Mechanisms of control in emergent interorganizational networks. *Policy Studies Journal*, 40(3), 516–546

McAndrew, C & Gore, J (2013) Understanding preferences in experience-based choice: A study of cognition in the 'wild'. *Journal of Cognitive Engineering and Decision Making*, 7(2), 179–197

Mintzberg, H & McHugh, A (1985) Strategy formation in an adhocracy. *Administrative Science Quarterly*, 160–197

Moynihan, D P (2008) Learning under uncertainty: Networks in crisis management. *Public Administration Review*, 68(2), 350–365

Moynihan, D P (2009a) The network governance of crisis response: Case studies of incident command systems. *Journal of Public Administration Research and Theory*, 19(4), 895–915

Moynihan, D P (2009b) *The Response to Hurricane Katrina.* Geneva (Italy): International Risk Governance Council, pp. 27–45

Munns, A K & Bjeirmi, B F (1996) The role of project management in achieving project success. *International Journal of Project Management*, 14(2), 81–87

Norio, O, Ye, T, Kajitani, Y, Shi, P & Tatano, H (2011) The 2011 eastern Japan great earthquake disaster: Overview and comments. *International Journal of Disaster Risk Science*, 2(1), 34–42

Pauchant, T C & Mitroff, I I (1992) Management by nosing around: Exposing the dangerous invisibility of technologies. *Journal of Management Inquiry*, 1(1), 70–78

Pearson, C M & Clair, J A (1998) Reframing crisis management. *Academy of Management Review*, 23(1), 59–76

Perrow, C (1984) *Normal accidents: Living with high risk technologies.* Princeton University Press

Perrow, C (1994) The limits of safety: The enhancement of a theory of accidents. *Journal of Contingencies and Crisis Management*, 2(4), 212–220

Powell, T C (1992) Organizational alignment as competitive advantage. *Strategic Management Journal*, 13(2), 119–134

Quarantelli, E L (1988) Disaster crisis management: A summary of research findings. *Journal of Management Studies*, 25(4), 373–385

Quarantelli, E L (2008) Conventional beliefs and counterintuitive realities. *Social Research: An International Quarterly*, 75(3), 873–904

Quarantelli, E L & Dynes, R R (1977) Response to social crisis and disaster. *Annual Review of Sociology*, 23–49

Rittel, H W (1972) *On the Planning Crisis: Systems analysis of the 'first and second generations'*. Institute of Urban and Regional Development, pp. 390–396

Rittel, H W & Webber, M M (1973) Dilemmas in a general theory of planning. *Policy Sciences*, 4(2), 155–169

Roberts, K H (1990) Managing high reliability organizations. *California Management Review*, 32(4), 101–113

Roberts, P S (2010) Private choices, public harms: The evolution of national disaster organizations in the United States. *Disaster and the Politics of Intervention*, 42–69

Roberts, K H & Rousseau, D M (1989) Research in nearly failure-free, high-reliability organizations: Having the bubble. *IEEE Transactions on Engineering Management*, 36(2), 132–139

Roberts, K H & Bea, R (2001) Must accidents happen? Lessons from high-reliability organizations. *Academy of Management Perspectives*, 15(3), 70–78

Rochlin, G I (1989) Informal organizational networking as a crisis-avoidance strategy: US naval flight operations as a case study. *Industrial Crisis Quarterly*, 3(2), 159–176

Rochlin, G I, La Porte, T R & Roberts, K H (1987) The self-designing high-reliability organization: Aircraft carrier flight operations at sea. *Naval War College Review*, 40(4), 76–92

Roe, E (2009) Preventing transboundary crises: The management and regulation of setbacks. *Review of Policy Research*, 26(4), 457–471

Rosenthal, U, Charles, M and 't Hart, P T (eds.) (1989) *Coping with Crises*. Springfield, IL: Charles C Thomas

Rosenthal, U & 't Hart, P T (1991) Experts and decision makers in crisis situations. *Knowledge*, 12(4), 350–372

Rosenthal, U & Kouzmin, A (1997) Crises and crisis management: Toward comprehensive government decision making. *Journal of Public Administration Research and Theory*, 7(2), 277–304

Rosenthal, U, Boin, A & Comfort, L K (2001) *Managing Crises: Threats, dilemmas, opportunities*. Charles C Thomas Publisher

Ross, K G, Klein, G A, Thunholm, P, Schmitt, J F & Baxter, H C (2004) The Recognition-Primed Decision Model. Army Combined Arms Center Fort Leavenworth Ks Military Review

Roux-Dufort, C (2007) Is crisis management (only) a management of exceptions? *Journal of Contingencies and Crisis Management*, 15(2), 105–114

Rubens, D (2016) The topology of crises. *Crisis Response Journal*, 12(2), December

Ryle, G (1976) Improvisation. *Mind*, 85(337), 69–83

Santella, N, Steinberg, L J & Parks, K (2009) Decision making for extreme events: Modeling critical infrastructure interdependencies to aid mitigation and response planning. *Review of Policy Research*, 26(4), 409–422

Schein, E H (1993) On dialogue, culture, and organizational learning. *Organizational Dynamics*, 22(2), 40–52

Schulman, P R (1993) The negotiated order of organizational reliability. *Administration & Society*, 25(3), 353–372

Schulman, P R (2004) General attributes of safe organisations. *Quality and Safety in Health Care*, 13(suppl 2), ii39–ii44

Schulman, P, Roe, E, Eeten, M V & Bruijne, M D (2004) High reliability and the management of critical infrastructures. *Journal of Contingencies and Crisis Management*, 12(1), 14–28

Shelanski, V B, Sills, D L & Wolf, C P (eds.) (1982) *Accident at Three Mile Island*. Westview Press

Smith, W & Dowell, J (2000) A case study of co-ordinative decision-making in disaster management. *Ergonomics*, 43(8), 1153–1166

Stallings, R A & Quarantelli, E L (1985) Emergent citizen groups and emergency management. *Public Administration Review*, 45, 93–100

Stark, A (2010) Legislatures, legitimacy and crises: The relationship between representation and crisis management. *Journal of Contingencies and Crisis Management*, 18(1), 2–13

Stern, E K (1999) *Crisis Decision Making: A cognitive institutional approach* (Vol 6). University of Stockholm, Department of Political Science

Tatham, P & Houghton, L (2011) The wicked problem of humanitarian logistics and disaster relief aid. *Journal of Humanitarian Logistics and Supply Chain Management*

't Hart, P, Rosenthal, U & Kouzmin, A (1993) Crisis decision making: The centralization thesis revisited. *Administration & Society*, 25(1), 12–45

Tierney, K J & Trainor, J E (2004) Networks and resilience in the World Trade Center disaster (pp. 157–172). MCEER

Toft, B & Reynolds, S (1994) *Learning from Disasters*, Butterworth-Heinemann

Turner, B A & Pidgeon, N F (1997) *Man-made Disasters*. Butterworth-Heinemann

Turoff, M, White, C, Plotnick, L & Hiltz, S R (2008) May. Dynamic emergency response management for large scale decision making in extreme events. In Proceedings of the 5th International ISCRAM Conference (pp. 462–470). ISCRAM Washington, DC, US

US Department of Homeland Security (2004) National Incident Management System. https://www.hsdl.org/?abstract&did=482966 (archived at https://perma.cc/V8GE-9U62)

Utoya Island Report. https://www.regjeringen.no/contentassets/bb3dc76229c64735b4f6eb4dbfcdbfe8/en-gb/pdfs/nou2012_14_eng.pdf (archived at https://perma.cc/559K-LKTY)

Van Bueren, E M, Klijn E-H & Koppenjan, J F M (2003) Dealing with wicked problems in networks: Analyzing an environmental debate from a network perspective. *Journal of Public Administration Research and Theory: J-PART*, 13(2), 193–212

Van Wart, M & Kapucu, N (2011) Crisis management competencies: The case of emergency managers in the USA. *Public Management Review*, 13(4), 489–511

Veil, S R (2011) Mindful learning in crisis management. *The Journal of Business Communication*, 48(2), 116–147

Wachtendorf, T & Kendra, J M (2004) Considering convergence, coordination, and social capital in disasters. https://udspace.udel.edu/handle/19716/737 (archived at https://perma.cc/JTD4-H4LX)

Waldenström, C (2008) What is difficult in naval sensemaking. In Proceedings of the 13th International Command and Control Research and Technology Symposium

Waugh, W L (2006) The political costs of failure in the Katrina and Rita disasters. *The Annals of the American Academy of Political and Social Science*, 604(1), 10–25

Weick, K E (1987) Organizational culture as a source of high reliability. *California Management Review*, 29(2), 112–127

Weick, K E (1993) The collapse of sensemaking in organizations: The Mann Gulch disaster. Administrative Science Quarterly, 628–652

Weick, K E, Sutcliffe, K M & Obstfeld, D (1999) Organizing for high reliability: Processes of collective mindfulness. *Crisis Management*, 3, 81–123

Weick, K E & Sutcliffe, K M (2001) *Managing the Unexpected* (Vol 9). San Francisco: Jossey-Bass.

Weinberg, R B (1989) Consultation and training with school-based crisis teams. *Professional Psychology: Research and Practice*, 20(5), 305

Weinberg, A M (1987) Science and its limits. In *De Minimis Risk*, Springer US, pp. 27–38

Wenger, D, Quarantelli, E L & Dynes, R R (1990) Is the incident command system a plan for all seasons and emergency situations. *Hazard Monthly*, 10(3), 8–12

White House (2006) The federal response to Hurricane Katrina. Chapter 5, Lessons learned. https://georgewbush-whitehouse.archives.gov/reports/katrina-lessons-learned/chapter5.html (archived at https://perma.cc/728J-T7ZF)

2

Corporate risk management in the 2020s

There is nothing permanent except change.

HERACLITUS (GREEK PHILOSOPHER, 5TH CENTURY BCE)

The world in which Heraclitus lived was undoubtedly simpler, and perhaps to our eyes more primitive, than the world we live in today. Yet, just like almost every generation before and since, he and his compatriots undoubtedly felt that they were living in a time of unprecedented change, and one that created challenges and dangers that had been unknown to the previous generation, which perhaps they in turn looked back on fondly as a simpler and less chaotic period.

It seems that there is almost no break in news of major events that have significant impacts on the world today. Whether it is the challenges of climate change, pollution, hurricanes, heatwaves, flooding or snowstorms, infrastructure failures, satellite dependency or supply change fragility, or in another context the challenges faced by corporations in adapting and responding to changes caused by Covid-19, every one of the above could plausibly be preceded by the word 'unprecedented'. The world as we know it today seems to have entered the age of crisis.[1]

Crises are certainly not new. It is possible that every period in history has considered itself living through 'The Age of Crises'. Although there is no such thing as a routine crisis,[2] it is reasonable to ask why we are not better prepared to deal with the challenges that the world throws at us, particularly considering the level of destructive impact that crises have when we fail to deal with them effectively. Traditional mechanisms regularly get overwhelmed by them.[3] This leads to the assumption that 21st-century crises are different from the ones that we have experienced before. But it is worthwhile asking whether in fact they do differ from past centuries crises and if so, what that means for us. If we use words such as transboundary, transjurisdictional and hyper-complex, what does that mean, what are the challenges in dealing with them, and what is it that is being asked from today's crisis managers?

This chapter aims to establish an understanding of the contexts within which 21st-century crises take place and sets the stage for developing an understanding of the issues and challenges that strategic risk and crisis managers will need to engage with.

Defining the crisis state

A traditional crisis is defined as a situation with low probability and a high impact. It has elements of threat, urgency and uncertainty at its core and is characterized by ambiguity of cause, effects and means of resolution.[4]

30 years ago, there was a belief that the world had become a safer place, thanks to advances in medicine, social safeguards, engineering and food security.[5] It is hard to believe that someone in the 2020s would have the same optimistic view. It seems that the nature of crises has changed. They are no longer singular events but are facets of fundamental infrastructural vulnerabilities, the symptoms of a planet that is no longer stable or centred. Today's crises would be 'better described in terms of a destruction of vital references and a dynamic of systemic implosions'.[6]

Just as our global networks can increasingly be seen as being woven into a dense, geographically dispersed, fragile, interdependent web of technical, organizational and economic infrastructure, the layers of complexity in crises increase.[7] It is often the case that rather than being clearly identifiable, the nature of the crisis and the ways that it manifests are themselves unclear.[8] Complexity is something that is inherent in both natural and social systems.[9] Complexity has become embedded into every aspect of our existence, meaning that crises by default are intrinsically dynamic and non-linear. Seemingly minor incidents can almost instantaneously become triggering events that can in turn escalate into major – and potentially planetary – disasters.[10] Rather than being isolated incidents that can be responded to, controlled and recovered from by the use of simplistic responses, modern crises are by their very nature *transboundary* when 'the functioning of multiple, life-sustaining systems, functions, or infrastructures is acutely threatened and the causes of failure or courses of redress remain unclear'.[11]

As well as the crises themselves, the nature of their impacts and consequences has also changed. Wicked problems are essentially unique: 'All true disasters contain elements of surprise – otherwise they would not warrant that classification'.[12] In addition to their complexity, modern crises have impacts that cross geographical borders (increasing adversity for larger numbers of population) and functions (which goes along with a heightened damage potential), impacting multiple aspects of the underlying infrastructures on which our critical infrastructures and daily lives depend. They have a snowball-like and unpredictable dynamic, both escalating and cascading through multiple interconnected systems in ways that cannot be modelled or predicted. They have the ability to cut off access to critical resources or emergency response systems that were supposed to respond to them. They have long durations and recovery times, combined with extreme uncertainty, many stakeholders (both responders and victims) and high stakes in terms of political pressure to 'get something done'.[13] The inherent risks associated with hyper-complex systems that are connected in multiple ways mean that a problem in any part of the system (however insignificant that component may be in the wider picture) can have immediate, total and potentially irrecoverable impacts across the system. This interconnectedness and the complexity that goes along with it is the defining element of the transboundary crises that define our current risk environment. It is what transforms the understanding of crisis events from one-off statistical outliers (a once-in-a-hundred-year event) to something that is endemic, a part of the ecosystem in which we are all operating.

Main trends in crisis management

Since the early 1980s, crisis management has consisted of two main trends: pre-event planning for crisis management on the one hand and post-event response management on the other. It has to a large extent consisted of:

- a dynamic interplay between the desire to develop theoretical models of crisis management that would allow organizations to prepare themselves both technically, in terms of skills, methods and capabilities, and from a more psychological perspective in order to be 'crisis ready', in order to respond effectively in the event that a crisis event was triggered; and

- post-event reviews that have tried to identify why the frameworks and capabilities that have been developed previously, often in preparation for exactly those events to which they were responding, were not effective and had failed, often catastrophically, in the face of the realities of an actual crisis response.

Hermann and Dayton[14] discovered in an investigation of 77 crisis cases with a high threat level that half of them were anticipated and provided extended time for action, a view Choo shares, defining the elements of anticipation failure as *epistemic blind spots*, *risk denial* and *structural impediment*.[15] Research by Corbacioglu and Kapucu[16] on five major earthquakes in Turkey showed that in three cases no significant organizational learning occurred, and Quarantelli emphasizes that the major source of problems in disasters is the organization's response.[17] Perrow, after having investigated many high-risk-related accidents, concludes: 'Time and time again warnings are ignored, unnecessary risks taken, sloppy work done, deception and downright lying practiced.'[18]

Hurricane Katrina, the category 5 hurricane that made landfall in the city of New Orleans on 29 August 2005, is the pivotal study of crisis events in the first part of the 21st century, and the lessons identified (multiple subsequent events have suggested that they were identified rather than learned) can be seen as a template for why crisis management fails even when there has been a concerted effort to create frameworks and capabilities that should be able to deal with exactly those incidents. The context of the response to Katrina was that New Orleans was known to be vulnerable to flooding, and in fact it was an integral part of its existence. In 2005, more than 50 per cent of New Orleans was below sea level, the ground itself was sinking given the additional weight caused by increased construction, all on top of a soil base that itself was unstable. Besides that, sea levels were rising because of global warming, all of which made it clear that any hurricane that did hit New Orleans would in all likelihood create widespread damage and high-cost impacts. At the same time, in the after-effects of the attacks on the World Trade Center and other targets on September 11 2001 (9/11), the US government had invested almost limitless amounts of time, energy and financial support to enhance the Federal Emergency Management Agency. At the time of Hurricane Katrina, FEMA was undoubtedly the most developed, supported and financed emergency response organization in the world. It is worthwhile asking, then, why it failed so critically in responding to a known and expected event in an American city when it had no other issues other than responding to the hurricane and ensuring the safety, security and well-being of the local population. 'No one anticipated the degree and scope of the destruction the storm would cause, even though many could and should have,' noted the Bipartisan Committee investigating the response to Hurricane Katrina.[19] This quote highlights a significant issue around all aspects of strategic risk and crisis management. The development of the ability to respond appropriately is only one part of crisis management. The Congressional report into Katrina identified a damning list of failures, all of which contributed to the overall failure:

- the lack of appropriate levels of preparedness;
- ignoring of warning signs; bad or missing intelligence and communication before, during and after the storm;
- a large population being unaware of the existing threats;
- federal concepts not properly exercised; and
- the failure of critical infrastructure, institutions and supply chains, all of which combined to create a complex, intertwined construct of elements.[20]

Piotrowski emphasizes that errors were repeated multiple times and lessons from previous events were ignored.[21] The scale, scope and intensity of Hurricane Katrina were not the cause of the crisis but rather the trigger that caught everyone by surprise;[22] these were the missing ingredients that triggered the chain reaction in a long-simmering cocktail of non-functioning elements, the tipping point in a 'series of connected crises'.[23]

Why are lessons not learned?

In corporate environments, the nature of crisis is often misunderstood; rather than being seen as the indication of systemic failures and vulnerabilities, an emerging crisis is seen as a threat that needs to be responded to in terms of incident control.[24] There is a seemingly in-built desire in organizations to not recognize that there are systemic issues that need to be addressed, even when it is clear that the incidents that are being dealt with are not one-off situations caused by error or oversight, and which can be corrected by a simple quick-fix solution. This is perhaps understandable, given the level of organizational response that would be required in the event that such vulnerabilities were acknowledged.[25] But focusing on current threats only ignores the red flags, the frequently hidden although present opportunities that can escalate into crises.[26] Lalonde identifies a lack of time for a proper analysis of a situation (which goes hand in hand with the prioritization of a return to business as usual in the aftermath of a crisis), sensitivity of the topic, managers avoiding responsibilities, lack of competence to transfer knowledge and silo-thinking among companies, sectors and countries.[27]

A review of 2021's top risks shows that transboundary crises have become the new normal. Infectious diseases, climate action failure, pressures on natural resources, extreme weather, fundamental economic changes and cyber security failure all make the list.[28] In 2014, 82 per cent of cities were in areas with a high risk of mortality related to natural disasters and 89 per cent were located in areas with a high vulnerability to economic losses caused by natural disasters.[29]

The snowstorms in February 2021 that caused significant infrastructural failures across Houston, Texas and the surrounding areas were a stark example of how even the most advanced and well-funded urban centres can fall victim to events that can decimate their infrastructures as well as their ability to respond. This is despite the fact that such events should be high on the risk register and a central part of the incident and crisis management programme. The sheer size of the region should make it a necessity: Houston is the fourth largest city in the US and Texas, as a stand-alone economy, is the ninth largest economy in the world – larger than Brazil, Canada or South Korea.

If crisis can be triggered by infrastructural failures that are an inevitable consequence of the highly interconnected hyper-complex systems that keep our world running, or by natural disasters that are the result of the increasing planetary instability we see as a consequence of global warming, then we also need to take into consideration the impacts of malicious attack. Cyber-attacks are a transboundary crisis triggered by active intent. Florida's city water supply system was hacked in February 2021 in an attempt to release toxic material into the water system. In May 2021, Colonial Pipeline faced a ransomware attack, causing a six-day shutdown of one of the major pipeline systems in the US. Meat producer JBS, one of the largest food companies in the world, experienced a ransomware attack in June 2021,[30] as did US nuclear weapons contractor Sol Oriens when it was attacked by the REvil ransomware gang.[31] The month after, Japanese digital imaging and high-tech medical kit producer Fujifilm experienced ransomware attacks.[32] While these were principally isolated cases, the consequences were complex and long-ranging for citizens, sectors, industries and even governments. With societies becoming more and more intertwined and therefore vulnerable to relatively small disturbances, the escalation power is immense: 'Modernization has created "highways for failure" that leverage the effects of emerging threats (be they man-made or natural)'.[33]

Modernization, in all its myriad forms, has created risk vectors that did not exist previously. The changing nature of threat agents is a significant consideration that needs to be addressed, and with a level of seriousness that allows us to understand the significance of those threats and the requirements of any system we would look to put in place to model and engage with them. Technology, terrorism, climate change, demographic and tightly coupled urbanization shifts, global power and economic shifts, organized crime, natural resources, media or complex companies may pose new opportunities and/or threats.[34] It has long been recognized that there are classes of events associated with particularly high-risk technology, such as chemical or nuclear plants, aircraft and air traffic control, ships, dams, nuclear weapons, space missions or genetic engineering, which give them special characteristics making accidents inevitable, regardless of the safeguards in place. This is not necessarily based on their inherent risk levels but on the way their systems are tied together and therefore the way that failure can be triggered by seemingly inconsequential actions in one part of the system that can have cascading effects across the entire network – including to critical infrastructures that did not even realize they were connected to the wider systems. The 2008 global financial collapse is a powerful example of how what can be seen as a powerful global network can at the same time be a potential house of cards, vulnerable to catastrophic systems failure at any time and in ways that are both unexpected and non-recoverable.

Normal accidents in extremely complex environments

The founding statement for this class of events comes from Charles Perrow: 'If interactive complexity and tight coupling – system characteristics – inevitably will produce an accident, I believe we are justified in calling it a normal accident, or a system accident.'[35] The Normal Accident Theory was used to describe events (together with the cultural and management failures that allowed the possibility of such failures to even exist) such as the interactive complexity that led to the Three Mile Island nuclear power plant incident, where within the first 30 seconds four mechanical failures of highly interdependent parts (although they were not in a direct operational sequence) led to a partial meltdown of reactor number two, leading to the largest accident in the US commercial power plant at that time.[36]

If the fact that 'interactive complexity and tight coupling inevitably will produce an accident' was true in the world of the 1980s and 2000s, then it is true to an exponentially greater degree in the world of the 2020s. As an example, global financial transactions are now run by high-frequency trading (HFT) programs that can run millions of commands a second, each of which can create trades worth hundreds of millions of dollars. Trades are completed in milliseconds and even microseconds.[37] Given the fact that such actions are completely automated and each command in turn impacts and influences other commands that are responding to it, it is clear that the possibility of a self-referencing feedback loop that creates a cascading failure could happen before there is the possibility of human intervention, and that could have impacts on the global economy beyond anything that has been seen previously.[38]

ATM cash machines and card payment systems, for example, are dependent on satellite communications, a fragile link connecting centralized databases with billions of data files and end users that are spread across the world. This means that a failure (for whatever reason and anywhere in the system) can have instantaneous effects not only across those systems but across the systems that are piggy-backing off them.

The failure of the entire ATM system in Indonesia,[39] the global failure of Facebook in 2021[40] and seemingly regular failures in, for example, airline booking systems are just an indicator of both how dependent and how fragile these systems are.

The Facebook failure, during which the entire global system went off-line for up to six hours, was a classic example of the issues that were identified and which caused such serious problems. The first issue was that Facebook's own systems all run through Facebook, so when the system goes off-line so does the systems' ability to talk among themselves or to access their own services and resources. The second was that this was an 'unprecedented' event. Although there had been regular outages of sections of the systems (which had therefore become recognized as routine emergencies), there had never been a total systems failure before. And the third was that it was not something that had been planned for.

The fragility of the systems can be seen in another outage that occurred in June 2021, when Fastly, an internet platform provider for some of the largest websites in the world, went off-line, the result of a single customer updating their settings, triggering a series of cascading events that resulted seconds later in a global outage.[41]

The New York power outage of 2003 and the European power outage of 2006 are classic examples of how a relatively minor incident in one position can trigger cascading events across multiple regions and jurisdictions. In the European outage, a standard response was initiated to manage a local power surge that was intended to decrease the pressure on the system. In fact, it had the opposite effect and within 28 seconds an electrical blackout had cascaded across Europe, extending from Poland in the north-east through the Benelux countries and France in the west, through to Portugal, Spain and Morocco in the south-west, and across to Greece and the Balkans in the south-east.[42]

In the New York blackout, the initial triggering event was overloaded power lines hitting unpruned tree foliage, causing a local cut-out. A software bug in the alarm system, located at a control room in Ohio, turned out to be the primary cause. The operators weren't made aware due to a lack of alarm, resulting in a missing redistribution of power once the overloaded transmission lines hit the foliage. This triggered a race condition in the control software. What would have been a manageable local blackout cascaded into massive widespread distress on the electric grid, affecting 45 million people in eight US states and 10 million people in Ontario, Canada.[43]

When a similar transboundary power outage affected almost all of Argentina and neighbouring Uruguay and Paraguay, the official response was that it was 'unprecedented'.[44] As in so many cases where the word unprecedented is used, what it actually meant was: *We were not ready.*

What can be done to tackle today's transboundary crises?

Preparation for today's crises requires a change of mindset, although there are multiple types of challenges along the way: political–administrative challenges, the fabric of society and its resilience capabilities, and the ability for the necessary level of deep thinking from policy makers.[45] Lagadec further mentions bureaucratic inertia[46] (to wait until the crisis fits its codes and rules) and the general loss of nerve both among the public and along the chain of command in terms of taking decisions that would have an impact in preventing, mitigating or responding to such events.

In crises, there is often the belief that there should be someone who 'knows the answers' and who can take control.[47] This is often in direct contrast to the skills and capabilities organizations need to run in conventional times, which requires the ability to develop structures and frameworks that follow processes and procedures. Crises, by definition, force leaders to break through silos and to be creative in finding new solutions. The higher the stakes, the more important is direct and determined leadership from the top – this requires mental preparedness, conviction and vision.[48]

The ability to be sensitive to the indicators of potential impending crises is a critical issue. These signals are often silent, hidden and elusive. There may be background noise that precludes them being identified, and alternatively there may be the desire to suppress bad news and to block messages about those signals being passed further up the management chain ('normalcy' bias and heuristics[49]) Both issues create a situation where it is the lack of sensitivity to potential warning signals that prevents an organization from either recognizing a potential crisis before it escalates to such a condition or having the readiness to respond in an appropriate and effective manner once such signals are detected.

The role of modern-day crisis management has changed. Ready-made answers, conventional tactics and interpretations are no longer robust enough to stand up in the face of the high-impact challenges associated with modern crisis events. An agile, integrated big-picture approach to risk assessment, preparedness, response and recovery, backed by a culture and technology that respect the seriousness of the issues and accept the responsibility to create a risk-sensitive and crisis-ready organization, is the starting point for the development of effective risk management. Holistic concepts with inter-organizational coordination, information exchange, resource allocation (e.g. professional personnel familiar with engaging with chaos and who are to be responsive to unstable situations) and non-linear response strategies (involving the integration of multiple stakeholders, both internal and external, formal and *ad hoc*, including both communities and non-profit sector organizations) are increasingly important in setting a perspective that is able to go beyond traditional linear, simplistic and bounded events that have clear boundaries and limited impacts.

The question now is: What does it take to move into the crisis-ready state?

Endnotes

1 Blythe, B T (2014) *Blindsided: A manager's guide to crisis leadership*. Brookfield: Rothstein Publishing

2 Boin, A & Lagadec, P (2000) Preparing for the future: Critical challenges in crisis management. *Journal of Contingencies and Crisis Management*, 8, 185–191

3 Lagadec, E (2007) Unconventional crises, unconventional responses: Reforming leadership in the age of catastrophic crises and hypercomplexity. Center for Transatlantic Relations, Paul H. Nitze School of Advanced International Studies, Johns Hopkins University

4 Lagadec, P (2009) A new cosmology of risks and crises: Time for a radical shift in paradigm and practice. *Review of Policy Research*, 26(4), 473–486

5 Wildavsky, A B (1988) Searching for safety (Vol. 10) Transaction publishers

6 Lagadec, P (2009) A new cosmology of risks and crises: Time for a radical shift in paradigm and practice. *Review of Policy Research*, 26(4), 473–486

7 Boin, A (2009) The new world of crises and crisis management: Implications for policymaking and research. *Review of Policy Research*, 26(4), 367–377

8 Blythe, B T (2014) *Blindsided: A manager's guide to crisis leadership*. Brookfield: Rothstein Publishing

9 Corbacioglu, S & Kapucu, N (2006) Organisational learning and selfadaptation in dynamic disaster environments. *Disasters*, 30(2), 212–233

10 Corbacioglu, S & Kapucu, N (2006) Organisational learning and selfadaptation in dynamic disaster environments. *Disasters*, 30(2), 212–233

11 Boin, A (2009) The new world of crises and crisis management: Implications for policymaking and research. *Review of Policy Research*, 26(4), 367–377

12 Tierney, K (2008) Structure and process in the study of disaster resilience. 14th World Conference on Earthquake Engineering, Beijing, China

13 Boin, A (2009) The new world of crises and crisis management: Implications for policymaking and research. *Review of Policy Research*, 26(4), 367–377

14 Hermann, M G & Dayton, B W (2009) Transboundary crises through the eyes of policymakers: Sense making and crisis management. *Journal of Contingencies and Crisis Management*, 17(4), 233–241

15 Choo, C W (2008) Organizational disasters: Why they happen and how they may be prevented. *Management Decisions*, 46(1), 32–45

16 Corbacioglu, S & Kapucu, N (2006) Organisational learning and self-adaptation in dynamic disaster environments. *Disasters*, 30(2), 212–233

17 Quarantelli, E L (1988) Disaster crisis management: A summary of research findings. *Journal of Management Studies*, 25(4), 373–385

18 Perrow, C (1999) Normal accidents: Living with high risk technologies. Princeton University Press

19 United States. Congress. House. Select Bipartisan Committee to Investigate the Preparation for and Response to Hurricane Katrina (2006) A failure of initiative: Final report of the select bipartisan committee to investigate the preparation for and response to Hurricane Katrina (Vol. 109) Government Printing Office

20 United States. Congress. House. Select Bipartisan Committee to Investigate the Preparation for and Response to Hurricane Katrina (2006) A failure of initiative: Final report of the select bipartisan committee to investigate the preparation for and response to Hurricane Katrina (Vol. 109) Government Printing Office

21 Piotrowski, C (2006) Hurricane Katrina and organization development: Part 1. Implications of chaos theory. *Organization Development Journal*, 24(3), 10

22 Hermann, M G & Dayton, B W (2009) Transboundary crises through the eyes of policymakers: Sense making and crisis management. *Journal of Contingencies and Crisis Management*, 17(4), 233–241

23 Moynihan, D P (2009) The response to hurricane Katrina. Geneva (Italy): International Risk Governance Council, 27–45

24 Blythe, B T (2014) *Blindsided: A manager's guide to crisis leadership*. Brookfield: Rothstein Publishing

25 Corbacioglu, S & Kapucu, N (2006) Organisational learning and selfadaptation in dynamic disaster environments. *Disasters*, 30(2), 212–233

26 Blythe, B T (2014) *Blindsided: A manager's guide to crisis leadership*. Brookfield: Rothstein Publishing

27 Lalonde, C (2007) Crisis management and organizational development: Towards the conception of a learning model in crisis management. Organization Development Journal, 25(1)

28 WEF (World Economic Forum) (2021) The Global Risks Report 2021, 16th Edition. Geneva

29 United Nations (2016) Department of Economic and Social Affairs, The world's cities in 2016

30 Duffy, C & Iyengar, R (2021) Hackers have a devastating new target. Available at: https://edition.cnn.com/2021/06/03/tech/ransomware-cyberattack-jbs-colonial-pipeline/index.html (archived at https://perma.cc/P52E-JVH9) (Accessed: 15 June 2021)

31 Abrams, L (2021) REvil ransomware hits US nuclear weapons contractor. Available at: https://www.bleepingcomputer.com/news/security/revil-ransomware-hits-us-nuclear-weapons-contractor/ (archived at https://perma.cc/4RGD-9TRL) (Accessed: 18 June 2021)

32 Page, C (2021) Fujifilm becomes the latest victim of a network-crippling ransomware attack. Available at: https://techcrunch.com/2021/06/03/fujifilm-becomes-the-latest-victim-of-a-network-crippling-ransomware-attack/ (archived at https://perma.cc/A477-M3FY) (Accessed: 16 June 2021)

33 Boin, A (2009) The new world of crises and crisis management: Implications for policymaking and research. *Review of Policy Research*, 26(4), 367–377

34 Blythe, B T (2014) *Blindsided: A manager's guide to crisis leadership*. Brookfield: Rothstein Publishing

35 Perrow, C (1984) *Normal accidents: Living with high risk technologies*. Basic Books

36 Perrow, C (1984) *Normal accidents: Living with high risk technologies*. Basic Books

37 A millisecond is 1/1,000th of a second. A microsecond is 1/1000th of a millisecond.

38 Aquilina, M, Budish, E & O'Neill, P (2021) Quantifying the high-frequency trading 'arms race'. *The Quarterly Journal of Economics*, 137(1), 493–564

39 Nangoy, F & Silviana, C (2017) Thousands of ATMs go down in Indonesia after satellite problems. Reuters (28 August) Available at: https://www.reuters.com/article/us-indonesia-telkom-indonesia-banking-idUSKCN1B80QP (archived at https://perma.cc/WH6H-DCFR) (Accessed: 20 June 2022)

40 Taylor, J (2021) Facebook outage: What went wrong and why did it take so long to fix after social platform went down? Available at: https://www.theguardian.com/technology/2021/oct/05/facebook-outage-what-went-wrong-and-why-did-it-take-so-long-to-fix (archived at https://perma.cc/P2D2-7YXM) (Accessed 1 May, 2022)

41 Hern, A (2021) Fastly says single customer triggered bug behind mass internet outage. Available at: https://www.theguardian.com/technology/2021/jun/09/fastly-says-single-customer-triggered-bug-that-caused-mass-outage (archived at https://perma.cc/Q7MV-XFBC) (Accessed: 1 May, 2022)

42 European Blackout (2006) Available at: https://en.wikipedia.org/wiki/2006_European_blackout (archived at https://perma.cc/JE2A-5CWU) (Accessed: 21 June 2022)

43 New York Blackout (2003) Blackout in the United States and Canada: Causes and Recommendations. Available at: https://www3.epa.gov/region1/npdes/merrimackstation/pdfs/ar/AR-1165.pdf (archived at https://perma.cc/PX97-VZR5) (Accessed 1 May, 2022)

44 BBC (2019) South American power cut. Argentina investigates 'unprecedented outage'. Available at: https://www.bbc.co.uk/news/world-latin-america-48662279 (archived at https://perma.cc/LBF7-RPUJ) (Accessed 1 May, 2022)

45 Boin, A (2009) The new world of crises and crisis management: Implications for policymaking and research. *Review of Policy Research*, 26(4), 367–377

46 Lagadec, P (2009) A new cosmology of risks and crises: Time for a radical shift in paradigm and practice. *Review of Policy Research*, 26(4), 473–486.

47 Ripley, A (2008) *The unthinkable: Who survives when disaster strikes – and why*. Crown Archetype

48 Lagadec, P (2009) A new cosmology of risks and crises: Time for a radical shift in paradigm and practice. *Review of Policy Research*, 26(4), 473–486

49 Choo, C W (2008) Organizational disasters: Why they happen and how they may be prevented. *Management Decisions*, 46(1), 32–45

Further reading

Abrams, L (2021) REvil ransomware hits US nuclear weapons contractor. Available at: https://www.bleepingcomputer.com/news/security/revil-ransomware-hits-us-nuclear-weapons-contractor/ (archived at https://perma.cc/4RGD-9TRL) (Accessed: 18 June 2021)

Aquilina, M, Budish, E & O'Neill, P (2021) Quantifying the high-frequency trading 'arms race'. *The Quarterly Journal of Economics*, 137(1), 493–564

AZ Quotes (1) (2021) Available at: https://www.azquotes.com/quote/521413 (archived at https://perma.cc/PQU3-XLPX) (Accessed: 10 June 2021)

AZ Quotes (2) (2021) Available at: https://www.azquotes.com/quote/366460 (archived at https://perma.cc/5CA3-CDTD) (Accessed: 10 June 2021)

BBC (2019) South American power cut. Argentina investigates 'unprecedented outage'. Available at: https://www.bbc.co.uk/news/world-latin-america-48662279 (archived at https://perma.cc/LBF7-RPUJ) (Accessed 1 May, 2022)

Betts, R K (1981) Surprise despite warning: Why sudden attacks succeed. *Political Science Quarterly*, 95, 551–572

Blythe, B T (2014) *Blindsided: A manager's guide to crisis leadership*. Brookfield: Rothstein Publishing

Boin, A (2009) The new world of crises and crisis management: Implications for policymaking and research. *Review of Policy Research*, 26(4), 367–377

Boin, A & Lagadec, P (2000) Preparing for the future: Critical challenges in crisis management. *Journal of Contingencies and Crisis Management*, 8, 185–191

Choo, C W (2008) Organizational disasters: Why they happen and how they may be prevented. *Management Decisions*, 46(1), 32–45

Cohen, W M & Levinthal, D A (1990) Absorptive capacity: A new perspective on learning and innovation. *Administrative Science Quarterly*, 128–152

Comfort, L K (2007) Crisis management in hindsight: Cognition, communication, coordination, and control. *Public Administration Review*, 67, 189–197

Corbacioglu, S & Kapucu, N (2006) Organisational learning and selfadaptation in dynamic disaster environments. *Disasters*, 30(2), 212–233

Duffy, C & Iyengar, R (2021) Hackers have a devastating new target. Available at: https://edition.cnn.com/2021/06/03/tech/ransomware-cyberattack-jbs-colonial-pipeline/index.html (archived at https://perma.cc/P52E-JVH9) (Accessed: 15 June 2021)

Dynes, R R & Aguirre, B E (1979) Organizational adaptation to crises: Mechanisms of coordination and structural change. *Disasters*, 3(1), 71–74

European Blackout (2006) Available at: https://en.wikipedia.org/wiki/2006_European_blackout (archived at https://perma.cc/JE2A-5CWU) (Accessed: 21 June 2022)

Hermann, M G & Dayton, B W (2009) Transboundary crises through the eyes of policymakers: Sense making and crisis management. *Journal of Contingencies and Crisis Management*, 17(4), 233–241

Hern, A (2021) Fastly says single customer triggered bug behind mass internet outage. Available at: https://www.theguardian.com/technology/2021/jun/09/fastly-says-single-customer-triggered-bug-that-caused-mass-outage (archived at https://perma.cc/Q7MV-XFBC) (Accessed 1 May 2022)

Lagadec, E (2007) Unconventional crises, unconventional responses: Reforming leadership in the age of catastrophic crises and hypercomplexity. Center for Transatlantic Relations, Paul H. Nitze School of Advanced International Studies, Johns Hopkins University

Lagadec, P (2009) A new cosmology of risks and crises: Time for a radical shift in paradigm and practice. *Review of Policy Research*, 26(4), 473–486

Lalonde, C (2007) Crisis management and organizational development: Towards the conception of a learning model in crisis management. *Organization Development Journal*, 25(1), 17

LaPorte, T R (2007) Critical infrastructure in the face of a predatory future: Preparing for untoward surprise. *Journal of Contingencies and Crisis Management*, 15(1), 60–64

Moynihan, D P (2009) The response to hurricane Katrina. Geneva (Italy): International Risk Governance Council, 27–45

Nangoy, F & Silviana, C (2017) Thousands of ATMs go down in Indonesia after satellite problems. Reuters (28 August) Available at: https://www.reuters.com/article/us-indonesia-telkom-indonesia-banking-idUSKCN1B80QP (archived at https://perma.cc/WH6H-DCFR) (Accessed: 20 June 2022)

NDB (Nachrichtendienst des Bundes) (2021) Sicherheit Schweiz 2021. Lagebericht des Nachrichtendienst des Bundes. BBL, Verkauf Bundespublikationen

New York Blackout (2003) Blackout in the United States and Canada: Causes and recommendations (2004) Available at: https://www3.epa.gov/region1/npdes/merrimackstation/pdfs/ar/AR-1165.pdf (archived at https://perma.cc/PX97-VZR5) (Accessed 1 May, 2022)

Page, C (2021) Fujifilm becomes the latest victim of a network-crippling ransomware attack. Available at: https://techcrunch.com/2021/06/03/fujifilm-becomes-the-latest-victim-of-a-network-crippling-ransomware-attack/ (archived at https://perma.cc/A477-M3FY) (Accessed: 16 June 2021)

Pearson, C M & Clair, J A (1998) Reframing crisis management. *Academy of Management Review*, 23(1), 59–76

Perrow, C (1984) *Normal accidents: Living with high risk technologies*. Basic Books

Piotrowski, C (2006*)* Hurricane Katrina and organization development: Part 1. Implications of chaos theory. *Organization Development Journal*, 24(3), 10

Quarantelli, E L (1988) Disaster crisis management: A summary of research findings. *Journal of Management Studies*, 25(4), 373–385

Ripley, A (2008) *The Unthinkable: Who survives when disaster strikes – and why*. Crown Archetype

Rosenthal, U, Boin, A & Comfort, L K (2001) *Managing crises: Threats, dilemmas, opportunities*. Charles C Thomas Publisher

Rosenthal, U, Charles, M T & Hart, P T (eds.) (1989) *Coping with crises: The management of disasters, riots, and terrorism*. Charles C Thomas Pub Limited

Rosenthal, U, Hart, P T, & Kouzmin, A (1991) The bureau-politics of crisis management. *Public Administration*, 69(2), 211–233

Taylor, J (2021) Facebook outage: What went wrong and why did it take so long to fix after social platform went down? Available at: https://www.theguardian.com/technology/2021/oct/05/facebook-outage-what-went-wrong-and-why-did-it-take-so-long-to-fix (archived at https://perma.cc/P2D2-7YXM) (Accessed 1 May, 2022)

United Nations. Department of Economic and Social Affairs (2016) The world's cities in 2016. UN.

United States. Congress. House. Select Bipartisan Committee to Investigate the Preparation for and Response to Hurricane Katrina (2006) A failure of initiative: Final report of the select bipartisan committee to investigate the preparation for and response to Hurricane Katrina (Vol. 109) Government Printing Office.

WEF (World Economic Forum) (2021) *The Global Risks Report 2021, 16th Edition*. Geneva

Wildavsky, A B (1988) *Searching for safety (Vol. 10)* Transaction Publishers

3

Black swans + grey rhinos – being ready

There seems to be something in the human condition that means that we prefer simplicity over complexity, even when simplicity often rolls over into being simplistic. While simplicity can be seen as a positive attribute – the absence or avoidance of that which is not necessary – simplistic has another and more negative meaning. It implies that rather than avoiding that which is unnecessary, it is more a case of ignoring that which is critical, especially if it is something which makes the observer feel uncomfortable or for which they do not have an appropriate toolbox, whether conceptual or operational, to deal with it.

Karl Weick identified the ability to be comfortable with complexity as one of the basic attributes of high-reliability organizations[1] and it is the inability to be comfortable with complexity or the desire to avoid it that often leads to a failure to grasp the true nature of challenging situations. This in turn sets the conditions that lead to the failure to develop effective or appropriate pre-emptive management or post-event response capabilities.

In 1992, following the fall of the Soviet Union and the end of the Cold War that had dominated global geopolitics since the end of the Second World War 45 years previously, Francis Fukuyama wrote a book called *The End of History and the Last Man*.[2] In it, he postulated that the end of the Cold War was not merely a natural ripple in the neverending tapestry of human history but was actually something much more powerful than that. In Fukuyama's opinion, the victory of the United States over the Soviet Union demonstrated the dominance of social democracy in the political sphere and market capitalism in the economic one. He did not hold back in giving a sense of the significance of these developments. 'What we may be witnessing is not the end of the Cold War, but the end of history as such; that is, the end point of man's ideological evolution and the universalization of Western liberal democracy.' It was a winner of the Los Angeles Times Book Prize and carried on its front cover a quote from a review in the *Washington Post*'s Book World: 'Awesome... A landmark work... Profoundly realistic and important... Supremely timely and cogent... The first book to fully fathom the depth and range of the changes now sweeping through the world.' From the perspective of 30 years later (though it is a point made widely at the time), the question has to be, 'I wonder how that worked out?' If there was one lesson to be learned from Fukuyama's book (and there are many, depending on the perspective you take) it is the fact that just because a book wins prizes and is on the *New York Times* bestseller list doesn't mean that it is correct.

In our generation, the equivalent of Fukuyama's review of history is *The Black Swan*, the global bestseller by Nassim Nicholas Taleb, published in 2010 with the strap line 'The impact of the highly improbable'. Taleb described black swans as the random events that underlie our lives, from bestsellers to world disasters.[3] Their impact is huge and they are impossible to predict, and yet after they happen we always try to rationalize them. In Taleb's view, there was a need to get away from the idea that everything could be predicted and to accept – and even embrace – the idea of the uncertain and unexpected.

Almost immediately the phrase 'black swan' became shorthand for everything associated with shock and unpreparedness – and in itself became a rallying cry for the fact that when black swan events did happen, they were so strange and unpredictable that no one could be held responsible for the fact that they hadn't predicted or prepared for them.

Misunderstanding the black swan

It is one of the principles of black swan events that they are unpredictable prior to them happening, but there is a realization that they were almost inevitable in hindsight. The 2008 global financial crash is one obvious example of a black swan event, the 2001 9/11 attacks are another and coronavirus/Covid-19 is a third. However, to label these events as black swan is to both misunderstand what a black swan event is and misinterpret what that means.

A black swan event is not one that is simply rare or unexpected but rather one that is paradigm-changing. Taleb in his book gave a succinct description of what a black swan is: 'First, it is an outlier, as it lies outside the realm of regular expectations, because nothing in the past can convincingly point to its possibility. Second, it carries an extreme "impact". Third, in spite of its outlier status, human nature makes us concoct explanations for its occurrence after the fact, making it explainable and predictable.' He then made the claim that a small number of black swans explains almost everything in our world, from the success of ideas and religions to the dynamics of historical events, to elements of our personal lives.

What a black swan event is *not*, and nor should it be, is an excuse for the rather more prosaic 'Sorry, I wasn't paying attention'. It is impossible to claim that Covid-19 was a black swan event given that we have had repeated examples of potential global pandemics over the past 20 years (Zika, SARS, MERS, swine flu, avian flu, Ebola). Emergent infectious diseases were listed on the UK National Risk Register in 2017 with a likelihood of four out of five of happening in the next five years (the same level of likelihood as pandemic influenza, which is considered an annual event in UK healthcare sectors) Although we could not know that the specific case of Covid-19 would happen, or that it would take place in the first part of 2020, the fact that something within the class of events labelled 'global pandemics' would happen at some stage was not only known but highlighted as something inevitable for which we should prepare.

The US Center for Strategic and International Studies published a report in November 2019 highlighting the lack of US capability to engage with, manage and respond to pandemics, citing the 2001 anthrax attacks, SARS in 2003, measles, dengue fever and recurring incidences of Ebola and influenza as warning signs that the system was failing.[4] It identified that a lack of strategic vision and leadership had left significant gaps and vulnerabilities in the US healthcare and crisis management systems. The message could not have been clearer: 'The American people are far from safe. To the contrary, the United States remains woefully ill-prepared to respond to global health security threats. This kind of vulnerability should not be acceptable to anyone. At the extreme, it is a matter of life and death. [We urge] the U.S. government to replace the cycle of crisis and complacency that has long plagued health security preparedness with a doctrine of continuous prevention, protection, and resilience.'

Yet this vulnerability was not something that had been realized suddenly. In 2014, following the outbreak of Ebola in West Africa, then president Barack Obama gave a presentation to the National Institutes of Health.[5] One of his key points was the call for a global – not local – infrastructure, allowing the detection, isolation and quick response to new diseases. He emphasized to pay it forward, so that when a new strain of flu or similar popped up in a few years, the world would be ready to react appropriately. 'We have to put in place an infrastructure – not just here at home but globally – that allows us to see it quickly, isolate it quickly, respond to it quickly. So that if and when a new strain of flu, like the Spanish flu, crops up five years from now or a decade from now, we've made the investment and we're further along to be able to catch it.'

This was not a knee-jerk reaction to an unexpected event or one that was designed to gain political points. He had written in an op-ed in *The New York Times* in 2005 about the recommendation to the administration to work with Congress, public health officials, the pharmaceutical industry, foreign governments and international organizations to build a steady framework.[6] This framework should curtail the spread of new infectious diseases. Passing emergency funding to fight Ebola and setting up a public health infrastructure, Obama continued, is arguably the best example for the world to agree on how to deal with potential future outbreaks.

Some of the points highlighted in the op-ed piece included:

- increasing international disease surveillance, response capacity and public education and coordination, especially in South East Asia;
- stockpiling enough antiviral doses to cover high-risk populations and essential workers;
- ensuring that at home health and human services and state governments put in place plans that address issues of surveillance, medical care, drug and vaccine distribution, communication, protection of the work force and maintenance of core public functions in case of a pandemic;
- accelerating research into avian flu vaccines and antiviral drugs; and
- establishing incentives to encourage nations to report flu outbreaks quickly and fully.

On 3 April 2015, Bill Gates gave a TEDx presentation entitled 'The next outbreak? We're not ready'.[7] As of June 2022 that had been viewed more than 35 million times according to YouTube. For those who would like a more historical perspective, in *A Dancing Matrix*, a 1993 book by Robin Henig, she quotes Nobel Prize Laureate Joshua Lederberg who said, 'The single biggest threat to man's continued dominance on the planet is the virus.'[8] (For readers who would like to see Henig's thoughts on our unpreparedness for Covid-19, see her article in the July 2020 edition of *National Geographic*.[9])

Understanding grey rhinos

It is clear that the model described as black swans by Taleb does not fit this model of almost wilful ignoring of signs. It was in response to the seemingly universal acceptance of the reality and ubiquity of black swans that a challenge to this approach appeared with the publication of *The Gray Rhino* by Michele Wucker. She used the analogy of the grey rhino.

By its very nature, a grey rhino is big, fast and aggressive, and it's very hard to ignore when it is standing on the path right in front of you, front foot pawing, snorting and ready to make its move. Wucker used this animal to describe the way many people react to crisis events that are not only not hidden but are screaming to be noticed.[10] As she points out, the whole premise of black swans, and one that is even highlighted in the title of the book, is that they are improbable events. On the classical impact/likelihood risk matrix, they are so far into the corner that identifies unlikely events that they have almost no mathematical value.

If these improbable events are becoming so frequent that almost any unpleasant experience can be described as a black swan, then this might be for two possible reasons. First, either our understanding of the concept of improbable is wrong, or second, the nature of the risk environment we are operating in has changed to such a degree that, just like aliens dropping into our planet from an unknown dimension in a science-fiction film, they do not follow any cause-and-effect patterns that would allow us to recognize, predict or pre-empt them. While it is entirely possible that in fact the nature of the risk environment is changing in such a way as to make what would previously have been considered black swan events part of our normal operating environment, it does not deny the truth that while black swan events are theoretical, a grey rhino standing in front of you is very real. As Wucker points out, under such circumstances it is not necessarily helpful to waste your time trying to work if it is in fact a grey rhino rather than a white, black, Sumatran, Javan or Indian rhino. What you really want to be concentrating on is:

- how I can predict how the rhino will behave;
- can I accentuate my behaviour that will placate it or make it go away; and
- can I minimize behaviour that could antagonize it and trigger an attack?

Of course, by far the better move would have been to have an awareness of the environment that you and the rhino are both operating in, to have intelligence available on the known movement of rhinos in general, to have checked out the path you were taking to see if there were in fact any rhinos there on that particular day. Then you could proceed in the knowledge that although you think there are no grey rhinos there, it is always possible that one could appear, in which case it is good to first maintain a level of awareness appropriate to the potential danger and second have a plan of action based on the guidance of people who have expert knowledge and personal experience of grey rhino behaviour.

When put in such terms, it can be seen that although grey rhinos are inherently potentially dangerous, by having an awareness of how they operate and an ability to spot them early – or to avoid them completely – the level of actual risk can be minimized to an extent that it can reasonably be considered as extremely low value in the risk matrix calculation. This is risk management in its purest and most effective form, and it's something that is not based on esoteric calculations and algorithms but on an ability to engage with the real world as it is rather than as we might wish it to be.

In the conclusion of her book, Wucker identifies five behaviours that could help you avoid being threatened by a charging rhino. Let's go through each of these in turn.

1. Recognize the rhino

Grey rhinos, and crisis events in general, are not easy to hide. The reason that people do not recognize them is because, in the main, they spend a huge amount of time and effort trying to pretend that they can't see exactly the threats that are causing them the greatest danger. Whether it is global warming, climate change, resource depletion, infrastructure fragility, global supply chain complexity or personal issues such as obesity, drug abuse or society-wide mental health issues, it is the reluctance to face up to the truth of the threats we are facing that prevents us from dealing with them in a realistic manner. And of course, there is also the secondary issue that the longer we try to pretend we cannot see the problem, it is in itself getting closer, more aggressive and more dangerous, and will undoubtedly leave us in greater peril by the time we do decide to pay attention – which in the case of the rhino is when it starts charging and in the cases of the global crises events mentioned above… well, the truth is, we haven't started to pay attention to them even now.

2. Define the rhino

We have a natural bias towards engaging with problems for which we have a set of potential solutions, or which we have dealt with before, rather than those which are seemingly intractable or are new to us. By breaking down a seemingly insoluble, or at least hard-to-define, problem into manageable components, we can downgrade it to a challenging but nevertheless rational problem, or at least one for which we think we might have a tool kit or set of options to deal with it.

Within the context of 2020s' risk and crisis management, we are faced with a range of problems which we seemingly lack the language or frameworks to define. Without such a shared definition, it is by its very nature hard to agree on what the significance of those problems is and what the potential range of solutions is that we could bring to the table to engage with them. If there is one central theme, it is that there is the necessity – one that is increasingly urgent and critical – to develop a language to describe the problems of the 2020s and to give us the ability to both conceptualize and articulate what appropriate response management measures might look like. The lack of such shared language and frameworks is in itself a sign that we will continue to be unable to engage with those issues in a meaningful way.

This comes back to Rittel and Webber's observation, that defining the problem is predefining the solution:[11] the definition of the problem will never be applicable the same way when you look at it from another perspective. Neither ideal is the solution. So the question remains: What is the problem – how do you define the rhino?

3. Don't stand still

There is nothing in nature that is static. Even if an animal is physically standing still, their antennae are undoubtedly checking the surrounding environment on an ongoing basis. In their context, losing awareness of your surroundings is one of the fastest ways of ending up as someone else's dinner. It is well known that the fight/flight syndrome caused by the adrenaline surge triggered by a dangerous or scary event is more accurately described as fight/flight/freeze. Fight and flight are learned actions. They are developed as repetitive behaviour patterns that need to be trained and embedded. The much more likely scenario is that the first time that you are put into a scary or threatening situation – even if you have practised and rehearsed that scenario multiple times – the adrenaline rush will mean you will lose the cognitive and motor skills that should have allowed you to deliver the performance in the same way that you did in the run-throughs. As a matter of fact, the adrenaline causes major parts of your system to shut down, meaning that you are not able to process information in such a way that you can start to engage with whatever the situation is throwing at you and start to build a picture, identify options and create a plan of action. You literally become disengaged from the reality of your immediate environment.

The way to break that adrenaline freeze is simply to do something. It doesn't have to be big or brave or dramatic. But the mere fact of moving, of doing something, whatever that might be, allows you to break out of the fight/flight/freeze box, which in turn is associated with decision inertia and failures to act,[12] and to regain control of your situation. It is the first step that is the hardest; once you have done something, then the next step(s) will be easier.

4. A crisis is a terrible thing to waste

Although Rahm Emanuel, Barack Obama's White House Chief of Staff and subsequently mayor of Chicago, is often cited as saying 'Never let a crisis go to waste', it was Winston Churchill who used the same words towards the end of the Second World War. Crises are by their very nature destructive. They often leave behind a trail of wreckage that means that a substantial rebuilding stage is a natural part of the post-crisis recovery process. It is exactly at the time of greatest destruction and dislocation that there are often the greatest opportunities to not only build back but build back better.

What this can look like in practice is visible best when we look at cities. London as we know it today, and particularly the great churches and cathedrals bequeathed to us by Sir Christopher Wren and his contemporaries, was a direct result of the opportunity to rebuild the city after the Great Fire of London in 1666 (which itself followed the Great Plague of 1665, which had killed an estimated 100,000 people – almost a quarter of London's population – in 18 months[13]) It was the cities of Japan and Germany that saw the great rebuilding after the destruction of the Second World War, which gave them the social and technical infrastructure that led them to becoming global economic powerhouses from the 1960s onwards.

In many ways, Covid-19 has had an impact as significant on the way we live our lives as the Great Plague did 350 years earlier. It has created complete disruption in the way we run our businesses, earn our livings and generally interact with each other in both social and business contexts. The WFH (work from home) phenomenon that was triggered by the global pandemic lockdown from March 2020 (although it had been around for some time before already) has seen revolutionary change in the way we do our work,[14] as well as the way we interact with our workmates, clients, employees and bosses. Despite some of the largest organizations in the world insisting that WFH was an 'aberration'[15] and that they fully expected their workers to return to an office-based routine[16] (even threatening them with pay reductions if they did not do so),[17] there was a parallel movement of the 'Great Resignation', when millions of people decided that the work they were doing, or at least the way that they were doing it, was not for them.[18]

These are what could be considered in their purest sense pivot moments. They are those points in time when a historical change occurs and within moments you are either part of the past or part of the future – and trying to straddle those two tectonic plates could have unfortunate results. Life is full of both examples and metaphors of what happens when you don't read the signs. The classic example of inefficiency are the dinosaurs. But actually, dinosaurs are exactly the opposite of what should be seen as inefficiency leading to extinction. From a historical perspective, dinosaurs (along with viruses and cockroaches) are the outstanding example of successful adaptation to their environment. The dinosaurs as a class lived for about 180 million years (as a comparison, humans have been around for 200,000 years and civilization as we know it for about 6,000 years) It is generally accepted that what wiped out the dinosaurs was a catastrophic planetary event, probably an asteroid crash.[19]

On one level, the crises that we are currently facing are perhaps in some ways as significant as that asteroid collision, particularly if we see the impacts of climate change on the planet as being as epoch-defining as the advent of the ice ages were in previous planetary eco-cycles. However, in most cases, crises are more likely to be temporal, and in that sense create opportunities for those organizations that have the necessary powers of agility, adaptability and innovation, along with leadership, organizational culture and the other softer qualities that would allow them to be aware of the changes and to make their moves accordingly.

Although we often consider crises to be sudden and unexpected, a closer reading leads to the conclusion that it was the failure to read the signs of on-coming change, and to try to stick with methods and processes that were demonstrably outmoded and inherently ineffective, that created the final collapse. Technology firm IBM is used as the standard case study for how failure to move with emerging trends can cause even the greatest beasts to fail – though perhaps not fatally. The onset of personal computers meant that the IBM business model of highly expensive mainframe computers quickly became outdated and in 1993 the company lost $8 billion in a single quarter.[20] It was only by holding a total review of what it was that they did as a company, and what it was that their customers wanted, that they were able to reinvent themselves as a systems integrator as much as a components seller. Photography film technology producer Kodak is another organization that went from being pre-eminent, and almost sector-defining given the scale of its dominance, to being outmoded and bankrupt a few years later.[21]

That was in a period when the great dinosaurs of industry were still seen to be the alpha beasts of their environments. In the current world, where organizations can go from zero to a unicorn status ($1 billion valuation) in months, and without ever having made a profit, or even actually produced anything, then the pace of change is even more dramatic and challenging. While most of us don't have the ambition to gain unicorn status, the rules that hold true for those organizations are equally true for those much lower down the food chain.

Just as military tacticians would talk of a 'target-rich environment', we are currently living in an age characterized by a 'crisis-rich environment'. Crises are no longer once-in-a-hundred-year events, outliers or anomalies. They are part of the background environment within which we are operating day in, day out. The ability to understand and accept that fact, and to begin to prepare yourself for the realities that creates, is one of the defining differences between those organizations that can consider themselves to be risk sensitive and those that don't.

5. *Stay downwind*

In Wucker's analysis, staying downwind of the rhino has two aspects. The first is, be aware of the environment you are operating in and make sure that the behaviour you use is appropriate. It might equally have been called 'Don't go waving red rags at bulls': Wucker mentions horizon scanning as a means for becoming aware of potential dangers as early as possible. Then, taking action in order to avoid walking further forwards towards danger, and ultimately to mitigate any potential risks that might be inherent in the situation you find yourself in.[22]

However, Wucker also discusses the 'meta-rhinos' that are the internal characteristics of an organization, preventing it from either being aware of the dangers of the environments it is operating in or having the decision-making capabilities in order to do something about those issues in a meaningful and timely manner. This can often be because the precise programmes that are in place to incentivize us (for example, short-term profit rewards rather than longer-term value-building processes) are those that prevent an organization from making exactly those decisions that will have most value in the long term.

If we believe that crises are sudden, unexpected and unprecedented, then we are in the position of the person walking down the path who believes that there is no value in scanning the horizon, or even in observing the immediate vicinity, for rhinos and who is continuously surprised when they repeatedly meet rhinos that are not only there but are territorial and aggressive. If they continuously ignore repeated warnings that this is an area where rhinos abound, then it is simply a matter of time until their luck runs out and they become just another statistic of rhino deaths that are unfortunate but entirely avoidable.

Be a rhino spotter; become a rhino keeper

If you ask anyone working in a zoo what are the most exciting animals there, they will almost certainly say whichever ones they are responsible for. To someone who looks after monkeys, then monkeys are incredibly exciting – but to the people who look after the penguins or the butterflies or the frogs, their lives are just as rewarding to observe and be a part of. The truth is that each species is equally compelling in the adventures they encounter as they go through their life cycles – but they are only apparent to those people who have the time to study them and become aware of the nuances of their existence.

To be able to spot the grey rhino, to understand what it means and what the appropriate responses are, both pre-emptively to prevent bad things happening and reactively in the event that the attack mode has already been triggered, it is necessary to study them in an appropriate way. To be effective, the lessons learned for that study – which is ongoing and dynamic and part of the natural development cycle of the organization itself – must be valued, embedded, prioritized and given the necessary level of support and encouragement from the leadership that will allow everyone, whatever their specific role, to become rhino spotters and rhino keepers.

In classical crisis management studies, critical significance is given to the ability to recognize soft signals.[23] That is, to be aware of the slight tremors that are telling you that an avalanche or earthquake is on its way. The truth is, not only are we often very bad at recognizing those signals, but even when certain people do recognize them, their voices are not heard. Given the nature of the risk environment that we are all operating in, the ability to be aware of changes in the wind that indicate that a storm is coming, or to feel the tremors beneath your feet that could be either the harbinger of an earthquake or the signal that a grey rhino is actually charging towards you, is a critical skill not only for management but for survival. Just as reading a book on fitness doesn't make you fitter – you need to go to the gym, change your diet or whatever it takes in order to get there – having another academic or management book on the shelf – even this one! – does not in itself make you safer. These are issues that are as real as tomorrow's headlines, and they are issues that affect every one of us, wherever we live and whatever we do.

Endnotes

1 Weick, K E, Sutcliffe, K M & Obstfeld, D (2008) Organizing for high reliability: Processes of collective mindfulness. *Crisis Management*, 3, 81–123

2 Fukuyama, F (1992) *The end of history and the last man*. Free Press

3 Taleb, N T (2007) The black swan: chapter 1: The impact of the highly improbable. *The New York Times* (22 April). Available at: https://www.nytimes.com/2007/04/22/books/chapters/0422-1st-tale.html (archived at https://perma.cc/399F-BBM6) (Accessed: 21 June 2022)

4 CSIS, Centre for Strategic and International Studies (2019) Ending the cycle of crisis and complacency in U.S. global health security. A report of the CSIS Commission on strengthening America's health security. Available at: https://csis-website-prod.s3.amazonaws.com/s3fs-public/publication/191122_EndingTheCycle_GHSC_WEB_FULL_11.22.pdf (archived at https://perma.cc/HK9M-3T58) (Accessed: 21 June 2022)

5 NowThis News (2020) Obama warned the U.S. to prepare for a pandemic back in 2014 | NowThis (9 April). Available at: https://www.youtube.com/watch?v=pBVAnaHxHbM (archived at https://perma.cc/WW5W-FYMM) (Accessed: 21 June 2022)

6 Lugar, R & Barack, O (2005) Grounding a pandemic. *The New York Times* (6 June). Available at: https://www.nytimes.com/2005/06/06/opinion/grounding-a-pandemic.html (archived at https://perma.cc/7CHG-7UFA) (Accessed: 21 June 2022)

7 Gates, B (2015) Bill Gates: The next outbreak? We're not ready. https://www.ted.com/talks/bill_gates_the_next_outbreak_we_re_not_ready?language=dz (archived at https://perma.cc/3PX8-F6CW)

8 Lederberg, J (1993) In Henig, R M, *A dancing matrix: How science confronts emerging viruses*. New York: Vintage Books

9 Henig, R M (2020) Experts warned of a pandemic decades ago. Why weren't we ready? *National Geographic* (July). Available at: https://www.nationalgeographic.com/science/article/experts-warned-pandemic-decades-ago-why-not-ready-for-coronavirus (archived at https://perma.cc/CCC9-FEXN) (Accessed: 21 June 2022)

10 Wucker, M (2016) *The gray rhino: How to recognize and act on the obvious dangers we ignore*. Macmillan

11 Rittel, H W & Webber, M M (1973) Dilemmas in a general theory of planning. *Policy Sciences*, 4(2), 155–169

12 Alison, L, Power, N, van den Heuvel, C, Humann, M, Palasinksi, M & Crego, J (2015) Decision inertia: Deciding between least worst outcomes in emergency responses to disasters. *Journal of Occupational and Organizational Psychology*, 88(2), 295–321

13 Great Plague of London (2022). Available at: https://en.wikipedia.org/wiki/Great_Plague_of_London (archived at https://perma.cc/Z5UW-AK8H) (Accessed: 21 June 2022)

14 Microsoft (2021) The next great disruption is hybrid work—are we ready? 2021 work trend index: Annual report. Available at: https://www.microsoft.com/en-us/worklab/work-trend-index/hybrid-work (archived at https://perma.cc/LUX7-8AM7) (Accessed: 21 June 2022)

15 BBC (2021) Goldman Sachs: Bank boss rejects work from home as the 'new normal'. BBC News (25 February). Available at: https://www.bbc.co.uk/news/business-56192048 (archived at https://perma.cc/XCT7-XQFQ) (Accessed: 21 June 2022)

16 Keegan, P (2021) Employees balk at end to remote work: 'Going back to the office is stupid'. *Newsweek Magazine* (13 April). Available at: https://www.newsweek.com/2021/04/30/employees-balk-end-remote-work-going-back-office-stupid-1583059.html (archived at https://perma.cc/G26R-PRJK) (Accessed: 21 June 2022)

17 Allegretti, A (2021) Civil servants in London could see pay cut if they resist return to office. *The Guardian* (9 August). Available at: https://www.theguardian.com/politics/2021/aug/09/civil-servants-in-london-could-see-pay-cut-if-they-resist-office-return (archived at https://perma.cc/L38Q-7L3D) (Accessed: 21 June 2022); Kaye, D (2021) Pay cut: Google employees who work from home could lose money. Reuters (10 August). Available at: https://www.reuters.com/world/the-great-reboot/pay-cut-google-employees-who-work-home-could-lose-money-2021-08-10/ (archived at https://perma.cc/M8QK-2KEF) (Accessed: 21 June 2022)

18 Cook, I (2021) Who is driving the great resignation? Harvard Business Review (15 September) Available at: https://hbr.org/2021/09/who-is-driving-the-great-resignation (archived at https://perma.cc/X9G4-QF6L) (Accessed: 21 June 2021)

19 Osterloff, E (2018) How an asteroid ended the age of the dinosaurs. Natural History Museum (13 June) Available at: https://www.nhm.ac.uk/discover/how-an-asteroid-caused-extinction-of-dinosaurs.html (archived at https://perma.cc/9ZM4-QC34) (Accessed: 21 June 2022)

20 Mathews, J (1993) IBM plans to cut 35,000 more jobs, report $8 billion quarterly loss, *Washington Post* (28 July). Available at: https://www.washingtonpost.com/archive/politics/1993/07/28/ibm-plans-to-cut-35000-more-jobs-reports-8-billion-quarterly-loss/ab29aa34-4e2a-4376-86ed-4efbe73cdd2a/ (archived at https://perma.cc/3URY-R53B)

21 Mui, C (2012) How Kodak failed. *Forbes* (18 January). Available at: https://www.forbes.com/sites/chunkamui/2012/01/18/how-kodak-failed/?sh=613a93506f27 (archived at https://perma.cc/S2VR-G4D4) (Accessed: 21 June 2022)

22 It goes without saying that a risk cannot be avoided completely, since this step would require total absence of the situation or activity related to this risk. However, reducing it to the lowest reasonably practicable level appears to be a solution that is enabling organizations rather than completely blocking them.

23 Boin, A, Hart, P T & Kuipers, S (2018) The crisis approach. In *Handbook of disaster research*, 23–38, Springer Nature

Further reading

Alison, L, Power, N, van den Heuvel, C, Humann, M, Palasinksi, M & Crego, J (2015) Decision inertia: Deciding between least worst outcomes in emergency responses to disasters. *Journal of Occupational and Organizational Psychology*, 88(2), 295–321

Allegretti, A (2021) Civil servants in London could see pay cut if they resist return to office. *The Guardian* (9 August). Available at: https://www.theguardian.com/politics/2021/aug/09/civil-servants-in-london-could-see-pay-cut-if-they-resist-office-return (archived at https://perma.cc/L38Q-7L3D) (Accessed: 21 June 2022)

BBC (2021) Goldman Sachs: Bank boss rejects work from home as the 'new normal'. BBC News (25 February). Available at: https://www.bbc.co.uk/news/business-56192048 (archived at https://perma.cc/XCT7-XQFQ) (Accessed: 21 June 2022)

Boin, A, Hart, P T & Kuipers, S (2018) The crisis approach. In *Handbook of disaster research*, 23–38, Springer Nature

COMAH, Control of Major Accident Hazards Regulations (1999) Application of QRA in operational safety issues. Available at: https://www.hse.gov.uk/research/rrpdf/rr025.pdf (archived at https://perma.cc/87ZJ-ZBTF) (Accessed: 21 June 2022)

Cook, I (2021) Who is driving the great resignation? Harvard Business Review (15 September). Available at: https://hbr.org/2021/09/who-is-driving-the-great-resignation (archived at https://perma.cc/X9G4-QF6L) (Accessed: 21 June 2021)

CSIS, Centre for Strategic and International Studies (2019) Ending the cycle of crisis and complacency in U.S. global health security. A report of the CSIS Commission on strengthening America's health security. Available at: https://csis-website-prod.s3.amazonaws.com/s3fs-public/publication/191122_EndingTheCycle_GHSC_WEB_FULL_11.22.pdf (archived at https://perma.cc/HK9M-3T58) (Accessed: 21 June 2022)

Forbes (2021) The CEO of Goldman Sachs called remote work an aberration – here's why his employees may disagree. Robert Glazer (11 May). https://www.forbes.com/sites/robertglazer/2021/05/11/the-ceo-of-goldman-sachs-called-remote-work-an-aberration-heres-why-his-employees-may-disagree/?sh=623731762377 (archived at https://perma.cc/XD35-82TX)

Fuller, J & Kerr, W (2022) The great resignation didn't start with the pandemic. Harvard Business Review (23 March). https://hbr.org/2022/03/the-great-resignation-didnt-start-with-the-pandemic (archived at https://perma.cc/X7NM-AWKH)

Gates, B (2015) Bill Gates: The next outbreak? We're not ready https://www.ted.com/talks/bill_gates_the_next_outbreak_we_re_not_ready?language=dz (archived at https://perma.cc/3PX8-F6CW)

Great Plague of London (2022) Available at: https://en.wikipedia.org/wiki/Great_Plague_of_London (archived at https://perma.cc/Z5UW-AK8H) (Accessed: 21 June 2022)

Kaye, D (2021) Pay cut: Google employees who work from home could lose money. Reuters (10 August). Available at: https://www.reuters.com/world/the-great-reboot/pay-cut-google-employees-who-work-home-could-lose-money-2021-08-10/ (archived at https://perma.cc/M8QK-2KEF) (Accessed: 21 June 2022)

Keegan, P (2021) Employees balk at end to remote work: 'Going back to the office is stupid'. *Newsweek Magazine* (13 April). Available at: https://www.newsweek.com/2021/04/30/employees-balk-end-remote-work-going-back-office-stupid-1583059.html (archived at https://perma.cc/G26R-PRJK) (Accessed: 21 June 2022)

Klotz, A (2022) The great resignation is still here, but whether it stays is up to leaders. OECD (3 June). Available at: https://www.oecd-forum.org/posts/the-great-resignation-is-still-here-but-whether-it-stays-is-up-to-leaders (archived at https://perma.cc/8KJH-DYY7)

Lederberg, J (1993) In Henig, R M, *A dancing matrix: How science confronts emerging viruses*. New York: Vintage Books

Lugar, R, & Barack, O (2005) Grounding a pandemic. *The New York Times* (6 June). Available at: https://www.nytimes.com/2005/06/06/opinion/grounding-a-pandemic.html (archived at https://perma.cc/7CHG-7UFA) (Accessed: 21 June 2022)

Microsoft (2021) The next great disruption is hybrid work – are we ready? 2021 Work Trend Index: Annual Report. Available at: https://www.microsoft.com/en-us/worklab/work-trend-index/hybrid-work (archived at https://perma.cc/LUX7-8AM7) (Accessed: 21 June 2022)

Mui, C (2012) How Kodak failed. *Forbes* (18 January). Available at: https://www.forbes.com/sites/chunkamui/2012/01/18/how-kodak-failed/?sh=613a93506f27 (archived at https://perma.cc/S2VR-G4D4) (Accessed: 21 June 2022)

NowThis News (2020) Obama warned the U.S. to prepare for a pandemic back in 2014 | NowThis (9 April). Available at: https://www.youtube.com/watch?v=pBVAnaHxHbM (archived at https://perma.cc/WW5W-FYMM) (Accessed: 21 June 2022)

Obama, B & Lugar, R (2006) Grounding a pandemic. *The New York Times* (6 June). Available at: https://www.nytimes.com/2005/06/06/opinion/grounding-a-pandemic.html (archived at https://perma.cc/7CHG-7UFA)

Osterloff, E (2018) How an asteroid ended the age of the dinosaurs. Natural History Museum (13 June). Available at: https://www.nhm.ac.uk/discover/how-an-asteroid-caused-extinction-of-dinosaurs.html (archived at https://perma.cc/9ZM4-QC34) (Accessed: 21 June 2022)

Rittel, H W & Webber, M M (1973) Dilemmas in a general theory of planning. *Policy Sciences*, 4(2), 155–169

Taleb, N T (2007) The black swan: Chapter 1: *The impact of the highly improbable. The New York Times* (22 April). Available at: https://www.nytimes.com/2007/04/22/books/chapters/0422-1st-tale.html (archived at https://perma.cc/399F-BBM6) (Accessed: 21 June 2022)

Weick, K E, Sutcliffe, K M & Obstfeld, D (2008) Organizing for high reliability: Processes of collective mindfulness. *Crisis Management*, 3, 81–123

Wucker, M (2016) *The Gray Rhino: How to recognize and act on the obvious dangers we ignore*. Macmillan

4

Causes of crisis management failure

The two central themes that repeatedly emerge from the study of disaster and crisis management failures were encapsulated in two phrases from the Congressional reports into 9/11 and Hurricane Katrina. The 9/11 Commission reported that 'the most important failure was one of imagination',[1] while the Congressional report into Katrina identified it as being primarily 'a failure of leadership'.[2] These two leitmotifs of failing to understand what exactly a 21st-century crisis would look like as part of the pre-event planning process, and a failure to respond effectively as part of the post-event emergency management operation, are repeatedly highlighted in post-crisis event reviews, whatever the nature of the event.

The way in which an emergency event is perceived is not merely of academic interest but is critical to how those in power implement appropriate changes. If the 'disaster' is perceived as an external event, lessons are unlikely to be learned and systemic errors of management and policy are likely to be repeated. If, however, it is accepted that the root causes of failure were within the system, then lessons can be learned and improvements made. Which path is chosen will decide whether the next crisis will see an improved response or escalation of the levels of impact and loss. A clear sign that lessons are not learned is the judgement by those in power that the disaster was the result of a 'one-off event' or a 'unique set of circumstances', and that there is little to fear from the possibility of future similar events. For those with an understanding of systems design and management, it is clear that when the systemic faults and vulnerabilities that led to the original disaster are left in place, those conditions not only could cause but, given time, will inevitably cause similar catastrophic failures, what Perrow called 'normal accidents'.[3] The inability to learn from such incidents is not only a sign of the management weaknesses that precede such failures but a root cause of them.

The question that increasingly lies at the heart of our current age's crisis management thinking, as the range of disruptive events continues to become higher impact, more destructive and with longer-lasting consequences that are often moving into the realm of 'non-recoverable', is whether a disaster is a truly random event, one that is outside the ability of the relevant authorities to influence, mitigate or prevent, or is in fact a signifier of the failures of community and government agencies to prepare effectively[4] and to learn lessons from the past. There is a growing awareness that any disaster, however dramatic and catastrophic its consequences, should be seen as part of an extended development process rather than a single event, and that the failure to prepare or to respond is a function of vulnerabilities and failures in the management systems rather than a direct consequence of the external event alone. The truth is that very few of the 'disasters' that have become crisis events are completely unexpected and many of them could be considered to be high-likelihood, high-impact events that should be considered not as sudden or random failures but rather as inevitable occurrences stemming from systemic vulnerabilities.

If we are to create a truly effective crisis management planning and response capability, it is those organizational planning and management failures that are the critical issues, rather than the specific aspects of the external event. Many of the major events that can be considered as catastrophic failures stem from the failure to identify potential issues that not only were known but should have been central to those organizations' risk management processes. It is those organizational planning and management failures that are the critical issue, rather than the specific aspects of the external event. We can look at the lessons learned from the classical case studies of:

- Hurricane Katrina;
- the failures of British Petroleum management in responding to the Deepwater Horizon oil spills in the Gulf of Mexico; or
- the vulnerabilities that led to the TEPCO nuclear reactor failure in the aftermath of the Fukushima earthquake and tsunami in Japan.

And we can look at the lessons learned from more recent events, such as:

- the failure to prepare for the disruption to global supply chains from the blocking of the Suez Canal;
- the failure to prepare for infrastructure failures;

- the failure of UK government agencies to learn from the lessons identified in the national-level Exercise Cygnus pandemic simulation in 2016;[5] or
- the inability to respond to adverse weather events that are becoming a normalized part of our risk environment.

While those specific events may have been unexpected, that is not to say that they could not have been planned for, or that the relevant management teams (and the organizations or agencies as a whole) should not have been prepared to respond to exactly such situations as part of their basic risk management responsibilities.

Cyber-attacks on critical infrastructure

Two attacks on major US infrastructure in 2021 capture the impacts of failing to engage with the nature of developing threats, which were not only known but were clearly identified. A hacking attack on the Colonial pipeline in May 2021, which originated in Texas but supplied fuel to much of the south-east United States, targeted the billing processes within the company's administration system. However, because of fears of the possibility of other areas of the management systems being compromised, including the management systems of the pipelines themselves, the company closed down its operations and within a few hours had paid a ransom of 75 Bitcoin, equivalent to $4.4 million at the time. The fact that the FBI helped facilitate the payment of the ransom shows the impact that was considered to have on US critical national infrastructure.[6]

The vulnerability that led to the hackers being able to gain access to the system was discovered to be a single compromised password that was discovered in a cache of stolen passwords available on the dark web.[7] That password lacked basic authentication procedures that would have prevented the initial breach being made and would have avoided the success of the attempted attack.

Although the vulnerability that led to the attack being successful was preventable and should have actually been managed by basic cyber-security protocols at the lowest level of the organization's operations, the response to the attack demonstrates some lessons that can be considered positive outcomes. The first is that the person discovering the initial problem – found in a ransom note in the company's IT network – reported it to their supervisor and within one hour that information had been escalated to the CEO of the company and he had made the decision to shut down the entire system. It would have been possible – and perhaps expected – that in such circumstances and given the impact of that decision not only on the company but also on the dependent networks, as well as the fact that such a decision had immediate and far-reaching national security implications, that the request would have been made to 'Give me more information'. It is to the credit of the organization, and to the CEO Joseph Blount, that such a path was not taken. The other positive was that the company informed the FBI of the threat immediately and their decision to close down a critical part of the US national infrastructure and involve them in the decision-making as to next steps.

In a separate incident, but one which demonstrates how similar incidents might be in their patterns, even if they are different in their details, a hacker infiltrated the IT systems of the Florida city water management program and tried to release the entire stock of a toxic agent into the water system. This action would have resulted in massive damage to the infrastructure and potentially thousands of poisonings across the city. Once again, the vulnerability of the entry point into the system was the use of outdated IT systems, under-maintained security, and the use of the same password by all of the plant's computers to gain access to the corporate TeamViewer application.[8] A water operator at the plant could only watch in real time as his computer mouse was taken over and attempted to release the stock of lye – a caustic chemical that is part of the water purification process – from 100 parts per million to 11,100 parts per million, a level that would have made the entire water system highly toxic.[9]

As one report had it, 'Luckily, the operator was able to restore chemical levels to normal once hackers exited the system, narrowly averting a disaster that could've poisoned 15,000 people in the small city of Oldsmar'[10] – but luck is not the thing you want to depend on when the potential consequences are so serious and when the defences that are designed to prevent such incidents are apparently so weak and porous.

The WannaCry ransomware attack that targeted the UK National Health system in May 2017,[11] and which either closed down hospital administration systems or caused them to be closed down in order to prevent further spread of the computer virus, was similarly able to take advantage of outdated and un-maintained IT security systems that in a very real way meant they were vulnerable to attack from anyone who had the necessary skills and motivation. This was despite the fact that the previous year the government department responsible for data management and security had published a report identifying cyber-attack as a real threat, identifying specifically the use of old and unpatched systems as a vulnerable attack point, and recommending that all health and care organizations needed to provide evidence that they were taking action to improve cyber security, including moving away from old operating systems.

Predicted disasters

These are not sudden or unexpected events or random attacks that have no pattern, or that can be considered as 'unprecedented'. They are in fact exactly the threats that should be at the very heart of corporate and operational risk registers. If organizations cannot keep themselves safe from potential attacks that are recognized and understood, and for which specific warnings have been given, then it is questionable as to whether they can claim to have any risk management frameworks in place that would be considered appropriate given the level of threat, the potential impacts and the duty to protect critical national infrastructures so as to maintain the safety, security and access to services of the entire population.

In its Quadrennial Review in January 2017,[12] the US Energy Department openly stated that the US Grid was in 'imminent danger'[13] from cyber-attack (as well as being increasingly vulnerable to high-impact adverse weather events). The report noted that increases in smart grid technology in itself creates greater vulnerability and that the threats from outside actors (as opposed to technical malfunctions, human error, natural disasters and other such causes) were becoming more sophisticated and had the potential to cause national-level disruption that would undermine both critical defence infrastructure and much of the economy. Any disruption of the national power grid would also automatically create a significant health, safety and security risk for significant parts of the population. While this is perhaps to be expected in a strategic review of a critical national infrastructure, and the failure to identify such threats itself would have become a signifier of a failure to understand the current and emerging risk environment, it was the response from the infrastructure operators that had the most chilling effect, when 'grid operators claimed that they were on top of the problem'. It is often the belief that 'we have this under control' that creates a corporate atmosphere in which it is presumed that current frameworks, protocols and capabilities would be enough to deal with existing problems, never mind future emergent challenges that are likely to be substantively different in the intensity of their impact, consequences and attack vectors.

The response of the Colonial Pipeline company to discovering the threat to the integrity of its systems might seem natural, and there would be few if any other options open to the decision-makers at the top of an organization that was providing a crucial service to its customers and clients, but which then discovered that it had a critical and potentially catastrophic fault within its systems. However, you can contrast and compare the decision taken by Colonial Pipeline with the decisions taken by the senior management of Boeing when it was discovered that there was a fault in the Boeing 737-Max automated flight control systems that had been upgraded without informing airlines or their pilots. It was a probably well-meant update that turned out to be very negative.[14] The new system meant that under certain circumstances automated procedures would override the pilot, preventing them from taking control, and would actually create a situation where the instructions given would lead to a catastrophic loss of flight management and an almost inevitable crash.

This is clearly a significant issue and one would imagine that the first – in fact only – response from Boeing management would be to ground the planes with immediate effect, inform all of their clients and partners of the issues and then work towards finding a solution that would correct the critical fault. But the company decided differently. In fact, they continued to claim that the technology itself was safe and encouraged their clients to continue to fly the planes. This went on even after there was a Boeing 737 MAX operated by the Indonesian airline Lion Air crashed in October 2018, killing all 189 passengers and crew. The Boeing response was to deny that the fault was in the flight management system and initially to blame pilot error. However, they went beyond that and pressured the Federal Aviation Authority (FAA) inspectors to avoid finding Boeing and its technology responsible. This was the policy until a second crash, involving Ethiopian Airlines Flight 302 on 10 March 2019, which killed all 157 people on board.[15]

The nature of the organizational cultural issues at the heart of the sequence of events that led to the tragic – and entirely avoidable – crashes was summed up in the official report from the US House Committee on Transportation and Infrastructure,[16] which found that Boeing had removed references to the faulty Maneuvering Characteristics Augmentation System (MCAS) from the pilot's Operations Manual. The company had failed to share results from its own tests that identified the fact that pilots were either unaware of or were not able to comply with the specified responses in the time available once the fault was activated, even though the pilot involved in testing the system identified the potential consequences as 'catastrophic'. Despite the fact that Boeing was aware that the alert program was not functioning on more than 80 per cent of its 737 MAX fleet, it failed to alert the FAA, its customers and the MAX pilots. During this time, it continued to both manufacture and deliver around 200 planes with this known non-functional component.

The outcome of the reviews was that Boeing agreed to pay $2.5 billion to settle criminal charges from the two crashes.[17] Still partly following the strategy of denial, Boeing continues to call them 'accidents' though actually there was nothing accidental about them. Under the agreement, Boeing did not admit guilt, which would have impacted the company's ability to bid for future government contracts, and no company executive faced any criminal charges for the actions they had taken. CEO Dennis Muilenburg was fired as a result of the 737 MAX crashes but nevertheless received a pay-off of $62 million.

The fact that the FAA monitoring and certification were built on a system where the processes were carried out by Boeing staff created a clear conflict of interest, as well as an in-built opportunity for the company to bypass or sideline exactly those guidelines and controls that were in place to prevent such an incident. The system itself created the situation whereby Boeing personnel felt pressured to accept sub-standard results and service delivery and to allow Boeing to believe that they could get away with it.

This was actually so deeply embedded into the system that in a completely unrelated set of incidents, the certification of the faulty lithium batteries that led to the grounding of Boeing's global fleet of 787 Dreamliners in 2013 after two aircraft experienced fires due to technical faults within the batteries, it was reported that FAA managers delegated 95 per cent of the certification of the Boeing 787 Dreamliner to Boeing personnel.[18] However, as well as the flawed testing regime, there had been multiple reports of previous battery failures and near-misses that had been ignored and had gone unreported.[19]

In a different context, the inability to benefit from lessons that have been clearly identified can be seen in the years immediately prior to the development of the coronavirus/Covid-19 pandemic. Rather than being an unexpected or black swan event, the possibility of a global pandemic had been widely flagged up and discussed at both national and global levels. The UK government ran a pandemic scenario exercise in 2016 called Exercise Cygnus. That was a national-level simulation of a flu outbreak, carried out to war-game the UK's pandemic readiness. It involved 950 officials from central and local government as well as multiple ancillary organizations, modelling a worst-case-scenario flu pandemic affecting up to 50 per cent of the population and causing up to 400,000 deaths.

The post-exercise report was frank about the state of the UK's readiness. 'The UK's preparedness and response, in terms of its plans, policies and capability, is currently not sufficient to cope with the extreme demands of a severe pandemic that will have a nationwide impact across all sectors.'[20]

As is often the case, the report found that each government body and agency had its own plans, policies and capabilities, which in theory would have allowed them to utilize their own expertise and resources in an effective and speedy manner. However, those plans were unknown both to the central coordinating teams and to the other agencies with which they were supposed to collaborate and interact. The lack of an integrated overarching framework meant that when the system was tested in reality by the outbreak of the coronavirus pandemic, there was an inability to respond to the changing nature of the events and to allow an effective deployment and utilization of available resources at the point where they were needed most.

Different failures, same mistakes

The two extracts below, from official reports into very different events, highlight the organizational shortcomings that led to the failure to either create a safety culture that would have prevented the crisis happening or develop organizational capabilities that would have allowed an effective response once the crisis had been triggered.

(From Fukushima Nuclear Accident Independent Investigation Commission[21]):

> The TEPCO Fukushima Nuclear Power Plant accident was the result of collusion between the government, the regulators and TEPCO, and the lack of governance by said parties. They effectively betrayed the nation's right to be safe from nuclear accidents. Therefore, we conclude that the accident was clearly 'manmade'. The direct causes of the accident were all foreseeable prior to March 11, 2011. The operator, the regulatory bodies and the government body promoting the nuclear power industry (METI) all failed to correctly develop the most basic security requirements, such as assessing the probability of damage, preparing for containing collateral damage from such a disaster, and developing evacuation plans for the public in case of serious radiation release.

(From Report of the 22nd July Commission into the Utoya island massacre[22]):

- The ability to acknowledge risk and learn from exercises has not been sufficient.
- The ability to implement decisions that have been made, and to use the plans that have been developed, has been ineffectual.
- The ability to coordinate and interact has been deficient.
- The potential inherent in information and communications technology has not been exploited well enough.
- Leadership's willingness and ability to clarify responsibility, set goals and adopt measures to achieve results have been insufficient.
- In the opinion of the Commission, these lessons learned are to a greater extent applicable to leadership, interaction, culture, and attitudes than to a lack of resources, a need for new legislation, organization, or important value choices.

A clear example of this phenomenon is the fact that in almost every crisis, an immediate, and seemingly almost inevitable, consequence of the triggering event is the failure of communication.[23] This then becomes a causal influence on many of the subsequent problems that are later identified as having a critical impact on the failure of the crisis response programme to deliver its core functions. The reasons for such failures can broadly be defined by three categories:

- the failure of communication systems on an infrastructural level, as when the radio systems of one agency do not interact with the systems of another, or the surge in the level of communications during a crisis event causes the communication infrastructure to collapse at the exact time when it is most critical;
- the inability to transfer critical information across the network of the emergency response framework; or
- simply when the level of information and communication associated with the emergency response operation overwhelms the management framework and those working within it.[24]

The causes of such failures are almost banal in their ordinariness, but their impact is potentially catastrophic. The emergency response to the July 7 terrorist bombings in London in 2005 was severely hampered by the fact that the emergency services radios didn't work in the underground tube system,[25] even though this had been previously identified as a critical issue in the 1987 King's Cross fire, which led to 37 deaths.[26] In Hurricane Katrina, 'the lack of survivable, interoperable communications [which was identified as the most critical problem at the state level] occurred because of an accumulation of decisions by federal, state, and local officials that left this long-standing problem unsolved'.[27]

Disasters aren't random

The question that lies at the heart of 21st-century crisis management thinking is whether a disaster is a truly random event, one that is outside the ability of the relevant authorities to influence, mitigate or prevent, or is in fact a signifier of the failures of community and government agencies to prepare effectively and to learn lessons from the past.

There is a growing awareness that any disaster, however dramatic and catastrophic its consequences, should be seen as part of an extended development process rather than a single event, and that the failure to prepare or respond is a function of vulnerabilities and failures in the management systems rather than a direct consequence of the external event alone. The truth is that very few of the 'disasters' that have become crisis events are completely unexpected, and many of them could be considered to be high-likelihood, high-impact events that approach Perrow's concept of inevitable occurrence.[28] Many of the major events that can be considered catastrophic failures stem from the failure to identify potential issues that were not only known but should have been central to those organizations' risk management processes. It is those organizational planning and management failures that are the critical issue rather than the specific aspects of the external event. Whether it is Hurricane Katrina, air traffic controllers responding to adverse weather conditions or the failures of British Petroleum management in responding to the oil spills in the Gulf of Mexico, while those specific events may have been unexpected, that is not to say that they could not have been planned for or that the relevant management teams (and the organizations as a whole) should not have been prepared to respond to exactly such situations.

The way in which an emergency event is perceived is not merely of academic interest but is critical to how those in power implement appropriate changes. If the disaster is perceived of as an external event, lessons are unlikely to be learned and systemic errors of management and policy are likely to be repeated. If, however, it is accepted that the root causes of failure were within the system, then lessons can be learned and improvements made. Which path is chosen will decide whether the next crisis will see an improved response or escalation of the levels of impact and loss.[29] A clear sign that lessons are not learned is the judgement by those in power that the disaster was the result of a 'one-off event' or a 'unique set of circumstances' and that there is little to fear from the possibility of future similar events. For those with an understanding of systems design and management, it is clear that when the systemic faults and vulnerabilities that led to the original disaster are left in place, those conditions not only could cause but, given time, will inevitably cause similar catastrophic failures, what Perrow called 'normal accidents'.[30] The inability to learn from such incidents is not only a sign of the management weaknesses that precede such failures but is a root cause of them.

Endnotes

1 National Commission on Terrorist Attacks upon the United States, (2004) The 9/11 Commission report: final report of the National Commission on Terrorist Attacks upon the United States. Washington, DC: National Commission on Terrorist Attacks upon the United States. Available at: https://www.9-11commission.gov/report/911Report.pdf (archived at https://perma.cc/9TZD-JXWG) (Accessed: 22 June 2022)

2 United States. Congress. House. Select Bipartisan Committee to Investigate the Preparation for, & Response to Hurricane Katrina (2006) A failure of initiative: Final report of the select bipartisan committee to investigate the preparation for and response to Hurricane Katrina (Vol. 109, No. 377) US Government Printing Office

3 Perrow, C (1984) *Living with high-risk technologies*. New York: Basic Books

4 Comfort, L K (2007) Crisis management in hindsight: Cognition, communication, coordination, and control. *Public Administration Review*, 67, 189–197

5 Public Health England (2017) Exercise Cygnus Report: Tier one command post exercise pandemic influenza 18 to 20 October 2016. Available at: https://assets.publishing.service.gov.uk/government/uploads/system/uploads/attachment_data/file/927770/exercise-cygnus-report.pdf (archived at https://perma.cc/8VX8-BLAQ) (Accessed: 22 June 2022); Pegg, D (2020) What was Exercise Cygnus and what did it find? *The Guardian* (7 May). Available at: https://www.theguardian.com/world/2020/may/07/what-was-exercise-cygnus-and-what-did-it-find (archived at https://perma.cc/R4TH-LEU9) (Accessed: 22 June 2022)

6 Wilkie, C (2021) Colonial Pipeline paid $5 million ransom one day after cyberattack, CEO tells Senate. CNBC (8 June). Available at: https://www.cnbc.com/2021/06/08/colonial-pipeline-ceo-testifies-on-first-hours-of-ransomware-attack.html (archived at https://perma.cc/Q42W-MHBX) (Accessed: 22 June 2022)

7 Mehrotra, K & Turton, W (2021) Hackers breached Colonial Pipeline using compromised password. Bloomberg Europe Edition (4 June). Available at: https://www.bloomberg.com/news/articles/2021-06-04/hackers-breached-colonial-pipeline-using-compromised-password (archived at https://perma.cc/YEN9-8G4Y) (Accessed: 22 June 2022)

8 Matthews, L (2021) Florida Water plant hackers exploited old software and poor password habits. *Forbes* (15 February). Available at: https://www.forbes.com/sites/leemathews/2021/02/15/florida-water-plant-hackers-exploited-old-software-and-poor-password-habits/?sh=3d2ffcc7334e (archived at https://perma.cc/E2J2-FJMU) (Accessed: 22 June 2022)

9 Warren, M S (2021) Florida water system hack offers lessons for other states. Government Technology (19 April). Available at: https://www.govtech.com/security/florida-water-system-hack-offers-lessons-for-other-states.html (archived at https://perma.cc/GR7D-5XGC) (Accessed: 22 June 2022)

10 Warren, M S (2021) N.J. water systems are exposed to hackers. A near-disaster in Florida shows the threat, NJ.com (18 April). Available at: https://www.nj.com/news/2021/04/nj-water-systems-are-exposed-to-hackers-a-near-disaster-in-florida-shows-the-threat.html?outputType=amp (archived at https://perma.cc/G5FB-Y8X4)

11 National Audit Office (2018) Investigation WannaCry cyber attack and the NHS. Available at: https://www.nao.org.uk/wp-content/uploads/2017/10/Investigation-WannaCry-cyber-attack-and-the-NHS.pdf (archived at https://perma.cc/HG3P-L49E)

12 US Department of Energy (2017) Quadrennial Energy Review – Transforming the nation's electricity system: The second installment of the QER. Available at: https://www.energy.gov/sites/prod/files/2017/02/f34/Quadrennial%20Energy%20Review--Second%20Installment%20%28Full%20Report%29.pdf (archived at https://perma.cc/4LFV-3522) (Accessed: 22 June 2022)

13 Chediak, M & Natter, A (2017) US grid in 'imminent danger' from cyber attack, study says. *Forbes* (6 January). Available at: https://www.bloomberg.com/news/articles/2017-01-06/grid-in-imminent-danger-from-cyber-threats-energy-report-says (archived at https://perma.cc/P3WY-29D5) (Accessed: 22 June 2022)

14 Another security measurement gone wrong from the aviation sector is the crash of Germanwings Flight 9525. According to the official investigation results, the co-pilot, who suffered from a mental disorder with psychotic symptoms, locked himself in the cockpit and disabled the code panel that would have allowed the captain to re-open the doors. Since the cockpit door was also hardened (a measurement following the 9/11-attacks), manual force wasn't of help either. The co-pilot, aiming to commit suicide, crashed the plane, killing 144 passengers and six crew.

15 Hradecky, S (2019) Crash: Ethiopian B38M near Bishoftu on Mar 10th 2019, impacted terrain after departure. *The Aviation Herald* (26 September). Available at: http://avherald.com/h?article=4c534c4a/0065 (archived at https://perma.cc/3VQN-DNAE) (Accessed: 22 June 2022)

16 House Committee on Transportation and Infrastructure (2020) Final Committee Report: The design, development & certification of the Boeing 737 MAX. Available at: https://transportation.house.gov/imo/media/doc/2020.09.15%20FINAL%20737%20MAX%20Report%20for%20Public%20Release.pdf (archived at https://perma.cc/3S5A-HBKL) (Accessed: 22 June 2022)

17 Claburn, T (2021) After deadly 737 Max crashes, damning whistleblower report reveals sidelined engineers, scarcity of expertise, more. The Register (15 December). Available at: https://www.theregister.com/2021/12/15/boeing_737_max_senate_report/ (archived at https://perma.cc/H5ZJ-E5LX) (Accessed: 22 June 2022)

18 Mouawad, J (2014) Report on Boeing 787 Dreamliner battery flaws finds lapses at multiple points. *The New York Times* (1 December). Available at: https://www.nytimes.com/2014/12/02/business/report-on-boeing-787-dreamliner-batteries-assigns-some-blame-for-flaws.html (archived at https://perma.cc/2N6E-Y79P) (Accessed: 22 June 2022)

19 Drew, C, Tabuchi, H & Mouawad, J (2013) Boeing 787 battery was a concern before failure. *The New York Times* (29 January). Available at: https://www.nytimes.com/2013/01/30/business/boeing-aware-of-battery-ills-before-the-fires.html (archived at https://perma.cc/8LPF-6KXB) (Accessed: 22 June 2022)

20 Public Health England (2017) Exercise Cygnus Report: Tier one command post exercise pandemic influenza 18 to 20 October 2016. Available at: https://assets.publishing.service.gov.uk/government/uploads/system/uploads/attachment_data/file/927770/exercise-cygnus-report.pdf (archived at https://perma.cc/8VX8-BLAQ)

21 Fukushima (2012) The official report of Executive Summary, The Fukushima Nuclear Accident Independent Investigation Commission. Available at: http://warp.da.ndl.go.jp/info:ndljp/pid/3856371/naiic.go.jp/wp-content/uploads/2012/09/NAIIC_report_lo_res10.pdf (archived at https://perma.cc/RB7W-9TRA) (Accessed: 10 July 2022)

22 Gjorv, A (2012) Rapport fra 22. juli-kommisjonen. Norges Offentlige Utredninger 14

23 Longstaff, P H & Yang, S U (2008) Communication management and trust: Their role in building resilience to 'surprises' such as natural disasters, pandemic flu, and terrorism. *Ecology and Society*, 13(1); Drabek, T E (1985) Managing the emergency response. *Public Administration Review*, 45, 85–92

24 Kapucu, N (2005) Interorganizational coordination in dynamic context: Networks in emergency response management. *Connections*, 26(2), 33–48; Kapucu, N, Arslan, T & Demiroz, F (2010) Collaborative emergency management and national emergency management network. *Disaster Prevention and Management*, 19(4), 452–468; Sagun, A, Bouchlaghem, D & Anumba, C J (2009) A scenario-based study on information flow and collaboration patterns in disaster management. *Disasters*, 33(2), 214–238

25 Allen, D K, Karanasios, S & Norman, A (2014) Information sharing and interoperability: The case of major incident management. *European Journal of Information Systems*, 23(4), 418–432; London Assembly (2006) Report of the 7 July Review Committee. Greater London Authority

26 Fennel, D (1988) Investigation into the King's Cross Fire. Available at: http://www.railwaysarchive.co.uk/documents/DoT_KX1987.pdf (archived at https://perma.cc/T96F-XN4B) (Accessed: 10 July 2022)

27 United States. Congress. House. Select Bipartisan Committee to Investigate the Preparation for, & Response to Hurricane Katrina (2006) A failure of initiative: Final report of the select bipartisan committee to investigate the preparation for and response to Hurricane Katrina, Vol. 109, No. 377, US Government Printing Office

28 Perrow, C (1984) *Normal accidents: Living with high-risk technologies*. New York: Basic Books

29 Comfort, L K (2007) Crisis management in hindsight: Cognition, communication, coordination and control. *Public Administration Review*, 67, 189–197

30 Perrow, C (1984) *Normal accidents: Living with high-risk technologies*. New York: Basic Books

Further reading

Allen, D K, Karanasios, S & Norman, A (2014) Information sharing and interoperability: The case of major incident management. *European Journal of Information Systems*, 23(4), 418–432

Chediak, M & Natter, A (2017) US grid in 'imminent danger' from cyber attack, study says. *Forbes* (6 January). Available at: https://www.bloomberg.com/news/articles/2017-01-06/grid-in-imminent-danger-from-cyber-threats-energy-report-says (archived at https://perma.cc/P3WY-29D5) (Accessed: 22 June 2022)

Claburn, T (2021) After deadly 737 Max crashes, damning whistleblower report reveals sidelined engineers, scarcity of expertise, more. The Register (15 December). Available at: https://www.theregister.com/2021/12/15/boeing_737_max_senate_report/ (archived at https://perma.cc/H5ZJ-E5LX) (Accessed: 22 June 2022)

Comfort, L K (2007) Crisis management in hindsight: Cognition, communication, coordination and control. *Public Administration Review*, 67, 189–197

Drabek, T E (1985) Managing the emergency response. *Public Administration Review*, 45, 85–92. https://doi.org/10.2307/3135002 (archived at https://perma.cc/7Q86-963R)

Drew, C, Tabuchi, H & Mouawad, J (2013) Boeing 787 battery was a concern before failure. *The New York Times* (29 January). Available at: https://www.nytimes.com/2013/01/30/business/boeing-aware-of-battery-ills-before-the-fires.html (archived at https://perma.cc/8LPF-6KXB) (Accessed: 22 June 2022)

Fennel, D (1988) Investigation into the King's Cross fire. Available at: http://www.railwaysarchive.co.uk/documents/DoT_KX1987.pdf (archived at https://perma.cc/T96F-XN4B) (Accessed: 10 July 2022)

Fukushima (2012) The official report of Executive Summary, The Fukushima Nuclear Accident Independent Investigation Commission. Available at: http://warp.da.ndl.go.jp/info:ndljp/pid/3856371/naiic.go.jp/wp-content/uploads/2012/09/NAIIC_report_lo_res10.pdf (archived at https://perma.cc/RB7W-9TRA) (Accessed: 10 July 2022)

Gjorv, A (2012) Rapport fra 22. juli-kommisjonen. *Norges Offentlige Utredninger* 14

House Committee on Transportation and Infrastructure (2020) Final Committee Report: The design development & certification of the Boeing 737 MAX. Available at: https://transportation.house.gov/imo/media/doc/2020.09.15%20FINAL%20737%20MAX%20Report%20for%20Public%20Release.pdf (archived at https://perma.cc/3S5A-HBKL) (Accessed: 22 June 2022)

Hradecky, S (2019) Crash: Ethiopian B38M near Bishoftu on Mar 10th 2019, impacted terrain after departure. *The Aviation Herald* (26 September). Available at: http://avherald.com/h?article=4c534c4a/0065 (archived at https://perma.cc/3VQN-DNAE) (Accessed: 22 June 2022)

Kapucu, N (2005) Interorganizational coordination in dynamic context: Networks in emergency response management. *Connections*, 26(2), 33–48

Kapucu, N, Arslan, T & Demiroz, F (2010) Collaborative emergency management and national emergency management network. *Disaster Prevention and Management*, 19(4), 452–468

London Assembly (2006) Report of the 7 July Review Committee. Greater London Authority

Longstaff, P H & Yang, S U (2008) Communication management and trust: Their role in building resilience to 'surprises' such as natural disasters, pandemic flu, and terrorism. *Ecology and Society*, 13(1)

Matthews, L (2021) Florida water plant hackers exploited old software and poor password habits. *Forbes* (15 February). Available at: https://www.forbes.com/sites/leemathews/2021/02/15/florida-water-plant-hackers-exploited-old-software-and-poor-password-habits/?sh=3d2ffcc7334e (archived at https://perma.cc/E2J2-FJMU) (Accessed: 22 June 2022)

Mehrotra, K & Turton, W (2021) Hackers breached Colonial Pipeline using compromised password. Bloomberg Europe Edition (4 June). Available at: https://www.bloomberg.com/news/articles/2021-06-04/hackers-breached-colonial-pipeline-using-compromised-password (archived at https://perma.cc/YEN9-8G4Y) (Accessed: 22 June 2022)

Mouawad, J (2014) Report on Boeing 787 Dreamliner battery flaws finds lapses at multiple points. *The New York Times* (1 December). Available at: https://www.nytimes.com/2014/12/02/business/report-on-boeing-787-dreamliner-batteries-assigns-some-blame-for-flaws.html (archived at https://perma.cc/2N6E-Y79P) (Accessed: 22 June 2022)

National Audit Office (2018) Investigation WannaCry cyber attack and the NHS. https://www.nao.org.uk/wp-content/uploads/2017/10/Investigation-WannaCry-cyber-attack-and-the-NHS.pdf (archived at https://perma.cc/HG3P-L49E)

Pegg, D (2020) What was Exercise Cygnus and what did it find? *The Guardian* (7 May). Available at: https://www.theguardian.com/world/2020/may/07/what-was-exercise-cygnus-and-what-did-it-find (archived at https://perma.cc/R4TH-LEU9) (Accessed: 22 June 2022)

Perrow, C (1983) *Normal accidents: Living with high-risk technologies*. New York: Basic Books

Public Health England (2017) Exercise Cygnus Report: Tier one command post exercise pandemic influenza 18 to 20 October 2016. Available at: https://assets.publishing.service.gov.uk/government/uploads/system/uploads/attachment_data/file/927770/exercise-cygnus-report.pdf (archived at https://perma.cc/8VX8-BLAQ) (Accessed: 22 June 2022)

Sagun, A, Bouchlaghem, D & Anumba, C J (2009) A scenario-based study on information flow and collaboration patterns in disaster management. *Disasters*, 33(2), 214–238

United States. Congress. House. Select Bipartisan Committee to Investigate the Preparation for, & Response to Hurricane Katrina (2006) A failure of initiative: Final report of the select bipartisan committee to investigate the preparation for and response to Hurricane Katrina (Vol. 109, No. 377) US Government Printing Office.

US Department of Energy (2017) Quadrennial energy review – Transforming the nation's electricity system: The second installment of the QER. Available at: https://www.energy.gov/sites/prod/files/2017/02/f34/Quadrennial%20Energy%20Review--Second%20Installment%20%28Full%20Report%29.pdf (archived at https://perma.cc/4LFV-3522) (Accessed: 22 June 2022)

Warren, M S (2021) Florida water system hack offers lessons for other states. Government Technology (19 April). Available at: https://www.govtech.com/security/florida-water-system-hack-offers-lessons-for-other-states.html (archived at https://perma.cc/GR7D-5XGC) (Accessed: 22 June 2022)

Wikipedia (2015) Germanwings Flight 9525. Available at: https://en.wikipedia.org/wiki/Germanwings_Flight_9525 (archived at https://perma.cc/V8PK-QKR3) (Accessed: 28 June 2022)

Wilkie, C (2021) Colonial Pipeline paid $5 million ransom one day after cyberattack, CEO tells Senate. CNBC (8 June). Available at: https://www.cnbc.com/2021/06/08/colonial-pipeline-ceo-testifies-on-first-hours-of-ransomware-attack.html (archived at https://perma.cc/Q42W-MHBX) (Accessed: 22 June 2022)

5

Incident command systems and hierarchical management

This chapter examines the traditional centralized hierarchical command-and-control systems that have emerged as the default framework for formal incident command systems. It starts by examining the relationship between ICS and the environments in which they are operating, then goes on to delineate the evolutionary link between current ICS frameworks and the highly managed processes associated with industrial production. It discusses the limitations that causes, particularly in terms of dealing with complexity and multi-organization responses. The subsequent section introduces some alternative concepts of 'command and control' based on an equal exchange of information between a community of embodied experts rather than the creation of pre-set frameworks which must then be imposed by those lower down the command chain. It discusses the inherent tension in centralization, where there is a single unified command system and integration, which is built around collaborative efforts of multiple players, within which the value of local participation is recognized. The chapter goes on to suggest ways in which that transformation can take place, taking into account the cultural restrictions that are inherent to command-based organizations, and finally identifies some of the issues that cause failures within ICS and which will need to be addressed if a truly effective management structure is to be developed.

Hierarchical command systems: removing uncertainty

Bureaucratic management systems are built upon accepted processes involving divisions of labour, with each person's roles, actions and authority being strictly limited; detailed guides and controls that are designed by people who are not involved in the actual decisions or actions that they are designed to control; and a general belief that people who are higher in the hierarchy know more and have greater understanding of the requirements than those lower than them. They are controlled by complex and often legalistic procedures that actively mitigate against deviance, creativity or individual decision-making. They are based on a multi-layered and highly differentiated development process, where it is often difficult, if not impossible, to know who to go to in order to get authorization for a non-standard action.

If we wanted a starker description of how the nature of standardized bureaucratic decision-making is not suited to the highly charged demands of a crisis event, it would be hard to find one. The nature of crises, involving severe threat, high uncertainty and time pressure, means that the decision-making processes associated with organizational bureaucracy are inherently incapable of responding to the challenges that such situations set. As noted in a study of the emergency response to 9/11, '[B]y their very nature, these highly unusual and perhaps unique situations are not amenable to unvarying procedures, checklists or protocols.'[1] This is exacerbated by the tendency for both corporate organizations and government agencies to further centralize control systems when under pressure. In fact, the expectation that such centralization will take place has become the cornerstone of both theoretical models of crisis management and the administrative frameworks that are activated once such crisis situations are triggered.[2] Although this model of centralized control has been increasingly challenged from both a theoretical and a practical perspective, it is still true that such reflexive responses are the norm rather than the exception once a crisis event takes place.

If one looks at the response to Covid-19 within the UK context, it soon becomes clear that the response to what was seen as a genuinely unprecedented event, in terms both of its complexity and the potential impact it could have on multiple aspects of our society, did not involve opening up the discussion to the broadest range of participants, many of whom had developed specific areas of expertise over a lifetime of practitioner experience and who could have given structure and support to the ongoing discussions. In an almost diametrically opposite approach, decision-making within the government structures was increasingly limited to a handful of people, many of those chosen on the basis of support for previous government policies (specifically Brexit and the removal of the UK from the European Union, which had held centre stage in British politics since the referendum on leaving the EU in 2016) and personal loyalty for and unquestioning support of the prime minister.

Although this was a highly public demonstration of the tendency to isolate decision-making at the centre and the top of any hierarchical management system, it is one that would be recognizable to many decision-makers – and perhaps even more starkly to those who have been excluded from that group and have had to look on from outside or afar as decisions were taken that to those decision-makers with more detailed and specialized knowledge of those subjects were clearly sub-optimal.

A legacy from the past

The hierarchical command systems that are currently considered appropriate to manage complex incident responses are directly traceable to a model of instructionist management that was developed at the start of the Industrial Revolution to oversee the delivery of a product, whether a mass-produced artefact or one-off bridges or ocean liners.[3] It was developed around a process-driven production-line system based on standardization, compartmentalization (division of labour) and a separation between the individual and the final product, and its ultimate objective was to remove any uncertainty from the production process. The reliability of the operating system was predicated specifically on the validity of the design process that created it, based on a process embodying efficiency, predictability, quantification and control. Within such a system, the human operator has no more significance than any other component of the machine, merely required to fulfil their roles as minor cogs within a greater whole, concerning which they neither had nor needed any understanding. Based on mechanistic principles, such modelling assumes that planners and systems analysts can break down problems into component parts, individual sections can be isolated and treated as self-contained units, and that there is a logical process based on identification of problem, analysis of needs and delivery of a 'correct' solution. However, when such industrial management systems are transposed to different operating environments, the determination to impose them on processes that cannot be reduced to highly differentiated de-skilled tasks can lead to a pathology that creates the exact opposite of the desired effect, where the 'best services' of yesterday turn into worst practices, and core competences turn into core rigidities,[4] creating inefficiency, lack of control and an inability to achieve the core objectives.

The following description of a basic structure of an incident command system appropriate for large-scale emergencies or disasters is a perfect example of the 'industrialization' of the crisis management arena and could have been used word for word to describe a 19th-century cotton mill:

> The system is highly formalized, characterized by extensive rules, procedures, policies, and instructions. Jobs within the system are specialized, are based on standardized routines, and require particularized training. Positions are arranged hierarchically and related to one another on the basis of formal authority.[5]

If the first stage of process management emerged from the Industrial Revolution, which maintained its fundamental structures and methodologies for almost 200 years, the next stage came with the development of computers and automated management systems. From this perspective, systems management was seen in terms of information processing, complete with information flow diagrams, input, output, processing and feedback loops.[6] Although there was a high level of complexity inherent in such systems, they were basically linear in nature, with a clear pattern of information transfer that could be mapped, directed and controlled. The fact that such systems were highly complex was seen as an advantage – allowing a much higher level of data to be managed than was previously possible – rather than a cause of potential catastrophic failures.

However, the attempt to transfer such a mechanistic design to the field of crisis planning and management carries seeds of failure. The 'paradox of rationality'[7] is that the validity of such a mechanistic, rationalistic systems management approach is predicated on the ability to use deductive reasoning to anticipate all possible consequences of a potential action and thereby to eliminate harmful or undesirable causal pathways. If this can be achieved, that would then leave a single causal pathway that leads inevitably and unavoidably to the desired optimal outcome. This is impossible outside of a highly engineered mechanistic system, and even systems science texts make it clear that their models and approaches are not applicable to 'real world phenomena such as social or organizational groups [which] are typically poorly structured or 'messy'.[8] In fact, not only are such tightly defined management processes no longer seen to be functional in a loosely structured environment, but the belief that they are – that one can set the parameters for determining how a crisis will develop and then make assumptions as to how it will respond tamely to your interventions – is regarded as dangerous and crisis-creating in itself, entering into the realm of moral responsibility.[9]

Developing the ICS further

The need to move away from a mechanistic model led to the third evolutionary stage of systems management, which introduced the concept of ecology to operations planning. Rather than seeing the situation as something that could be isolated and approached as a bounded event, the relationship between the event, the responder and the surrounding environment was recognized as consisting of a dynamic ecosphere, within which any action would produce primary and secondary effects with cascading consequences on every other component of the system. In terms of interaction with its environment and adapting to it, such an organization could be classed as 'vitalistic'. Although organizations operating within such a dynamic biosphere were not without structure, that structure could no longer be described in traditional terms of hierarchies and linear relationships and was more analogous to a living entity than to a cold machine.

Given the evolving models of systems management, the issue with centrally directed, hierarchically structured command-and-control frameworks is not that they are unnecessary or ineffective, but rather that they are used to deliver the wrong task. In multiple post-event reports, it becomes clear that the role of the centralized command system is not to control or direct operations but rather to coordinate communication, data sharing and sense-making.[10] In this sense, we can see the transition for the role of the centralized command system from 'command and control' to 'support and adapt'. The ability of the command system to manage the flow of what could easily become overwhelming amounts of complex information is a critical factor in any crisis situation. This is a task that, if managed correctly, the centralized command system is uniquely able to manage, but if it fails can lead to catastrophic consequences.[11]

The developments of the incident command system in the US, and a similar though more loosely defined JESIP (Joint Emergency Services Interoperability Principles) programme in the UK, are both attempts to codify the principles of collaborative operations in a way that supports the delivery of effective multi-agency operations, while at the same time acknowledging and respecting the necessity of each of those agencies to maintain its autonomy in deciding how it can best deliver its own specialist services within the demands of the immediate operating environment.

The effectiveness of a centralized command system, as exemplified in the ICS framework, is predicated on two defining and limiting criteria, both of which have been identified as failing under crisis conditions. The first is that rather than dealing with genuinely crisis situations (that is, those which significantly exceed an organization's capability to adapt and respond), the scenarios that are used as evidence of ICS value are often positioned within the 'normal operating environment' of the responding agencies, involving pre-planned organizational solutions to meet the more predictable aspects of an evolving incident.[12] This is the classic crisis management failure where once a crisis response programme has been triggered and then has failed to deliver its expected results, the conclusion is 'that is not what we were thinking about' (see Chapter 5 for more on this).

The UK preparation for global pandemics, and the response to coronavirus/Covid-19 when it did occur, is a classic example of this failure to understand the meaning or significance of the events that are being modelled. In the 2017 National Risk Register published by the UK Cabinet Office, Pandemic Influenza was given the highest ranking, with the likelihood of 4/5 happening in the next five years and an impact of 5/5, considering the effect that would have on already overloaded national healthcare systems (and the already overstretched and under-resourced National Health Service in particular).

In the same risk register, Emergent Infectious Diseases was given the same level of likelihood (4/5 over the next five years) but with an impact level of 3/5. Based on extrapolations from figures that had been seen in the SARS/MERS attacks in South East Asia in 2003, the UK government's official assessment of the number of deaths from a global pandemic hitting the country was 150–250 deaths. In reality, the number of fatalities rose to 150,000. It is clear that in such a situation, and under such circumstances, traditional process-driven response mechanisms are unlikely to be robust enough to adapt to the needs of what is an overwhelming event. Some mechanisms also fail to manage resources, both their own and those integrated from external sources, into a fast-moving response framework in the face of hyper-challenging events.

In fact, ICS frameworks (and to be effective, they should be exactly that, frameworks that can offer guidance rather than detailed plans that need to be adhered to) are designed to be utilized in exactly those situations which are known and understood and for which the responding agencies can be considered to be acting within accepted operating parameters. In these contexts, the role of the ICS is not to direct the agencies as to what they need to be doing but to create a shared common operating picture or situational awareness that allows them to understand exactly what is needed and how they can make the greatest contribution to the incremental stages and the overarching objectives.

A general misunderstanding

By definition, the scenarios covered by an ICS are situations where those utilizing those procedures and frameworks are official responders, part of a professional community developed through years of training and shared experiences, where the demands being responded to are routine to them, and where social and cultural dilemmas are at a minimum.[13] In other words – these are not crisis events.

This means that a crisis is almost exactly not what is being described within the ICS context. A crisis is chaotic and unstable, demanding the utilization of skills, resources and responses that are not part of the normal operating environment of both the agencies and the individuals associated with them. Above all, these scenarios do not involve the loss of sense-making that is at the centre of a true crisis and which is the significant characteristic that turns a major incident into a crisis event.

To discuss the issues described so far in the standard rationalistic language of normal responses, where the crisis can be conceptualized as an incident which, despite a potential for destructive consequences, can be approached in isolation and be solved with the application of the correct (and known) solution,[14] demonstrates a critical misunderstanding of the nature of crises and the danger that comes from using terminology in an undefined or casual manner.

The second criterion for judging ICS effectiveness involves inter-agency integration. Although the management of inter-agency coordination is often cited as the reason for the need for ICS, case studies are often limited to operations involving coordination between agencies of a similar nature, in particular fire departments with other fire departments.[15] This is visible also in roots of the original ICS system: it was based on the first formal multi-agency coordination programme, FIRESCOPE (**FI**refighting **RES**ources of

California Organized for Potential Emergencies), which was specifically designed for the benefit of fire teams. Bigley and Roberts' widely cited 2001 paper concerning high-reliability organizing for complex and volatile task environments focuses exclusively on fire department responses. Although these are undoubtedly complex organizations and respond both speedily and effectively to highly challenging and often personally dangerous events, their complexity is internal, and their ability to respond so effectively is based on a shared language, terminology, culture and the collective individual and organizational experience that allows fellow professionals to create a shared understanding of a situation with little if any formal communication.

It is questionable as to what extent this situation is analogous to the challenges of creating interoperability with other agencies which may not benefit from a common operational language, basis of crisis cognition, organizational culture or shared embodied knowledge.

Studies on the challenges of increasingly complex organizational frameworks[16] or the emergent multi-organization networks that came together in response to 9/11 and Hurricane Katrina[17] demonstrate that from both a theoretical and an empirical perspective, the usefulness of centralized command systems is strongly bounded by issues of size and organizational complexity, and is quickly called into question once the scale and composition of the response operation moves beyond what might be considered 'enhanced normality'.[18] It is this complexity, particularly when positioned in a social context rather than the highly defined delineations of an incident response one, where there are multiple overlapping jurisdictions, each with its own pre-existing patterns of authority and each with the necessity for simultaneous action and autonomous decision-making, that suggests that not only is it impossible to create a centralized authority system, but such a centralized, hierarchical, command-centred approach is probably not necessary and is unlikely to be successful.[19]

While centralized command systems theoretically offer a framework for managing conglomerations of agencies that share common values, their effectiveness in responding to challenges outside strictly normative conditions can be less than optimal.[20] However, it is precisely at the point that crisis response operations move beyond 'routine emergencies',[21] to a highly volatile crisis situation which requires innovative solutions, that the weaknesses of hierarchically managed command systems become clear.

The problem with the distance

An instructionist/hierarchical system is predicated on decisions being made and then disseminated through the command chain of a relatively small and homogenous group of actors with similar backgrounds, within an administrative framework that assumes stable operating conditions.[22] In fact, the traditional division between strategic and operational roles, based on the concept that strategists work out solutions and operational managers deliver them, tends to imbue the strategic commanders with an omniscience on which all decisions will be based.[23] However, distance from the crisis location inhibits their decision-making power. The command chain will be operating in a highly complex and unstable environment, dependent on fragile technical systems and being held hostage to the likelihood that detailed information will be misheard, mis-transmitted or misunderstood at some stage in the communications chain.[24] Given the time needed to assimilate information, develop solutions and transmit them back down the communication chain, the reality is that by the time the latest strategic decisions have reached the ground, the situation will have changed to such a degree that the local teams will have already created their own solutions to the original problem and are already managing a new set of problems.

The classic example of this tendency towards commanding from distance was the policy labelled 'the 6,000-mile screwdriver', whereby Donald Rumsfeld, US Secretary of Defense in the George Bush administration, tried to set operating guidelines for troops in the field in Iraq. Those guidelines may have made sense when discussed in a situation room in the Pentagon or the White House. However, within the realities of on-the-ground operating conditions, they were not only not viable, they were actively counter-productive. In his 2009 book *Wiser in Battle*, Lt Gen Ricardo Sanchez[25] described the challenges that having operational directives issued from Washington created. In the run-up to the preparation for deployment, the issue of whether his unit (the 1st Armoured Division, then based in Germany) would actually be deployed or not was continuously in question, and if so whether that would be as a reserve force or a post-combat support unit. Each of the possible roles required completely different skill sets, and yet the fact that the unit role was being changed on a regular basis meant that not only was time being wasted in preparing for what their actual role might be, but the constant readjustments were having a significant impact on the mental state of battle readiness that is as critical as the physical readiness.

Sanchez makes the point that although the US constitution specifically puts the control of the military in civilian hands, that is not the same as putting military command in civilian hands. As non-military (and beyond that, political) personnel, they did not have the necessary level of understanding to be able to make decisions that could help support the achievement of the overall aims, at the same time supporting and empowering the individual units to be in the best possible state in order to fulfil their own missions within the realities of the environments that they were operating in. Whereas there was a legitimate (and necessary) role for the political leadership to set the policy goals and strategic aims, that does not justify them trying to influence – and even dominate – operational command.

In December 2020, at the height of the second wave of Covid-19, and at a time when the hospitality industry was under immense pressure due to the ever-changing government guidance on what was or was not permissible, the UK government issued a directive that pubs could allow people to drink as long as they had a substantive meal (with the threat of fines of up to £10,000 for those breaking the rules). There then followed a series of statements, clarifications, U-turns and clarification of the U-turns as to what constituted a substantial meal, with the focus of conversation being on whether the traditional pub snack of a scotch egg was one or not. The various views on that were that:

- it was if it was eaten with a knife and fork rather than with hands;
- it was if there were two of them;
- it was if it was served with condiments; or
- it was if it came with table service (that is, delivered by a waiter).[26]

A senior government minister then declared, 'Everyone knows what a substantial meal is, that is well established in law', without actually being able to describe what that was. This might be seen as being no more than a fairly typical example of government incompetence, if it was not symptomatic of a wider tendency of trying to impose operational directives from a policy level. At a time when the impact of newly emergent strains of the virus was a fear, there were concerns about the NHS being overwhelmed by the overlap of Covid-19 with seasonal influenza, and there was a serious policy decision to be made as to whether the UK should go into lockdown over the Christmas period (it was later decided that it should, with the most restrictive conditions put in place since the start of the Covid-19 outbreak in March that year), the focus on something as seemingly insignificant as the specific definition of 'substantial meal' creates the impression of a senior management structure that is unsure of its own specific policy-setting role, and an almost desperate desire to be engaged in something that they can actually understand and influence.

Leadership is not only about decision and actions – it is equally about culture. The culture of the organization sets the tone for all activities that take place within its remit, and if the culture is one of centralization, the concentration of decision-making in a small group of inner personnel, micromanagement and 'leadership by directive', then that is a critical issue that will impact every other aspect of the organization and its activities. The fact that so much time and effort was spent on trying to define the exact status of a scotch egg is an indicator of the approach that the UK government at the time would be taking in other aspects of the Covid-19 response, and that is borne out by government reviews.

The House of Lords Public Service Committee report 'A critical juncture for public services: lessons from Covid-19', published in November 2020, stated, 'The overall public health response was at times hampered by over-centralized, poorly coordinated and poorly communicated policies that were designed and delivered by central Government, even though local-level providers were often better equipped.'[27] Given that this was at a time of national emergency, and that pandemic influenza and emergent viruses had appeared prominently on recent national risk registers, this is a significant indictment of the decision-making culture that was embedded into government practices.

Given that the role of the strategic leadership is to create a space where multiple stakeholders can bring their collective experience, insight and capabilities in order to create a multi-stranded response based on their collaborative and coordinated efforts, it is an indication of the failure to learn lessons that more than six months later, when the UK was still in the grip of Covid-19 and its impacts and consequences, the British Medical Association took the steps of writing to the Health Secretary, complaining about the 'micromanagement of general practice.... involving SOPs, directives and damaging comments to the press.... [which] undermined the confidence and morale of the whole workforce'.[28]

These are not insignificant issues – and equally they are not issues that can be either engaged with or changed easily. The culture of an organization is much like the oxygen we breathe – it is something that we are completely unaware of until it starts to go wrong. That can be something analogous to inner-city pollution that in itself goes almost unnoticed but actually has a slowly evolving but nevertheless significant and corrosive impact on everyone living and working there, or it can be the equivalent of a toxic spill that creates immediate danger for everyone in its area of influence. It is often the case that the cultural issues that create the organizational weaknesses become evident only when the organization is put under pressure for a crisis event – but at that stage, the vulnerabilities within that system become critical failure points that impact the entirety of the organization and its response operations.

Centralization vs integration

The debate concerning the appropriateness or otherwise of 'centralization' and 'integration' is not just a matter of semantics, but on a much deeper level reflects the world view of the opinion holder.[29] For the centralist, the role of the 'command structure' may be considered to control and direct, to impose options and responses onto communities that are not only not involved in the decision-making process but may well come to be seen as either a nuisance, an obstacle or outrightly hostile both to the policies that are imposed and to the agencies at the ground level that are implementing them. Although centralized command-and-control systems are often seen as inflexible, that is not necessarily an inherent quality. If centralized command systems are considered as systems architecture, setting a framework within which different sections can work on a commonly shared basis,[30] there is no reason why that architecture cannot accommodate new entrants, new working relationships and the ability to adapt and respond to external challenges. Rather than being seen as restrictive, from this perspective a crisis management framework can act as the host for a 'system of systems' fundamental to the success of the network-based nature of modern crisis management.[31] This in turn would engender the qualities of robustness, responsiveness, flexibility and adaptation that could contribute to the necessary level of C2 (command and control) agility.[32] However, even though it is perfectly possible for leadership to be directive, supportive, participative and achievement-oriented,[33] it is more likely that most people involved in such systems will be more familiar with a management framework that is characterized by its hierarchical pattern of interaction, its grudging and minimalistic delegation of decision rights and its relatively tight control over the distribution of information.[34]

Management models such as Structural Contingency Theory (SCT) suggest that the structure of an organization, rather than being set in stone, should be able to adapt according to the demands of specific tasks.[35] As such, the structure of an organization is a reflection of the values that it sets itself, as well as acting as a framework and boundary within which decisions are made and actions are delivered. The spectrum of such organizations ranges from those which are entirely mechanistic (such as a factory assembly line) through to the entirely organic, where decision-making can be seen as spontaneous, innovative and unstructured at all levels of operation. However, even within a highly controlled environment such as a nuclear power station, there is a range of management systems that include both highly directive and more open, semi-structured options.[36] Whatever decision-making model is chosen, it is the ability of the coordinated command structure to set commonly shared superordinate goals[37] and an agreed agenda of strategic objectives that sets the framework for all subsequent activity. This effort to create sense-making at the highest level, that will then cascade down and influence all other decisions along the command chain, complements the traditional understanding of sense-making in terms of 'data – information – knowledge – understanding'[38] that starts at the operational level and is then communicated up the command chain to the strategic commanders.[39]

In general, centralized command-based systems are better suited to the range of tame problems that are tightly defined, have limited impact and which are conducive to clearly defined solutions, while organic systems are more appropriate to decision-making arenas where the problems themselves are less structured and more likely to require adaptive and potentially innovative responses. While it is a generalization, it can be said that centralized organizations are more suited to decision-making environments where accuracy and adherence to a commonly agreed policy is required, while decentralized organizations are more effective in environments[40] where the situations they are dealing with are more dynamic and unstable and where time is of the essence in making decisions concerning specific operational requirements. Decentralized systems are also more effective when there is an implied need for dynamic learning associated with unstable and fast-developing situations.[41] When put in such simple terms, it becomes clear why attempts to impose a centralized system onto situations that demand innovative decision-making and fast-learning adaptability are unlikely to produce positive results.

From command to collaboration

The value of collaboration has been well-recognized,[42] but despite the many academic works on different aspects of collaboration in crisis management decision-making,[43] we still have little understanding of what exactly allows organizations to develop collaborative arrangements in the heat of a crisis situation.[44] While it is acknowledged that collaborative decision-making organizations are qualitatively different from hierarchical, command-based organizations, and that there may even be a tendency for collaborative structures to replace command structures in many organizations,[45] the present challenge is not necessarily how to create a more democratic form of decision-making within command-based organizations but how to allow collaboration between organizations from different cultures.[46] As an example from a US context, although there is the expectation that local response teams should interact with police or National Guard units for larger events, the American Red Cross and the Salvation Army are the principal sources of assistance to US disaster victims,[47] and 72 per cent of all fire fighters in the US are volunteers.[48] While this does not affect their professional capabilities, it does mean that there may be problems when they come into contact with hierarchically command-orientated police or military units, especially within the pressurized context of a high-level emergency response.

The desire to impose a military-style command-and-control system on emergency management networks indicates a misunderstanding of both the nature of the problems that emergency managers face and the nature of the solutions that they are required to develop and deliver.[49] The heterogeneous, locally based, multiple-organization nature of emergency management means that a centrally managed command style is not only ineffective but encroaches on the ability of service deliverers to achieve their own aims, which are often clear, local and immediate.

This perspective is immediately transferable to a corporate environment, where personal and professional networks, both formal and recognized and informal and unspoken, are actually the framework on which much of the work gets done. This is particularly true within non-standard events where the need to develop innovative solutions based on available resources and in the face of constantly changing demands means that a pre-set one-size-fits-all approach is simply not applicable. There is a clear desire to impose solutions both from above and from outside the normal working frameworks, which means that any solutions that are offered are not only not likely to be applicable or effective but will actually disrupt the existing frameworks and relationship that could have allowed effective solutions to be found and put in place. But in turn, it is questionable why senior management still insist on trying to impose solutions from the executive suite rather than trusting the people on the ground to have the experience, insight and judgement to understand what is most appropriate within that context.

While there is no doubt that an information and communication system is critical to the success of any operation beyond the most simple,[50] the role of that system should be 'to support creative, adaptive behaviour throughout a distributed decision-making network'.[51] As such, it should be supporting decision-making rather than issuing commands, or in other words enhance collaboration and coordination, not support organizational control.[52]

Those valuing integration over hierarchical command systems recognize the inherent value that is brought to the response programme through local knowledge, shared decision-making and the belief that the focus of the response lies at the community level. This is not just a matter of 'political correctness' or theoretical posturing but reflects a deeply held belief that what the community needs is the support of those with authority to allocate resources and make things happen, rather than being seen as an impersonal problem that needs to be solved through centralist intervention. From this perspective, emergency management agencies thus act as consultants to communities rather than directing the change process.[53] The tendency to centralize limits the access to a wide range of knowledge, experience and insight that could be critical to the development of effective solutions, given that centralization and integration are in themselves often mutually antagonistic and exclusive in nature.[54]

From a hierarchical command perspective, the host community of the disaster has often been seen in terms of a nuisance/distraction[55] to the professional responders who are trying to follow the protocols set out in their response manuals, which often do not take account of the realities imposed by the presence of actual people in the disaster zones. Such tensions can cause distrust and even active antagonism on the part of both the responding agency and the local community.[56] However, there is a growing awareness of the negative impact of the imposition of a centralized command-style system controlled by outside agencies which often have little, if any, understanding of the local environment, whether physical, geographical or social, and which impose the 'expertise' of emergency response managers in one context or management consultants in another. Under such a regime, '[t]he real experts, the state and local officials who are first to the scene of natural disasters, and from whom we have a great deal to learn, have been subordinated to the "expertise" of federal law enforcement officials, military officers, and, often, civilian contractors, many of which have little to no experience in any sort of disaster or emergency management'.[57] In their desire to impose external solutions onto local communities, they will almost certainly either ignore or antagonize those community-based organizations and networks that are best positioned to deliver first-response services, whether in terms of accommodation, local skills or the ability to quickly reconstruct some sort of social network.[58] This is especially true if the ability to work with (or as it may be seen from the community perspective, submit to) the ICS system is a condition of acceptance into the network.[59] In one sense, all emergencies are inherently local,[60] involving a system of disaster response emerging from a ground-level effort of schools, faith groups and voluntary organizations as well as more formal agencies which have shared cultural and community memories and experiences which can be utilized when similar events occur.[61]

Within corporate environments, almost all organizations will claim that they trust their people. There is a belief that empowering people to make decisions in the areas that have direct impact on their own operations, especially if those decisions are taken at the lowest appropriate level, adds value to the organization and its operations, and is overall a good thing to do. And yet, when the pressure of an actual non-standard or potentially high-level disruptive event occurs, it is exactly at that time of greatest stress, when it would be hoped that the normal operating procedures that have been developed over years, and which are tried and tested and are known to all participants, would have been utilized, that they are replaced by untried and untested protocols which are then themselves highly disruptive and have a significant impact on the organization's ability to manage its own affairs, never mind the external event.

Adaptability within the command system

Even within the most tightly managed centralized command systems, there is usually the understanding that, as a human activity interacting with the external environment, it will involve some level of decision-making and creativeness.[62] In that sense, just as any organization lies somewhere on the spectrum of centralized/hierarchical and devolved/networked, so the individual command culture will set a balance between the boundary within which decisions can be made more or less freely, depending on the demands of the specific situation and the defining command culture of the respective organization. The fact that operations are highly designed and defined in concept does not necessarily mean that that micro-management reaches to the molecular level. Within each stage there is a degree of freedom of decision-making, the 'outer envelope'[63] within which acceptably autonomous decision-making can be made.

As an example of the modelling of such transactional complexity, the NATO SAS-050 programme[64] was an attempt to unify the issues surrounding the nature of the management system, the information-rich or information-poor environment it was operating in, and the nature of the problem itself. The three axes (dimensions) that are used to model such decision-making processes range from centralized to decentralized, from tightly managed to relatively unrestrained, and from information withholding to information distributing. There are also three variables relating to the nature of the problem, namely the familiarity or otherwise of the problem, the stability/instability of the problem and the amount of information available concerning the problem. This was then set against two classes of problems, either decomposable, in that they can be broken down into component parts and formally distributed to different stakeholders, or non-decomposable, in that they must be treated as a single organic event; and those that can be seen as predictable, in that effective planning and preparation will lead to enhanced response capabilities and effectiveness, and those that cannot be predicted, which call for a much higher level of innovative response development. Each of these axes must also be analysed in the light of other aspects of organizational interoperability,[65] such as institutional, functionality and technological comparisons, or social, technological, and temporal pressures.

Given that most problems in the real world are neither totally random nor totally predictable,[66] it is clear that an unthinking adherence to one 'pure' system would be neither appropriate nor optimal. Whatever the official doctrine may be, the likelihood is that any organization is a hybrid of centralized mechanistic command systems and more autonomous, free-moving organic organizations.[67] From a systems management perspective, a crisis management system is an open system, combining a high degree of non-linearity in the environment in which it is operating with a high level of non-linearity within its own operating framework. This requires a high level of integration and optimization between the different participating organizations in order to create an ability to cope with high levels of complexity, instability, disruption and dynamism.[68] It can be said that these are the results of the tensions created from balancing the pressures between competing demands, based on the need to make decisions both quickly and accurately, to have a well-defined hierarchy but also to integrate lower levels of the organization into the decision-making process, and to manage the balance between having masses of information and getting trapped in an 'information quagmire'.[69] The ability to manage the balancing act between creating a framework that can interact with such unstable complexity and maintain the freedom to adapt as the situation changes can be characterized as 'operating on the edge of chaos'.[70] The ability to move from a highly centralized hierarchical management framework during times of normal activity to a decentralized and flat decision-making framework[71] during times of heightened tension is one of the characteristics that is common to effective crisis response operations, whatever context they are operating in.

There is nothing intrinsic to any single management system that precludes it from utilizing different management styles, even if only on a case-by-case basis. Although it is clearly in an organization's interest to be able to switch smoothly between different systems or styles, there is not an equal balance in the ability to make that switch. Described as 'asymmetric adaptability',[72] in all cases that were studied it was easier for a more controlled system to move to a more relaxed mode than it was the other way around. Thus, it was easier for a centralized command-based structure to delegate decision-making responsibilities and give local decision-makers greater autonomy and authority than it was for an organic system to impose centralized command discipline. The reality is that any incident that goes beyond the most basic will require some level of adaptive decision-making. The question is not 'whether...?' but rather 'how much...?'.

Why hierarchical command systems fail

For any researcher of emergency management, one of the earliest and perhaps most stark lessons that becomes clear is that the cause of failures in emergency response and management, rather than being genuinely unexpected, are typically not only foreseeable but actually were predicted, often with remarkable accuracy.[73] It is in the nature of emergency response that the characteristics associated with chaos and the breakdown of normative management frameworks within the crisis event are reflected absolutely within the incident command systems themselves. This is why incident command systems are extremely effective at responding to limited and tightly defined incidents, have significant challenges when dealing with situations which require a higher level of innovative response, and fail miserably (and actually are seen to have been completely inappropriate) when there is a collapse of the underpinning operational frameworks.[74] As repeated post-disaster reviews have demonstrated, although the range of crises is perhaps unlimited, the causes of the failure of effective response are remarkably similar.[75]

In the US Federal emergency management framework in particular, the trust in the effectiveness of the centralized ICS is so inbuilt into the system that it seems hard to believe that its efficacy is doubted.[76] And yet when it comes to actual incident management, the ICS itself is often the first point of failure. One of the single most significant issues raised by experienced crisis response commanders in New Orleans following Hurricane Katrina was the lack of unified command. The command structures that were in place were 'unclear, multiple, conflicting, uncooperative, and isolated'.[77] As one fire commander described it, 'In New Orleans, you couldn't go two blocks without running into somebody's incident command post. But there was no coordination between them. Everyone assumes there'll be a graduation up to some larger structure, but nobody knows how to get to that.' In many cases, the cause of the failure is simply the inability to manage the level of information that is created by a disaster event.[78] The Oklahoma bombing of a single office building in 1995, targeted by an individual US extremist because it housed federal agencies, created a situation that involved response teams from across the US, fire fighters from more than 75 Oklahoma communities and more than 35 other fire departments from various other states, as well as over 1,000 FEMA agents and hundreds from other federal agencies.[79] The need to create an overarching ICS that could manage that level of interaction was simply beyond the capabilities of the existing infrastructure to handle.

The idea that a hierarchical command-centred emergency management framework was either necessary or appropriate has been questioned for at least 70 years. The end of the Second World War, which saw the transition of emergency management from a branch of war-footing civil defence to a more community-based collaborative approach, brought a growing realization that not only did distance-managed central-command response systems not work, they actually disrupted the much more local and informal response frameworks that developed spontaneously when a crisis event occurred.[80] This differentiation between organizational and collective responses has been documented across a wide range of events.[81] Despite the level of time, funding and resources that has been pumped into the development of effective multi-agency command systems, many of the people who are tasked with managing those systems lack either actual experience or the personal and professional background[82] that would allow them to work effectively under the pressures that a crisis situation brings. As one interviewee commented, their training was too simplistic to allow them to understand the demands of a crisis event[83] and once the crisis was in full flow, that was not the time to start learning.

In many cases, rather than failures in crisis management leading to the acceptance of the need for a non-hierarchical management system more appropriate to the demands of the crisis, there is the tendency for the 'solution' to such problems to involve yet another level of bureaucratic oversight being put in place.[84] A growth in external complexity is matched by increasing the organization's internal complexity, often involving the creation of more staff functions, which leads inevitably to even more complicated decision-making and reporting structures, often characterized by a lack of clarity as to who effectively has ownership of the problem. Once the shared command or information framework goes beyond its core members, it also presumes that all of the logistical issues associated with shared information exchange, such as interoperability of communications systems, practised and known operating procedures, a shared understanding of terminology, the equivalence of authority across different ranks in different agencies, and a shared understanding of risk and acceptable working practice, can be managed without impacting the effectiveness of the communications and information exchange itself. As we have seen on multiple occasions, not only are these assumptions liable to fail, but the inability to maintain communications across multiple agencies, or even between multiple respondents from the same agency, is not only a high likelihood failure point but is perhaps an inevitable one once the pressure and complexity of the event reach a certain critical point.

The defining demonstration of the failure of the traditional centralized command system was Hurricane Katrina and the aftermath of its landfall in New Orleans in 2005. This occurred four years after the events of 9/11, following an unprecedented level of political, human, technological and above all financial investment to develop an agency that would be fit to respond to the challenges of 21st-century emergency management. The US government's tone in describing the post-Katrina management failures was one of apologetic regret. As the Congressional report put it, 'There is no question that the Nation's current incident management plans and procedures fell short of what was needed and that improved operational plans could have better mitigated the Hurricane's tragic effects.'[85] To President Bush, speaking from New Orleans in the immediate aftermath of the event and in the midst of the ongoing disaster, the solution was clear: 'A challenge on this scale requires greater federal authority and a broader role for the armed forces – the institution of our government most capable of massive logistical operations on moment's notice.'[86]

The then Secretary of State Michael Chertoff announced that FEMA's preparedness function (as opposed to its response function) should be severed from FEMA and assigned to a newly created Preparedness Directorate.[87] This tendency to increase organizational complexity rather than simplify it is in direct contrast to an approach that could be labelled as 'simple organizations and complex jobs'. That would describe the quality of the organization that gives it its ability to deal with a complex and continuously changing environment while at the same time maintaining an appropriate level of organizational simplicity and effectiveness within its own management frameworks.

The comments from the Congressional report and President Bush's remarks seem to suggest that the issue was not in the intrinsic nature of the command-and-control structure but had not been implemented properly, and that a greater degree of control and operational management would allow those weaknesses to be corrected. This was in stark contrast to the directness of language used in one of the most influential papers written in the aftermath of the Hurricane Katrina failure,[88] according to which the response to Hurricane Katrina proved beyond doubt that the fundamental organizational issues involving sharing of information, development of a unified 'task vision' and the ability of 'the system' to deliver emergency response in what was, after all, a relatively benign environment, on United States home territory, in a situation that was both known and expected, were so overwhelming as to call into question every aspect of the fundamental principles and assumptions on which US crisis management and homeland security was based:

> The obvious collapse of the intergovernmental system in emergency management under the strains of the catastrophic events initiated by Hurricane Katrina provides an unquestioned demonstration of the failure of hierarchical control in the dynamic context of an actual disaster... This task

> requires rethinking the terms of communication and coordination to dispel the myth of hierarchical control... It means redefining the terms of cognition, communication, coordination and control in ways that fit the reality of practice in extreme events... The record of operations from Hurricane Katrina compels a redefinition of organizational framework and standard terms of emergency management.[89]

Given the absolutist nature of this assessment, the following question needs to be asked: Why is there such a continued commitment to centralist command systems and what impact does this have on possible alternative models of management systems?

Conclusion

The intrinsically creative nature of crisis management is acknowledged in the recognition of the importance of personal 'craftmanship' in dealing with what are unique situations. The belief that such events can be best managed by pre-planned response programmes, and that it is the role of local commanders to simply implement those plans rather than to assess the local situation in order to develop the most appropriate response based on specific local conditions, is both short-sighted and counterproductive.

The nature of crisis response within such an unstable and highly dynamic environment involves intuitive decision-making and optimal guesswork rather than highly defined and managed responses. Any management framework that would be expected to maintain operational relevance within a crisis management context would need to have these values at its very heart. Hurricane Katrina demonstrated beyond doubt the limitations of traditional militaristic command systems, and yet despite this there is still the ingrained belief that centrally controlled hierarchical command chains are the best (and even the natural) form of emergency response management. As this chapter points out, such failures can be seen as the outcome of the inability to use such centrally managed systems effectively and that, if they are used correctly, such frameworks not only have their place but are invaluable in creating a management structure appropriate for highly complex and geographically defused operations. However, it is the local, collaborative and innovative solution development that is at the heart of crisis management, and it will be the ability of hierarchical command systems to adapt to that reality, and to act as a support system to such local activities, that will determine their relevance in future crisis management situations.

Endnotes

1 Kendra, J M & Wachtendorf, T (2003) Elements of resilience after the world trade center disaster: Reconstituting New York City's Emergency Operations Centre. *Disasters*, 27(1), 37–53

2 't Hart, P, Rosenthal, U & Kouzmin, A (1993) Crisis decision: Making the centralization thesis revisited. *Administration & Society*, 25(1), 12–45

3 Burns, T (1963) *Mechanistic and organismic structures. Organization theory. Selected readings*, 4th ed. Penguin Books, London

4 Malhotra, Y (2000) Knowledge management and new organization forms: A framework for business model innovation. *Information Resources Management Journal*, January–March, 13(1), 5–14

5 Bigley, G A & Roberts, K H (2001) The incident command system: High reliability organizing for complex and volatile task environments. *Academy of Management Journal*, 44(6), 1281–1299

6 Cooke, N J, Gorman, J C & Rowe, L J (2004) An ecological perspective on team cognition. Cognitive Engineering Research Inst Mesa Az; Eysenck, M W & Keane, M T (2015) *Cognitive psychology: A student's handbook*. Psychology Press

7 Rittel, H W (1972) On the planning crisis: Systems analysis of the 'first and second generations'. Institute of Urban and Regional Development, 390–396. http://courses.cs.vt.edu/cs4634/reading/Rittel.pdf (archived at https://perma.cc/88ZT-JLK6) (Accessed: 10 July 2022)

8 Flood, R L & Carson, E R (1993) *Dealing with complexity: An introduction to the theory and applications of the systems science*. Plenum Press

9 Clarke, L (1999) *Mission improbable: Using fantasy documents to tame disaster*. University of Chicago Press
Rittel, H W & Webber, M M (1973) Dilemmas in a general theory of planning. *Policy Sciences*, 4(2), 155–169; Wexler, M N (2009) Exploring the moral dimension of wicked problems. *International Journal of Sociology and Social Policy*, 29(9/10), 531–542

10 Trnka, J & Jenvald, J (2006) Role-playing exercise – a real-time approach to study collaborative command and control. *International Journal of Intelligent Control and Systems*, 11(4), 218–228; Waldenström, C (2008) What is difficult in naval sensemaking. In Proceedings of the 13th International Command and Control Research and Technology Symposium

11 De Dreu, C K (2007) Cooperative outcome interdependence, task reflexivity, and team effectiveness: A motivated information processing perspective. *Journal of Applied Psychology*, 92(3), 628

12 Bigley, G A & Roberts, K H (2001) The incident command system: High reliability organizing for complex and volatile task environments. *Academy of Management Journal*, 44(6), 1281–1299. Howitt, A M & Leonard, H B (2006) Katrina and the core challenges of disaster response. *Fletcher Forum of World Affairs*, 30(1), 215–221. https://www.hks.harvard.edu/sites/default/files/centers/research-initiatives/crisisleadership/files/katrina_core_challenges.pdf (archived at https://perma.cc/X2AN-EEN7) (Accessed: 11 September 2014)

13 Buck, D A, Trainor, J E & Aguirre, B E (2006) A critical evaluation of the incident command system and NIMS. *Journal of Homeland Security and Emergency Management*, 3(3)

14 Lagadec, E (2007) Unconventional crises, unconventional responses: Reforming leadership in the age of catastrophic crises and hypercomplexity. Center for Transatlantic Relations, Paul H Nitze School of Advanced International Studies, Johns Hopkins University

15 Bigley, G A & Roberts, K H (2001) The incident command system: High reliability organizing for complex and volatile task environments. *Academy of Management Journal*, 44(6), 1281–1299; Klein, G A, Calderwood, R & Clinton-Cirocco, A (1986, September) Rapid decision making on the fire ground. In Proceedings of the human factors society annual meeting, 30(6), 576–580. Los Angeles, CA: Sage Publications; Moynihan, D P (2009) The network governance of crisis response: Case studies of incident command systems. *Journal of Public Administration Research and Theory*, 19(4), 895–915; Weick, K E (1993) The collapse of sensemaking in organizations: The Mann Gulch disaster. *Administrative Science Quarterly*, 628–652

16 Dynes, R R (1970) Organized behavior in disaster: Analysis and conceptualization (No. 3) Disaster Research Center, Ohio State University

17 Comfort, L K (2007) Crisis management in hindsight: Cognition, communication, coordination and control, *Public Administration Review*, 67, 189–197; Kapucu, N (2005) Interorganizational coordination in dynamic context: Networks in emergency response management. *Connections*, 26(2), 33–48; Marcum, C S, Bevc, C A & Butts, C T (2012) Mechanisms of control in emergent interorganizational networks. *Policy Studies Journal*, 40(3), 516–546

18 Wenger, D, Quarantelli, E L & Dynes, R R (1990) Is the incident command system a plan for all seasons and emergency situations? *Hazard Monthly*, 10(3), 8–12

19 Dynes, R R (1983) Problems in emergency planning. *Energy*, 8(8–9), 653–660

20 Howitt, A M & B'Duth'Leonard, H (2005) A command system for all agencies? *Crisis Response Journal*, 1(2), 40–42

21 Lutz, L D & Lindell, M K (2008) Incident command system as a response model within emergency operation centers during Hurricane Rita. *Journal of Contingencies and Crisis Management*, 16(3), 122–134

22 Comfort, L K (2007) Crisis management in hindsight: Cognition, communication, coordination and control. *Public Administration Review*, 67, 189–197; Moynihan, D P (2009) The network governance of crisis response: Case studies of incident command systems. *Journal of Public Administration Research and Theory*, 19(4), 895–915

23 Burns, T & Stalker, G M (1961) Mechanistic and organic systems. *Classics of Organizational Theory*, 209–214; Daft, R L & Weick, K E (1984) Toward a model of organizations as interpretation systems. *Academy of Management Review*, 9(2), 284–295; Dynes, R R (1994) Community emergency planning: False assumptions and inappropriate analogies. *International Journal of Mass Emergencies and Disasters*, Vol. 12, No. 2, 141–158

24 Butts, C T, Petrescu-Prahova, M & Remy Cross, B (2007) Responder communication networks in the World Trade Center disaster: Implications for modeling of communication within emergency settings. *Mathematical Sociology*, 31(2), 121–147; Garnett, J L & Kouzmin, A (2007) Communicating throughout Katrina: Competing and complementary conceptual lenses on crisis communication. *Public Administration Review*, 67, 171–188; Van Wart, M & Kapucu, N (2011) Crisis management competencies: The case of emergency managers in the USA. *Public Management Review*, 13(4), 489–511

25 Sanchez, R S (2009) *Wiser in battle: A soldier's story*. HarperCollins

26 Bland, A (2020) Scotch egg is definitely a substantial meal, says Michael Gove. *The Guardian* (1 December). https://www.theguardian.com/world/2020/dec/01/scotch-egg-is-definitely-a-substantial-meal-says-michael-gove (archived at https://perma.cc/7WAS-TFLG); House of Lords Public Service Committee (2019) A critical juncture for public services: Lessons from Covid 19. 1st Report of Session (November 2020). https://committees.parliament.uk/publications/3438/documents/32865/default/ (archived at https://perma.cc/ZCC9-KDVB); Wilkonson, E (2021) BMA urges Health Secretary to address 'micromanagement' of GPs by NHS England. Pulse (21 July). https://www.pulsetoday.co.uk/news/politics/bma-urges-health-secretary-to-address-micromanagement-of-gps-by-nhs-england/ (archived at https://perma.cc/7Q7M-MCTZ)

27 House of Lords Public Services Committee (2020) A critical juncture for public services: lessons from COVID-19, parliament.uk. Available at: https://publications.parliament.uk/pa/ld5801/ldselect/pubserv/167/167.pdf (archived at https://perma.cc/BZ85-MMJT)

28 Wilkonson, E (2021) BMA urges Health Secretary to address 'micromanagement' of GPs by NHS England. Pulse (21 July). https://www.pulsetoday.co.uk/news/politics/bma-urges-health-secretary-to-address-micromanagement-of-gps-by-nhs-england/ (archived at https://perma.cc/7Q7M-MCTZ)

29 Dynes, R R (1994) Community emergency planning: False assumptions and inappropriate analogies. *International Journal of Mass Emergencies and Disasters*, Vol. 12, No. 2, 141–158

30 McNeese, M D, Pfaff, M S, Connors, E S, Obieta, J F, Terrell, I S & Friedenberg, M A (2006, October) Multiple vantage points of the Common Operational Picture: Supporting international teamwork. In Proceedings of the Human Factors and Ergonomics Society Annual Meeting, 50(3), 467–471. Sage Publications

31 Jungert, E, Derefeldt, G, Hallberg, J, Hallberg, N, Hunstad, A & Thurén, R (2004) Architecture-based model for preventive and operative crisis management. Swedish Defence Research Agency Foi Tumba (Sweden); Miller, L E (2005) Wireless Technologies and the SAFECOM SoR for Public Safety Communications. NIST Technical Report, Available at: https://www.nist.gov/document/wirelessandsor060206pdf (archived at https://perma.cc/63R5-7WU5) (Accessed: May 2015); McChrystal, Gen Stanley, et al (2015) *Team of teams: New rules of engagement for a complex world*. Penguin

32 Kalloniatis, A C, Macleod, I D G & La, P (2009) Process versus battle-rhythm: Modelling operational command and control. Online

33 Moon, H, Hollenbeck, J R, Humphrey, S E, Ilgen, D R, West, B, Ellis, A P & Porter, C O (2004) Asymmetric adaptability: Dynamic team structures as one-way streets. *Academy of Management Journal*, 47(5), 681–695

34 Walker, G H, Stanton, N A, Salmon, P M & Jenkins, D P (2008) A review of sociotechnical systems theory: A classic concept for new command and control paradigms. *Theoretical Issues in Ergonomics Science*, 9(6), 479–499

35 Beersma, B, Hollenbeck, J R, Humphrey, S E, Moon, H, Conlon, D E & Ilgen, D R (2003) Cooperation, competition, and team performance: Toward a contingency approach. *Academy of Management Journal*, 46(5), 572–590; Moon, H, Hollenbeck, J R, Humphrey, S E, Ilgen, D R, West, B, Ellis, A P & Porter, C O (2004) Asymmetric adaptability: Dynamic team structures as one-way streets. *Academy of Management Journal*, 47(5), 681–695; Pennings, J M (1998) Structural contingency theory. *Organizational Psychology*, 4, 39–60

36 Boulier, J F (1996) Que valent les options cachées? *Revue d'Économie Financière*, 37(2), 189–201

37 Alison, L, Power, N, van den Heuvel, C, Humann, M, Palasinksi, M and Crego, J (2015) Decision inertia: Deciding between least worst outcomes in emergency responses to disasters. *Journal of Occupational and Organizational Psychology*, 88: 295–321. doi: 10.1111/joop.12108; Cannon-Bowers, J A, Salas, E, Tannenbaum, S I & Mathieu, J E (1995) Toward theoretically based principles of training effectiveness: A model and initial empirical investigation. *Military Psychology*, 7(3), 141–164

38 Waldenström, C (2008) What is difficult in naval sensemaking. In Proceedings of the 13th International Command and Control Research and Technology Symposium

39 McNeese, M D, Pfaff, M S, Connors, E S, Obieta, J F, Terrell, I S & Friedenberg, M A (2006, October) Multiple vantage points of the Common Operational Picture: Supporting international teamwork. In Proceedings of the Human Factors and Ergonomics Society Annual Meeting, 50(3), 467–471. Sage Publications

40 Hollenbeck, J R, Ilgen, D R, LePine, J A, Colquitt, J A & Hedlund, J (1998) Extending the multilevel theory of team decision making: Effects of feedback and experience in hierarchical teams. *Academy of Management Journal*, 41(3), 269–282; Ellis, A P, Hollenbeck, J R, Ilgen, D R & Humphrey, S E (2003) The asymmetric nature of structural changes in command and control teams: The impact of centralizing and decentralizing on group outcomes. In 8th Annual International Command and Control Research Technology Symposium, Washington, DC; Moon, H, Hollenbeck, J R, Humphrey, S E, Ilgen, D R, West, B, Ellis, A P & Porter, C O (2004) Asymmetric adaptability: Dynamic team structures as one-way streets. *Academy of Management Journal*, 47(5), 681–695

41 Jundt, D K, Ilgen, D R, Hollenbeck, J R, Humphrey, S E, Johnson, M D & Meyer, C J (2004) The impact of hybrid team structures on performance and adaptation: Beyond mechanistic and organic prototypes; Mintzberg, H (1980) Structure in 5s: A synthesis of the research on organization design. *Management Science*, 26(3), 322–341; Wise, C R (2006) Organizing for homeland security after Katrina: Is adaptive management what's missing? *Public Administration Review*, 66(3), 302–318

42 Hill, B (2010) Diagnosing co-ordination problems in the emergency management response to disasters. *Interacting with Computers*, 22(1), 43–55

43 Allen, D K, Karanasios, S & Norman, A (2014) Information sharing and interoperability: The case of major incident management. *European Journal of Information Systems*, 23(4), 418–432; Devitt, K R & Borodzicz, E P (2008) Interwoven leadership: The missing link in multi-agency major incident response. *Journal of Contingencies and Crisis Management*, 16(4), 208–216; Mishra, J L, Allen, D K & Pearman, A D (2011) Information sharing during multi-agency major incidents. Proceedings of the American Society for Information Science and Technology, 48(1), 1–10; Samurçay, R & Rogalski, J (1991) A method for tactical reasoning (MTR) in emergency management: Analysis of individual acquisition and collective implementation. *Distributed decision making: Cognitive models for cooperative work*, Wiley, 287–297

44 Ansell, C, Boin, A & Keller, A (2010) Managing transboundary crises: Identifying the building blocks of an effective response system. *Journal of Contingencies and Crisis Management*, 18(4), 195–207

45 Powell, W W (1990) Neither market nor hierarchy. *Sociology of Organizations: Structures and Relationships*, Sage, 30–40

46 Kapucu, N (2005) Interorganizational coordination in dynamic context: Networks in emergency response management. *Connections*, 26(2), 33–48

47 Waugh, W L & Streib, G (2006) Collaboration and leadership for effective emergency management. *Public Administration Review*, 66(s1), 131–140

48 Schafer, W A, Carroll, J M, Haynes, S R & Abrams, S (2008) Emergency management planning as collaborative community work. *Journal of Homeland Security and Emergency Management*, 5(1)

49 Drabek, T E (1985) Managing the emergency response. *Public Administration Review*, 85–92; Ohder, C & Sticher, B (2013) Approaches towards a community-oriented and enabling disaster management model. Unger, C, Mitschke, T & Freudenberg, D (eds.), Crisis management–Emergency planning–Civil Protection. Festschrift on the occasion of, 60

50 Chua, A Y, Kaynak, S & Foo, S S (2007) An analysis of the delayed response to Hurricane Katrina through the lens of knowledge management. *Journal of the American Society for Information Science and Technology*, 58(3), 391–403; Comfort, L K, Woods, T R & Nesbitt, J E (1989) Designing an emergency information system: The Pittsburgh experience; Moynihan, D P (2009) The response to Hurricane Katrina. Geneva (Italy): International Risk Governance Council, 2

51 Harrald, J & Jefferson, T (2007, January) Shared situational awareness in emergency management mitigation and response. *System Sciences*. HICSS 2007. 40th Annual Hawaii International Conference, 23–23. IEEE

52 Harrald, J & Jefferson, T (2007, January) Shared situational awareness in emergency management mitigation and response. *System Sciences*. HICSS 2007. 40th Annual Hawaii International Conference on, 23–23. IEEE

53 Paton, D & Johnston, D (2001) Disasters and communities: Vulnerability, resilience and preparedness. *Disaster Prevention and Management*, 10(4), 270–277

54 United States Commission on National Security/21st Century (2001) Road Map for National Security: Imperative for Change: the Phase III Report of the US Commission on National Security/21st Century. The Commission

55 Dynes, R R (1994) Community emergency planning: False assumptions and inappropriate analogies. *International Journal of Mass Emergencies and Disasters*, 12(2), 141–158

56 Kapucu, N (2005) Interorganizational coordination in dynamic context: Networks in emergency response management. *Connections*, 26(2), 33–48; Waugh, D (2000) *Geography: An integrated approach*. Nelson Thornes

57 Birkland, T A (2009) Disasters, catastrophes, and policy failure in the homeland security era1. *Review of Policy Research*, 26(4), 423–438

58 McEntire, D A (2002) Coordinating multi-organisational responses to disaster: Lessons from the March 28, 2000, Fort Worth tornado. *Disaster Prevention and Management: An International Journal*, 11(5), 369–379

59 Moynihan, D P (2009) The response to Hurricane Katrina. Geneva (Italy): International Risk Governance Council, 2

60 Schafer, W A, Carroll, J M, Haynes, S R & Abrams, S (2008) Emergency management planning as collaborative community work. *Journal of Homeland Security and Emergency Management*, 5(1)

61 Stratton, R M (1989) *Disaster relief: The politics of intergovernmental relations*. University Press of America

62 Pigeau, R & McCann, C (2000) Redefining command and control. In *The human in command*, 163–184. Springer US

63 Kalloniatis, A, Iain Macleod, P L & Fairbairn, D E (2009) 14th ICCRTS 'C2 and agility' bounding wicked problems: The C2 of military planning topic 3: Information sharing and collaboration processes and behaviors

64 NATO (2006) Technical Report TR-SAS-050 (2007): Exploring new command and control concepts and capabilities. NATO, Neuilly-sur-Seine Cedex; Walker, G, Stanton, N A, Salmon, P, Jenkins, D, Revell, K & Rafferty, L (2009) Measuring dimensions of command and control using social network analysis: Extending the NATO SAS-050 model. *The International C2 Journal*, 3(2), 1–46

65 Mishra, J L, Allen, D K & Pearman, A.D (2011) Information sharing during multi-agency major incidents. Proceedings of the American Society for Information Science and Technology, 48(1), 1–10

66 Kalloniatis, A, Iain Macleod, P L & Fairbairn, D E (2009) 14th ICCRTS 'C2 and agility' bounding wicked problems: The C2 of military planning topic 3: Information sharing and collaboration processes and behaviors

67 Jundt, D K, Ilgen, D R, Hollenbeck, J R, Humphrey, S E, Johnson, M D & Meyer, C J (2004) The impact of hybrid team structures on performance and adaptation: Beyond mechanistic and organic prototypes

68 Walker, G H, Stanton, N A, Salmon, P M & Jenkins, D P (2008) A review of sociotechnical systems theory: A classic concept for new command and control paradigms. *Theoretical Issues in Ergonomics Science*, 9(6), 479–499

69 Turner, B A (1994) Causes of disaster: Sloppy management. *British Journal of Management*, 5(3), 215–219

70 Waldrop, M M (1993) *Complexity: The emerging science at the edge of order and chaos*. Simon & Schuster.

71 Mannarelli, T, Roberts, K H & Bea, R G (1996) Learning how organizations mitigate risk. *Journal of Contingencies and Crisis Management*, 4(2), 83–92

72 Hollenbeck, J R, Moon, H, Ellis, A P, West, B J, Ilgen, D R, Sheppard, L, .. & Wagner III, J A (2002) Structural contingency theory and individual differences: Examination of external and internal person-team fit. *Journal of Applied Psychology*, 87(3), 599; Moon, H, Hollenbeck, J R, Humphrey, S E, Ilgen, D R, West, B, Ellis, A P & Porter, C O (2004) Asymmetric adaptability: Dynamic team structures as one-way streets. *Academy of Management Journal*, 47(5), 681–695

73 Wise, C R (2006) Organizing for homeland security after Katrina: Is adaptive management what's missing? *Public Administration Review*, 302–318

74 Comfort, L K (2007) Crisis management in hindsight: cognition, communication, coordination and control. *Public Administration Review*, 67, 189–197

75 Pollock, K (2013) Review of persistent lessons identified relating to interoperability from emergencies and major incidents since 1986

76 Quarantelli, E L & Dynes, R R (1977) Response to social crisis and disaster. *Annual Review of Sociology*, 23–49; Wenger, D, Quarantelli, E L & Dynes, R R (1990) Is the incident command system a plan for all seasons and emergency situations? *Hazard Monthly*, 10(3), 8–12

77 Donahue, A K & Tuohy, R V (2006) Lessons we don't learn: A study of the lessons of disasters, why we repeat them, and how we can learn them. *Homeland Security Affairs*, Vol II, July

78 Kapucu, N (2005) Interorganizational coordination in dynamic context: Networks in emergency response management. *Connections*, 26(2), 33–48
Kapucu, N, Arslan, T & Demiroz, F (2010) Collaborative emergency management and national emergency management network. *Disaster Prevention and Management*, 19(4)

79 Waugh, W L & Streib, G (2006) Collaboration and leadership for effective emergency management. *Public Administration Review*, 66(s1), 131–140

80 Waugh, W L & Streib, G (2006) Collaboration and leadership for effective emergency management. *Public Administration Review*, 66(s1), 131–140

81 Moynihan, D P (2009) The network governance of crisis response: Case studies of incident command systems. *Journal of Public Administration Research and Theory Journal of Public Administration Research and Theory*, 19(4), 895–915

82 Ross, K G, Klein, G A, Thunholm, P, Schmitt, J F & Baxter, H C (2004) The recognition-primed decision model. Army Combined Arms Center Fort Leavenworth Ks Military Review; US General Accounting Office (2003) Major management challenges and program risks: Department of Homeland Security. Government Printing Office, Washington. Available at http://www.gao.gov/assets/240/236953.pdf (archived at https://perma.cc/58BW-R97Q) (Accessed: 11 June 2022)

83 Donahue, A K & Tuohy, R V (2006) Lessons we don't learn: A study of the lessons of disasters, why we repeat them, and how we can learn them. *Homeland Security Affairs*, Vol II, July

84 Birkland, T A (2009) Disasters, catastrophes, and policy failure in the homeland security era1. *Review of Policy Research*, 26(4), 423–438; Dynes, R R (1994) Community emergency planning: False assumptions and inappropriate analogies. *International Journal of Mass Emergencies and Disasters*, 12(2), 141–158

85 United States. Executive Office of the President, Etats-Unis. Assistant to the President for homeland security, counterterrorism, Superintendent of Documents, President of the United States Staff, United States. Assistant to the President for Homeland Security, ... & Superintendent of Documents Staff (2006) The federal response to Hurricane Katrina: Lessons learned. Government Printing Office

86 United States. Executive Office of the President, Etats-Unis. Assistant to the President for homeland security, counterterrorism, Superintendent of Documents, President of the United States Staff, United States. Assistant to the President for Homeland Security, ... & Superintendent of Documents Staff (2006) The federal response to Hurricane Katrina: Lessons learned. Government Printing Office

87 Sitter, L U, Dankbaar, B & Hertog, J F (1994) Designing simple organisations and complex jobs. Maastricht, Maastricht Economic Research Institute on Innovation and Technology. https://collections.unu.edu/eserv/UNU:994/rm1994-012.pdf (archived at https://perma.cc/4E2M-3NUV) (Accessed: 10 July 2022); Wise, C.R (2006) Organizing for homeland security after Katrina: Is adaptive management what's missing? *Public Administration Review*, 302–318

88 Comfort, L K (2007) Crisis management in hindsight: Cognition, communication, coordination and control. *Public Administration Review*, 67, 189–197

89 Comfort, L K (2007) Crisis management in hindsight: Cognition, communication, coordination and control. *Public Administration Review*, 67, 189–197

Further reading

Alison, L, Power, N, van den Heuvel, C, Humann, M, Palasinksi, M and Crego, J (2015) Decision inertia: Deciding between least worst outcomes in emergency responses to disasters. *Journal of Occupational and Organizational Psychology*, 88, 295–321

Allen, D K, Karanasios, S & Norman, A (2014) Information sharing and interoperability: The case of major incident management. *European Journal of Information Systems*, 23(4), 418–432

Ansell, C, Boin, A & Keller, A (2010) Managing transboundary crises: Identifying the building blocks of an effective response system. *Journal of Contingencies and Crisis Management*, 18(4), 195–207

Beersma, B, Hollenbeck, J R, Humphrey, S E, Moon, H, Conlon, D E & Ilgen, D R (2003) Cooperation, competition, and team performance: Toward a contingency approach. *Academy of Management Journal*, 46(5), 572–590

Bigley, G A & Roberts, K H (2001) The incident command system: High reliability organizing for complex and volatile task environments. *Academy of Management Journal*, 44(6), 1281–1299

Birkland, T A (2009) Disasters, catastrophes, and policy failure in the homeland security era1. *Review of Policy Research*, 26(4), 423–438

Bland, A (2020) Scotch egg is definitely a substantial meal, says Michael Gove. *The Guardian* (1 December). Available at: https://www.theguardian.com/world/2020/dec/01/scotch-egg-is-definitely-a-substantial-meal-says-michael-gove (archived at https://perma.cc/7WAS-TFLG) (Accessed: 22 June 2022)

Boulier, J F (1996) Que valent les options cachées? *Revue d'Économie Financière*, 37(2), 189–201

Buck, D A, Trainor, J E & Aguirre, B E (2006) A critical evaluation of the incident command system and NIMS. *Journal of Homeland Security and Emergency Management*, 3(3)

Burns, T & Stalker, G M (1961) Mechanistic and organic systems. *Classics of Organizational Theory*, Oxford University Press, 209–214

Burns, T (1963) Mechanistic and organismic structures. *Organization Theory. Selected readings*, 4th ed. London: Penguin Books

Butts, C T, Petrescu-Prahova, M & Remy Cross, B (2007) Responder communication networks in the world trade center disaster: Implications for modeling of communication within emergency settings. *Mathematical Sociology*, 31(2), 121–147

Cannon-Bowers, J A, Salas, E, Tannenbaum, S I & Mathieu, J E (1995) Toward theoretically based principles of training effectiveness: A model and initial empirical investigation. *Military Psychology*, 7(3), 141–164

Chua, A Y, Kaynak, S & Foo, S S (2007) An analysis of the delayed response to Hurricane Katrina through the lens of knowledge management. *Journal of the American Society for Information Science and Technology*, 58(3), 391–403

Clarke, L (1999) *Mission improbable: Using fantasy documents to tame disaster*. University of Chicago Press

Comfort, L K, Woods, T R & Nesbitt, J E (1989) Designing an emergency information system: The Pittsburgh experience. UC Berkeley: Institute of Governmental Studies. Retrieved from https://escholarship.org/uc/item/31h237sn (archived at https://perma.cc/PH2U-22TP)

Comfort, L K (2007) Crisis management in hindsight: Cognition, communication, coordination and control. *Public Administration Review*, 67, 189–197

Cooke, N J, Gorman, J C & Rowe, L J (2004) An ecological perspective on team cognition. Cognitive Engineering Research Inst Mesa Az

Daft, R L & Weick, K E (1984) Toward a model of organizations as interpretation systems. *Academy of Management Review*, 9(2), 284–295

De Dreu, C K (2007) Cooperative outcome interdependence, task reflexivity, and team effectiveness: A motivated information processing perspective. *Journal of Applied Psychology*, 92(3), 628

Devitt, K R & Borodzicz, E P (2008) Interwoven leadership: The missing link in multi-agency major incident response. *Journal of Contingencies and Crisis Management*, 16(4), 208–216

Donahue, A K & Tuohy, R V (2006) Lessons we don't learn: A study of the lessons of disasters, why we repeat them, and how we can learn them. *Homeland Security Affairs*, Vol II, July

Drabek, T E (1985) Managing the emergency response. *Public Administration Review*, 85–92

Dynes, R R (1970) *Organized behavior in disaster: Analysis and conceptualization* (No. 3) Disaster Research Center, Ohio State University

Dynes, R R (1983) Problems in emergency planning. *Energy*, 8(8–9), 653–660

Dynes, R R (1994) Community emergency planning: False assumptions and inappropriate analogies. *International Journal of Mass Emergencies and Disasters*, Vol. 12, No. 2, 141–158

Ellis, A P, Hollenbeck, J R, Ilgen, D R & Humphrey, S E (2003) The asymmetric nature of structural changes in command and control teams: The impact of centralizing

Eysenck, M W & Keane, M T (2015) *Cognitive psychology: A student's handbook*. Psychology Press

Flood, R L & Carson, E R (1993) *Dealing with complexity: An introduction to the theory and applications of the systems science*. Plenum Press

Garnett, J L & Kouzmin, A (2007) Communicating throughout Katrina: Competing and complementary conceptual lenses on crisis communication. *Public Administration Review*, 67, 171–188

Harrald, J & Jefferson, T (2007) Shared situational awareness in emergency management mitigation and response. *System Sciences*. HICSS 2007. 40th Annual Hawaii International Conference, 23–23. IEEE

Hill, B (2010) Diagnosing co-ordination problems in the emergency management response to disasters. *Interacting with Computers*, 22(1), 43–55

Hollenbeck, J R, Ilgen, D R, LePine, J A, Colquitt, J A & Hedlund, J (1998) Extending the multilevel theory of team decision making: Effects of feedback and experience in hierarchical teams. *Academy of Management Journal*, 41(3), 269–282

Hollenbeck, J R, Moon, H, Ellis, A P, West, B J, Ilgen, D R, Sheppard, L, … & Wagner III, J A (2002) Structural contingency theory and individual differences: Examination of external and internal person-team fit. *Journal of Applied Psychology*, 87(3), 599

House of Lords Public Services Committee (2019) A critical juncture for public services: Lessons from COVID 19. 1st Report of Session. Available at: https://committees.parliament.uk/publications/3438/documents/32865/default/ (archived at https://perma.cc/BZ85-MMJT) (Accessed: 22 June 2022)

Howitt, A M & B'Duth'Leonard, H (2005) A command system for all agencies? *Crisis Response Journal*, 1(2), 40–42

Howitt, A M & Leonard, H B (2006) Katrina and the core challenges of disaster response. *Fletcher Forum of World Affairs*, 30(1), 215–221. Available at: http://www.hks.harvard.edu/index.php/content/download/67396/1242394/version/1/file/katrina_core_challenges.pdf (Accessed: 22 June 2022)

Jundt, D K, Ilgen, D R, Hollenbeck, J R, Humphrey, S E, Johnson, M D & Meyer, C J (2004) The impact of hybrid team structures on performance and adaptation: Beyond mechanistic and organic prototypes

Jungert, E, Derefeldt, G, Hallberg, J, Hallberg, N, Hunstad, A & Thurén, R (2004) *Architecture-based model for preventive and operative crisis management*. Swedish Defence Research Agency Foi Tumba (Sweden)

Kalloniatis, A C, Macleod, I D G & La, P (2009) Process versus battle-rhythm: Modelling operational command and control

Kalloniatis, A, Macleod, I & Fairbairn, D E (2009) 14th ICCRTS 'C2 and agility' bounding wicked problems: The C2 of military planning topic 3: Information sharing and collaboration processes and behaviors

Kapucu, N (2005) Interorganizational coordination in dynamic context: Networks in emergency response management. *Connections*, 26(2), 33–48

Kapucu, N, Arslan, T & Demiroz, F (2010) Collaborative emergency management and national emergency management network. *Disaster Prevention and Management: An International Journal*, 19(4)

Kendra, J M & Wachtendorf, T (2003) Elements of resilience after the World Trade Center disaster: Reconstituting New York City's emergency operations centre. *Disasters*, 27(1), 37–53

Klein, G A, Calderwood, R & Clinton-Cirocco, A (1986, September) Rapid decision making on the fire ground. In Proceedings of the Human Factors Society Annual Meeting, 30(6), 576–580. Los Angeles, CA: Sage Publications

Lagadec, E (2007) Unconventional crises, unconventional responses: Reforming leadership in the age of catastrophic crises and hypercomplexity. Center for Transatlantic Relations, Paul H Nitze School of Advanced International Studies, Johns Hopkins University

Lutz, L D & Lindell, M K (2008) Incident command system as a response model within emergency operation centers during Hurricane Rita. *Journal of Contingencies and Crisis Management*, 16(3), 122–134

Malhotra, Y (2000) Knowledge management and new organization forms: A framework for business model innovation. *Information Resources Management Journal*, January–March, 13(1), 5–14

Mannarelli, T, Roberts, K H & Bea, R G (1996) Learning how organizations mitigate risk. *Journal of Contingencies and Crisis Management*, 4(2), 83–92

Marcum, C S, Bevc, C A & Butts, C T (2012) Mechanisms of control in emergent interorganizational networks. *Policy Studies Journal*, 40(3), 516–546

McChrystal, Gen Stanley, et al (2015) *Team of teams: New rules of engagement for a complex world.* Penguin

McEntire, D A (2002) Coordinating multi-organisational responses to disaster: Lessons from the March 28, 2000, Fort Worth tornado. *Disaster Prevention and Management*, 11(5), 369–379

McNeese, M D, Pfaff, M S, Connors, E S, Obieta, J F, Terrell, I S & Friedenberg, M A (2006, October) Multiple vantage points of the common operational picture: Supporting international teamwork. Proceedings of the Human Factors and Ergonomics Society Annual Meeting, 50(3), 467–471, Sage Publications

Miller, L E (2005) Wireless technologies and the SAFECOM SoR for public safety communications. NIST Technical Report. http://www.antd.nist.gov/wctg/manet/docs/WirelessAndSoR060206.pdf (archived at https://perma.cc/373W-Z4BG) (Accessed: May 2015)

Mintzberg, H (1980) Structure in 5s: A Synthesis of the research on organization design. *Management Science*, 26(3), 322–341

Mishra, J L, Allen, D K & Pearman, A D (2011) Information sharing during multi-agency major incidents. *Proceedings of the American Society for Information Science and Technology*, 48(1), 1–10

Moon, H, Hollenbeck, J R, Humphrey, S E, Ilgen, D R, West, B, Ellis, A P & Porter, C O (2004) Asymmetric adaptability: Dynamic team structures as one-way streets. *Academy of Management Journal*, 47(5), 681–695

Moynihan, D P (2009a) The network governance of crisis response: Case studies of incident command systems. *Journal of Public Administration Research and Theory Journal of Public Administration Research and Theory*, 19(4), 895–915

Moynihan, D P (2009b) The response to Hurricane Katrina. Geneva (Italy): International Risk Governance Council, 2

NATO (2006) Technical Report TR-SAS-050 (2007) Exploring new command and control concepts and capabilities. NATO, Neuilly-sur-Seine Cedex

Ohder, C & Sticher, B (2013) Approaches towards a community-oriented and enabling disaster management model. Chr. Unger, Th. Mitschke & D. Freudenberg (eds.), Crisis management–Emergency planning–Civil Protection. Festschrift on the occasion of, 60

Paton, D & Johnston, D (2001) Disasters and communities: Vulnerability, resilience and preparedness. *Disaster Prevention and Management: An International Journal*, 10(4), 270–277

Pennings, J M (1998) Structural contingency theory. *Organizational Psychology*, 4, 39–60

Pigeau, R & McCann, C (2000) Redefining command and control. In *The human in command*, Springer US, 163–184

Pollock, K (2013) Review of persistent lessons identified relating to interoperability from emergencies and major incidents since 1986. https://www.jesip.org.uk/uploads/media/pdf/Pollock_Review_Oct_2013.pdf (archived at https://perma.cc/94ZZ-XERG)

Powell, W W (1990) Neither market nor hierarchy. *Sociology of Organizations: Structures and Relationships*, 30–40

Quarantelli, E L & Dynes, R R (1977) Response to social crisis and disaster. *Annual Review of Sociology*, 23–49

Rittel, H W (1972) *On the planning crisis: Systems analysis of the' first and second generations'* (390–396) Institute of Urban and Regional Development. Available at: http://courses.cs.vt.edu/cs4634/reading/Rittel.pdf (archived at https://perma.cc/88ZT-JLK6) (Accessed: 10 July 2022)

Rittel, H W & Webber, M M (1973) Dilemmas in a general theory of planning. *Policy Sciences*, 4(2), 155–169

Ross, K G, Klein, G A, Thunholm, P, Schmitt, J F & Baxter, H C (2004) The recognition-primed decision model. Army Combined Arms Center Fort Leavenworth Ks Military Review

Samurçay, R & Rogalski, J (1991) A method for tactical reasoning (MTR) in emergency management: Analysis of individual acquisition and collective implementation. *Distributed Decision Making: Cognitive Models for Cooperative Work*, 287–297

Sanchez, R S (2009) *Wiser in battle: A soldier's story*. HarperCollins

Schafer, W A, Carroll, J M, Haynes, S R & Abrams, S (2008) Emergency management planning as collaborative community work. *Journal of Homeland Security and Emergency Management*, 5(1)

Sitter, L U, Dankbaar, B & Hertog, J F (1994) Designing simple organisations and complex jobs. Maastricht, Maastricht Economic Research Institute on Innovation and

Technology. Available at: http://citeseerx.ist.psu.edu/viewdoc/download?doi=10.1.1.195.6931&rep=rep1&type=pdf (archived at https://perma.cc/DKW8-EASN) (Accessed: 10 July 2022)

Stratton, R M (1989) *Disaster relief: The politics of intergovernmental relations*. University Press of America

't Hart, P, Rosenthal, U & Kouzmin, A (1993) Crisis decision: Making the centralization thesis revisited. *Administration & Society*, 25(1), 12–45

Trnka, J & Jenvald, J (2006) Role-playing exercise – a real-time approach to study collaborative command and control. *International Journal of Intelligent Control and Systems*, 11(4), 218–228

Turner, B A (1994) Causes of disaster: sloppy management. *British Journal of Management*, 5(3), 215–219

United States Commission on National Security/21st Century (2001) Road Map for National Security: Imperative for Change: the Phase III Report of the US Commission on National Security/21st Century. The Commission

United States Executive Office of the President, Etats-Unis. Assistant to the President for homeland security, counterterrorism, Superintendent of Documents, President of the United States Staff, United States. Assistant to the President for Homeland Security, ... & Superintendent of Documents Staff (2006) The federal response to Hurricane Katrina: Lessons learned. Government Printing Office

United States General Accounting Office (2003) Major Management Challenges and Program Risks: Department of Homeland Security. Government Printing Office, Washington. Available at http://www.gao.gov/assets/240/236953.pdf (archived at https://perma.cc/58BW-R97Q) (Accessed: 11 June 2022)

Van Wart, M & Kapucu, N (2011) Crisis management competencies: The case of emergency managers in the USA. *Public Management Review*, 13(4), 489–511

Waldenström, C (2008) What is difficult in naval sensemaking. In Proceedings of the 13th International Command and Control Research and Technology Symposium

Waldrop, M M (1993) *Complexity: The emerging science at the edge of order and chaos*. Simon & Schuster

Walker, G H, Stanton, N A, Salmon, P M & Jenkins, D P (2008) A review of sociotechnical systems theory: A classic concept for new command and control paradigms. *Theoretical Issues in Ergonomics Science*, 9(6), 479–499

Walker, G H, Stanton, N A, Salmon, P M, Jenkins, D P, Revell, K & Rafferty, L (2009) Measuring dimensions of command and control using social network analysis: Extending the NATO SAS-050 model. *The International C2 Journal*, 3(2), 1–46

Waugh, D (2000) *Geography: An integrated approach*. Nelson Thornes

Waugh, W L & Streib, G (2006) Collaboration and leadership for effective emergency management. *Public Administration Review*, 66(s1), 131–140

Weick, K E (1993) The collapse of sensemaking in organizations: The Mann Gulch disaster. *Administrative Science Quarterly*, 628–652

Wenger, D, Quarantelli, E L & Dynes, R R (1990) Is the incident command system a plan for all seasons and emergency situations? *Hazard Monthly*, 10(3), 8–12

Wexler, M N (2009) Exploring the moral dimension of wicked problems. *International Journal of Sociology and Social Policy*, 29(9/10), 531–542

Wilkinson, E (2021) BMA urges Health Secretary to address 'micromanagement' of GPs by NHS England. Pulse (21 July). Available at: https://www.pulsetoday.co.uk/news/politics/bma-urges-health-secretary-to-address-micromanagement-of-gps-by-nhs-england/ (archived at https://perma.cc/7Q7M-MCTZ) (Accessed: 22 June 2022)

Wise, C R (2006) Organizing for homeland security after Katrina: Is adaptive management what's missing? *Public Administration Review*, 302–318

6

Leadership

Leadership has been a subject of deep study and analysis almost since the beginning of human history. While there have been notable works on political leadership (Machiavelli is still considered a standard work, even 500 years after it was published in Italy), and more recently a whole section of any bookshop will be devoted to corporate leadership, from a crisis management perspective we still tend to couch the situation in terms of battles and victory, and therefore it is no surprise that the exemplars we look for in terms of offering a template for crisis leadership still come from a military context. Whether it is Moses, King David and King Saul in the Old Testament, Sun Tsu and the *Art of War* from the 5th century BCE in China, Clausewitz's *On War* written from a Prussian perspective in the 19th century but still studied today at every military academy in the world, or the work of General Stanley McChrystal in our own times, leadership has been considered the final intangible that creates the opportunity to plan effective campaigns, to inspire others to follow, to grab victory when the tide of war seems to be against you and on occasion, to create loss and disaster when it seems that victory was inevitable.

While every leader (at least, every honest leader) will tell you that the final outcome was a mixture of unquenchable belief, effective strategies and good fortune, it is the leadership pillar of that triumvirate that seems to attract the most attention.

There is a desire to believe in the leader as heroic symbol. Someone who by the power of their personality alone can take destiny and turn it to their favour. Joan of Arc, Winston Churchill and in more recent times Rudi Giuliani, mayor of New York at the time of the 9/11 attacks in 2001, are examples of the heroic leader. And yet there is much to be said for the leader as an effective administrator, as someone who recognizes skills in others and creates a space for them to add their own contribution to the collective efforts that will lead to the final outcome. It was Napoleon who said, 'An army marches on its stomach,' that is, they must be fed in order to function. It was General Omar Bradley in the Second World War who famously said, 'Amateurs talk strategy. Professionals talk logistics.' In a different context, Jürgen Klinsmann, a member of the 1990s' World Cup-winning German football team and later its manager, responded to a question as to why the German team was so consistent in doing well in international competitions by saying, 'In the first part of the competition, you can get by on passion and energy. But in the later part, you need tactics and discipline.'

In almost every crisis event, the question of effective leadership quickly becomes a significant issue – either as the successful campaign is recognized in the lauding of the leader as a hero or, perhaps more frequently, when the failed leader is held responsible for events over which they often have little if any control.

It is easy when we think of crisis management frameworks to presume that a top-down, command-orientated 'command-and-control' system is the natural form of such programmes. Whether it is the corporate C-Suite crisis management team, a government cabinet office of ministers making decisions and issuing edicts, or an emergency response team dependent on the command chain to let them know what needs to be done, the idea of a centralized command system seems to give order to chaos and a sense of unified purpose at a time of maximum confusion.

The truth, as confirmed both theoretically and empirically, is that the hierarchical command-centred control systems that we can think of as 'natural' are part of a world view that is significantly different from the one that we operate in today. To give two simple examples, the development of communication technology means that it is rare that anyone has 'control' of a situation in the same way that might have been true 20 or 50 years ago. Given the multiplicity of organizations, departments, divisions, agencies, ministries and various groups at every level of an operation, from strategic through tactical and down to operational, as well as the plethora of local agencies and community bodies that would be part of an on-ground engagement of any nature, it has become clear that the role of the 'command' system is not so much 'command and control' but rather 'support and adapt'.

The second point is the speed of events that happen in the present world. Although we can look at events such as Covid-19, which has developed across the world over years, it is still true that many events happen so quickly that there is little if any time to activate the formal crisis management framework and gather information, assess the situation and make a range of decisions that can be shared with participants and stakeholders in a structured manner according to the protocols laid out in the crisis management handbook.

Crisis management: a skill or an art?

As the crisis events that we are facing become ever more challenging, destructive and chaotic, there is a growing awareness that crisis management is no longer confined to merely a bureaucratic role delivering pre-formed emergency response programmes, an act that can be managed from a control room or a command centre using closely defined protocols and frameworks.

It has been widely recognized that both emergency management and crisis management are as much arts as they are technical skills. That is, of course, not to say that technical skills are not important. If you take the classical crisis management situation of a fire service responding to a major fire in a range of contexts (think the Beirut port explosion in 2021 or the Grenfell Tower fire in London in 2017), then it is clear that the technical experience, capabilities, equipment, protocols and leadership are all pre-requisites for any chance of success. But that on its own is no longer enough. If a traditional incident could be considered linear – there is a series of problems or challenges, and when you have dealt with them all you can consider the problem as over and then you can go back to base – modern crises are much more complex and messy and require a different mindset to engage with them, and with the multiple other stakeholders who will be involved in the response and recovery operations.

By taking crisis management away from a technical perspective and placing it firmly in the softer skills of an art, or even a craft, we see that it is not just the skill sets that change but the language used to describe them. Hurricane Katrina was an event that caused many organizations to reassess their skills capabilities and overall approach, not least FEMA. In his 2006 paper published in Public Administration Review in the aftermath of Katrina, Charles Wise asked questions about 'adaptive leadership' and 'managerial craftmanship'.[1]

The protocols and frameworks that were used for the first time in responding to an actual live crisis event in 2005 were the direct outcome of decisions taken across the US emergency management and national security arenas following the 9/11 attacks in 2001. The stated aim of those changes was to create an overarching multi-agency framework that would allow all responding agencies, as well as the peripheral organizations that would be involved at local levels, to be integrated into a unified information-sharing and command-orientated organization.

Although the objective of the programme was to create a shared understanding of response protocols and a shared common operating picture across the multiple agencies, the truth as seen in the test of an actual event was different.[2] In fact, the desire to create protocols that were centralized, hierarchical and command-orientated meant that many of the responding organizations had little if any understanding of the protocols, the communications frameworks or their roles or positions in the wider multi-agency operation.

Most planning programmes are based on a number of basic assumptions that are so fundamental that we are often not even aware of their existence or critical significance. The first is that we are operating in a relatively stable environment. In fact, it can be claimed that one of the overriding objectives of any planning programme is to remove as much as possible any source of randomness or deviance. It is actually the desire to create and then maintain a completely controlled environment that is the critical issue in achieving the aim of technical planning, namely efficiency.

Efficiency can be described as finding the optimal way of doing something with the least effort and the greatest output and then to be able to replicate that in order to achieve scalability. This was true of the first industrial processes in the mid-1700s, with the introduction of factories and production lines. It is what allowed Henry Ford to develop the first mass-produced car, McDonald's to ensure that a hamburger bought anywhere in the world is exactly the same, and Amazon to become the largest company to ever exist based on storing, accessing and then dispatching billions of pieces of goods from warehouses across the world. In their essence, these systems all share the same fundamental approach: the development of a reductionist, mechanistic model based on the centralized control of increasingly small components of activity, where the individual input is de-skilled as much as possible.

The issue, of course, is whether planning principles that are based on the ability to both create and replicate stability are transferable to the highly chaotic and unstable world of crisis management. The language used to describe these working environments gives a strong clue as to how appropriate tightly managed control systems might be or not be in such contexts. The truth is that this is not new to the last 20 years. 'Fuzzy thinking' was considered revolutionary in the 1970s, 'messy problems' were introduced in the 1990s and Patrick Lagadec wrote widely about the challenges of hyper complexity in the 2000s. Each in their own way examined the challenges created by problems that were not only not linear but not even rational.

With the growing acceptance that such challenges required a new approach in terms of management, there was the recognition that management in this sense was not the oversight of a standardized production line (in whatever context that might operate) but qualities that could be considered to demonstrate organizational craftsmanship. This included the ability to respond to the ever-changing demands created by the interaction of social, technological and natural systems,[3] a sense for the similarities and differences from previous experiences, so that innovative solutions can be found to previously unknown situations, and an ability to incorporate fast learning into every aspect of an organization's response framework so that fluidity and adaptability are at the centre of all management protocols.

Under this model of 'management as an art', there is a recognition that responses to complex crisis scenarios are based on emergent *ad hoc* interactions between differentiated groups, each with their own organizational culture, language and wealth of embodied experience. The need is not to command or direct them but rather to create the space which would allow these groups, each with its own highly developed but highly focused expertise, to develop collaborative relationships based on trust, communication and recognition of shared values.

Dealing with crises is a difficult and twisted task, writes Kapucu.[4] The potential domino effect, a high-speed spread of a crisis across geographies or functions, can create a power vacuum that is difficult to manage. Blurred territories, shared power and interactivity between the crisis's drivers leave room for tensions between states, organizations, responders, citizens in all thinkable combinations. Leadership is essential in crisis response and requires imagination and initiative, both before and during a situation: the fundamental nature of complex problems is that no answer exists[5] and although there may be experts who have specialist insight into specific aspects of the crisis, there are no experts who can claim to know how to solve them.

What makes it even more complex is that not everything is complex by default: the leaders' task is to understand which parts of a situation are in order or un-order, embracing that both states interact and intertwine, and probably are difficult to distinguish. Solutions are not so much managed as brought into existence through an iterative decision-making process that is in a constant state of flux. This perspective assumes that solutions to crisis situations must be pragmatic and situationally responsive, rather than being predicated on pre-planned, process-based templates.[6] The people who are interacting with the crisis environment are constantly monitoring and assessing changing situations and then creating new decision paths, which in turn are monitored, assessed and adapted. This process is dependent on the interaction of experienced practitioners who are the repositories of specialized knowledge that is in itself tacit, intangible and context dependent. Such knowledge, by its very nature, resists attempts to codify it into universally applicable 'guides to practice'.

The fact that the external environment is itself unstable and dynamic – and will respond to interventions in ways that cannot be modelled or predicted – changes the whole crisis management process from one of a tightly managed mechanistic procedure which leads to the finished article ('the solution') to one where the project itself is seen as inherently innovative, experimental and ambiguous. Within such a working space, project management strategies are more likely to be focused on a 'probe and learn' methodology, based on 'clumsy solutions', or even 'fuzzy gambling', where the project itself is seen as a learning, reflective process, progressing through a series of failures and improvement, and where managers can only 'grope along' towards organizational goals. This 'science of muddling through' stands in contrast to the classical understanding of strategic decision-making, which is focused on developing a 'deliberate conscious set of guidelines that determines decisions into the future'.

In wicked problems, there is no one correct answer because there is no way of testing the outcomes or consequences of any particular option. The general tone is one of consultancy between peers holding embodied knowledge rather than a predetermined response delivered through a hierarchical command system. In such a situation, the role of the central command team is to coordinate actions and to support them in appropriating resources and resolving conflict, rather than cascading instructions through a hierarchical chain of command. The challenges of responding to either unthinkable (9/11) or highly predicted but nevertheless surprising (Hurricane Katrina) events led to the realization that whatever the formal emergency response plan might have described, the reality on the ground was that in the early, chaotic stages, spontaneous self-organizing teams were created that worked together with other empowered individuals to develop solutions to the most immediate challenges, using resources that were close to hand.[7]

The relevance of this concept of the understanding, modelling and responding to crisis events as an incrementally developing emergent process, in which at all times decisions are made on 'best available evidence' and on a conditional basis, given that those making the decisions can have no way of knowing what the outcomes of those decisions might be, has clear parallels to the challenges facing administrators and decision-makers all over the world in response to the Covid-19 pandemic. Although politicians like to say 'We will follow the science', that was often used as a way to off-load responsibility for hard decision-making to others, who could then be used as a catch-all *get out of jail* card in the (likely) event that situations did not develop as planned.

The truth is that such decisions, whether in a government or a corporate context, are always political. They are decisions based on the judgement associated with multiple competing – and often conflicting – priorities, each of which has its own set of supporters. In such a situation, any decision that is finally made will be open to questioning and attack, and as long as the outcome has not been formally recognized, it is impossible to know what that final outcome might be.

Given the issues and challenges associated with making decisions in situations characterized and defined by uncertainty, a lack of clarity and no obvious solution, it can be legitimately asked on what basis any decision can be made.

One of the critical lessons learned from Hurricane Katrina, and the failure to respond effectively to what had been a long-planned-for event, was the recognition of the value of what came to be called emergent multi-organizational networks. In fact, they came to be seen as a crucial stage in creating effective solutions within the context of high-stress, highly unstable and fast-mutating threat environments.

In such environments, the words associated with sense-making and decision-making are no longer hierarchical, centralized or command and control, but rather discursive, collaborative and emergent. The criticality of such self-forming and often spontaneous EMONs in creating innovative solutions is now widely offered as an alternative theoretical model to tightly controlling centralized management systems, but their fundamental need – and nature – were described more than 50 years ago as follows:

> Organismic systems are adapted to unstable conditions where new and unfamiliar problems and requirements continually arise which cannot be broken down and distributed amongst specialist roles within a hierarchy… Responsibilities and functions and even methods and powers have to be constantly redefined through interactions with others participating in common tasks or in the solutions to common problems.[8]

The organizational frameworks described by Burns, which he considered to be a natural outcome of the nature of the environment they were operating in, are in stark contrast to the hierarchical command system which sees the external environment as something to be controlled, through the imposition of a predetermined and highly structured management system. However, despite the *ad hoc* nature of such non-hierarchical, decentralized, free-forming emergent groupings, they are neither random nor without foundations. Whether they are purely emergent multi-organizational networks, more structured planned multi-organizational networks or mixed multi-organizational networks, the efficiency of both the individual components and the interconnected whole is still dependent on the amount of training and inter-agency practice undertaken by participating agencies, as well as the capabilities and motivation of critical individuals. The question for such unstructured social groupings, as it is for any organization preparing itself with the capabilities that would allow it to respond effectively to a challenging event, is how capabilities can be developed that are both institutionally and organizationally sound, yet flexible enough to adapt to the challenges of chaotic crisis situations.

The often-unspoken issue is that even if the critical nature of such *ad hoc* collaboration is acknowledged, there is little understanding of how the knowledge and insight embodied in experienced practitioners can be encoded and transferred to organizational frameworks and then utilized in a range of contexts. Without such an understanding, and the frameworks and methodologies that can flow from such an understanding, it is no surprise that those who talk of such issues often sound as though they are searching for the correct terminology to convey exactly what is required. In their 2003 study of the role of social interactions in the management of knowledge, Mike Bresnan from the University of Warwick Business School and colleagues identified the problems associated with articulating what are often highly amorphous concepts:

> In case of process innovation... what is learned is often tacit, intangible and context-dependent... Such learning is not only difficult to measure and evaluate, it is also difficult to capture in explicit forms, in ways that can be understood and applied in new contexts... How is the organisation able to capture learning and deploy it over the long term, when it is so embedded in the individual and manifested in their particular expertise and range of contacts... The individual embodiment of engineering knowledge and expertise militated against the transfer of such knowledge.[9]

Although we like to believe that management systems can impose control frameworks that ensure everything gets done in the way that it should be done, when it should be done and by the people who should be doing it, the truth is that within even the most tightly controlled environments, there is the need for an understanding of the system – and even an empathy to its needs – that cannot be captured in standardized guidelines. Even in such a highly controlled environment as a nuclear power station, there was a recognition by system planners that in parallel to the highly striated and delineated management and decision-making structures, there was another network of personal connections that created a 'fuzzy, informal and context-dependent nature of much of organizational knowledge', in which 'what we do around here doesn't always make sense'.

It is clear from the discussion above that we are moving away from a mechanistic understanding of management into one where the questions are as much philosophical as technical, and where the belief that there is a single correct answer, or that there is a single person who has the solution, is in itself a category error that precludes the possibility of developing non-traditional approaches which might be able to balance the needs to engage with complexity and uncertainty with the equally pressing issue of actually being able to get things done. Because the underlying truth behind all of these discussions is the simple fact that the ability or otherwise to engage with these issues in a way that is appropriate and effective – and above all, timely – has consequences. These are not merely philosophical questions to be discussed as theoretical challenges in an academic programme but have real consequences in the real world – and consequences that in an instant can escalate from the challenging to the critical and then to potentially being catastrophic.

The discussion shows that there is an equal need for both management skills and characteristics bound to personality. In answering, or at least engaging with, the seemingly paradoxical question as to how that which cannot be articulated can be shared, and that which cannot be described can be taught, we need to have something which acts as a foundation from which further discussion can evolve. This is even more necessary when we look at the future workforce: every generation has its own strengths, fears, skills and way to understand and look at issues – and each has its own language (verbally and non-verbally), trending apps, technologies: each has its own identity. How do current wicked problems impact the generations of tomorrow – the workforce, the leaders, the consumers, the citizens? And what can a response to such wicked problems look like?

However, just as with any paradox, the answer lies not in confronting mutually self-negating contradictions but in rephrasing the question. The issue is not so much concerned with facilitating the transfer of explicit knowledge from one 'knowledge holder' to another 'knowledge receiver', much less to command and direct, but rather with how we can create a working environment that supports a truly interactive community, one which can collectively develop and explore the innovative solutions that are at the heart of modern crisis response.

Endnotes

1 Wise, C R (2006) Organizing for homeland security after Katrina: Is adaptive management what's missing? *Public Administration Review*, 66(3), 302–318

2 Boin, A (2009) The new world of crises and crisis management: Implications for policymaking and research. *Review of Policy Research*, 26(4), 367–377; Comfort, L K (1999) *Shared risk: Complex systems in seismic response*. New York: Pergamon; Lagadec, E (2007) Unconventional crises, unconventional responses: Reforming leadership in the age of catastrophic crises and hypercomplexity. Center for Transatlantic Relations, Paul H Nitze School of Advanced International Studies, Johns Hopkins University; Lagadec, P (2009) A new cosmology of risks and crises: Time for a radical shift in paradigm and practice. *Review of Policy Research*, 26(4), 473–486; Longstaff, P (2009) Managing surprises in complex systems: Multidisciplinary perspectives on resilience. *Ecology and Society*, 14(1); Rosenthal, U & Kouzmin, A (1997) Crises and crisis management: Toward comprehensive government decision making. *Journal of Public Administration Research and Theory*, 7(2), 277–304; Perrow, C (1984) *Normal accidents: Living with high risk technologies*. New York: Basic Books; Wagner, D & Disparte, D (2016) *Global risk agility and decision making: Organizational resilience in the era of man-made risk*. Palgrave Macmillan

3 van Bueren, E M, Klijn, E H & Koppenjan, J F (2003) Dealing with wicked problems in networks: Analyzing an environmental debate from a network perspective. *Journal of Public Administration Research and Theory*, 13(2), 193–212

4 Kapucu, N (2005) Interorganizational coordination in dynamic context: Networks in emergency response management. *Connections*, 26(2), 33–48

5 Wagner, D & Disparte, D (2016) *Global risk agility and decision making: Organizational resilience in the era of man-made risk*. Palgrave Macmillan

6 Van Bueren, E M, Klijn, E H & Koppenjan, J F (2003) Dealing with wicked problems in networks: Analyzing an environmental debate from a network perspective. *Journal of Public Administration Research and Theory*, 13(2), 193–212

7 Tatham, P & Houghton, L (2011) The wicked problem of humanitarian logistics and disaster relief aid. *Journal of Humanitarian Logistics and Supply Chain Management*, 1(1), 51–31

8 Burns, T & Stalker, G M (1961) Mechanistic and organic systems. *Classics of Organizational Theory*, 209–214

9 Bresnen, M, Edelman, L, Newell, S, Scarbrough, H & Swan, J (2003) Social practices and the management of knowledge in project environments. *International Journal of Project Management*, 21(3), 157–166

Further reading

Boin, A (2009) The new world of crises and crisis management: Implications for policymaking and research. *Review of Policy Research*, 26(4), 367–377

Boin, A & Lagadec, P (2000) Preparing for the future: Critical challenges in crisis management. *Journal of Contingencies and Crisis Management*, 8(4), 185–191

Comfort, L K (1999) *Shared risk: Complex systems in seismic response*. New York: Pergamon

de Sitter, L U, Dankbaar, B & den Hertog, F (1994) *Designing simple organizations and complex jobs*. https://collections.unu.edu/eserv/UNU:994/rm1994-012.pdf (archived at https://perma.cc/ZZ2V-ETRY)

Drabek, T E (1985) Managing the emergency response. *Public Administration Review*, 45, 85–92

Goldin, I & Mariathasan, M (2014) *The butterfly defect. How globalization creates systemic risks, and what to do about it*. Princeton University Press

Kapucu, N (2005) Interorganizational coordination in dynamic context: Networks in emergency response management. *Connections*, 26(2), 33–48

Kapucu, N (2009) Public administrators and cross-sector governance in response to and recovery from disasters. *Administration and Society*, 41(7), 910–914

Kurtz, C F & Snowden, D J (2003) The new dynamics of strategy: Sense-making in a complex and complicated world. *IBM Systems Journal*, 42(3), 462–483

Lagadec, E (2007) Unconventional crises, unconventional responses: Reforming leadership in the age of catastrophic crises and hypercomplexity. Center for Transatlantic Relations, Paul H. Nitze School of Advanced International Studies, Johns Hopkins University

Lagadec, P (1997) Learning processes for crisis management in complex organizations. *Journal of Contingencies and Crisis Management*, 5(1), 24–31

Lagadec, P (2005) Crisis management in the 21st century - 'unthinkable' events in 'inconceivable' contexts. https://hal.archives-ouvertes.fr/file/index/docid/242962/filename/2005-03-14-219.pdf (archived at https://perma.cc/6S98-6ZMM)

Lagadec, P (2009) A new cosmology of risks and crises: Time for a radical shift in paradigm and practice. *Review of Policy Research*, 26(4), 473–486

Longstaff, P (2009) Managing surprises in complex systems: Multidisciplinary perspectives on resilience. *Ecology and Society*, 14(1)

Perrow, C (1984) *Normal accidents: Living with high risk technologies*. New York: Basic Books

Quarantelli, E L (1988) Disaster crisis management: A summary of research findings. *Journal of Management Studies*, 25(4), 373–385

Rosenthal, U & Kouzmin, A (1997) Crises and crisis management: Toward comprehensive government decision making. *Journal of Public Administration Research and Theory*, 7(2), 277–304

Sammut-Bonnici, T (2014) Complexity theory. Available at: https://www.um.edu.mt/library/oar/bitstream/123456789/21687/1/complexity%20theory.pdf (archived at https://perma.cc/G6FT-6DRT) (Accessed: 15 December 2021)

Tatham, P & Houghton, L (2011) The wicked problem of humanitarian logistics and disaster relief aid. *Journal of Humanitarian Logistics and Supply Chain Management*, 1(1), 51–31

't Hart, P, Heyse, L & Boin, A (2001) New trends in crisis management practice and crisis management research: Setting the agenda. *Journal of Contingencies and Crisis Management*, 9(4), 181–188

United States. Congress. House. Select Bipartisan Committee to Investigate the Preparation for, & Response to Hurricane Katrina (2006) A failure of initiative: Final report of the select bipartisan committee to investigate the preparation for and response to Hurricane Katrina, 109(377) US Government Printing Office

Van Bueren, E M, Klijn, E H & Koppenjan, J F (2003) Dealing with wicked problems in networks: Analyzing an environmental debate from a network perspective. *Journal of Public Administration Research and Theory*, 13(2), 193–212

Wagner, D & Disparte, D (2016) *Global risk agility and decision making: Organizational resilience in the era of man-made risk*. Palgrave Macmillan

7

Resilience

Resilience is a word that has come to encapsulate our ideas associated with risk engagement, preparation, response and management. It is something that is all pervasive and seems to have become the default position for anyone trying to describe what our future risk capacities should consist of. But it is also necessary to understand the process of resilience as much as the outcome.

An outstanding (and in many senses frightening) reflection of the lack of understanding as to what resilience actually is comes in the foreword to the 2017 UK National Risk Register, the document in which the threat of emergent infectious diseases was highlighted as having a likelihood of 4/5 of impacting the UK in the next five years.

The foreword was written by Caroline Nokes MP, at the time Minister for Government Resilience and Efficiency. She wrote:

> It is an unfortunate fact of life that emergencies do happen. However, our awareness, preparedness readiness and response to those emergencies are very much in our own hands. I encourage you to consider that as you read this document.
>
> Resilience does not come easily but the UK has a long experience. Call it what you will, but whether through the fabled 'stiff upper lip', 'Blitz spirit' or just stubborn determination, our resilience can be seen at the forefront of our handling of emergencies.'[1]

The fact that this was the document that set out the doctrine by which the UK would develop its resilience capabilities offers a suggestion as to why our resilience capacities have failed so often and in so many ways (though that is not an issue that is limited to the UK, by any means).

Classically, resilience is an engineering term. It is the quality of an organization to absorb stress, to maintaining functionality and then to return to its previous state. In this sense steel is resilient (in that it can absorb heat and maintain its functionality) whereas ice is not (in that it melts if the necessary conditions are not maintained). Within the engineering metaphor, it is often seen in terms of the ability of a structure to withstand those natural forces around it. It is the ability of a bridge to stay standing despite the wind, rain, erosion, tidal movement, sedimentation and all of the other natural processes which seem determined to wear it away. Within that context, a bridge can be considered to be highly resilient, as long as the fundamental assumptions that were made during its construction remain stable. That is, the level of salt in the water doesn't rise, the force of tidal movement doesn't increase, or the material itself maintains its integrity and, for example, the rust-proof paint used to protect it is up to the job and is replaced every 10 years as it was meant to be. If any of those assumptions change then so does the fundamental resilience of that structure. However, even within that, there are often high levels of redundant capability built into structures that allow them to deal with stresses that would have been unknown – and even unthinkable – to their original designers. The Ponte Vecchio bridge in Florence has stood in its present form since 1345, and it has maintained both its structure and function since then through wars, storms, pestilence and floods that have washed away other, more modern bridges.

Although we talk about corporate reliance or societal resilience, and often act as though they are separate branches that need to be approached from different perspectives and with different tools, they are in fact remarkably similar. The factors and qualities that allow a society to be considered resilient in many ways are the very same qualities that would be required for a corporate organization (or any other organization) to be resilient. If we see them in the sense of complex organic organisms, with a high level of interaction, exchange and dependency, then it starts to become clearer as to how that could work.

If, famously, the definition of madness is to do the same thing time after time and expect a different outcome, perhaps the recurring theme of this book is the question as to why, if we think we understand the fundamental principles and methodologies of risk management, we keep getting things wrong, and in such a catastrophic way.

A constant feature of post-event reviews is that the crisis management frameworks tasked with responding to major incidents are simply not robust enough to deal with the chaotic environments they are operating in. Rather than responding to repeated failures by creating more guidelines, regulations and management structures, this chapter suggests that a new approach is needed, based on ecological and organizational resilience. Under this model, it is not so much the technical details of an organization's capabilities that are critical to success but their ability to deliver those services within the reality of a crisis event. The chapter examines the qualities associated with resilience, its relevance to the concept of recovery, and the concept of 'community capital' which includes the social and inter-personal relationships which underpin effective multi-team and multi-agency collaboration. It concludes with an example of the impact of positive social capital in developing resilient response capabilities, which suggests that social capital is the quality that acts as the foundation for all other collaborative action.

Resilience as a metaphor for crisis management

One of the emergent concepts of the last 20 years has been resilience, and the metaphor of resilience has been adapted by many disparate fields of research.[2] Resilience has come to be accepted as a fundamental term within, for example, psychology and psychotherapy, whether in terms of individual survival/recovery from personal trauma (death, assault, emotional abuse) or post-disaster individual and community resilience, as in Hurricane Katrina.[3] Resilient systems are beginning to be studied in a wider range of non-traditional areas, such as business, political science, emergency management, human physiology, human development, engineering,[4] as well as material science, psychology, sociology and economics.[5]

If we are to develop the ability to actually deliver emergency responses in the scenarios where they are most needed, then operational resilience needs to become a core concept in all aspects of the planning, preparation and delivery of those services.[6] That is not to say that resilience is unknown in the world of crisis management.[7] Wildavsky introduced the concept of resilience as a post-event factor, together with pre-event anticipation, as a strategy for reducing risk in uncertain conditions. Comfort, one of the leading authorities on crisis management, has taken resilience as one of her leitmotifs.[8] Resilience as a factor of emergency management saw a surge in interest after both 9/11[9] and Hurricane Katrina.[10] Nevertheless, the repeated failures of crisis management operations for exactly the reasons that are associated with a lack of resilience highlight both the reality of its subsidiary status in crisis planning and the impact that the failure to build in resilience as a central feature of crisis management has on subsequent response operations.

The value of the resilience approach to disaster and crisis management is that it changes the perspective from 'control of an incident' to 'management of multiple consequences'. The movement away from the tightly controlled mechanistic model of crisis management does not deny the responsibility of crisis managers, at every level, to ensure that their systems management processes are in order. The ability to create a level of systems sustainability is dependent on the availability of resources, but also on the ability of that organism/organization to be able to access and utilize those resources. In order for a community or an emergency response operation to be resilient it needs a functioning infrastructural framework, whether it is the heart/lungs/brain/spine if we take the analogy of the human body, or the equivalent in the ecology model or systems framework.

Qualities of resilience

Resilience has many qualities, but the fundamental concept implies some aspect of 'bounceback-ability'.[11] Originally coming from material engineering, resilience denoted the ability of a material to absorb stress, maintain functionality and then return to its original state. In this sense, a rubber ball is resilient, a china plate is not. Typical definitions include:

- the ability of an individual or organization to expeditiously design and implement positive adaptive behaviours matched to the immediate situation, while enduring minimal stress;[12]
- the ability of a community to anticipate, prepare for, respond to and recover quickly from impacts of disasters;[13]
- the capacity of a system to absorb disturbance and reorganize while undergoing change so as to still retain essentially the same function, structure, identity, and feedbacks;[14] and
- a fundamental quality of individuals, groups, organizations and systems as a whole to respond to significant change that disrupts the expected pattern of events without engaging in excessive regressive behaviour.

Kendra et al[15] described resilience as consisting of features such as redundancy, resourcefulness, effective communications and the capacity for self-organizing in the face of extreme demands. Bruneau et al[16] were almost minimalistic as they defined resilience in terms of three simple functions: reduced failure probabilities, reduced consequence from failures and reduced time to recovery. Weick went further and characterized resilience simply as 'coping skills'.[17] Whatever definition of resilience one takes, they all imply a high level of adaptability[18] and often tend to come back to the widely cited qualities as set out by the Multidisciplinary Center for Earthquake Engineering Research (MCEER), which are Robustness, Resourcefulness, Redundancy and Rapidity.[19] Bruneau et al describe these four qualities in terms of processes (resourcefulness and redundancy) and ends (robustness and rapidity).[20]

Robustness describes the ability to deal with a range of sub-optimal operational environments, continuing to maintain service delivery capability despite the challenges that the surrounding environment may cause. Mayunga noted that resilience is a buffer,[21] allowing the system to absorb a high level of disruption without losing its basic functionality. Resilience, under this understanding, is not just a matter of recovery post-event but how it interacts with its environment on an ongoing basis.

Resourcefulness relates to the ability to develop solutions that will allow the maintenance of operational functions despite internal and external disruptions to various aspects of those operations and is associated with learning and coping.

Redundancy is the quality that allows the organization to continue functioning despite the failure of any specific part of the operation. Redundancy, which can be understood as spare capacity, is one of the critical aspects of organizational management, in that if managed correctly it ensures that identified critical failure points have multiple alternative delivery pathways that will allow operational status and service delivery to be maintained. It is a critical vulnerability of many emergency or crisis response plans that they are full of single-path failure points, so that if one aspect of the operation fails, then the operation itself becomes non-viable.

Rapidity is the ability of the organization to adapt to changing circumstances in a speedy manner, developing innovative solutions and integrating them into their wider operating framework so as to minimize any potential disruption.

Crises do not develop smoothly, but much like biological development, they are 'episodic'[22] in that they undergo 'surges' that are of much greater intensity, and have greater evolutionary significance, than the background activity that is the normal state of affairs. It is the ability of the response teams to recognize, understand and then adapt to these rapidly changing events that allows them to maintain an effective presence in the midst of a rapidly evolving crisis that otherwise would either overwhelm them or pass them by. A flood surge in a river, an avalanche or a mud slide, a power-surge that can destroy support systems are all 'crises within crises' that require fast-action responses, often at exactly the time when there is the greatest loss of 'sense-making', situational awareness and organizational capability.

Resilience and recovery

We can see from the above that although resilience is associated with 'robustness, vulnerability and risk',[23] the association of resilience as an antonym for 'vulnerability' is simplistic and misleading. Resilience as a concept should not only allow an organization to recover better after a potentially catastrophic event but should allow it to function more effectively in its environment to minimize the risk of that catastrophic event occurring. As such, resilience should be seen as a fundamental value for any community[24] rather than merely being used as 'a sloppy synonym for flexibility'.[25]

Holling was perhaps the first person to see resilience in terms of complex systems adaptation[26] when he took the term out of its traditional engineering environment and looked at in terms of complex systems interplay in the world of ecology. He identified that all dynamic systems are sustained through the tension between the forces of stability (efficiency, constancy and predictability) and change (persistence, change and unpredictability), pointing out that the characteristics associated with stability are those of the engineer, while those associated with change are those of the biologist. As such, organizational resilience, or the attempt to manage it, runs in a continuum from bureaucratic control (which stifles creativity and punishes attempts to create innovative solutions to crisis events) to chaotic disorganization, in which all organizational capabilities disintegrate in the face of rapidly changing environments, leading to 'avalanches of disorder'.[27]

One of the significant differences between engineering resilience and ecological resilience is in the approach to the concept of 'recovery'.[28] In engineering terms, recovery specifically refers to a return to the pre-event state, so that if a metal is heated, when it cools it should maintain the form, function and qualities it possessed beforehand. In an ecological sense, however, resilience includes three separate qualities – resilience, adaptability and transformability.[29] In this sense, rather than comparing 'what is' to 'what was', ecological resilience allows for an organism or organization to transform itself post-event but maintain functionality, even if in a changed way or at sub-optimum levels.[30] Part of this transformational capability goes so far as to include the ability to 'degrade gracefully when it must'.[31] There is a direct parallel between the abilities of communities to recover post-disaster, the abilities of emergency response teams to overcome problems, and the path of recovery for individuals following traumatic events, namely, functioning despite distress, rapid recovery from distress, removal of distress, and then post-event growth and development.[32]

Developing resilience: community capital

Whether it is within a community context or a crisis emergency response team, the development of resilience is always a multi-faceted portfolio approach as it requires individual components as well as system-wide functions to be fully integrated in order to achieve a desired level of operational effectiveness. This approach extends to the long-term development, as there needs to be a parallel process for creating specific resilience measures as well as creating the underlying infrastructure that allows for a more resilient organization or society in general.[33] However, the development of the inter-agency working relationships that underpin the development of resilient working procedures is not something that can be achieved in the midst of a crisis event but is the result of ongoing relationship developments through high-repetition interactions, whether in training environments or on joint operations.

Mayunga's study of community-based resilience identifies qualities of 'community capital'[34] that could be considered universally applicable within any emergency response environment. These qualities that 'could reduce vulnerability and increase community resilience... include economic resources, assets and skills, information and knowledge, support and supportive networks, access to services and community values'.[35] This understanding of resilience suggests that 'resilience is achieved by preparing, not for any particular event, but rather for the maintenance of a range of capabilities or functions that will be needed after any kind of event'.[36] This conceptual framework of social capital can be easily adapted to the needs of a critical incident management system, or any corporate business continuity/resilience framework,[37] and the ability to understand such issues and introduce them as part of a sustainable development process on a policy level can have significant benefits.[38]

The five factors associated with community capital are social, economic, physical, human and natural. This can be compared with the model proposed by Bruneau et al, in which the four dimensions of community resilience were listed as technical, organizational, social and economic. The concept of community capital suggests that the greater the development of such capital, then almost as a side-effect that community will inherently have greater resilience. In the event that a crisis situation does arise, there is a natural nexus formed by social capital, sustainability and disaster resilience. This is all directly applicable to the ability of post-event multi-agency response teams to maintain the highest level of operational capability in the face of highly unpredictable, challenging and unstable conditions.

Social capital reflects the integration of the community. It is the way that members see themselves as parts of the greater whole, that they are interested in each other's success and are committed to create the greatest good for the greatest number. Breakdowns due to the lack of social capital are usually one of the first issues highlighted in many post-disaster reviews.

Economic capital refers to the financial resources that are used to support the community in general. It is one of the simplest ways of measuring the likely level of resilience of any organization to a sudden, unexpected outside impact. In its bluntest terms, the more resources a community has, the more likely it is to minimize the impact of the original event and to return to a higher level of normal functionality quicker and more effectively. As a basic rule of thumb, 'an unhealthy or declining economy is an indicator of increasing vulnerability',[39] a lesson that is immediately applicable to the maintenance of crisis management capabilities in a time of budgetary and resource cutbacks.

Physical capital consists of the critical infrastructure that supports the other functions of the organization, such as IT, communications and data storage. In terms of managing a post-event scenario, the physical capital becomes a defining issue in determining the ability of the organization to stabilize, take control and then recover from the crisis event. Lack of physical capital and the resources associated with it has a direct negative impact on the ability of an organization to respond to unexpected events.

Human capital is the collective experience, insight, knowledge, skills and wisdom embodied in the personnel associated with the organization. This is usually gained through education, training and experience, though it is also associated with how that resource is recognized and utilized as well as with the mere fact of its existence.

Natural capital consists of those resources that nature provides, such as the landscape, water and the general ecosystem within which the event is taking place. While it is difficult to control natural capital, the ability to understand and work with it in a holistic manner is a significant aspect of community resilience.

A model for success: Fort Worth tornado response (2000)

One of the features of disaster management studies is that they tend to be failure-focused. The Fort Worth tornado response in 2000 is considered one of the few beacons of a successful emergency response operation, as discussed in detail by McEntire.[40]

The tornado that took place on 28 March 2000 could not be described as a major catastrophic event. It was of short duration, had relatively tight geographical and jurisdictional spread and caused relatively little damage (8 buildings destroyed and 52 significantly damaged). The aftermath of the tornado was limited to overturned cars, a city-wide power outage and a 'significant amount of debris in the streets'. However, the event was reported to have caused $450 million worth of damage, enough for one observer to comment that 'it looked like a war zone'. The immediate human cost was 5 deaths and 48 injured. Still, in terms of a community working together both pre-emptively through planning and preparation and during the event itself, the Fort Worth response seems to offer an almost textbook case of what went right.

The first thing that set the foundation for the successful response, according to McEntire,[41] was a general attitude that emergency management was important, that something could be done about it, and that managers in various departments should accept the responsibility for ensuring that they had the networks in place to do what was needed. There was a proactive and supportive stance by city managers that fed down into all subsidiary agencies. Regular preparation and training were an integrated part of the city management calendar. Training was also task specific and realistic, and concentrated on incident command processes that involved information management and multi-agency integration. The training was so well designed that in the post-event review, 'one respondent commented on the value of the experience by noting that the person who had scheduled the training activities must have "foreseen the future"'.[42]

Previous experience, although not on the same scale, included a severe hailstorm and a church shooting. These experiences had been used to learn lessons and to develop a multi-agency framework that was able to adapt to the different challenges of a high-impact storm.[43] The EOC (emergency operations centre) was not only properly equipped with sufficient space for all the relevant teams but was also well managed. The EOC commander would ask for everyone's attention every two hours and each team or agency would update the room on what they were doing and what help they might need. Key leaders would also hold a planned meeting each afternoon (for between 45 minutes and 2 hours) for an update on the bigger picture, identification of potential issues and reassignment of key tasks. This was seen by everyone as being of real value in helping develop a 'big picture' of overall situational awareness beyond their own particular activities.

One paragraph in McEntire's paper encapsulates all that is positive in community-based disaster response and as such merits being framed and put on the wall in every emergency manager's office:

> One respondent stated that he knew the other directors by name and could talk to them about 'fishing, deer hunting and that kind of stuff'. He also added, 'this makes all the difference in the world... When you walk in [to the EOC] and have a pretty good idea of who they are'. Others affirmed that they also interact quite frequently with the different department leaders 'who are wonderful to work with'. Respondents were also well aware of the resources and contribution of each department as 'people assumed their roles and fulfilled them beautifully'. Moreover, it was reported that the various agencies were willing to work together: 'It was so nice to pick up the phone and say 'I need 500 mats' and they say 'when and where do you want them?'. It was also noted that there were 'no egos involved... [to say] it is not my job'.[44]

Resilience is at the heart of strategic risk management

Many crisis management plans seem, in their very nature, to be fragile and brittle, in that once a crisis event has occurred, they lack the ability to adapt to the pressures of the external environment in which they are operating, and the underlying assumptions on which they are built often fail to survive first contact with the reality of the crisis situation. As such, they lack the critical quality of resilience. The underlying metaphor of resilience is that of responding and adapting to the external environment (of which they themselves are a small component), rather than trying to control that environment or impose solutions on it. In that sense, it is a dramatic change from the mechanistic command models that see control as both the means and the ends of any solution.

By putting resilience at the heart of crisis management, it acknowledges the reality of the likelihood of significant (and potentially catastrophic) impacts on its own delivery systems rather than assuming that such delivery capabilities will themselves be unaffected by the external event, and a focus on resilience factors in the assumption that such impacts will occur, and therefore it is the ability to deliver solutions within such challenging circumstances that is the critical issue.

The concept of 'community capital', which is as equally relevant to the response agencies as to the communities that they are attempting to support, creates a framework through which such resilience can be developed and will have multiple other benefits beyond the limited (and hopefully rare) confines of emergency response and crisis management. The characteristic of resilience associated with 'learning organizations' means that an adherence to the values of resilience can create organizations that in their nature are less susceptible to failure and therefore, in a Darwinian sense, have a higher chance of survival than other organizations around them that do not have those qualities.

As was demonstrated in the Fort Worth tornado scenario, the benefits of community capital can be seen in terms of immediate return and significant impact once a disruptive event of any sort has occurred. Given that such capital is developed on the personal and individual basis, there is the opportunity to introduce and normalize such relationships on an ongoing and progressive basis rather than trying to develop them once a crisis event has occurred.

Even after countless red flags, that usually go unnoticed, it sadly takes some communities experiencing a crisis and its aftermath to truly appreciate the importance of a resilient community. The results do not lie. Even if a community and its leadership say they are resilient because it looks good financially and politically, response and recovery ultimately are the deciding factors. When researching their article on failed planning efforts during times of crisis, Boin and McConnell[45] share a colleague's sentiment when he says, 'contingency plans often amount to little more than fancy documents'. Furthermore, those 'fancy documents' usually end up shelved, both physically and virtually, without even so much as a glance until warranted or until questions need to be asked as to why the recovery took so long and how come certain aspects were not followed a certain way. The aforementioned, which is more prevalent in business culture, is still an unnecessary waste of energy to proceed into the crisis aftermath stage. Bruneau et al explain that a truly resilient system, or in this case community, is one that is 'robust, redundant, resourceful, and rapid'.[46]

How does one accomplish this? Make connections, network and liaise with as many leaders involved in the crisis well before it occurs. An example is the public/private collaboration established by the New Jersey Police Department. Standing directly in front of where the World Trade Center towers once stood, city emergency management officials, property/security managers meet quarterly for waterfront security meetings in surrounding corporate buildings to strengthen community engagement with first responders, and to give updates on current area threats and risks and what the response plans will look like. A running theme is communication, allowing groups from different sectors to share real-time best practices and answer questions.

These issues are not unknown. They have been at the centre of every government review ever taken. The US National Infrastructure Advisory Council published a report in 2010 that stated clearly: 'Our nation faces an increasingly complex set of risks that are interwoven into all facets of our businesses, infrastructures, and communities. The threat of hurricanes, financial instability, pandemics, cyber-crime, social unrest, terrorism, and other disruptive events that flow from our participation in a global economy has become a part of our everyday lives. Extreme weather events force many utilities to reassess their emergency practices, business continuity plans, and system design. Now, a new set of risks such as targeted physical and cyber-attacks, geomagnetic disturbances, and pandemics is emerging. Many of these risks are beyond the purview of a single company or even the entire industry and will require collaborative foresight.'[47]

Resilience is quite rightly a word that has been at the centre of the strategic risk management discourse for the last decade – but that in itself is not going to make our infrastructures, networks or communities any stronger. Rhetoric is not enough. There needs to be an understanding of what exactly is required to create the frameworks that will have the strength, durability and overall robustness to stand up to the challenges that they – we – will be facing in the coming years.

Endnotes

1 Cabinet Office (2017) National risk register of civil emergencies, 2017 edition. Available at: https://assets.publishing.service.gov.uk/government/uploads/system/uploads/attachment_data/file/644968/UK_National_Risk_Register_2017.pdf (archived at https://perma.cc/Y5Z7-3SQ9)

2 Norris, F H, Stevens, S P, Pfefferbaum, B, Wyche, K F & Pfefferbaum, R L (2008) Community resilience as a metaphor, theory, set of capacities, and strategy for disaster readiness. *American Journal of Community Psychology*, 41, 127–150

3 Dohrenwend, B S (1978) Social stress and community psychology. *American Journal of Community Psychology*, 6(1), 1

4 Longstaff, P H (2009) Managing surprises in complex systems: Multidisciplinary perspectives on resilience. *Ecology and Society*, 14(1), 49

5 Bruneau, M, Chang, S E, Eguchi, R T, Lee, G C, O'Rourke, T D, Reinhorn, A M, Shinozuka, M, Tierney, K, Wallace, W A & von Winterfeldt, D (2003) A framework to quantitatively assess and enhance the seismic resilience of communities. *Earthquake Spectra*, 19(4), 733–752

6 Godschalk, D R (2003) Urban hazard mitigation: Creating resilient cities. *Natural Hazards Review*, 4(3), 136–143; Weick, K E (1993) The collapse of sensemaking in organizations: The Mann Gulch disaster. *Administrative Science Quarterly*, 628–652

7 Wildavsky, A B (1988) *Searching for safety, 10.* Transaction Publishers

8 Comfort, L K (1994) Self-organization in complex systems. *Journal of Public Administration Research and Theory*, 393–410; Comfort, L K, Sungu, Y, Johnson, D & Dunn, M (2001) Complex systems in crisis: Anticipation and resilience in dynamic environments. *Journal of Contingencies and Crisis Management*, 9(3), 144–158; Comfort, L K, Oh, N & Ertan, G (2009) The dynamics of disaster recovery: Resilience and entropy in hurricane response systems 2005–2008. *Public Organization Review*, 9(4), 309–323; Comfort, L K, Boin, A & Demchak, C C (eds.) (2010). *Designing resilience: Preparing for extreme events*. University of Pittsburgh Press

9 Burke, R J (2005) Effects of 9/11 on individuals and organizations: Down but not out! *Disaster Prevention and Management: An International Journal*; Tierney, K J (2003) Conceptualizing and measuring organizational and community resilience: Lessons from the emergency response following the September 11, 2001 attack on the World Trade Center

10 Boin, A & McConnell, A (2007) Preparing for critical infrastructure breakdowns: The limits of crisis management and the need for resilience. *Journal of Contingencies and Crisis Management*, 15(1), 50–59; Norris, F H, Stevens, S P, Pfefferbaum, B, Wyche, K F & Pfefferbaum, R L (2008) Community resilience as a metaphor, theory, set of capacities, and strategy for disaster readiness. *American Journal of Community Psychology*, 41, 127–150

11 Longstaff, P H & Yang, S U (2008) Communication management and trust: Their role in building resilience to 'surprises' such as natural disasters, pandemic flu, and terrorism. *Ecology and Society*, 13(1)

12 Mallak, L A (1998) Measuring resilience in health care provider organizations. *Health Manpower Management*, 24(4), 148–152

13 Mayunga, J S (2007) Understanding and applying the concept of community disaster resilience: A capital-based approach. Summer Academy for Social Vulnerability and Resilience Building, 1–16

14 Walker, B, Holling, C S, Carpenter, S R & Kinzig, A (2004) Resilience, adaptability and transformability in social–ecological systems. *Ecology and Society*, 9(2)

15 Kendra, J M & Wachtendorf, T (2003) Elements of resilience after the World Trade Center disaster: Reconstituting New York City's emergency operations centre. *Disasters*, 27(1), 37–53

16 Bruneau, M, Chang, S E, Eguchi, R T, Lee, G C, O'Rourke, T D, Reinhorn, A M, Shinozuka, M, Tierney, K, Wallace, W A & von Winterfeldt, D (2003) A framework to quantitatively assess and enhance the seismic resilience of communities. *Earthquake Spectra*, 19(4), 733–752

17 Weick, K E (1993) The collapse of sensemaking in organizations: The Mann Gulch disaster. *Administrative Science Quarterly*, 628–652

18 Norris, F H, Stevens, S P, Pfefferbaum, B, Wyche, K F & Pfefferbaum, R L (2008) Community resilience as a metaphor, theory, set of capacities, and strategy for disaster readiness. *American Journal of Community Psychology*, 41, 127–150

19 Kapucu, N (2005) Interorganizational coordination in dynamic context: Networks in emergency response management. *Connections*, 26(2), 33–48; Kendra, J M & Wachtendorf, T (2003) Elements of resilience after the World Trade Center disaster: Reconstituting New York City's emergency operations centre. *Disasters*, 27(1), 37–53; MCEER (2006) Multidisciplinary Center for Earthquake Engineering Research. MCEER Resilience Framework.

20 Bruneau, M, Chang, S E, Eguchi, R T, Lee, G C, O'Rourke, T D, Reinhorn, A M, Shinozuka, M, Tierney, K, Wallace, W A & von Winterfeldt, D (2003) A framework to quantitatively assess and enhance the seismic resilience of communities. *Earthquake Spectra*, 19(4), 733–752

21 Mayunga, J S (2007) Understanding and applying the concept of community disaster resilience: A capital-based approach. Summer Academy for Social Vulnerability and Resilience Building, 1–16

22 Hollings, R L (1996) *Reinventing government: An analysis and annotated bibliography*. Nova Science Pub Incorporated; Weick, K E (1993) The collapse of sensemaking in organizations: The Mann Gulch disaster. *Administrative Science Quarterly*, 628–652

23 Walker, B, Holling, C S, Carpenter, S R & Kinzig, A (2004) Resilience, adaptability and transformability in social–ecological systems. *Ecology and Society*, 9(2)

24 Paton, D & Johnston, D (2001) Disasters and communities: Vulnerability, resilience and preparedness. *Disaster Prevention and Management: An International Journal*, 10(4), 270–277

25 Boin, A, Hart, P T, McConnell, A & Preston, T (2010) Leadership style, crisis response and blame management: The case of Hurricane Katrina. *Public Administration*, 88(3), 706–723

26 Holling, C S (1973) Resilience and stability of ecological systems. *Annual Review of Ecology and Systematics*, 1–23

27 Comfort, L K (1994) Self-organization in complex systems. *Journal of Public Administration Research and Theory*, 393–410

28 Holling, C S (1973) Resilience and stability of ecological systems. *Annual Review of Ecology and Systematics*, 1–23

29 Walker, B, Holling, C S, Carpenter, S R & Kinzig, A (2004) Resilience, adaptability and transformability in social – ecological systems. *Ecology and Society*, 9(2)

30 Bonanno, G A (2004) Loss, trauma, and human resilience: Have we underestimated the human capacity to thrive after extremely aversive events? *American Psychologist*, 59(1), 20

31 Allenby, B & Fink, J (2005) Toward inherently secure and resilient societies. *Science*, 309(5737), 1034–1036

32 Bonanno, G A (2005) Resilience in the face of potential trauma. *Current Directions in Psychological Science*, 14(3), 135–138; Norris, F H & Alegria, M (2005) Mental health care for ethnic minority individuals and communities in the aftermath of disasters and mass violence. *CNS Spectrums*, 10(2), 132–140

33 Schafer, W A, Carroll, J M, Haynes, S R & Abrams, S (2008) Emergency management planning as collaborative community work. *Journal of Homeland Security and Emergency Management*, 5(1)

34 Mayunga, J S (2007) Understanding and applying the concept of community disaster resilience: a capital-based approach. Summer Academy for Social Vulnerability and Resilience Building, 1–16

35 Mayunga, J S (2007) Understanding and applying the concept of community disaster resilience: a capital-based approach. Summer Academy for Social Vulnerability and Resilience Building, 1–16

36 Kendra, J M & Wachtendorf, T (2003) Elements of resilience after the World Trade Center disaster: Reconstituting New York City's emergency operations centre. *Disasters*, 27(1), 37–53

37 Kapucu, N (2005) Interorganizational coordination in dynamic context: Networks in emergency response management. *Connections*, 26(2), 33–48

38 Waugh, W L & Streib, G (2005) Collaboration and leadership for effective emergency management. *Public Administration Review*, 66(s1), 131–140

39 Buckle, P, Marsh, G & Smale, S (2001) *Assessing resilience and vulnerability: Principles, strategies and actions*. Victorian Government Publishing Services

40 McEntire, D A (2002) Coordinating multi-organisational responses to disaster: Lessons from the March 28, 2000, Fort Worth tornado. *Disaster Prevention and Management: An International Journal*, 11(5), 369–379

41 McEntire, D A (2002) Coordinating multi-organisational responses to disaster: Lessons from the March 28, 2000, Fort Worth tornado. *Disaster Prevention and Management*, 11(5), 369–379

42 McEntire, D A (2002) Coordinating multi-organisational responses to disaster: Lessons from the March 28, 2000, Fort Worth tornado. *Disaster Prevention and Management*, 11(5), 369–379

43 Chua, A Y, Kaynak, S & Foo, S S (2007) An analysis of the delayed response to Hurricane Katrina through the lens of knowledge management. *Journal of the American Society for Information Science and Technology*, 58(3), 391–403

44 McEntire, D A (2002) Coordinating multi-organisational responses to disaster: Lessons from the March 28, 2000, Fort Worth tornado. *Disaster Prevention and Management*, 11(5), 369–379

45 Boin, A & McConnell, A (2007) Preparing for critical infrastructure breakdowns: the limits of crisis management and the need for resilience. *Journal of Contingencies and Crisis Management*, 15(1), 50–59

46 Bruneau, M, Chang, S E, Eguchi, R T, Lee, G C, O'Rourke, T D, Reinhorn, A M, Shinozuka, M, Tierney, K, Wallace, W A & von Winterfeldt, D (2003) A framework to quantitatively assess and enhance the seismic resilience of communities. *Earthquake Spectra*, 19(4), 733–752

47 National Infrastructure Advisory Council (2010) A framework for establishing critical infrastructure resilience goals. Final report and recommendations by the Council. Available at: https://www.dhs.gov/xlibrary/assets/niac/niac-a-framework-for-establishing-critical-infrastructure-resilience-goals-2010-10-19.pdf (archived at https://perma.cc/WH2N-HZ4E)

Further reading

Allenby, B & Fink, J (2005) Toward inherently secure and resilient societies. *Science*, 309(5737), 1034–1036

Boin, A, Hart, P T, McConnell, A & Preston, T (2010) Leadership style, crisis response and blame management: The case of Hurricane Katrina. *Public Administration*, 88(3), 706–723

Boin, A & McConnell, A (2007) Preparing for critical infrastructure breakdowns: The limits of crisis management and the need for resilience. *Journal of Contingencies and Crisis Management*, 15(1), 50–59

Bonanno, G A (2004) Loss, trauma, and human resilience: Have we underestimated the human capacity to thrive after extremely aversive events? *American Psychologist*, 59(1), 20

Bonanno, G A (2005) Resilience in the face of potential trauma. *Current Directions in Psychological Science*, 14(3), 135–138

Bruneau, M, Chang, S E, Eguchi, R T, Lee, G C, O'Rourke, T D, Reinhorn, A M, Shinozuka, M, Tierney, K, Wallace, W A & von Winterfeldt, D (2003) A framework to quantitatively assess and enhance the seismic resilience of communities. *Earthquake Spectra*, 19(4), 733–752

Buckle, P, Marsh, G & Smale, S (2001) *Assessing resilience and vulnerability: Principles, strategies and actions*. Victorian Government Publishing Services

Burke, R J (2005) Effects of 9/11 on individuals and organizations: down but not out! *Disaster Prevention and Management*, 14(5)

Chua, A Y, Kaynak, S & Foo, S S (2007) An analysis of the delayed response to Hurricane Katrina through the lens of knowledge management. *Journal of the American Society for Information Science and Technology*, 58(3), 391–403

Comfort, L K (1994) Self-organization in complex systems. *Journal of Public Administration Research and Theory*, 393–410

Comfort, L K, Boin, A & Demchak, C C (eds.) (2010) *Designing resilience: Preparing for extreme events*. University of Pittsburgh Press

Comfort, L K, Oh, N & Ertan, G (2009) The dynamics of disaster recovery: Resilience and entropy in hurricane response systems 2005–2008. *Public Organization Review*, 9(4), 309–323

Comfort, L K, Sungu, Y, Johnson, D & Dunn, M (2001) Complex systems in crisis: Anticipation and resilience in dynamic environments. *Journal of Contingencies and Crisis Management*, 9(3), 144–158

Dohrenwend, B S (1978) Social stress and community psychology. *American Journal of Community Psychology*, 6(1), 1

Godschalk, D R (2003) Urban hazard mitigation: Creating resilient cities. *Natural Hazards Review*, 4(3), 136–143

Holling, C S (1973) Resilience and stability of ecological systems. *Annual Review of Ecology and Systematics*, 1–23

Hollings, R L (1996) *Reinventing government: An analysis and annotated bibliography*. Nova Science Pub Incorporated

Home, J F & Orr, J E (1997) Assessing behaviors that create resilient organizations. *Employment Relations Today*, 24(4), 29–39

Kapucu, N (2005) Interorganizational coordination in dynamic context: Networks in emergency response management. *Connections*, 26(2), 33–48

Kendra, J M & Wachtendorf, T (2003) Elements of resilience after the World Trade Center disaster: Reconstituting New York City's emergency operations centre. *Disasters*, 27(1), 37–53

Longstaff, P H (2009) Managing surprises in complex systems: Multidisciplinary perspectives on resilience. *Ecology and Society*, 14(1), 49

Longstaff, P H & Yang, S U (2008) Communication management and trust: Their role in building resilience to 'surprises' such as natural disasters, pandemic flu, and terrorism. *Ecology and Society*, 13(1)

Mallak, L A (1998) Measuring resilience in health care provider organizations. *Health Manpower Management*, 24(4), 148–152

Mayunga, J S (2007) Understanding and applying the concept of community disaster resilience: a capital-based approach. Summer Academy for Social Vulnerability and Resilience Building, 1–16

MCEER (2006) Multi-Discipline Centre for Earthquake Engineering Research. MCEER Resilience Framework. Available at http://mceer.buffalo.edu/research/resilience/resilience_10-24-06.pdf (Accessed: 14 June 2015)

McEntire, D A (2002) Coordinating multi-organisational responses to disaster: Lessons from the March 28, 2000, Fort Worth tornado. *Disaster Prevention and Management*, 11(5), 369–379

Norris, F H & Alegria, M (2005) Mental health care for ethnic minority individuals and communities in the aftermath of disasters and mass violence. *CNS Spectrums*, 10(2), 132–140

Norris, F H, Stevens, S P, Pfefferbaum, B, Wyche, K F & Pfefferbaum, R L (2008) Community resilience as a metaphor, theory, set of capacities, and strategy for disaster readiness. *American Journal of Community Psychology*, 41, 127–150

Paton, D & Johnston, D (2001) Disasters and communities: vulnerability, resilience and preparedness. *Disaster Prevention and Management*, 10(4), 270–277

Schafer, W A, Carroll, J M, Haynes, S R & Abrams, S (2008) Emergency management planning as collaborative community work. *Journal of Homeland Security and Emergency Management*, *5*(1)

Tierney, K J (2003) Conceptualizing and measuring organizational and community resilience: Lessons from the emergency response following the September 11, 2001 attack on the World Trade Center

Walker, B, Holling, C S, Carpenter, S R & Kinzig, A (2004) Resilience, adaptability and transformability in social–ecological systems. *Ecology and Society*, 9(2)

Waugh, W L & Streib, G (2005) Collaboration and leadership for effective emergency management. *Public Administration Review*, 66(s1), 131–140

Weick, K E (1993) The collapse of sensemaking in organizations: The Mann Gulch disaster. *Administrative Science Quarterly*, 628–652

Weick, K E & Roberts, K H (1993) Collective mind in organizations: Heedful interrelating on flight decks. *Administrative Science Quarterly*, 357–381

Wildavsky, A B (1988) *Searching for safety*, *10*. Transaction Publishers

8

The regulatory system – a failing safety net

If the proverbial Martian was to land on Planet Earth today, as part of their gap year 'Interplanetary cultural studies' programme, the report that they would send back at the end of their stay would undoubtedly comment on that fact that, at least to an educated observer, it seems that the world is ruled on the basis of two principles. The first is *The Golden Rule*, namely, whoever has the gold makes the rules. The second is that in every area of public activity that has major impact on the lives of the vast numbers of citizens, whether it is global financial matters, domestic banking, political management, public safety management, critical national infrastructures or pandemic management, despite the fact that all of these actors are supposedly working within tightly legislated and managed regulatory frameworks, they are in fact working to the *Law of the Jungle*, where those that are supposed to be governed by the rules are seemingly free to make up new rules if they don't like the present ones and to ignore even those if they decide that it is in their interest to do so.

The golden rule

It is probably one of the most outstanding facts about many of the major headline stories of strategic risk and crisis management – the Columbia and Challenger space shuttle disasters, Three Mile Island and Fukushima meltdowns, Boeing 737-Max and Volkswagen emission scandals, multiple transgressions by major banking and financial institutions, the Grenfell Tower disaster and multiple other examples – that all of these operations were taking in place in regulated environments that should have had alarm bells ringing in every regulatory office in the land. Yet these situations were not only left to carry on their ultimately destructive – and self-destructive – activities. Even worse, it subsequently became clear that it was done with a high level of collusion, if not outright manipulation, between the regulators themselves and those they were tasked with overseeing.

It has become common practice to state that we are living in what has increasingly become a 'Regulatory State', with every aspect of our lives now governed by rules and regulations. Often, they are backed up with the threat of punitive action, whether it is failing to leave the household rubbish in the correct bag or in the correct position on the pavement, the need for tens of thousands of community-based volunteers to go through criminal record checks, or the ability of increasing numbers of otherwise unauthorized people to claim access to both our private data and, in many cases, our homes and property. And yet when the self-interested and clearly irresponsible, if not actually illegal, actions of high-powered individuals lead to a meltdown in the institutions that underpin every aspect of our social fabric and daily life, it seems that they can merely walk away – often with multi-million-pound pay-offs – and there is nothing that anyone can do to even question them about their activities, never mind punish them for their transgressions.

We have become used to the sight of senior politicians, who are ultimately responsible for creating the regulatory frameworks that are supposedly responsible for preventing these failures, standing up in Parliament or at public enquiries to decry the clearly irresponsible behaviour that has led to the problems, to promise an enquiry as to how it happened, and to introduce new regulations and frameworks that will prevent any such occurrence happening in the future. And yet, if regulation is failing, then merely putting up more regulation is not likely to be the solution. In many cases, the activities that have led to the need for the enquiry are manifestly undesirable, almost certainly unethical, and quite often actually illegal. The question is not what more needs to be done to increase regulation, but why the systems that are already in place, and which have often been through multiple rounds of review and improvement, are clearly not fulfilling the single function for which they were developed, namely the protection of the public and wider society from the self-interested actions of those that put their own benefit ahead of the need to observe the rules and regulations within which they are supposed to be operating.

The law of the jungle

For our visiting Martian, there would be one other factor that would undoubtedly be highlighted in their report, with a brief, and probably perplexed, background essay on the strange habits of alien cultures. And that is, that in the midst of global pandemics, nuclear disasters, financial meltdowns and growing social disruption, with the complexity of global institutions reaching such a level of inter-dependence that it is literally impossible to calculate the impact and implications of any one specific failure of the wider local, national and global network, both the sector leaders and the political leadership in general are calling not for greater and more closely managed oversight but for actual deregulation,[1] claiming that the need to adhere to instructionist government diktats is the one thing that is preventing the growth and prosperity that would be of general benefit to us all.

The complexity of the interdependent systems can be seen in the fact that:

- a tsunami in Japan can trigger a breakdown in global supply-chain management of car manufacturing components, leading to the closures of factories across north-east England; or
- a single navigation error of a super-tanker in the Suez Canal can disrupt a third of global commerce; or
- an undersea volcanic eruption near Tonga can create a tidal wave that causes an oil tanker to spill its cargo on the coast of Peru, over 10,000 kilometres away, creating an immediate environmental crisis that impacts the livelihoods of entire fishing communities.

In this highly unstable global environment, where the risks of disaster are ever present and the impact of systems failures is both catastrophic and irreversible, the fact that our global and local systems are themselves being undermined for the benefit of a few corporations is both unbelievable and indefensible.

Another notable aspect of the government response to recent issues is the realization that in many cases the behaviour that seems to us both demonstrably wrong and morally abhorrent is actually separate from any punitive framework that would allow those in power to bring the perpetrators to a court of law, charge and then prosecute them as they would any other person who acted against the laws of the country. In fact, when it comes to the ordinary citizen, the range of activities that have been criminalized is increasing on a daily basis, and the technical ability to have increased surveillance of all of our activities is likely to cause that tendency to grow. However, when it comes to bankers fixing international inter-banking rates for their own advantage (as happened in the Libor scandal, dismantled in 2012, where the rates had been manipulated at least since 1991), or global corporations asset striping critical national infrastructures and leaving the shells of those organizations to manage – and mismanage – those infrastructures in ways that threaten the fabric of the society within which those organizations are operating, it seems that the authorities are left impotent. It appears to be impossible to do anything more than plaintively claim that it is the duty of the corporate shareholders to oversee the actions of their executives, and it seems like the shame of doing nothing would be enough to persuade global institutions to take the necessary steps to prevent these situations happening in the future.

About interests and profit

It is perhaps not surprising that those organizations that are subject to regulatory oversight are exactly the same ones that claim that such restrictions on their abilities to act in their self-interest are in fact damaging to the wider society. The response of major banks to Covid-19 was to claim that in the face of such unprecedented pressures, it was the government and regulatory oversight restrictions that were limiting their abilities to respond appropriately to the challenges that situation was creating, and to act in ways that could support faltering economies. However, if we go on past history (or even current activities), it becomes clear that the idea that banks should be considered responsible enough to manage their known adherence to the rules becomes almost laughable.

A simple review of the list of the fines meted out to banks in 2020 alone[2] gives an indication of the level to which malfeasance is inbuilt into the fundamental operating systems of such institutions. It is part of their operating system that they maximize their own benefit over any other consideration, including global financial stability, international terrorism, human trafficking and child sexual exploitation:

- Goldman Sachs (fined $5.4 billion): The bank had actively supported the 1MDB scandal in Indonesia that saw multi-million-dollar scams being used to loot the state investment fund by corrupt officials and their accomplices.
- Wells Fargo (fined $3 billion): Wells Fargo employees had set up a string of fake accounts that would allow them to meet their own internal sales targets.
- JPMorgan (fined $920 million): JPMorgan agreed to pay $920 million and admit misconduct tied to manipulation of precious metals.
- Westpac (fined $920 million): The bank agreed to pay the largest fine in Australian corporate history to settle a lawsuit that revealed more than 23 million breaches of the country's terrorism financing and money laundering rules as well as a failure to spot transfers that may have been connected to child exploitation in Asia.
- Bank Hapoalim (fined $874 million): Israel's largest bank agreed an $874 million penalty with US authorities as part of an agreement to settle a probe into its facilitation of US tax evasion, admitting that Hapoalim and its Swiss subsidiary conspired with US citizens and others to hide more than $7.6 billion in secret Swiss and Israeli bank accounts.
- Citigroup (fined $400 million): Citigroup was fined $400 million by US regulators and ordered to fix its risk management systems in the light of 'significant ongoing deficiencies'.
- Swedbank (fined $397 million): Swedish regulators hit Swedbank with a 4 billion Swedish krona fine in March after it concluded the bank's Baltic operation had serious deficiencies in its anti-money laundering measures, involving its operations in Sweden, Estonia, Latvia and Lithuania.
- JPMorgan (fined $250 million): JPMorgan was fined $250 million by US regulators over deficiencies in internal controls and internal audit practices that had continued over a period of years.

- Scotiabank (fined $127 million): The Canadian bank paid the fine to settle civil and criminal allegations in connection with its role in what authorities called a massive price-manipulation scheme stemming from thousands of manipulative orders for precious metals futures contracts placed on US exchanges. This included claims that Scotiabank made false statements and incomplete disclosures about alleged price manipulation by its traders in connection with a previous investigation by the regulator.

There are a number of things that become clear when this list is examined not on a case-by-case basis but as something that is seemingly endemic to the global banking sector. The first is that it is remarkably easy to be numbed by the scale of such large figures. After they are repeated enough times, it seems that £500 million fines seems a reasonable number, until you start asking, 'What is the business model that can accept repeated fines in their hundred millions and even billions – and continue to see that as merely a cost of doing business that can be written off against bottom-line profits?'

These are not one-off events, or mistakes, or errors, or oversights. They are in-built into the fabric[3] of the way that these institutions do business – and it is in fact questionable whether their business model would be sustainable if these highly profitable (and completely illegal) activities were not carried out. Reports in 2020 that $2,000 billion worth of illicit funds were moved and laundered through the US financial system over two decades give a feel for the level of activity and profitability of these actions. That included $514 billion at JPMorgan[4] and $1.3 trillion at Deutsche Bank. The fact that they are so critical to the banks' operating model, and that fines and other sanctions aren't effective, can be seen by the fact that they carry on with those activities even when they have been caught, fined and sanctioned for exactly the same activities previously. These are not meaningless transactions but the basis on which international criminals, terrorists and oligarchs move their money around.[5]

It is not just in the banking industry that we see such activities. It is the mix of the illegal, collusion between all parties, including the regulators, and an inbuilt culture over decades that allows such activities to become normalized and then to be an embedded part of the operating model. In fact, across multiple sectors, it is the collusion with the regulators that allows that system to be maintained – given that it is the role of the regulators to identify and prevent such behaviour.

The Boeing 737-MAX disaster was a classic example of where behaviours that are known to be dangerous are accepted as part of a normal operating procedure. It was only the collusion between senior executives across the organization, and the turning of a blind eye by regulators on numerous occasions and as part of the sector-accepted practices, even after it was clear that such illegal activity was taking place, that allowed it to continue.

There was a perfect storm of deficiencies. It was the fact that the regulators allowed Boeing to self-certify[6] as to the safety of its airplanes, even when new technology was introduced that was known to be faulty, that allowed such activity to take place. Additionally, it was within the confines and culture of a technology company that can be considered to be at the forefront of some of the most advanced and complex technical systems in the world, and that had built a reputation over more than 100 years of being world-leading in all aspects of excellence in design, innovation and delivery.

The complexity of the systems themselves meant that there were only very few people who understood them with enough insight to be aware of the possibility of things going wrong.[7] In that sense, they were dependent on the people who really knew the systems – that is, the engineers who designed and built them – to keep them up to date with the developments in the delivery process. This is a pattern that is repeated in all high-end technology systems, whether it is nuclear power stations in Japan (TEPCO and Fukushima), car manufacturing plants in Germany (Volkswagen), or space-shuttle development in America (NASA and space shuttles Columbia and Challenger).

The algorithmic systems that underpin the high-frequency trading platforms which make up a significant part of global finance are an example of systems that are so hyper-complex that no one has a true understanding of them, and certainly no one has control. Given the impacts of the 2008 financial crash, in what seems from today's perspective to be a simpler and certainly slower world, the impacts of a systems crash under present trading conditions are almost literally incalculable. On one side, those tasked with overseeing the management of these systems, and at the same time ensuring that the outcomes of any failures do not impact catastrophically on the rest of the world, would tell us that there are control mechanisms in place to ensure that the systems are used for the purposes and in the ways for which they were designed. On the other side, history and experience would tell us that in fact there is a high level of malfeasance, incompetence and collusion at every level of the system – and that there are known inbuilt vulnerabilities that at some stage will result in a systems-wide crash.

Accidents waiting to happen

The reports for the failures of these organizations, and the culture of deception and collusion that allowed them to happen, are so common as to allow them to be seen as a single undifferentiated phenomenon.

The US Congressional Committee Report[8] on the Boeing 737-MAX disaster clearly stated that the Federal Aviation Authority's delegation of certification function to Boeing's own personnel impacted effectiveness and public safety. Boeing failed to report critical issues to the FAA, and in some cases actively ignored directives from the FAA in order to maintain its business interests.

The Aviation Safety organization (AVS) within the FAA heard a report that 'AVS senior leadership's response to and management of industry pressure is at the heart of the organization's core safety culture challenges: lack of trust, inconsistent accountability, FAA role confusion, and the perception that AVS is moving further away from its safety mission'.

The final point in the section summary on 'FAA Oversight and Delegation of Authority' was that 'the Committee's investigation had identified sweeping and systemic problems revolving around the ability of the FAA to effectively engage in regulatory activity and robust oversight of Boeing to ensure the safety of the flying public and the aviation community'.[9]

As is so often the case, in retrospect it is clear that the Boeing 737-MAX was an accident that was waiting to happen. A report of the US Office of Inspector General for the Department of Transportation[10] found that the FAA oversight system was itself not fit for purpose:

- The organization was over-tasked and under-resourced.
- There was a lack of clarity as to what its primary role was (certification or oversight – they are often in conflict).
- There was a capability gap, meaning that FAA inspectors did not have the level of technical expertise to be able to make considered judgements as to either the efficacy of the systems or the veracity of the information that they were receiving.
- There were the activities of Boeing management teams who failed to share information that was significant and potentially critical, meaning that there was a fog of ignorance over the whole operation.

Both the report into the Boeing 737-MAX and the culture across the organization that allowed those issues to be embedded into every aspect of their operational activities are replicated across multiple similar events. Much as with a trick picture where a forest hides a herd of hidden zebras, and then once your eye clicks into that you start seeing zebras everywhere, once you understand what the language of cultural denial and cover-up feels like, you can see it almost everywhere you look.

The Volkswagen emissions scandals followed the pattern almost to the letter. Again, we are looking at a major global company, one that is both world-leading in its innovation and process management and implicitly trusted to deliver cars that are safe and roadworthy, acting in such a way that calls into question every aspect of its management culture, social responsibility and, at a fundamental level, basic humanity.

The simple facts are that Volkswagen devised a 'cheat system' that would allow the levels of emissions created during testing processes to be substantively lower than what would be seen in actual road-driving conditions. This technology was deployed in roughly 11 million cars in models from 2009 to 2015. Despite the fact that a car manufacturing process is one of the most highly controlled environments in the world, and that any slightest amendment to any part of the system needs multiple reviews, authorizations, tests and approvals across multiple sections of the organization and at every level in the process management hierarchy, VW claimed that the emissions-cheating technology was the result of a handful of rogue engineers who had acted without either consultation or authorization, and that they had managed to keep it secret from its inception in 2005 until US inspectors questioned it in 2015.[11]

It hardly inspires confidence that such events could not be repeated: even when it is acknowledged that Volkswagen engaged in a massive fraud[12] with dire consequences for the company and its stakeholders alike, and its corporate culture facilitated both the conception and perpetuation of the charade, it nevertheless remains an open question as to whether Volkswagen's auditors and lawyers might have missed opportunities to prevent the scandal.

The pattern that characterized the culture of failure during the various phases of the conspiracy, collusion and cover-up that continued into the post-discovery period, when the organization was held up to public shaming and then tried to regain its position of trust, can be seen step by step in both the Boeing and Volkswagen responses. Volkswagen chairman Hans Dieter Pötsch[13] finally admitted that the emissions scandal was the result of corporate failures rather than a few rogue engineers, though he made it clear that he felt that the existence of the cheat technology had not been known at the higher levels of the organizations, stating, 'We are relentlessly searching for those responsible for what happened and you may rest assured we will bring these persons to account.'

Volkswagen chief executive Matthias Müller apologized for cheating diesel car emissions tests. 'We know that we have let down customers, authorities, regulators and the general public here in America. We are – I am – truly sorry for that and I would like to apologize once again for what went wrong at Volkswagen.'[14] He added that 'our most important task in 2016 is to win back trust. It's not only our cars we have to fix. We have to repair our credibility, too'. Müller then went on to state, 'We are not a criminal brand or group', claiming that Volkswagen had made huge technical mistakes but had no intention of deceiving the US public or regulators. Given that that was the specific objective of the technology, it is hard to understand what exactly this statement means.

In a similar vein, Kevin McAllister, president and CEO of Boeing's commercial aircraft division, also apologized for the 'accidents'. 'It is a pivotal moment for all of us. It's a time for us to make sure that accidents like this never happen again. These accidents have only intensified our efforts to ensure the highest level of safety and quality in everything that we do. Safety's a shared priority amongst government regulators, suppliers, manufacturers, and operators, and we are dedicated to working in the broad industry to make aviation even safer.'[15]

Following the $3 billion fine imposed because of systematic mis-selling and the development of fake accounts, Wells Fargo's CEO Charles Scharf stated that 'the conduct at the core of today's settlements — and the past culture that gave rise to it — are reprehensible and wholly inconsistent with the values on which Wells Fargo was built'.[16]

Given the similarities that are evidenced in these examples from three of the most highly regulated spaces in the global economy – banking, automobile production and aviation – it seems reasonable to presume that these are attributes of a class of actions that have common themes, rather than one-off and isolated incidents that should be seen as anomalies and not indicative of a fundamental underlying weakness. In fact, we see a culture that creates a space where such actions can take place[17] – or more accurately, where such actions are not only encouraged to take place but are expected to take place – in a way that maximizes the benefit to the organization at the cost of the wider community. The situation in which individual bonuses are directly related to the ability to bypass regulations that would have limited profitability or to create solutions that will maximize profitability is not something that is extraneous to these issues. It is in fact deeply embedded in the organizational culture and management models that create such results not as unintended consequences but as the desired outcomes from highly incentivized reward systems.

As a final example of the egregiousness of such actions were the issues identified in the official report into the failures associated with the TEPCO nuclear reactor meltdown immediately following the tsunami that hit north-east Japan in March 2012. The instinctive response to deny, deflect and deceive[18] was evidenced in the TEPCO response to both the original reactor meltdown, following an undersea earthquake followed by a catastrophic tsunami that overwhelmed the flood defence systems of the wider community and of the nuclear reactor itself, and the subsequent government enquiry.

It might be considered that an undersea earthquake caused by shifting tectonic plates, a subsequent tsunami that reached heights of 11 metres, and the impact that had in the TEPCO Number 1 nuclear reactor, were genuinely beyond the abilities of planners and managers to prepare for or defend against. However, the Japanese government's Kurokawa Report[19] into the events makes it clear from the outset that it was not the case.

It is worth reading the chairman's foreword to the report as it seems to encapsulate everything that is of significance for every other event that we have discussed. The truth is that besides the specific details concerning the TEPCO nuclear meltdown, and the failure of the relevant authorities to either prepare for and mitigate such events or to develop response capabilities that could be deployed in the event that they were to happen, it is the cultural acceptances that are the underlying issues. As has been identified repeatedly in multiple post-crisis reports, from multiple sectors and contexts, these cultural failures are so common that they can be considered as almost offering a universal template for organizational failure:

> The earthquake and tsunami of March 11, 2011 were natural disasters of a magnitude that shocked the entire world. Although triggered by these cataclysmic events, the subsequent accident at the Fukushima Daiichi Nuclear Power Plant cannot be regarded as a natural disaster. It was a profoundly manmade disaster – that could and should have been foreseen and prevented. And its effects could have been mitigated by a more effective human response. How could such an accident occur in Japan, a nation that takes such great pride in its global reputation for excellence in engineering and technology? This Commission believes the Japanese people – and the global community – deserve a full, honest and transparent answer to this question. Our report catalogues a multitude of errors and willful negligence that left the Fukushima plant unprepared for the events of March 11. And it examines serious deficiencies in the response to the accident by TEPCO, regulators and the government. For all the extensive detail it provides, what this report cannot fully convey – especially to a global audience – is the mindset that supported the negligence behind this disaster. What must be admitted – very painfully – is that this was a disaster 'Made in Japan'. Its fundamental causes are to be found in the ingrained conventions of Japanese culture: our reflexive obedience; our reluctance to question authority; our devotion to 'sticking with the program'; our groupism; and our insularity. Had other Japanese been in the shoes of those who bear responsibility for this accident, the result may well have been the same. Following the 1970s' 'oil shocks', Japan accelerated the development of nuclear power in an effort to achieve national energy security. As such, it was embraced as a policy goal by government and business alike, and pursued with the same single-minded determination that drove Japan's postwar economic miracle. With such a powerful mandate, nuclear power became an unstoppable force, immune to scrutiny by civil society. Its regulation was entrusted to the same government bureaucracy responsible for its promotion. At a time when Japan's self-confidence was soaring, a tightly knit elite with enormous financial resources had diminishing regard for anything 'not invented here'. This conceit was reinforced by the collective mindset of Japanese bureaucracy, by which the first duty of any individual bureaucrat is to defend the interests of his organization. Carried to an extreme, this led bureaucrats to put organizational interests ahead of their paramount duty to protect public safety. Only by grasping this mindset can one understand how Japan's nuclear industry managed to avoid absorbing the critical lessons learned from Three Mile Island and Chernobyl; and how it became accepted practice to resist regulatory pressure and cover up small-scale accidents. It was this mindset that led to the disaster at the Fukushima Daiichi Nuclear Plant. This report singles out numerous individuals and organizations for harsh criticism, but the goal is not – and should not be – to lay blame. The goal must be to learn from this disaster, and reflect deeply on its fundamental causes, in order to ensure that it is never repeated. Many of the lessons relate to policies and procedures, but the

> most important is one upon which each and every Japanese citizen should reflect very deeply. The consequences of negligence at Fukushima stand out as catastrophic, but the mindset that supported it can be found across Japan. In recognizing that fact, each of us should reflect on our responsibility as individuals in a democratic society. As the first investigative commission to be empowered by the legislature and independent of the bureaucracy, we hope this initiative can contribute to the development of Japan's civil society. Above all, we have endeavored to produce a report that meets the highest standard of transparency. The people of Fukushima, the people of Japan and the global community deserve nothing less.

The issues highlighted in the Kurokawa report, and the manifestations that we see across multiple sectors in multiple contexts, are not merely individual acts that are taken by the leaders of individual enterprises. Rather, they can be seen as nothing else but the reflection of a deeply held belief that their only responsibility is to maximize their own reward. It might have been easier to say that they are acting in this way in order to create benefit for their organizations, but in the longer term it is possible to see that in fact these actions have significant, and potentially catastrophic, impacts on their organizations as well.

Profit over responsibility

The belief that their responsibility goes no further than maximizing profits, and therefore share value, can be traced back to one of the most influential economists of the 20th century, Milton Friedman, who won the Nobel Prize for Economics in 1976. His view on the idea that businessmen have a wider social responsibility may sound dated in its language, but the concepts are nevertheless at the heart of what we still perceive of as market capitalism:

> Businessmen believe that they are defending free enterprise when they declaim that business is not concerned 'merely' with profit but also with promoting desirable 'social' ends; that business has a 'social conscience' and takes seriously its responsibilities for providing employment, eliminating discrimination, avoiding pollution and whatever else may be the catchwords of the contemporary crop of reformers. In fact they are – or would be if they or anyone else took them seriously – preaching pure and unadulterated socialism. Businessmen who talk this way are unwitting puppets of the intellectual forces that have been undermining the basis of a free society these past decades.[20]

Even within the context of the pressures that have been created by the Covid-19 pandemic, global warming and other high-impact events, and (perhaps) the realization that these are potentially existential issues that requires a 'whole of humanity' response, one doesn't have far to look to see major corporations prioritizing their profits over what may be considered as wider social benefits – or even their own legal responsibilities. The Covid-19 pandemic has been perhaps the first truly global threat within our living memory. It undoubtedly created challenges that could not be confined to individual communities, countries or regions, or that could be engaged with or managed on a 'case-by-case' basis limited by national borders. And yet that is exactly the approach that has been taken across the world and over the course of two years of multiple stages of the pandemic. It became clear from the start that this was something that affected the global community, and one of the phrases that became associated with the responses to the pandemic was 'No one is safe until everyone is safe'.[21] And yet when we look at the actions of the organizations that had the capabilities to develop vaccines, for many of them their overarching objective was to use that opportunity to maximize their profits.

Although the manufacturers claimed that they would ensure their vaccines would be made equally available to poor countries as well as rich, a year after the start of the pandemic (when, as an example, the vaccine was responsible for Pfizer making a $900 million profit on $3.5 billion revenue in the first quarter of 2021), 87 per cent of the 700 million doses distributed worldwide[22] had gone to rich countries and 0.2 per cent to poor ones. This was despite the fact that the underlying research that supported the development of the vaccines was government funded[23] and that Pfizer, along with all other vaccine producers, directly benefited from that support. The claims that Pfizer was working for the public good was called out as 'one of the great public relations triumphs of recent corporate history'.[24]

Although there are clearly other issues at play in what is undoubtedly one of the most complex global operations ever undertaken, high prices were identified as one of the main factors[25] behind the widening vaccine inequality a year into the world's biggest inoculation campaign. The thought that global conglomerates would collaborate to defeat a common enemy, one that threatened mankind as a whole, was perhaps idealistic. As a World Trade Organization counsellor said, 'It could just be an incentive for companies to come forward and collaborate. But if left to the choice of companies, usually companies will refuse to collaborate and share what knowledge they have.'[26]

One does not have to look to the global stage to see such actions being repeated, in ways that have immediate and damaging effects on communities, and yet are not considered from anything but a profit-driven perspective.

The water sector in the UK is a privatized sector that has allowed multinational infrastructure management and investment companies to take over ownership of large parts of the UK's national infrastructure and to see that as a way of maximizing profit-taking while minimizing either active investment or social responsibility. One of the stated aims of the privatization, 30 years ago, was to allow for higher levels of investment in the upgrade of infrastructure and management technology. However, by late 2021 the ability of UK water companies to manage their finances, never mind investing in infrastructure upgrades, was under severe threat. This was regardless of the fact that from the 1990s until today, capital expenditure by the 10 biggest water and sewage monopolies had declined by 15 per cent from £5.7 billion to £4.8 billion a year,[27] a period during which those same companies had borrowed £53 billion, with £72 billion being paid out in dividends to shareholders. As a local speaker said in front of Westminster Council in London in 2021 after yet another rainstorm had created another high-impact flood (together with untreated sewage, dead rats, and other detritus from an overwhelmed system): 'This is the richest borough, in one of the world's wealthiest countries, and yet it lacks a functioning sewage system.'[28]

If we are to create a system that allows the global infrastructures we all are dependent on to operate in a safe, reliable and sustainable manner, we must accept the fact that these examples are not isolated incidents of misjudgement, fallibility or even occasional malfeasance. They are in fact so deeply embedded into the culture of these organizations that they can be considered to be present in their very DNA. It is their sheer size and complexity that allow them not only to create a culture of deceit that is the enabling agency that allows these events to happen, and to be maintained over time, often decades, but the fact that there is no form of oversight or responsibility that holds individuals to account. Until this is changed, the underlying culture that supports those actions will also not change.

The challenges that we are facing as we move into the third decade of the 21st century are of a scale, scope and impact that are substantively different from anything we have faced until now. The world itself is fragile, as are all of the fundamental infrastructures on which we are all so dependent. The belief that a few people can use the system for their own benefit, at the cost to everyone else on the planet, is one that is simply unsustainable. It may be that we do not do anything to manage those issues, but if we don't, that will have consequences that will be at least as catastrophic as the triggering events that might cause the collapse of the house of cards that those systems have been built on.

Endnotes

1 Dabo, M (2020) US banks call for deregulation to combat coronavirus. *Retail Banker International* (24 March). Available at: https://www.retailbankerinternational.com/news/us-banks-call-for-deregulation-to-combat-coronavirus/ (archived at https://perma.cc/A9PB-ETW9) (Accessed: 22 June 2022)

2 Booth, J (2020) From tax evasion to terrorism: These are the 10 biggest bank fines of 2020. *Financial News* (30 December). Available at: https://www.fnlondon.com/articles/from-tax-evasion-to-terrorism-these-are-the-10-biggest-bank-fines-of-2020-20201230 (archived at https://perma.cc/7HE2-RCJT) (Accessed: 22 June 2022)

3 Briançon, P (2020) Opinion: Global banks hit by new corruption allegations. Why authorities are unlikely to act this time. MarketWatch (22 September). Available at: https://www.marketwatch.com/story/global-banks-hit-by-new-corruption-allegations-why-authorities-are-unlikely-to-act-this-time-2020-09-21 (archived at https://perma.cc/BHK6-6QNE) (Accessed: 22 June 2022)
4 ICIJ, International Consortium of Investigative Journalists (2020) Global banks defy U.S. crackdowns by serving oligarchs, criminals and terrorists. Available at: https://www.icij.org/investigations/fincen-files/global-banks-defy-u-s-crackdowns-by-serving-oligarchs-criminals-and-terrorists/ (archived at https://perma.cc/LF96-RVGY) (Accessed: 22 June 2022)
5 ICIJ, International Consortium of Investigative Journalists (2020). Global banks defy U.S. crackdowns by serving oligarchs, criminals and terrorists. Available at: https://www.icij.org/investigations/fincen-files/global-banks-defy-u-s-crackdowns-by-serving-oligarchs-criminals-and-terrorists/ (archived at https://perma.cc/LF96-RVGY) (Accessed: 22 June 2022)
6 US Department of Transportation, Office of Inspector General (2021) Weaknesses in FAA's certification and delegation processes hindered its oversight of the 737 MAX 8. Available at: https://www.oig.dot.gov/sites/default/files/FAA%20Certification%20of%20737%20MAX%20Boeing%20II%20Final%20Report%5E2-23-2021.pdf (archived at https://perma.cc/HXG2-N4SV) (Accessed: 22 June 2022)
7 Willis, P (2020) What broke the 737 Max? Aerospace Testing International (27 August). Available at: https://www.aerospacetestinginternational.com/features/what-broke-the-737-max.html (archived at https://perma.cc/GH2Y-2QY9) (Accessed: 22 June 2022)
8 House Committee on Transportation and Infrastructure (2020) Final committee report: The design development & certification of the Boeing 737 MAX. Available at: https://transportation.house.gov/imo/media/doc/2020.09.15%20FINAL%20737%20MAX%20Report%20for%20Public%20Release.pdf (archived at https://perma.cc/VDK9-KYTQ) (Accessed: 22 June 2022)
9 House Committee on Transportation and Infrastructure (2020) Final committee report: The design development & certification of the Boeing 737 MAX. Available at: https://transportation.house.gov/imo/media/doc/2020.09.15%20FINAL%20737%20MAX%20Report%20for%20Public%20Release.pdf (archived at https://perma.cc/VDK9-KYTQ), page 64
10 US Department of Transportation, Office of Inspector General (2021) Weaknesses in FAA's certification and delegation processes hindered its oversight of the 737 MAX 8. Available at: https://www.oig.dot.gov/sites/default/files/FAA%20Certification%20of%20737%20MAX%20Boeing%20II%20Final%20Report%5E2-23-2021.pdf (archived at https://perma.cc/HXG2-N4SV) (Accessed: 22 June 2022)
11 EPA, United States Environmental Protection Agency (2021) Learn about Volkswagen violations. Available at: https://www.epa.gov/vw/learn-about-volkswagen-violations (archived at https://perma.cc/LH83-6QCP) (Accessed: 22 June 2022)
12 Jacobs, D & Kalbers, L P (2019) The Volkswagen diesel emissions scandal and accountability. Where were the auditors and attorneys during the sustainability charade? *The CPA Journal* (22 July). Available at: https://www.cpajournal.com/2019/07/22/9187/ (archived at https://perma.cc/C2RX-D85Q) (Accessed: 22 June 2022)

13 Ruddick, G (2015) VW admits emissions scandal was caused by 'whole chain' of failures. *The Guardian* (10 December). Available at: https://www.theguardian.com/business/2015/dec/10/volkswagen-emissions-scandal-systematic-failures-hans-dieter-potsch (archived at https://perma.cc/V8VA-2R3K) (Accessed: 22 June 2022)

14 The Guardian (2016) Volkswagen boss apologises to America for cheating diesel emissions tests (11 January). Available at: https://www.theguardian.com/business/2016/jan/11/volkswagen-boss-apologises-to-america-for-cheating-diesel-emissions-tests (archived at https://perma.cc/X78D-DGS8) (Accessed: 22 June 2022)

15 Winsor, M (2019) Boeing executives apologize for 737 Max crashes 17th June, 2019. ABC News (17 June). Available at: https://abcnews.go.com/International/boeing-apology/story?id=63756662 (archived at https://perma.cc/MY72-ZGS3) (Accessed: 22 June 2022)

16 Reisinger, S (2020) Wells Fargo Agrees to $3B Penalty to Resolve Fake Bank Account Scandal (22 February). Available at: https://www.treasuryandrisk.com/2020/02/22/wells-fargo-agrees-to-3b-penalty-to-resolve-fake-bank-account-scandal-411-21948/ (archived at https://perma.cc/5D3M-YJU8)

17 Waldersee, V (2021) VW culture to blame for silence over emissions scandal, ex-manager says in trial. Reuters (23 September). Available at: https://www.reuters.com/business/autos-transportation/vw-culture-blame-silence-over-emissions-scandal-ex-manager-says-trial-2021-09-23/ (archived at https://perma.cc/2PWP-QHSW) (Accessed: 22 June 2022)

18 CBS News (2016) Fukushima meltdown apology: 'It was a cover-up.'. CBS News (21 June). Available at: https://www.cbsnews.com/news/fukushima-tepco-power-japan-nuclear-meltdown-apologizes-cover-up/ (archived at https://perma.cc/GA4A-C4W9) (Accessed: 22 June 2022)

19 National Diet of Japan (2012) The official report of the Fukushima nuclear accident independent investigation commission. Available at: https://www.nirs.org/wp-content/uploads/fukushima/naiic_report.pdf (archived at https://perma.cc/97TZ-ZZQ5) (Accessed: 22 June 2022)

20 Friedman, M (1970) A Friedman doctrine – the social responsibility of business is to increase its profits. *The New York Times* (13 September). Available at: https://www.nytimes.com/1970/09/13/archives/a-friedman-doctrine-the-social-responsibility-of-business-is-to.html (archived at https://perma.cc/5ZAW-FQGW) (Accessed: 22 June 2022)

21 USGLC, US Global Leadership Coalition (2020) Fact sheet: No one is safe until everyone is safe. Available at: https://www.usglc.org/blog/fact-sheet-no-one-is-safe-until-everyone-is-safe/ (archived at https://perma.cc/U3PT-W5DE) (Accessed: 22 June 2022); Berkley, S (2021) No one is safe until everyone is safe. VaccinesWork (29 October). Available at: https://www.gavi.org/vaccineswork/no-one-safe-until-everyone-safe (archived at https://perma.cc/LFW6-CBQW) (Accessed: 22 June 2022); United Nations, Department of Economic and Social Affairs (2020) 'No one is safe, until everyone is.' Available at: https://www.un.org/en/desa/%E2%80%9Cno-one-safe-until-everyone-%E2%80%9D (archived at https://perma.cc/58W7-UJMT) (Accessed: 22 June 2022)

22 United Nations, UN News (2021) Low-income countries have received just 0.2 per cent of all Covid-19 shots given. Available at: https://news.un.org/en/story/2021/04/1089392 (archived at https://perma.cc/JY7K-D53K) (Accessed: 22 June 2022)

23 Goodman, P S & Robbins, R (2021) Pfizer reaps hundreds of millions in profits from Covid vaccine. *The New York Times* (4 May). Available at: https://www.nytimes.com/2021/05/04/business/pfizer-covid-vaccine-profits.html (archived at https://perma.cc/6EVS-DY6P) (Accessed: 22 June 2022)

24 Goodman, P S & Robbins, R (2021) Pfizer reaps hundreds of millions in profits from Covid vaccine. *The New York Times* (4 May). Available at: https://www.nytimes.com/2021/05/04/business/pfizer-covid-vaccine-profits.html (archived at https://perma.cc/6EVS-DY6P) (Accessed: 22 June 2022)

25 Mancini, D & Stabe, M (2021) Covid boosters in rich countries outnumber all jabs among poor nations. *Financial Times* (19 December). Available at: https://www.ft.com/content/5144cd19-2c67-46d0-a37d-a869006bfbdb (archived at https://perma.cc/KQX3-4UGF) (Accessed: 22 June 2022)

26 Goodman, P S & Robbins, R (2021) Pfizer reaps hundreds of millions in profits from Covid vaccine. *The New York Times* (4 May). Available at: https://www.nytimes.com/2021/05/04/business/pfizer-covid-vaccine-profits.html (archived at https://perma.cc/6EVS-DY6P) (Accessed: 22 June 2022)

27 Hollowood, E & Plimmer, G (2021) Sewage spills highlight decades of under-investment at England's water companies. *Financial Times* (28 December). Available at: https://www.ft.com/content/b2314ae0-9e17-425d-8e3f-066270388331 (archived at https://perma.cc/6RLM-F6V9) (Accessed: 22 June 2022)

28 Hollowood, E & Plimmer, G (2021) Sewage spills highlight decades of under-investment at England's water companies. *Financial Times* (28 December). Available at: https://www.ft.com/content/b2314ae0-9e17-425d-8e3f-066270388331 (archived at https://perma.cc/6RLM-F6V9)

Further reading

Berkley, S (2021) No one is safe until everyone is safe. VaccinesWork (29 October). Available at: https://www.gavi.org/vaccineswork/no-one-safe-until-everyone-safe (archived at https://perma.cc/LFW6-CBQW) (Accessed: 22 June 2022)

Booth, J (2020) From tax evasion to terrorism: These are the 10 biggest bank fines of 2020. *Financial News* (30 December). Available at: https://www.fnlondon.com/articles/from-tax-evasion-to-terrorism-these-are-the-10-biggest-bank-fines-of-2020-20201230 (archived at https://perma.cc/7HE2-RCJT) (Accessed: 22 June 2022)

Briançon, P (2020) Opinion: Global banks hit by new corruption allegations. Why authorities are unlikely to act this time. MarketWatch (22 September). Available at: https://www.marketwatch.com/story/global-banks-hit-by-new-corruption-allegations-why-authorities-are-unlikely-to-act-this-time-2020-09-21 (archived at https://perma.cc/BHK6-6QNE) (Accessed: 22 June 2022)

CBS News (2016) Fukushima meltdown apology: 'It was a cover-up.' CBS News (21 June). Available at: https://www.cbsnews.com/news/fukushima-tepco-power-japan-nuclear-meltdown-apologizes-cover-up/ (archived at https://perma.cc/GA4A-C4W9) (Accessed: 22 June 2022)

Dabo, M (2020) US banks call for deregulation to combat coronavirus. *Retail Banker International* (24 March). Available at: https://www.retailbankerinternational.com/news/us-banks-call-for-deregulation-to-combat-coronavirus/ (archived at https://perma.cc/A9PB-ETW9) (Accessed: 22 June 2022)

EPA, United States Environmental Protection Agency (2021) Learn about Volkswagen violations. Available at: https://www.epa.gov/vw/learn-about-volkswagen-violations (archived at https://perma.cc/LH83-6QCP) (Accessed: 22 June 2022)

Friedman, M (1970) A Friedman doctrine – the social responsibility of business is to increase its profits. *The New York Times* (13 September). Available at: https://www.nytimes.com/1970/09/13/archives/a-friedman-doctrine-the-social-responsibility-of-business-is-to.html (archived at https://perma.cc/5ZAW-FQGW) (Accessed: 22 June 2022)

Goodman, P S & Robbins, R (2021) Pfizer reaps hundreds of millions in profits from Covid vaccine. *The New York Times* (4 May). Available at: https://www.nytimes.com/2021/05/04/business/pfizer-covid-vaccine-profits.html (archived at https://perma.cc/6EVS-DY6P) (Accessed: 22 June 2022)

The Guardian (2016) Volkswagen boss apologises to America for cheating diesel emissions tests (11 January). Available at: https://www.theguardian.com/business/2016/jan/11/volkswagen-boss-apologises-to-america-for-cheating-diesel-emissions-tests (archived at https://perma.cc/X78D-DGS8) (Accessed: 22 June 2022)

Hollowood, E & Plimmer, G (2021) Sewage spills highlight decades of under-investment at England's water companies. *Financial Times* (28 December). Available at: https://www.ft.com/content/b2314ae0-9e17-425d-8e3f-066270388331 (archived at https://perma.cc/6RLM-F6V9) [(Accessed: 22 June 2022)

House Committee on Transportation and Infrastructure (2020) Final committee report: The design development & certification of the Boeing 737 MAX. Available at: https://transportation.house.gov/imo/media/doc/2020.09.15%20FINAL%20737%20MAX%20Report%20for%20Public%20Release.pdf (archived at https://perma.cc/VDK9-KYTQ) (Accessed: 22 June 2022)

ICIJ, International Consortium of Investigative Journalists (2020) Global banks defy U.S. crackdowns by serving oligarchs, criminals and terrorists. Available at: https://www.icij.org/investigations/fincen-files/global-banks-defy-u-s-crackdowns-by-serving-oligarchs-criminals-and-terrorists/ (archived at https://perma.cc/LF96-RVGY) (Accessed: 22 June 2022)

Jacobs, D & Kalbers, L P (2019) The Volkswagen diesel emissions scandal and accountability. Where were the auditors and attorneys during the sustainability charade? *The CPA Journal* (22 July). Available at: https://www.cpajournal.com/2019/07/22/9187/ (archived at https://perma.cc/C2RX-D85Q) (Accessed: 22 June 2022)

Mancini, D & Stabe, M (2021) Covid boosters in rich countries outnumber all jabs among poor nations. *Financial Times* (19 December). Available at: https://www.ft.com/content/5144cd19-2c67-46d0-a37d-a869006bfbdb (archived at https://perma.cc/KQX3-4UGF) (Accessed: 22 June 2022)

National Diet of Japan (2012) The official report of the Fukushima nuclear accident independent investigation commission. Available at: https://www.nirs.org/wp-content/uploads/fukushima/naiic_report.pdf (archived at https://perma.cc/97TZ-ZZQ5) (Accessed: 22 June 2022)

Ruddick, G (2015) VW admits emissions scandal was caused by 'whole chain' of failures. *The Guardian* (10 December). Available at: https://www.theguardian.com/business/2015/dec/10/volkswagen-emissions-scandal-systematic-failures-hans-dieter-potsch (archived at https://perma.cc/V8VA-2R3K) (Accessed: 22 June 2022)

United Nations, Department of Economic and Social Affairs (2020) 'No one is safe, until everyone is.' Available at: https://www.un.org/en/desa/%E2%80%9Cno-one-safe-until-everyone-%E2%80%9D (archived at https://perma.cc/58W7-UJMT) (Accessed: 22 June 2022)

United Nations, UN News (2021) Low-income countries have received just 0.2 per cent of all Covid-19 shots given. Available at: https://news.un.org/en/story/2021/04/1089392 (archived at https://perma.cc/JY7K-D53K) (Accessed: 22 June 2022)

US Department of Transportation, Office of Inspector General (2021) Weaknesses in FAA's certification and delegation processes hindered its oversight of the 737 MAX 8. Available at: https://www.oig.dot.gov/sites/default/files/FAA%20Certification%20of%20737%20MAX%20Boeing%20II%20Final%20Report%5E2-23-2021.pdf (archived at https://perma.cc/HXG2-N4SV) (Accessed: 22 June 2022)

USGLC, US Global Leadership Coalition (2020) Fact sheet: No one is safe until everyone is safe. Available at: https://www.usglc.org/blog/fact-sheet-no-one-is-safe-until-everyone-is-safe/ (archived at https://perma.cc/U3PT-W5DE) (Accessed: 22 June 2022)

Waldersee, V (2021) VW culture to blame for silence over emissions scandal, ex-manager says in trial. Reuters (23 September). Available at: https://www.reuters.com/business/autos-transportation/vw-culture-blame-silence-over-emissions-scandal-ex-manager-says-trial-2021-09-23/ (archived at https://perma.cc/2PWP-QHSW) (Accessed: 22 June 2022)

Willis, P (2020) What broke the 737 Max? Aerospace Testing International (27 August). Available at: https://www.aerospacetestinginternational.com/features/what-broke-the-737-max.html (archived at https://perma.cc/GH2Y-2QY9) (Accessed: 22 June 2022)

Winsor, M (2019) Boeing executives apologize for 737 Max crashes 17th June, 2019. ABC News (17 June). Available at: https://abcnews.go.com/International/boeing-apology/story?id=63756662 (archived at https://perma.cc/MY72-ZGS3) (Accessed: 22 June 2022)

9

Global urban resilience in the 2020s

Setting the scene

Even before the onset of Covid-19 at the start of 2020, and the impact that the subsequent global shutdown had on urban centres across the world, it was becoming clear that our models of cities as the centre of human activity and development were being challenged on multiple levels. Hyper-pollution, traffic management, infrastructure failures, increased polarization between extreme wealth and extreme poverty and the fact that the vast majority of global cities are located on the coast, which means that they are particularly sensitive and vulnerable to climate change and rising sea levels, all combined to create the impression that they were collapsing under the weight of their own success.

The status of the city as the highest form of human social organization has been an idea and ideal that has maintained pre-eminence since at least the time of the Greeks. Cities are not only drivers of economic growth and development, they create a framework that drives progress in all aspects of cultural, intellectual and social activity.

It is perhaps both a symptom and a cause of a modern global malaise that not only are the role and function of cities being questioned but also the viability of their very continued existence. Like anything in nature that aspires to be gargantuan, cities have moved beyond the bounds whereby the structures and frameworks that first allowed them to prosper and thrive can continue to support the monsters that they have become. With the rate of growth predicted to rise on Malthusian scales (the global urban population is estimated to grow by 70 million people a year[1]), the ability of city managers to continue to supply basic life-management structures is going to be increasingly challenged beyond breaking point.

Cities are not only beginning to fail in their fundamental purposes – as anyone will know who has sat in a traffic jam on a road system designed for a slower and simpler age – they are actually killing the people who live there,[2] whether it is from pollution or the ever-present stress of overcrowded urban life. The question now is how the next stage of city development will play out.

Cities and the Malthusian challenge

The city has always been the scene of worries about over-populations and the impacts of a growth rate out of control. The Malthusian concept, that resources grow linearly while population grows exponentially, has been a constant background fear.

The world of urban deprivation described by Charles Dickens in the 1860s would not be far removed from the description on the opening page of *The Population Bomb*, the book published in 1968 that first laid out the impact of poverty, over-breeding and slums. 'One stinking hot night in Delhi, we entered a crowded slum area. The streets seemed alive with people. People eating, people washing, people sleeping. People visiting, arguing and screaming. People thrusting their hands through the taxi window begging. People defecating and urinating ... Since that night I've known the feel of overpopulation.'[3]

40 years later, the author of that book revisited the issue of population explosion (by which time the Earth's population had doubled to 7 billion) and doubled down, stating that perhaps the most serious flaw in *The Population Bomb* was that it was too optimistic about the future.[4] His vision had not changed and remained rooted in famine, drought, poverty and conflict.[5]

However, the fear that population growth is a never-ending upward spiral may be over-simplistic. The movement from rural to urban settlement in itself is acting to reduce the population growth, as people in cities tend to have fewer children than those in farms and villages. In fact, in Delhi and Mumbai, the average birth-rate is less than in London (1.6 and 1.5 as compared to 1.72[6]). Even in China, where the 1979 removal of the 'one child' policy was expected to lead to a population boom (a significant issue in a country with the largest population in the world, of 1.6 billion people), in 2018 the number of births actually fell.[7] In Japan as well, the main problem is not one of population growth but actual population decline, combined with a rapidly aging demographic. In 2021, Japan recorded its lowest number of births in more than a century.[8] The post-Second World War generations are living longer, and in greater numbers, putting pressures on all aspects of society, from care home and dementia services to the tax burden on the declining working population to support a mushrooming 'silver generation'. In Portugal, the population has been shrinking since 2010, Spain's since 2012, and Germany had the lowest birth-rate in the world, 8.2 per 1,000 population between 2008 and 2013.[9]

Global growth rates will be dramatically different depending on the region. Eastern and south-eastern Asia as well as Europe and North America will see a decline in population starting around 2030. Central and southern Asia will become the most populated region of the world and India is expected to surpass China as the most populous country as early as 2023. However, the largest population growth will be in sub-Saharan Africa, where it is expected that the population will double from 2022 to 2050. Global population growth will be largely driven by eight countries: the Democratic Republic of the Congo, Egypt, Ethiopia, India, Nigeria, Pakistan, the Philippines and the United Republic of Tanzania. Additionally, they are among the 46 of the least developed countries, of which many are projected to double their population between 2022 and 2050.[10] With rapid population growth there will be rapid urbanization, with its own set of challenges that will be further complicated by an inability to properly prepare for and mitigate natural disasters and climate change.

Urban resilience in the megacity context

Megacities are not a new phenomenon. In fact, every generation has seen the growth of the city as being something that is moving beyond sustainable limits. Megacities are currently defined as those that have populations of more than 10 million people, though it had previously been set at 8 million.[11] However, in many cases it is increasingly hard to differentiate between individual urban entities and regional conglomerates that see major cities becoming a single seamless spread that has neither boundaries nor limits. A French geographer, Jean Gottmann, was the first person to describe these new advancements to the human urban development, coining the word 'Megalopolis' as the title for his 1961 book to describe the 500-mile-long region stretching from Boston to Washington along the United States' eastern coastal region.[12]

There were five megacities in 1975, 26 in 2015 and a projected 43 by 2030.[13] Much of the growth is in the developing world, where a mix of demographic growth aligned with the lack of jobs to support economic activity in the rural environment means that a large part of the population expansion will be based on internal immigration from rural to urban centres, creating a largely informal and unmanaged urban population that is in stark contrast to the gleaming megacities of the hyper-connected smart cities that often seem to be the *de facto* vision of the future. Throughout history, cities have been the driving force of business, arts, culture and whatever modernism looks like in each generation, but at the same time they have also been seen as mixing threats and vulnerability with opportunities, at both the individual and the national level. They are places where diseases spread, where there are natural hazards, ecological disasters, food scarcity and the additional pressures on increased traffic, resource scarcity, supply change management and failing infrastructure that come together to create the perfect storm of potential apocalyptic collapse.[14] One of the leading advocates of the 'cities as the end of civilization' school of thought was Lewis Mumford. In his 1938 book *The Culture of Cities*,[15] he saw their inexorable growth and domination of all aspects of social integration, resource utilization and political and economic concentrations as a reflection of a fundamental disharmony with the natural order of things, leading to inevitable collapse, as well as high levels of suffering among their citizens but also in the wide ecosphere which would be ultimately impacted by their excesses. A Japanese researcher wrote similarly about Tokyo that 'not only is the air of megalopolis polluted with automobile exhaust and factory fumes, but the rivers are filled with industrial waste products. The environment of megalopolis is noisy and ugly. Its settlements are expanding haphazardly, spoiling the landscape and obliterating man's contacts with nature'.[16]

The idea that the megacity is a place that is designed, managed and led is one that reflects our desire for control, but in fact megacities tend to grow organically, as complex organisms operating in an equally complex and multi-dimensional biosphere rather than as some form of engineered entity. The United Nations has been focusing on the growth of megacities as an issue of concern since the 1992 United Nations Conference on Environment and Development (UNCED), when it recognized the need to promote the concept of sustainable development based on economic, social and ecological frameworks that could allow the growth that was already taking place to exist within a globally aware and socially conscious context.[17]

The growth of megacities, while often seen as something that is out of control, is actually something that has been widely studied from multiple perspectives, and with often surprisingly accurate projections as to how megacity growth trends will develop. Bugliarello predicted that the 11 largest megacities[18] would grow from a combined population of 162 million in 1992 to 240 million in 2026, while the 2016 United Nations review of world cities listed the population of the top 10 as 243 million.[19] Another source put the 2015 figures as 600 million people in about 60 megacities worldwide (that is, in metropolises with more than 5 million population). Given that it is unlikely that the growth trend in urban populations will change radically (although that may be challenged in a post-Covid world), by 2030 an estimated 60 per cent of the world's population will be living in urban areas. That figure will keep rising until mid-century when over 65 per cent of the world's population is projected to live in cities.[20]

UN Habitat identifies 2,000 global urban centres where one third of the global population lives. The move is not just from rural areas into cites, which can be considered as well-defined and self-contained geographical and physical entities, but into metropolitan areas – never-ending conglomerations of major cities that have spread so that their edges overlap and then become inextricably interlinked. They create a seamless urban landscape where the only identifier of geographical space is the changing postcodes.[21] By 1990, the Tokyo Megalopolis which included Tokyo itself, as well as Saitama, Chiba and Kanagawa prefectures,[22] had a combined population of 31 million.

Urban resilience tends to see the focus of the problem as being one of scale – gargantuanism – that is the root cause of both the vulnerabilities and the challenges of megacities, and that therefore they are considered as a class apart from other lesser cities, that have neither the scale, the grandeur nor the global attention that their bigger cousins might have. However, the smaller urban centres are facing exactly the same challenges and given that a city of 2 million or 5 million people, when disrupted by high-impact events, whether externally or internally triggered, will face exactly the same problems, it is disingenuous to presume that the impacts of crises in urban centres is one of scale alone.[23]

While megacities attract the attention of both urban planners and strategic risk managers, it is easy to forget that they are concentrated in only 20 countries, with the majority of them located in Asia. The majority of the urban population continues to live in cities that are below 500,000 inhabitants.

Even though it is projected that roughly two thirds of the global population will live in urban areas by 2050, the vast majority will be in cities with between 1 million and 5 million inhabitants which are expected to increase by over 100 by 2030 to number almost 600 worldwide. The majority of these cities will develop in the coastal regions of Asia and Africa as a consequence of rapid population growth and will not only face many of the challenges associated with urbanization but most likely will also be affected by a wide range of disruptive and potentially catastrophic events, whether natural or man-made.[24]

Urban development: a comparative approach

Urban development has different characteristics in different environments. The major cities of North America are different from the cities of Africa, which in turn are different from those of Asia. It is not merely a matter of differentiating between those that have strong, centralized managed systems and those which are fragmented, ad hoc and largely unmanaged.[25] We are increasingly seeing an overlap of the two (and every combination of hybrid management chaos): shared and overlapping spaces are created by the juxtaposition of extreme wealth and extreme poverty. There is also the overlay of the struggling professional and middle classes which are the ones who have the responsibility for maintaining the functioning of the urban behemoths at the same time as they are struggling with exactly the same problems as the rest of their co-inhabitants in terms of housing, transport, pollution, access to services and a slowly (and occasionally rapidly) declining level of functionality across all aspects of the supporting infrastructure, both physical and administrative.

In these environments, informal settlements are often the largest part of the urban landscape and yet are often unnoticed either in official population figures or in the discussions around planned, managed and integrated development programmes. This in turn creates increased pressures on all aspects of society in terms of health, environmental and public safety issues.[26]

Although cities have always been associated with trade and commerce, and therefore the necessity of creating connections with other cities, their networks are often bypassing and ignoring the local communities that surround them as an irrelevance. In the modem context this tendency was accelerated in the 1970s due to a global economic modelling of the internationalization of the division of labour. This meant that it was economically viable to outsource production processes to low-wage (and often low-regulation) regions, combined with the developments in communications technology that meant that physical distance was increasingly irrelevant as global communications could be close to instantaneous irrespective of physical location.[27]

There are a number of common aspects to global cities, wherever they might be in physical reality:

- ties to the world economy;
- agglomeration and scale, combined with concentration of skills and services;
- high-level services, together with a suitable educated and skilled workforce;
- locational concentration and 'glamour zones' that reflect both the reality and the aspiration of those cities to associate themselves with futuristic planning and development;
- 'quartering', which sees an increasingly entrenched division between those that are seen as productive and value-adding and those that are marginalized and disempowered – even though it may well be their labour that keeps the city running.[28]

In this brave new world of global connectivity, global cities are often seen as being more connected to each other than they are to the countries that they are situated in, just as the global technology companies that support them, whether through information, communications or finance, have no physical reality in any geographic zone.[29]

There is an almost bipolar conceptualization of the megacity, with one part of the global consciousness thinking of it in terms of smart cities, where everything is hyper-connected and cyber-enabled, and where artificial intelligence and cutting-edge and futuristic technology will ensure the maximum utilization of resources for a usefully employed population. At the same time, we see them as a post-apocalyptic dystopian vision of a spiral of over-population, failing infrastructures and the creation of disempowered and disenfranchised under-classes that would not be out of place in a Dickensian novel.[30] The truth is that both of those visions are not only true, in their own contexts, but are the reality for the next generations, that will need to find a way of living in a world that encapsulates both visions, often intermingling within the same physical space but operating in entirely different existences.

It is the ability to develop both a vision and a methodology that can embrace both branches of that development and can square the paradox of the question as to what the city of the future will look like that will set the foundation for the wellbeing or otherwise of billions of people both living and as yet unborn.

Managing megacities

There is also the fact that while we understand the problems of megacities, there is little understanding of what we can do to manage them effectively, particularly in the face of the increasing high-stress situations that they are finding themselves in. We are repeatedly seeing examples of high-impact disruptions to city infrastructures for which the authorities seem to simply have no response. We have traditionally considered issues such as flooding, drought, earthquakes and landslides to be anomalous events, disruptors that have disturbed the otherwise well-ordered way we live our lives, in a dynamic but fundamentally sustainable exchange between urban construction, the natural environment and human inhabitants. The major events that caught global attention were, from a developed (northern/Western) world's perspective, 'over there'. They were events that took place in other places and for which Western nations could offer help and support from their privileged position of being both safe and resource-enabled. What we have seen in recent years is that these events are no longer part of a distant narrative but are in fact part of the daily lives that we live. Just as deserts encroach on fields and rising sea levels encroach on coastal plains, so the global risk environment has encroached on what we had previously perceived to be safe areas, where human ingenuity and never-ending technical innovation had kept out the wildness of nature.

Countries that 'lived in crisis', for example Bangladesh and flooding or East Africa and drought, are suddenly no longer outliers that have little relevance to the way we live our lives, and in fact are the harbingers of a new future, where the lessons that have been learned over generations in response to their disasters are now a road map – or at least a warning system – for the major advanced cities of the world.

Traditionally, it has been the megacities of the developing world, characterized as low- and middle-income countries (LMIC), that were seen as being particularly vulnerable to major disruptions, whether they were created by external events (adverse weather events, climate change issues), infrastructural failure, or simply the result of massive numbers of people living in high-density environments with little or no formal support or infrastructure (such as access to clean water). Such conditions would inherently lead to rapidly escalating failures with rapidly cascading effects. In this scenario, it was not the specific events that caused high levels of disruption and dislocation but the absence of well-structured management and response frameworks.[31]

The snowstorm in Houston, Texas, in February 2021 was one example of a natural event that caught city managers completely unawares and knocked a hyper-modern city off the grid in a matter of hours, but there are multiple others, such as the bush fires that have attacked large parts of the highly populated west coast of Australia or the ultra-high temperatures and unprecedented flooding that have hit many European cities.

Although we often look at megacities from the perspective of stand-alone studies, they do of course operate in the wider sphere of national governance and other structures. It is the case that the megacities often attract the majority of political attention, commercial investment and national support, sucking the oxygen out of efforts to produce alternative options for those gravitating to the megacities out of either ambition or desperation.[32] As well as the question of how we manage the megacities, the parallel question to be asked is, 'How do we create alternative options for those wishing to live their lives in an environment which offers the benefits and opportunities that living in a megacity undoubtedly brings but without adding to the already overwhelming burden that creates on both cities and national resources?'

Natural disasters and urban environments

The nature of the events that the world is facing and the level of destruction and dislocation that they are causing are growing exponentially. This is not a new phenomenon. In the report issued to mark the end of the United Nations International Decade for Natural Disaster Reduction (1990–99[33]), it was noted that the cost of weather-related disasters in 1998 alone was more than the total cost of all such disasters across the 1980s. It was also noted at the time that the impact of those events, in terms of deaths and impact on lives and livelihoods, was predominantly felt by poor people.

Although we are quick to claim that 'natural disasters' are to blame for the level of destruction and disruption, a closer reading makes it clear that in fact it is often human inaction to either prepare for or to adequately respond to such events that is the root cause of the escalation of the external event to a disaster situation. As the UN IDNDR report makes clear, it is the tendency of those who are poorest to live in areas that are most vulnerable, and therefore do not have even the most basic mitigation and defence measures in place that would be available to more affluent communities in their society, that creates such levels of impact.[34] The development of urban centres often creates the very environments that make them more vulnerable to natural disasters and increases the likelihoods that those events, when they do happen, will have a higher level of impact because of those activities.[35] While major flooding is increasingly a problem across much of Europe, the level of soil erosion that is caused by the denuding of the natural forest, combined with the inability of urbanized concreted areas to absorb water as they did when they were still green fields, in itself increases both the volume and the speed of water flow, which in turn increases the level of impacts that such flooding causes. Although such events can be blamed on climate change, it is often the case that in fact it is the planning and management failures that have increased the propensity to flooding, and the failure to develop appropriate or effective management measures which escalates the situation from a manageable outlier event to an actual human catastrophe.[36]

The floods in Germany in 2021, which led to the deaths of more than 180 people, were a classic example of this phenomenon. While experts were quick to blame climate change for the high levels of rain,[37] in parallel to that the collapse of a major dam was caused by the build-up of a level of pressure of water for which it had simply not been designed. Local streams had been turned into fast-flowing rivers because banks had been straightened and what had been water-absorbing greenery had been turned into concreted residential areas.[38] In language that reflects the findings that were published following the snowstorms in Houston in February 2021,[39] questions were asked as to why Germany, the fourth largest economy in the world and a country known for both its technological innovation and its engineering efficiency, could not devise a system that could warn people of floods before they created the level of destruction seen here.[40] Given the complex nature of German politics, combining national, state and city governance systems, it is perhaps not surprising that there was an effort to avoid responsibility both for the flooding event itself and the level of human destruction it caused.

The guidance of the UK government's adviser on the effects of adapting to global warming, following the unprecedented flooding of 2015 coming after the wettest December ever seen, was 'although recent flooding has caused houses and other buildings to be inundated, property could continue to be constructed on flood plains. He said that the attendant risks and the possible devastation would have to be made clear to households, local government and developers'.[41]

This was despite the fact that clear warning had been given concerning the dangers of the increased likelihood of flooding and the failure to learn similar lessons following the floods of 2013–14. This had followed on from cuts to flood defence funds in the previous government.[42]

Although there is a tendency to see natural disasters as 'something that just happens', there is the need to differentiate between the external event (the earthquake, flood or landslide, for example) and the impacts that causes for the local population. In fact, it has been clearly identified that it is not the nature, scale or scope of the event itself that is the critical issue in assessing the likelihood of damage or destruction (including to human life), but rather the maturity of the governance frameworks within which it is taking place. Between 1980 and 2002, India experienced 14 earthquakes that killed a total of 32,117 people while the United States experienced 18 earthquakes that killed only 143 people.[43]

An IPCC report found that of the global population exposed to natural hazards such as earthquakes, cyclones, floods and droughts, only 11 per cent are found in countries with a low Human Development Index (HDI), yet these countries disproportionately accounted for 53 per cent of all disaster fatalities from 1980 to 2000.[44] In contrast, the economic cost for such events, unsurprisingly, is found in those areas which have the highest level of economic development. However, in terms of absolute economic impact (based on percentage of GDP impacted by the event), it is once again the smaller and more vulnerable nations that are at greatest risk. It is the small islands that can see the totality of their infrastructure and economic production wiped out in a single event that can have the highest impact in absolute terms. The costliest disasters relative to GDP are the 2010 Haiti earthquake (167 per cent of GDP), the 2004 Grenada cyclone (149 per cent of GDP), the 2005 Guyana flood (56 per cent of GDP) and the 2004 Maldives earthquake and tsunami (45 per cent of GDP).[45]

The 2019 World Economic Forum Global Risk Report[46] identified that two thirds of the world population was expected to live in cities by 2050 and that their growth only exacerbated the risks that already exist by putting increased pressure on the surrounding environment, destroying natural sources of resilience and creating greater and more significant points of failure, each of which could have a set of cascading consequences that are almost impossible to model or predict.

While there is no doubt that on a global scale the impacts of the planetary-level changes that we are seeing manifest on a daily basis will have a significant, and in many cases catastrophic, impact on rural communities, it is in the cities that the most dramatic impacts will be felt. Just as urban centres are dependent on the rural hinterlands that supply and support them, so the world is dependent on its cities, both as independent units of activity and as part of the global network of interconnections and interdependencies. However, the challenges caused by increased urbanization, and the pressure it creates on systems designed for an older, slower lifestyle, are not new.

The first cases of complaints of air pollution in London were recorded in the 13th century, and as Peter Ackroyd points out in his magisterial autobiography of London, issues of overcrowding poverty and waste disposal were never far away from the thoughts of the elders.[47] The growth of London in the mid-19th century was at a pace that had never been seen before in any stage of history. Between 1850 and 1899 the population grew from 2 million to over 6.5 million. The development of the first railway systems, that allowed workers from outside the city to become the world's first commuters, created serious problems of congestion.[48] In 1900, almost every vehicle on London's streets was horse-drawn, with over 300,000 horses needed to keep the city on the move.[49] The traffic created such a level of congestion in London that many of the bridges became impassable and it was felt that they would cause the collapse of the London structures that had survived for the previous centuries.

Even earlier than that, the ancient Greeks were already concerned with the concept of over-population and the impact that had both on the possibility of civil unrest and the need to introduce policies to reduce population expansion to a zero-growth rate. Balance was one of the fundamental pillars of good order in the Greek conception of a balanced universe, which in turn leads to both societies and individuals being comfortable and at ease with themselves.[50]

The metaphor of the human body is often used to describe cities – we talk about the heart of the city or parks being the lungs of the city, and the internal roads and railways as well as the networks of multi-lane highways that connect one city to another are the blood circulation system that, just as in the body, can be blocked and collapse just as our veins and arteries can, and with much the same effect.[51] And yet we are increasingly seeing cities not as entities in themselves but as points in a global matrix, where the cyber-aspects of the city – virtual, disconnected, non-corporeal – means that they lose their individual identity and increasingly become seen from the context of the global network.[52] In the post-Covid age, we have seen the realization of a futuristic (or perhaps apocalyptic) vision of the end of the city as we have traditionally known it and the work from home phenomenon changing the city from a pulsating centre of politics, arts and industry to a decolonized husk, where it is primarily maintenance people who still see it as the fundamental focus of their working lives.

On a wider perspective, a famous paper delivered to the Club of Rome in 1972 predicted that given the continued population growth and the subsequent demand on resources that would create, there was a limit to the amount of growth it is possible to model before catastrophic rebalancing mechanisms kick in.[53]

The five trends that were considered are as real today as they were then:

- accelerating industrialization;
- rapid population growth;
- widespread malnutrition;
- depletion of non-renewable resources; and
- a deteriorating environment.

The conclusions were stark: 'If the present growth trends in world population, industrialization, pollution, food production, and resource depletion continue unchanged, the limits to growth on this planet will be reached sometime within the next one hundred years. The most probable result will be a rather sudden and uncontrollable decline in both population and industrial capacity.'[54] The paper ends on a slightly hopeful note, that humankind has both the knowledge and the ingenuity to develop such a society – one that is in equilibrium with the planet-wide systems we are part of and can be constructed on a concept of equilibrium rather than never-ending growth. However, there was also the recognition that the minimum requirements to achieve that would be a realistic, long-term goal that can act as the guideline for such an effort, and the human will to achieve it. There was an additional warning. Due to the time-lag effect of any intervention that might be made (for example, in increased birth control that might need 30 years to have an impact), the time to engage with such issues is before they become critical. The time lag from any action taken to significant impact is such that 'if the global society waits until those constraints are unmistakably apparent, it will have waited too long'.[55]

Megacities, fragility and imminent failure

We have always been aware of cities as being fragile and brittle, and the need to find the balance between modelling the vulnerability of the city and sustainability is not new.[56] While cities were traditionally the refuge that people used when disasters hit rural areas, they subsequently came to be seen as the place where in fact the potential large-scale events and disruptive and destructive impacts and consequences could be seen and felt. The rise of the megacity has seen the growth of problems and challenges that cannot be modelled or engaged with using traditional planning and management tools.

Although the impacts of Covid-19 hit cities in a way and with a speed that had not been seen before, the vision of the 'end of the city' is not a new phenomenon. In the 1970s we saw the financial as well as the physical collapse of cities, with New York as the epitome of the city of the future that had become a relic of the past. Of course, there was then renewal and reconstruction in the never-ending cycle of boom and bust that hits cities as they hit every other aspect of our lives.[57]

Disruption within the mega-city and other urban conurbations has traditionally been seen from two separate perspectives. One is the collapse of the failing cities, those that are traditionally in the emerging south and are characterized by high levels of informal communities and economies, a lack of planned development and the failure to have the range of governance and management structures in place that could allow the maintenance of the city to be managed on a sustained basis.[58] This model of the city sees it as a place of continuous micro-negotiations that take place within the context of a place of chaos, continuously on the edge of collapse, but somehow almost miraculously maintaining itself even in the face of ever-increasing challenges in terms of numbers, structures and resources. The opposing view of this is the modern city, one that is self-confident, future-looking and both grounded and cocooned in an all-embracing network of supportive systems, networks and agencies that work tirelessly and ceaselessly to maintain the needs of the ever-growing monster, often in ways unseen by and unknown to the citizens and visitors who are completely dependent, without their knowing, on the never-ending machinations of the equivalent of the life support system that keeps them alive.

It is only when these the support systems of the modern cities collapse, whether because of an external event such as an earthquake or flooding, or the breakdown of the global supply chains that keep them fed, or an internal one like the collapse of a bridge or the failure of the power system, that suddenly the vulnerability of the city without the protective cocoon becomes clear. The blackouts across the north-east US and parts of Canada in 2003,[59] the impacts on Tokyo in 2011,[60] following the tsunami around Fukushima that led to the release of a radioactive cloud from the failed TEPCO Daiichi nuclear reactor, or the failure of Houston[61] to be prepared for or able to respond to the challenges caused by a snowstorm in 2021, were stark warnings that the facade of urban invincibility is exactly that – no more than a sheen over the potential chaos of millions of inter-tangled lives that is as fragile as the sheets of glass that cover their hyper-modernistic skyscrapers.

Although we consider cities to be managed entities or organisms, depending on whether you see them from an design/engineering perspective or an ecosystem perspective, the truth is that there is often little if any understanding of how cities actually work and what are the fundamental issues around maintaining their functionality and mitigating or responding to systems failures when they do happen.[62]

The nature of urban risk

Urban risk is not new. Since people first started gathering in concentrated centres of population, there have been risks associated with that, whether dependent on weather-assisted food supplies, the volcanic destruction of Pompeii, the plague-ridden cities of the Middle Ages, the issues of poverty in 19th-century London or the hyper-pollution of the 21st century. There have been climate-related events on a regular basis, with storms, flooding, droughts and earthquakes a common feature of urban life. And yet, there is no doubt that the nature, scale, frequency and impact of the scenes that we are now seeing suggest a genuine paradigm shift in both the nature of the threats that we are facing and the demands that creates on every aspect of our governance and daily lives.

Urban growth has been one of the most dramatic and influential trends of the 20th and 21st centuries and urban centres are both the embodiment of the challenges that we are facing on a global scale and the petri dish in which potential solutions can be developed and deployed.[63] In discussing urban and social resilience, we can look at it through the lens of vulnerability. From this perspective the three components that make up the vulnerability model can be described in various ways, for example exposure, sensitivity and resilience,[64] people, places and ecosystems,[65] or risk, exposure and vulnerability.[66] This of course does not take into account the changing nature of the threat environment itself. Given the fundamental changes in the nature, scale and scope of the adverse events that we are witnessing across the world, it needs to be asked to what extent the classical understanding of vulnerability in terms in the context of what, from an academic perspective, could be considered as a relatively stable environment is still valid. It seems clear that the modelling of adverse events in which they could be considered a rational part of the background operating environment needs to be changed in light of what are increasingly overwhelmingly destructive events that either bypass or totally invalidate traditional mitigation, defence or response frameworks.

While we often see the response to disruptive events in terms of emergency response and crisis management (in other words, the restoration of order through planned and managed interventions), the truth is that in less-well developed environments there is little if any expectation that local or central government agencies or representatives will make an appearance, and as such rather than a centralized, process-driven and agency-led response, there is a much more informal approach of 'coping'.[67] This is increasingly becoming recognized as an approach that needs to be seen in even advanced environments, given the level of demands in both numbers of incidents and the demands that they make and the increasingly limited resources that are available to respond to them.

The announcement by the Australian government in 2022, following a series of unprecedented floods and fires, that citizens should not expect that the government would be able to come and help them and that they would need to make their own arrangements to ensure their safety and wellbeing at the personal and community level, seemingly broke the unspoken contract that said the government would come and help you if you were in trouble.

The risks that cities are facing are not unknown. From one perspective, they are exactly the same issues that faced the inhabitants of the earliest cities – how to maintain them when they were so dependent on a constant influx of supplies and support from an extended external network system, and how to manage the lives of those citizens in the face of never-ending challenges to the stability and sustainability of urban life. While we might claim that the levels of complexity of the modern day have undoubtedly taken those challenges and their potential impacts to the next level, that is exactly the attitude and phrasing that would have been used in every generation, in that every generation sees itself as the epitome of modernization, burdened by the legacy of the past at the same time as it prepares itself to be the cutting edge into the future.

The nature of the failures of cities to prepare for the challenges they are facing can almost always be seen in terms of a failure to learn from past events.[68] In something as complex as a city, systems failure must always be considered as a possibility on the high-impact risk register. The fact is that once some aspect of a city fails, whether for internal or external reasons, then the impacts and consequences are going to be increasingly high-impact themselves, crossing multiple geographical, organizational and jurisdictional boundaries and requiring a multi-tiered, multi-organizational response that can both model and understand the nature and range of the challenges associated with that incident. If there is an inability to deal with the lower-level incidents that are the signs of a system moving closer to collapse, and that are the precursors to a major systemic failure, then it is certain that there will not be the capability in terms of leadership, coordination and resources to deal with a major incident when it does finally – and inevitably – occur.

Climate change

As with so many of the existential risks that humanity is facing – and it's no exaggeration to say that climate change is an existential risk[69]) – it is not something that has not been known, modelled or discussed for the last 50 years. There have been multiple warnings of 'the last chance saloon', and as the second hand clicks ever closer to midnight, we still seem to think that there will be a magic answer that will make it all go away.

The fact that the nature of the hazards we are facing is changing, and the significance of the range of impacts that could cause, was at the heart of the United Nations-sponsored International Decade for Natural Disaster Reduction (1990–2000) Study Group on the Disaster Vulnerability. '*[T]he universe of hazard is now undergoing fundamental changes that may invalidate previous research findings*' (italics in the original).[70]

The growing levels of impact of planetary-level climate changes are themselves creating a higher level of complexity in both the individual and the compound impacts for multiple sources. It is increasingly difficult to project the measures that will need to be taken to engage with these issues or to mitigate/prevent them.[71] For instance, more than 90 per cent of all urban areas are coastal, which puts most cities across the globe at risk of flooding from sea-level rise and powerful storms.[72]

The Australian Security Leaders Climate Group report in 2021 summed it up with the quote on its cover: 'Australia has repeatedly ignored the risks and is ill-prepared for the security implications of devastating climate impacts at home and in the Asia-Pacific, the highest risk region in the world.'[73]

The era of the Lucifer heatwave

Multiple reports have repeatedly made the point that while the dangers we are facing are severe and the impacts and consequences will change the nature of the way we live, there are solutions at hand that would be both applicable and effective, as long as we act now. The problem is that those warnings are never heeded and the actions are never taken. In fact, despite the lip service to the commitment to change, policies are often produced that actively militate against such actions being introduced and instead take decisions that actively worsen the situation.

What unites all the reports and warnings is a sense of urgency,[74] combined with an authoritative voice that makes it clear that these are not issues based on theoretical models of future developments but are descriptions of often irreversible planetary changes that are taking place as we speak.

While it might seem that the changes we need to make are becoming increasingly out of reach, it is also clear that any impact we can have on the ever-rising heat levels would have significance. As the World Meteorological Organization report on global climate change states, 'Every fraction of a degree of warming makes a difference.'[75] Of course, that statement works both ways and every time we allow the global temperature to rise, whether through passive inaction or active wilfulness, that has a significance that will lead to further cascading consequences, for good or bad.

We are now seeing heatwaves that are, from any perspective, both unprecedented and at levels that were previously considered almost inconceivable. The rate of change has grown exponentially so that record heatwaves are not breaking records in increments of fractions of degrees but by multiple degrees at a time. The summer of 2022 saw heat records set at levels never seen before. The United Kingdom saw previous records of 38.7 degrees being superseded by heatwaves of over 40 degrees. This was accompanied, for the first time ever, by a Red Heat Warning, which included Danger of Death.[76]

The heatwave that covered much of Europe in 2022 was labelled 'Lucifer', while in Canada record heatwaves meant that previous records that had failed to reach 45 degrees were broken by temperatures that not only breached the 45 degree level but soared to over 49 degrees. It was not merely a matter of the suffering that created for the populations who had never experienced such temperatures, but the impact that had on the entire infrastructure system,[77] including global internet providers such as Google[78] and Oracle.[79] The UCCRN report identified the major issue[80] as increased heat, and for increasingly extended periods of time, especially for those living in poverty who do not have the wherewithal to mitigate the impact of that heat in ways that are available to the more affluent sections of the community. That included a decline in access to fresh water, decline in food security due to the impact of climate change on global food production, coastal flooding due to rises in sea levels and the knock-on effects of that in terms of impacts on aspects like power supply.

Flood management

In January 2022, the Indonesian government announced a plan to relocate the capital from Jakarta, a city that is habitually hit with flooding and other adverse events, to Borneo, where it would be called Nusantara. The need to relocate major cities because of the impacts of climate change, and rising sea levels in particular, is not a problem that is going to go away. As in Jakarta, the issue of coastal flooding is not only due to rising sea levels but also to the fact that the cities themselves are sinking. With around 90 per cent of coastal areas being impacted,[81] this is a reality that has already started to impact the way we live our lives in the major urban centres of the world.

One response has been to go for engineering solutions, which are designed to protect the coastal urban centres from the rising water levels. In this sense, they are little different from the famous act of King Canute, who in order to demonstrate his lack of ability to influence the natural world around him, tried to demand of the tide that it retreat.[82] These attempts are not new. The city of Rotterdam built a 400 m dam to keep the waters back as long ago as the 13th century. The current iteration is the Maeslant Barrier, which is the size of two Eiffel Towers on their side. However, the engineering aspect is only one part of a wider engagement with the reality of what water management looks like in the 21st century. The truth is that you can't make water go away, and you can only keep it back for a certain amount of time. Although the Dutch have created a flood management plan that they believe will be effective against a once in 10,000 (ten thousand!) year storm,[83] one of their approaches has been to stop trying to hold back the water and rather letting it come into what were previously inhabited areas, so that its force is dissipated and creating what is in effect a water reserve area that protects the further back and higher standing land from its impacts.[84]

A similar mixed-methods approach has been tried in China, where the issue of coastal flooding is so severe that it is estimated that 641 out of China's 654 largest cities are subject to regular flooding.[85] As well as massive engineering works (including a 520 km protective seawall), they have introduced a 'sponge city' concept. Under this regime, 80 per cent of their land is expected to be able to absorb or recycle 70 per cent of storm water.[86] As in all issues to do with urban resilience, there is no solution that can be considered an isolated option, and the impact or effectiveness of sponge city policies is dependent on an integrated and long-term approach to urban planning that includes issues such as low-impact development, sustainable drainage systems, green infrastructure and, perhaps above all, a recognition from the general population that such policies are not only necessary but critical. It is only with an all-of-society approach, including buy-in and acceptance from individuals and communities, that such approaches can be expected to have a chance of influencing and mitigating the impact of the climate changes that are taking place all around us.

The ability to learn from others, share developments and create a global understanding of best practices is something that is perhaps applicable to urban flooding management more than any other aspect of global urban resilience. Studies in Denmark, Vietnam, India, Australia and the United States,[87] among others, offer a range of options that are embedded in their own specific social and cultural issues but are also widely applicable to multiple other contexts.

The level of knowledge, experience and insight that has been developed on an individual basis across multiple cities is a resource that can (must!) be used to develop best practices that can be introduced in urban centres.[88] It is only by acknowledging and accepting the threats, and the need for proactive action, that such learning can be utilized and effective flood management programmes introduced before the catastrophic impact is experienced and such plans are introduced on a post-event and reactive basis.

While it was written specifically from a US perspective, the words from a 2012 paper on flood plain management are applicable to any urban planner looking at this issue and wondering why we cannot engage with and manage what is one of the most immediate and critical challenges we are facing, and one that will have more impact on a greater percentage of the global population than any other. 'The most striking aspect of United States flood policy is the growing gap between, on the one hand, the increasing sophistication of flood and hazard mapping and risk assessment and communication, and on the other, the failure to incorporate these developments into law and policy. We continue to rely on uncoordinated, structural defences, even as our understanding of the limits of that policy increases and we continue to encourage floodplain development.'[89]

Migration and urban security

We are witnessing a world that will continue to urbanize over the next three decades – from 56 per cent in 2021 to 68 per cent in 2050. This translates into an increase of 2.2 billion urban residents, living mostly in Africa and Asia.[90] Globally, 1.6 billion people, or 20 per cent of the world's population, live in inadequate housing, of which 1 billion reside in slums and informal settlements.[91]

Many of the cities with a population of 1 million and more in the developing global south that will emerge as a result of rapid population growth will face challenges that are already apparent today and could hypercharge in the coming years. Some of the African countries which will double their population by 2050, such as Nigeria, already have to deal with decaying infrastructure and increased vulnerability to external events. Lagos massively suffered from the oil crisis in May 2015 due to scarcity of a working national electric grid and a reliance on private diesel generators. When fuel became either unobtainable or too expensive, business, transport and communication infrastructure effectively came to a halt. Furthermore, the cost of living in these cities is often underestimated and more expensive than in comparable low- and middle-income countries by a staggering 11–18 per cent.[92] Urban food and water insecurity is linked to poor health and the informal or simply brutal character of policing systems has contributed to what has been called an 'urbanization of violence'.[93] While there are opportunities created in the informal economies from the urbanization processes discussed in Chapter 10, the impact of climate change and its cascading consequences could have a devastating effect on urban security.[94]

The worst-case scenario envisages cities – mainly in the developing global south – as being denuded of the infrastructures that would support their current populations, as well as the loss of economic foundations that support basic or even rudimentary infrastructure and service deliveries. They would become, in very real terms, dystopian landscapes without hope. However, as well as imposing lives of desperation, suffering and misery on their own populations, they would create rippling effects that would impact on the global community. This would be either in terms of the impacts of mass migrations from failing states to those that are perceived to be comparatively prosperous and successful, or in the imposition of increasingly authoritarian and exclusionary policies that see outsiders as 'others' who are a threat to the wellbeing of the local population and who must be excluded, criminalized and, using language that we are already seeing, dehumanized.[95]

Conclusion

The city is going to be the backdrop to global development for the rest of this century, as it was for the past three millennia. Cities are where the solutions to the challenges we are facing will be found and implemented. At the same time, the likelihood is that the cities of our globalized world, whether megacities of multiple tens of millions of people or smaller cities that are more able to create their differentiated identity, will be facing challenges that will create existential levels of risk and potentially systems-level catastrophic collapse. The city management models that have supported the growth of cities from the start of the industrial revolution have always been tested by increasing pressures from multiple directions, but it seems that the challenges being created by the issues discussed in this chapter have pushed those abilities to the edge of their current capabilities.

It is possible, like so many times before in history, that this is merely the precursor to a new period of growth, development and the creation of a generation of urban reality that will be as different from the city experience of today as the horse-and-cart periods were from the cities of the motor cars that followed them.

Destruction and renewal are always intertwined, as are chaos and opportunity. Having explored some of the challenges facing modern global cities, we can now look at some of the options that are available to engage with them, whether from the perspective of a hyper-modern future or one where the reality of the informal urban settlement becomes the defining narrative.

Endnotes

1 Statistics Times, https://statisticstimes.com/demographics/world-urban-population.php (archived at https://perma.cc/Q5LG-EVQR); https://population.un.org/wup/Download/ (archived at https://perma.cc/U8SU-FU5F); UN (2018) Department of Economic and Social Affairs Population Dynamics. World Urban Population Dynamics 2018. https://population.un.org/wup/Download/ (archived at https://perma.cc/U8SU-FU5F)

2 Mahmood, S A I (2011) Air pollution kills 15,000 Bangladeshis each year: The role of public administration and governments integrity. *Journal of Public Administration and Policy Research*, 3(4), 129–140; WHO (2010) Urbanization and health. https://www.scielosp.org/pdf/bwho/2010.v88n4/245-246 (archived at https://perma.cc/S3HY-PZSN)

3 Ehrlich, P (1968) The population bomb. https://projectavalon.net/The_Population_Bomb_Paul_Ehrlich.pdf (archived at https://perma.cc/LGR3-C67F)

4 Ehrlich, P R and Ehrlich, A H (2009) The population bomb revisited. *The Electronic Journal of Sustainable Development*, 1(3), 63–71

5 Jowit, J (2011) Paul Ehrlich, a prophet of global population doom who is gloomier than ever. *The Guardian*, 23 October. https://www.theguardian.com/environment/2011/oct/23/paul-ehrlich-global-collapse-warning (archived at https://perma.cc/NG9S-9KDA)

6 Pearce, F (2018) Is the way we think about overpopulation racist? *The Guardian*, 19 March. https://www.theguardian.com/cities/2018/mar/19/overpopulation-cities-environment-developing-world-racist-paul-ehrlich (archived at https://perma.cc/P5MC-2L4M)

7 UN DESA (2022) World population prospects 2022: Summary of results. United Nations Department of Economic and Social Affairs

8 Parker, C (2022) Japan records its largest natural population decline as births fall. *Washington Post*, https://www.washingtonpost.com/world/2022/06/03/japan-low-births-population-decline-2021/ (archived at https://perma.cc/AL2L-QWSP)

9 The Observer (2015) Europe needs many more babies to avert a population disaster. https://www.theguardian.com/world/2015/aug/23/baby-crisis-europe-brink-depopulation-disaster (archived at https://perma.cc/H9ZV-N4VH)

10 UN (2022) World population prospects 2022: Summary of results. United Nations Department of Economic and Social Affairs

11 Uitto, J I (1998) The geography of disaster vulnerability in megacities: A theoretical framework. *Applied Geography*, 18(1), 7–16 UN (1987) Population growth and policies in megacities. Available at: https://www.un.org/development/desa/pd/sites/www.un.org.development.desa.pd/files/files/documents/2020/Jan/un_1987_population_growth_and_policies_in_megacities_-_bangkok.pdf (archived at https://perma.cc/R4A7-Z56V) (Accessed: 8 August 2022).

12 Gottmann, J (1961) *Megalopolis: The urbanized northeastern seaboard of the United States* (Vol. 8). New York: Twentieth Century Fund

13 UN DESA (2018a) The world's cities in 2018 – data booklet. United Nations Department of Economic and Social Affairs. Available at: https://www.un.org/en/development/desa/population/publications/pdf/urbanization/the_worlds_cities_in_2018_data_booklet.pdf (archived at https://perma.cc/U4FZ-K8FZ)

14 Bugliarello, G (1999) Megacities and the developing world. *Urbanization & Engineering*, 29(4), 19–26

15 Mumford, L (2016) The culture of cities. Open Road Media. Available at: https://monoskop.org/images/5/5a/Mumford_Lewis_The_Culture_of_Cities.pdf (archived at https://perma.cc/G25X-NSFM) (Accessed: 8 August 2022)

16 Nagashima, C (1967) Megalopolis in Japan. Ekistics; *Reviews on the Problems and Science of Human Settlements*, 24(140), 6–14

17 UN (1992) Agenda 21. United Nations Conference on Environment and Development, Rio de Janeiro, Brazil, 3–14 June 1992. Available at: https://sustainabledevelopment.un.org/content/documents/Agenda21.pdf (archived at https://perma.cc/Y77U-36S5) (Accessed: 8 August 2022)

18 Bugliarello, G (1999) Megacities and the developing world. *Urbanization & Engineering*, 29(4), 19–26

19 UN DESA, Population Division (2016) The world's cities in 2016 – data booklet. United Nations Department of Economic and Social Affairs

20 IPCC (2014) Climate change 2014: Synthesis report. Contribution of Working Groups I, II and III to the Fifth Assessment Report of the Intergovernmental Panel on Climate Change. IPCC, Geneva, Switzerland; UN Habitat (2020) The New Urban Agenda Illustrated, United Nations Human Settlements Programme. Available at: https://unhabitat.org/sites/default/files/2020/12/nua_handbook_14dec2020_2.pdf (archived at https://perma.cc/9QHQ-DQQX)

21 UN Habitat (2020) The New Urban Agenda Illustrated, United Nations Human Settlements Programme. Available at: https://unhabitat.org/sites/default/files/2020/12/nua_handbook_14dec2020_2.pdf (archived at https://perma.cc/9QHQ-DQQX)

22 Uitto, J I (1998) The geography of disaster vulnerability in megacities: A theoretical framework. *Applied Geography*, 18(1), 7–16

23 Robinson, J (2006) *Ordinary cities: Between modernity and development*. Routledge

24 UN DESA (2018a) The world's cities in 2018 – data booklet. United Nations Department of Economic and Social Affairs. Available at: https://www.un.org/en/development/desa/population/publications/pdf/urbanization/the_worlds_cities_in_2018_data_booklet.pdf (archived at https://perma.cc/U4FZ-K8FZ)
UN DESA (2018b) World urbanization prospects: The 2018 revision. New York, United Nations. Available at: https://population.un.org/wup/Publications/Files/WUP2018-Report.pdf (archived at https://perma.cc/MS2C-Y3ZE)

25 UN Habitat (2020) The New Urban Agenda Illustrated, United Nations Human Settlements Programme. Available at: https://unhabitat.org/sites/default/files/2020/12/nua_handbook_14dec2020_2.pdf (archived at https://perma.cc/9QHQ-DQQX)

26 UN Habitat (2020) The New Urban Agenda Illustrated, United Nations Human Settlements Programme. Available at: https://unhabitat.org/sites/default/files/2020/12/nua_handbook_14dec2020_2.pdf (archived at https://perma.cc/9QHQ-DQQX)

27 Taylor, P (2004) *World city network: A global urban analysis*. London: Routledge

28 Vedula, A (2007) Blueprint and reality: Navi Mumbai, the city of the 21st century. *Habitat International*, 31(1), 12–23

29 Sassen, S (2013) *The global city: New York, London, Tokyo*. Princeton University Press

30 Kraas, F (2007) Megacities and global change in East, Southeast and South Asia. *Asien*, 103(4), 9–22

31 Butsch, C, Kraas, F, Namperumal, S & Peters, G (2016) Risk governance in the megacity Mumbai/India: A complex adaptive system perspective. *Habitat International*, 54(2), 100–111; Uitto, J I (1998) The geography of disaster vulnerability in megacities: A theoretical framework. *Applied Geography*, 18(1), 7–16

32 Bugliarello, G (1999) Megacities and the developing world. *Urbanization & Engineering*, 29(4), 19–26
Kraas, F (2007) Megacities and global change in East, Southeast and South Asia. *Asien*, 103(4), 9–22

33 IDNDR (1999) International Decade for Natural Disaster Reduction. Proceedings, Programme Forum

34 Braun, B & Aßheuer, T (2011) Floods in megacity environments: Vulnerability and coping strategies of slum dwellers in Dhaka/Bangladesh. *Natural Hazards*, 58(2), 771–787

35 Uitto, J I (1998) The geography of disaster vulnerability in megacities: A theoretical framework. *Applied Geography*, 18(1), 7–16

36 Braun, B & Aßheuer, T (2011) Floods in megacity environments: vulnerability and coping strategies of slum dwellers in Dhaka/Bangladesh. *Natural Hazards*, 58(2), 771–787

37 National Geographic (2021) Sarah Gibbens. Experts fear Germany's deadly floods are a glimpse into climate future. Available at: https://www.nationalgeographic.com/environment/article/experts-fear-germany-deadly-floods-glimpse-into-climate-future (archived at https://perma.cc/3SUH-XAEY) (Accessed: 8 August 2022)

38 RS21 (2021) Mark Bergfeld. Flooding in Germany is a man-made disaster. Available at: https://www.rs21.org.uk/2021/07/23/flooding-in-germany-is-a-man-made-disaster/ (archived at https://perma.cc/9ZRM-227L) (Accessed: 8 August 2022)

39 Donald, J (2021) Winter Storm Uri 2021: The economic impact of the storm. Available at: https://comptroller.texas.gov/economy/fiscal-notes/2021/oct/winter-storm-impact.php (archived at https://perma.cc/MC2P-QYNB) (Accessed: 8 August 2022)

40 BBC (2021) Europe's floods: Lessons from German tragedy. 29 October. Available at: https://www.bbc.co.uk/news/world-europe-58992093 (archived at https://perma.cc/CLX4-GXEG) (Accessed: 8 August 2022)

41 Harvey, F (2016) Build on flood plains despite the risks, say UK government advisers. *The Guardian*, 27 January. Available at: https://www.theguardian.com/environment/2016/jan/27/homes-and-companies-should-be-built-on-flood-plains-despite-risks-says-panel (archived at https://perma.cc/79Z7-KMFW)

42 Carrington, D & Wintour, P (2015) Cameron government rejected flood risk warnings from climate advisers. *The Guardian*, 9 December. Available at: https://www.theguardian.com/environment/2015/dec/09/cameron-government-rejected-flood-risk-warnings-from-climate-advisers (archived at https://perma.cc/62SU-VRN3) (Accessed: 8 August 2022)

43 Khan, M E (2005) The death toll from natural disasters: The role of income, geography and institutions. *The Review of Economics and Statistics*, 87(2), 271–284

44 UNDP (United Nations Development Programme) (2004) Human development report 2004: Cultural liberty in today's diverse world. New York

45 Mochizuki, J, Mechler, R, Hochrainer-Stigler, S, Keating, A & Williges, K (2014) Revisiting the 'disaster and development' debate – toward a broader understanding of macroeconomic risk and resilience. *Climate Risk Management*, 3, 39–54; World Economic Forum (2019b) The world's coastal cities are going under. Here's how some are fighting back. Available at: https://www.weforum.org/agenda/2019/01/the-world-s-coastal-cities-are-going-under-here-is-how-some-are-fighting-back/ (archived at https://perma.cc/9NCR-LL7D)(Accessed: 8 August 2022)

46 https://www.weforum.org/reports/the-global-risks-report-2019/ (archived at https://perma.cc/B22W-J6KK)

47 Ackroyd, P (2001) *London: The biography*. Random House

48 History of London (nd) In brief – late Victorian London. Available at: https://www.thehistoryoflondon.co.uk/in-brief-late-victorian-london/ (archived at https://perma.cc/L3N6-F3LZ) (Accessed: 8 August 2022)

49 London Transport Museum (nd) On the surface 1900–1945. Available at https://www.ltmuseum.co.uk/visit/museum-guide/surface-1900-1945#:~:text=In%201900%2C%20almost%20every%20vehicle,were%20unreliable%20and%20short%2Dlived (archived at https://perma.cc/C94T-2W7R) (Accessed: 8 August 2022)

50 Feen, R H (1996) Keeping the balance: Ancient Greek philosophical concerns with population and environment. *Population and Environment*, 17(6), 447–458

51 Godschalk, D R (2003) Urban hazard mitigation: Creating resilient cities. *Natural Hazards Review*, 4(3)

52 Cairncross, A (1998) *Living with the century*. iynx Publishing; Gandy, M (2006) Planning, anti-planning, and the infrastructure crisis facing metropolitan Lagos. *Cities in contemporary Africa, 247264*. New York: Palgrave Macmillan

53 Meadows, D H (1972) The limits to growth: A report to the Club of Rome. Available at: http://ask-force.org/web/Global-Warming/Meadows-Limits-to-Growth-Short-1972.pdf (archived at https://perma.cc/7B2J-AQS6) (Accessed: 8 August 2022)

54 Meadows, D H (1972) The limits to growth: A report to the Club of Rome. Available at: http://ask-force.org/web/Global-Warming/Meadows-Limits-to-Growth-Short-1972.pdf (archived at https://perma.cc/7B2J-AQS6) (Accessed: 8 August 2022)

55 Meadows, D H (1972) The limits to growth: A report to the Club of Rome. Available at: http://ask-force.org/web/Global-Warming/Meadows-Limits-to-Growth-Short-1972.pdf (archived at https://perma.cc/7B2J-AQS6) (Accessed: 8 August 2022)

56 Mitchell, J K (1999) Megacities and natural disasters: A comparative analysis. *GeoJournal*, 49(2), 137–142; Lavalle, C, Demicheli, L, Turchini, M, Casals-Carrasco, P & Niederhuber, M (2001) Monitoring megacities: The Murbandy/Moland approach. *Development in Practice*, 11(2–3), 350–357

57 Gandy, M (2006) *Planning, anti-planning, and the infrastructure crisis facing metropolitan Lagos. Cities in contemporary Africa*, 247–264. New York: Palgrave Macmillan

58 Lavalle, C, Demicheli, L, Turchini, M, Casals-Carrasco, P & Niederhuber, M (2001) Monitoring megacities: The Murbandy/Moland approach. *Development in Practice*, 11(2–3), 350–357

59 Minkel, J R (2008) The 2003 northeast blackout-five years later. Available at: https://www.scientificamerican.com/article/2003-blackout-five-years-later/ (archived at https://perma.cc/NBP8-MD2F) (Accessed: 8 August 2022)

60 Kingston, J (2014) Mismanaging risk and the Fukushima nuclear crisis. In *Human security and Japan's triple disaster* (pp. 51–70). Routledge

61 Busby, J W , Baker, K, Bazilian, M D, Gilbert, A Q, Grubert, E, Rai, V, Rhodes, J D, Shidore, S, Smith, C A & Webber, M E (2021) Cascading risks: Understanding the 2021 winter blackout in Texas. *Energy Research & Social Science*, 77, 102–106

62 Mitchell, J K (1999) Megacities and natural disasters: A comparative analysis. *GeoJournal*, 49(2), 137–142

63 UN Habitat (2020) The new urban agenda illustrated, United Nations human settlements programme. Available at: https://unhabitat.org/sites/default/files/2020/12/nua_handbook_14dec2020_2.pdf (archived at https://perma.cc/9QHQ-DQQX)

64 Braun, B & Aßheuer, T (2011) Floods in megacity environments: Vulnerability and coping strategies of slum dwellers in Dhaka/Bangladesh. *Natural Hazards*, 58(2), 771–787

65 Turner, B T, Matsond, P A, McCarthye, J J, Corellf, R W, Christensend, L, Eckleyg, N, Hovelsrud-Brodah, G K, Kaspersonb, J X, Kaspersonb, R E, Luersd, A & Martellof, M L (2003) Illustrating the coupled human–environment system for vulnerability analysis: Three case studies. *PNAS*, 100(14)

66 Mitchell, J K (1999) Megacities and natural disasters: A comparative analysis. *GeoJournal*, 49(2), 137–142

67 Braun, B & Aßheuer, T (2011) Floods in megacity environments: Vulnerability and coping strategies of slum dwellers in Dhaka/Bangladesh. *Natural Hazards*, 58(2), 771–787

68 Mitchell, J K (1999). Megacities and natural disasters: A comparative analysis. *GeoJournal*, 49(2), 137–142

69 ASLCG (2021) Missing in action: Responding to Australia's climate and security failure. Available at: https://www.aslcg.org/missinginaction/ (Accessed: 8 August 2022); UN Habitat (2022) Envisaging the future of cities, 2022. United Nations human settlements programme. Available at: https://unhabitat.org/sites/default/files/2022/06/wcr_2022.pdf (archived at https://perma.cc/H5TP-LMAR)

70 Mitchell, J K (1999) Megacities and natural disasters: A comparative analysis. *GeoJournal*, 49(2), 137–142

71 IPCC (2022) Summary for policymakers (H-O Pörtner, D C Roberts, E S Poloczanska, K Mintenbeck, M Tignor, A Alegría, M Craig, S Langsdorf, S Löschke, V Möller, A Okem (eds.)) Climate change 2022: Impacts, adaptation, and vulnerability. Contribution of Working Group II to the Sixth Assessment Report of the Intergovernmental Panel on Climate Change. Cambridge University Press

72 UCCRN (2018) The future we don't want: How climate change could impact the world's greatest cities. Urban Climate Change Research Network. Available at: https://www.c40.org/wp-content/uploads/2021/08/1789_Future_We_Dont_Want_Report_1.4_hi-res_120618.original.pdf (archived at https://perma.cc/54YB-QQ3Q) (Accessed: 8 August 2022)

73 ASLCG (2021) Missing in action: Responding to Australia's climate and security failure. Available at: www.aslcg.org/wp-content/uploads/2021/09/ASLCG_MIA_Report.pdf (archived at https://perma.cc/N6AH-4FEJ) (Accessed: 8 August 2022)

74 WMO (2018) WMO statement on the state of the global climate in 2018. Available at: https://library.wmo.int/doc_num.php?explnum_id=5789 (archived at https://perma.cc/PWX6-258N) (Accessed: 8 August 2022); IPCC (2022) Summary for policymakers (H-O Pörtner, D C Roberts, E S Poloczanska, K Mintenbeck, M Tignor, A Alegría, M Craig, S Langsdorf, S Löschke, V Möller, A Okem (eds.)). Climate change 2022: Impacts, adaptation, and vulnerability. Contribution of Working Group II to the Sixth Assessment Report of the Intergovernmental Panel on Climate Change. Cambridge University Press

75 WMO (2018) WMO statement on the state of the global climate in 2018. Available at: https://library.wmo.int/doc_num.php?explnum_id=5789 (archived at https://perma.cc/PWX6-258N) (Accessed: 8 August 2022)

76 Met Office (2022) Record breaking temperatures for the UK. Met Office, 19 July. Available at: https://www.metoffice.gov.uk/about-us/press-office/news/weather-and-climate/2022/red-extreme-heat-warning-ud (archived at https://perma.cc/7VX3-ASKW) (Accessed: 8 August 2022); Ridgewell, H (2021)'Lucifer' heat wave scorches Mediterranean; dozens die in wildfires (12 August). https://www.voanews.com/a/europe_lucifer-heat-wave-scorches-mediterranean-dozens-die-wildfires/6209502.html (archived at https://perma.cc/78KJ-NDTA); Bawden, T (2021) A 'Lucifer' style heatwave of nearly 50C will happen every three years in Europe, says Met Office (3 November). https://inews.co.uk/news/environment/lucifer-heatwave-50c-happen-every-three-years-climate-change-europe-1280225 (archived at https://perma.cc/X5SQ-BGWY); BBC News (2021) Canada weather: Dozens dead as heatwave shatters records (30 June). https://www.bbc.co.uk/news/world-us-canada-57654133 (archived at https://perma.cc/2FDK-4K7T)

77 Mathiesen, K, Weuse, Z & Haeck, P (2022) Europe's not ready for a hotter world. https://www.politico.eu/article/europe-climate-change-global-warming-heat-wave-adaptation/ (archived at https://perma.cc/9ZPT-HP2X)

78 Google Cloud (2022) Multiple Cloud products experiencing elevated error rates, latencies or service unavailability in europe-west2. https://status.cloud.google.com/incidents/fmEL9i2fArADKawkZAa2 (archived at https://perma.cc/7NCF-KT3W)

79 Multiple Services | UK South (London) | CN-764094. https://ocistatus.oraclecloud.com/#/incidents/ocid1.oraclecloudincident.oc1.phx.amaaaaaavwew44aa7zoskanlspjh4ll6wxhwxrbkbed4d4cnupxexzqzvlyq (archived at https://perma.cc/9R4E-4WJJ)

80 UCCRN (2018) The future we don't want: How climate change could impact the world's greatest cities. Urban Climate Change Research Network. Available at: https://www.c40.org/wp-content/uploads/2021/08/1789_Future_We_Dont_Want_Report_1.4_hi-res_120618.original.pdf (archived at https://perma.cc/54YB-QQ3Q) (Accessed: 8 August 2022); Ratcliffe R (2022) Indonesia names new capital Nusantara, replacing sinking Jakarta. *The Guardian*, 18 January. https://www.theguardian.com/world/2022/jan/18/indonesia-names-new-capital-nusantara-replacing-sinking-city-of-jakarta (archived at https://perma.cc/56WW-EAKY)

81 World Economic Forum (2019a) The Global Risks Report 2019. Available at: https://www.weforum.org/reports/the-global-risks-report-2019 (archived at https://perma.cc/B22W-J6KK) (Accessed: 8 August 2022)

82 King Canute (nd) King Canute and the tide. Available at: https://en.wikipedia.org/wiki/King_Canute_and_the_tide (archived at https://perma.cc/S4XB-L4HL) (Accessed: 8 August 2022)

83 CBS (2017) Sea change: How the Dutch confront the rise of the oceans. CBS News, 21 May. Available at: https://www.cbsnews.com/news/sea-change-how-the-dutch-confront-the-rise-of-the-oceans/ (archived at https://perma.cc/WGF2-RJG7) (Accessed: 8 August 2022)

84 Kimmelman, M (2017) The Dutch have solutions to rising seas. The world is watching. *The New York Times*, 15 June. Available at: https://www.nytimes.com/interactive/2017/06/15/world/europe/climate-change-rotterdam.html (archived at https://perma.cc/QTN6-LLUN) (Accessed: 8 August 2022)

85 World Economic Forum (2019) The world's coastal cities are going under. Here's how some are fighting back. Available at: https://www.weforum.org/agenda/2019/01/the-world-s-coastal-cities-are-going-under-here-is-how-some-are-fighting-back/ (archived at https://perma.cc/9NCR-LL7D) (Accessed: 8 August 2022)

86 Zevenbergen, C, Fu, D & Pathirana, A (2018) Transitioning to sponge cities: Challenges and opportunities to address urban water problems in China. *Water*, 10(9), 1230

87 Arnbjerg-Nielsen, K (2011) Past, present, and future design of urban drainage systems with focus on Danish experiences. *Water Science and Technology*, 63(3), 527–535; Shannon, K (2008) Water urbanism: Hydrological infrastructure as an urban frame in Vietnam. Water and urban development paradigms, 73–84. CRC Press; van Rooijen, D J, Turral, H & Wade Biggs, T (2005) Sponge city: Water balance of mega-city water use and wastewater use in Hyderabad, India. *Irrigation and Drainage: The Journal of the International Commission on Irrigation and Drainage*, 54(S1), S81–S91; Mitchell, V G (2006) Applying integrated urban water management concepts: A review of Australian experience. *Environmental Management*, 37(5), 589–605; Tarlock, A D (2012) United States flood control policy: The incomplete transition from the illusion of total protection to risk management. *Duke Envtl. L. & Pol'y F.*, 23, 151

88 Seymoar, N K, Mullard, Z & Winstanley, M (2009) *City-to-city learning*. International Centre for Sustainable Communities: Vancouver, BC, Canada

89 Tarlock, A D (2012) United States flood control policy: The incomplete transition from the illusion of total protection to risk management. *Duke Envtl. L. & Pol'y F.*, 23, 151

90 UN Habitat (2022) Envisaging the future of cities, 2022. United Nations Human Settlements Programme. Available at: https://unhabitat.org/sites/default/files/2022/06/wcr_2022.pdf (archived at https://perma.cc/H5TP-LMAR)

91 UN Habitat (2022) Envisaging the future of cities, 2022. United Nations Human Settlements Programme. Available at: https://unhabitat.org/sites/default/files/2022/06/wcr_2022.pdf (archived at https://perma.cc/H5TP-LMAR)

92 Dodman, D, Leck, H, Rusca, M & Colenbrander, S (2017) African urbanisation and urbanism: Implications for risk accumulation and reduction. *International Journal of Disaster Risk Reduction*, 26, 7–15. https://doi.org/10.1016/j.ijdrr.2017.06.029 (archived at https://perma.cc/6WCL-6AXU)

93 Dodman, D, Leck, H, Rusca, M & Colenbrander, S (2017) African urbanisation and urbanism: Implications for risk accumulation and reduction. *International Journal of Disaster Risk Reduction*, 26, 7–15. https://doi.org/10.1016/j.ijdrr.2017.06.029 (archived at https://perma.cc/6WCL-6AXU)

94 Currie, P K & Musango, J K (2017) African urbanization: Assimilating urban metabolism into sustainability discourse and practice. *Journal of Industrial Ecology*, 21(5), 1262–1276. https://doi.org/10.1111/jiec.12517 (archived at https://perma.cc/XB6S-SV6H)

95 Elgot, J (2016) How David Cameron's language on refugees has provoked anger. 27 January. Available at: https://www.theguardian.com/uk-news/2016/jan/27/david-camerons-bunch-of-migrants-quip-is-latest-of-several-such-comments (archived at https://perma.cc/8TQ6-8E53) (Accessed: 8 August 2022)

Further reading

Ackroyd, P (2001) *London: The biography*. Random House

Arnbjerg-Nielsen, K (2011) Past, present, and future design of urban drainage systems with focus on Danish experiences. *Water Science and Technology*, 63(3), 527–535

ASLCG (2021) Missing in action: responding to Australia's climate and security failure. Available at: www.aslcg.org/wp-content/uploads/2021/09/ASLCG_MIA_Report.pdf (archived at https://perma.cc/N6AH-4FEJ) (Accessed: 8 August 2022)

Bawden, T (2021)A 'Lucifer' style heatwave of nearly 50C will happen every three years in Europe, says Met Office. https://inews.co.uk/news/environment/lucifer-heatwave-50c-happen-every-three-years-climate-change-europe-1280225 (archived at https://perma.cc/X5SQ-BGWY), INews, 3 November

BBC (2021) Europe's floods: Lessons from German tragedy. 29 October. Available at: https://www.bbc.co.uk/news/world-europe-58992093 (archived at https://perma.cc/CLX4-GXEG) (Accessed: 8 August 2022)

BBC News (2021) Canada weather: Dozens dead as heatwave shatters records. 30 June. https://www.bbc.co.uk/news/world-us-canada-57654133 (archived at https://perma.cc/2FDK-4K7T)

Braun, B & Aßheuer, T (2011) Floods in megacity environments: Vulnerability and coping strategies of slum dwellers in Dhaka/Bangladesh. *Natural Hazards*, 58(2), 771–787

Bugliarello, G (1999) Megacities and the developing world. *Urbanization & Engineering*, 29(4), 19–26

Busby, J W, Baker, K, Bazilian, M D, Gilbert, A Q, Grubert, E, Rai, V, Rhodes, J D, Shidore, S, Smith, C A and Webber, M E (2021) Cascading risks: Understanding the 2021 winter blackout in Texas. *Energy Research & Social Science*, 77, 102–106

Butsch, C, Kraas, F, Namperumal, S and Peters, G (2016) Risk governance in the megacity Mumbai/India: A complex adaptive system perspective. *Habitat International*, 54(2), 100–111

Cairncross, A (1998) *Living with the century*. iynx Publishing

Carrington, D & Wintour, P (2015) Cameron government rejected flood risk warnings from climate advisers. *The Guardian*, 9 December. Available at: https://www.theguardian.com/environment/2015/dec/09/cameron-government-rejected-flood-risk-warnings-from-climate-advisers (archived at https://perma.cc/62SU-VRN3) (Accessed: 8 August 2022)

CBS (2017) Sea change: How the Dutch confront the rise of the oceans. CBS News, 21 May. Available at: https://www.cbsnews.com/news/sea-change-how-the-dutch-confront-the-rise-of-the-oceans/ (archived at https://perma.cc/WGF2-RJG7) (Accessed: 8 August 2022)

Currie, P K & Musango, J K (2017) African urbanization: Assimilating urban metabolism into sustainability discourse and practice. *Journal of Industrial Ecology*, 21(5), 1262–1276. https://doi.org/10.1111/jiec.12517 (archived at https://perma.cc/XB6S-SV6H)

Dodman, D, Leck, H, Rusca, M & Colenbrander, S (2017) African urbanisation and urbanism: Implications for risk accumulation and reduction. *International Journal of Disaster Risk Reduction*, 26, 7–15. https://doi.org/10.1016/j.ijdrr.2017.06.029 (archived at https://perma.cc/6WCL-6AXU)

Donald, J (2021) Winter Storm Uri 2021: The economic impact of the storm. Available at: https://comptroller.texas.gov/economy/fiscal-notes/2021/oct/winter-storm-impact.php (archived at https://perma.cc/MC2P-QYNB) (Accessed: 8 August 2022)

Ehrlich, P (1968) The population bomb. Available at: https://projectavalon.net/The_Population_Bomb_Paul_Ehrlich.pdf (archived at https://perma.cc/LGR3-C67F) (Accessed: 8 August 2022)

Elgot, J (2016) How David Cameron's language on refugees has provoked anger. 27 January. Available at: https://www.theguardian.com/uk-news/2016/jan/27/david-camerons-bunch-of-migrants-quip-is-latest-of-several-such-comments (archived at https://perma.cc/8TQ6-8E53) (Accessed: 8 August 2022)

Feen, R H (1996) Keeping the balance: Ancient Greek philosophical concerns with population and environment. *Population and Environment*, 17(6), 447–458

Gandy, M (2006) Planning, anti-planning, and the infrastructure crisis facing metropolitan Lagos. *Cities in contemporary Africa*, 247–264. New York: Palgrave Macmillan

Godschalk, D R (2003) Urban hazard mitigation: Creating resilient cities. *Natural Hazards Review*, 4(3)

Gottmann, J (1961) *Megalopolis: The urbanized northeastern seaboard of the United States* (Vol. 8). New York: Twentieth Century Fund

Harvey, F (2016) Build on flood plains despite the risks, say UK government advisers. *The Guardian*, 27 January. Available at: https://www.theguardian.com/environment/2016/jan/27/homes-and-companies-should-be-built-on-flood-plains-despite-risks-says-panel (archived at https://perma.cc/79Z7-KMFW)

History of London (nd) In brief – late Victorian London. Available at: https://www.thehistoryoflondon.co.uk/in-brief-late-victorian-london/ (archived at https://perma.cc/L3N6-F3LZ) (Accessed: 8 August 2022)

IDNDR (1999) International Decade for Natural Disaster Reduction. Proceedings, Programme Forum

IPCC (2014) Climate change 2014: Synthesis report. Contribution of Working Groups I, II and III to the Fifth Assessment Report of the Intergovernmental Panel on Climate Change. IPCC, Geneva, Switzerland

IPCC (2022) Summary for policymakers (H-O Pörtner, D C Roberts, E S Poloczanska, K Mintenbeck, M Tignor, A Alegría, M Craig, S Langsdorf, S Löschke, V Möller, A Okem (eds.)) Climate change 2022: Impacts, adaptation, and vulnerability. Contribution of Working Group II to the Sixth Assessment Report of the Intergovernmental Panel on Climate Change. Cambridge University Press

Jowit, J (2011) Paul Ehrlich, a prophet of global population doom who is gloomier than ever. *The Guardian*, 23 October. Available at: https://www.theguardian.com/environment/2011/oct/23/paul-ehrlich-global-collapse-warning (archived at https://perma.cc/NG9S-9KDA) (Accessed: 8 August 2022)

Khan, M E (2005) The death toll from natural disasters: The role of income, geography and institutions. *The Review of Economics and Statistics*, 87(2), 271–284

Kimmelman, M (2017) The Dutch have solutions to rising seas. The world is watching. *The New York Times*, 15 June. Available at: https://www.nytimes.com/interactive/2017/06/15/world/europe/climate-change-rotterdam.html (archived at https://perma.cc/QTN6-LLUN) (Accessed: 8 August 2022)

King Canute (n.d.) King Canute and the tide. Available at: https://en.wikipedia.org/wiki/King_Canute_and_the_tide (archived at https://perma.cc/S4XB-L4HL) (Accessed: 8 August 2022)

Kingston, J (2014) Mismanaging risk and the Fukushima nuclear crisis. In *Human security and Japan's triple disaster* (pp. 51–70). Routledge

Kraas, F (2007) Megacities and global change in East, Southeast and South Asia. *Asien*, 103(4), 9–22

Lavalle, C, Demicheli, L, Turchini, M, Casals-Carrasco, P & Niederhuber, M (2001) Monitoring megacities: the Murbandy/Moland approach. *Development in Practice*, 11(2–3), 350–357

London Transport Museum (n.d.) On the surface 1900–1945. Available at: https://www.ltmuseum.co.uk/visit/museum-guide/surface-1900-1945#:~:text=In%201900%2C%20almost%20every%20vehicle,were%20unreliable%20and%20short%2Dlived (archived at https://perma.cc/C94T-2W7R) (Accessed: 8 August 2022)

Mahmood, S A I (2011) Air pollution kills 15,000 Bangladeshis each year: The role of public administration and governments integrity. *Journal of Public Administration and Policy Research*, 3(4), 129–140

Meadows, D H (1972) The limits to growth: A report to the Club of Rome. Available at: http://ask-force.org/web/Global-Warming/Meadows-Limits-to-Growth-Short-1972.pdf (archived at https://perma.cc/7B2J-AQS6) (Accessed: 8 August 2022)

Met Office (2022) Record breaking temperatures for the UK. Met Office, 19 July. Available at: https://www.metoffice.gov.uk/about-us/press-office/news/weather-and-climate/2022/red-extreme-heat-warning-ud (archived at https://perma.cc/7VX3-ASKW) (Accessed: 8 August 2022)

Minkel, J R (2008) The 2003 northeast blackout-five years later. Available at: https://www.scientificamerican.com/article/2003-blackout-five-years-later/ (archived at https://perma.cc/NBP8-MD2F) (Accessed: 8 August 2022)

Mitchell, J K (1999) Megacities and natural disasters: A comparative analysis. *GeoJournal*, 49(2), 137–142

Mitchell, V G (2006) Applying integrated urban water management concepts: A review of Australian experience. *Environmental Management*, 37(5), 589–605.

Mochizuki, J, Mechler, R, Hochrainer-Stigler, S, Keating, A & Williges, K (2014) Revisiting the 'disaster and development' debate – toward a broader understanding of macroeconomic risk and resilience. *Climate Risk Management*, 3, 39–54

Mumford, L (2016) The culture of cities. Open Road Media. Available at: https://monoskop.org/images/5/5a/Mumford_Lewis_The_Culture_of_Cities.pdf (archived at https://perma.cc/G25X-NSFM) (Accessed: 8 August 2022)

Nagashima, C (1967) Megalopolis in Japan. Ekistics; *Reviews on the Problems and Science of Human Settlements*, 24(140), 6–14

National Geographic (2021) Sarah Gibbens. Experts fear Germany's deadly floods are a glimpse into climate future. Available at: https://www.nationalgeographic.com/environment/article/experts-fear-germany-deadly-floods-glimpse-into-climate-future (archived at https://perma.cc/3SUH-XAEY) (Accessed: 8 August 2022)

The Observer (2015) Europe needs many more babies to avert a population disaster. *The Observer*, 23 August. Available at: https://www.theguardian.com/world/2015/aug/23/baby-crisis-europe-brink-depopulation-disaster (archived at https://perma.cc/H9ZV-N4VH) (Accessed: 8 August 2022)

Parker, C (2022) Japan records its largest natural population decline as births fall. *Washington Post*, 3 June. Available at: https://www.washingtonpost.com/world/2022/06/03/japan-low-births-population-decline-2021/ (archived at https://perma.cc/AL2L-QWSP)

Pearce, F (2018) Is the way we think about overpopulation racist? *The Guardian*, 19 March. Available at: https://www.theguardian.com/cities/2018/mar/19/overpopulation-cities-environment-developing-world-racist-paul-ehrlich (archived at https://perma.cc/P5MC-2L4M) (Accessed: 8 August 2022)

Ridgewell, H (2021)'Lucifer' heat wave scorches Mediterranean; dozens die in wildfires. VOA News, 12 August https://www.voanews.com/a/europe_lucifer-heat-wave-scorches-mediterranean-dozens-die-wildfires/6209502.html (archived at https://perma.cc/78KJ-NDTA)

RS21 (2021) Mark Bergfeld. Flooding in Germany is a man-made disaster. Available at: https://www.rs21.org.uk/2021/07/23/flooding-in-germany-is-a-man-made-disaster/ (archived at https://perma.cc/9ZRM-227L) (Accessed: 8 August 2022)

Sassen, S (2013) *The global city: New York, London, Tokyo*. Princeton University Press.

Seymoar, N K, Mullard, Z & Winstanley, M (2009) *City-to-city learning*. International Centre for Sustainable Communities: Vancouver, BC, Canada

Shannon, K (2008) Water urbanism: Hydrological infrastructure as an urban frame in Vietnam. *Water and Urban Development Paradigms*, 73–84. CRC Press

Statistics Times. https://statisticstimes.com/demographics/world-urban-population.php (archived at https://perma.cc/Q5LG-EVQR) https://population.un.org/wup/Download/ (archived at https://perma.cc/U8SU-FU5F)

Tarlock, A D (2012) United States flood control policy: The incomplete transition from the illusion of total protection to risk management. *Duke Envtl. L. & Pol'y F.*, 23, 151

Taylor, P (2004) *World city network: A global urban analysis*. London: Routledge

Turner, B T, Matsond, P A, McCarthye, J J, Corellf, R W, Christensend, L, Eckleyg, N, Hovelsrud-Brodah, G K, Kaspersonb, J X, Kaspersonb, R E, Luersd, A & Martellof, M L (2003) Illustrating the coupled human–environment system for vulnerability analysis: Three case studies. *PNAS*, 100(14)

UCCRN (2018) The future we don't want: How climate change could impact the world's greatest cities. Urban Climate Change Research Network. Available at: https://www.c40.org/wp-content/uploads/2021/08/1789_Future_We_Dont_Want_Report_1.4_hi-res_120618.original.pdf (archived at https://perma.cc/54YB-QQ3Q) (Accessed: 8 August 2022)

Uitto, J I (1998) The geography of disaster vulnerability in megacities: A theoretical framework. *Applied Geography*, 18(1), 7–16

UN (1987) Population growth and policies in megacities. Available at: https://www.un.org/development/desa/pd/sites/www.un.org.development.desa.pd/files/files/documents/2020/Jan/un_1987_population_growth_and_policies_in_megacities_-_bangkok.pdf (archived at https://perma.cc/R4A7-Z56V) (Accessed: 8 August 2022)

UN (1992) Agenda 21. United Nations Conference on Environment and Development, Rio de Janeiro, Brazil, 3–14 June 1992. Available at: https://sustainabledevelopment.un.org/content/documents/Agenda21.pdf (archived at https://perma.cc/Y77U-36S5) (Accessed: 8 August 2022)

UN (2018) Department of Economic and Social Affairs Population Dynamics World Urban Population Dynamics 2018. https://population.un.org/wup/Download/ (archived at https://perma.cc/U8SU-FU5F)

UN DESA (2015) Below-replacement fertility in China: Policy response is long overdue. United Nations Department of Economic and Social Affairs. Available at: https://www.un.org/en/development/desa/population/events/pdf/expert/24/Policy_Briefs/PB_China.pdf (archived at https://perma.cc/NXG9-PW73) (Accessed: 8 August 2022)

UN DESA, Population division (2016) The world's cities in 2016 – data booklet. United Nations Department of Economic and Social Affairs

UN DESA (2018a) The world's cities in 2018 – data booklet. United Nations Department of Economic and Social Affairs. Available at: https://www.un.org/en/development/desa/population/publications/pdf/urbanization/the_worlds_cities_in_2018_data_booklet.pdf (archived at https://perma.cc/U4FZ-K8FZ)

UN DESA (2018b) World urbanization prospects: The 2018 revision. New York, United Nations. Available at: https://population.un.org/wup/Publications/Files/WUP2018-Report.pdf (archived at https://perma.cc/MS2C-Y3ZE)

UN DESA (2022) World population prospects 2022: Summary of results. United Nations Department of Economic and Social Affairs

UN Habitat (2020) The new urban agenda illustrated, United Nations human settlements programme. Available at: https://unhabitat.org/sites/default/files/2020/12/nua_handbook_14dec2020_2.pdf (archived at https://perma.cc/9QHQ-DQQX)

UN Habitat (2022) Envisaging the future of cities, 2022. United Nations human settlements programme. Available at: https://unhabitat.org/sites/default/files/2022/06/wcr_2022.pdf (archived at https://perma.cc/H5TP-LMAR)

UNDP (United Nations Development Programme) (2004) Human Development Report 2004: Cultural Liberty in Today's Diverse World. New York

van Rooijen, D J, Turral, H & Wade Biggs, T (2005) Sponge city: Water balance of mega-city water use and wastewater use in Hyderabad, India. *Irrigation and Drainage: The Journal of the International Commission on Irrigation and Drainage*, 54(S1), S81–S91

Vedula, A (2007) Blueprint and reality: Navi Mumbai, the city of the 21st century. *Habitat International*, 31(1), 12–23

WHO (2010) Urbanization and health. https://www.scielosp.org/pdf/bwho/2010.v88n4/245-246 (archived at https://perma.cc/S3HY-PZSN)

WMO (2018) WMO statement on the state of the global climate in 2018. Available at: https://library.wmo.int/doc_num.php?explnum_id=5789 (archived at https://perma.cc/PWX6-258N) (Accessed: 8 August 2022)

World Economic Forum (2019a) The Global Risks Report 2019. Available at: https://www.weforum.org/reports/the-global-risks-report-2019 (archived at https://perma.cc/B22W-J6KK) (Accessed: 8 August 2022)

World Economic Forum (2019b) The world's coastal cities are going under. Here's how some are fighting back. Available at: https://www.weforum.org/agenda/2019/01/the-world-s-coastal-cities-are-going-under-here-is-how-some-are-fighting-back/ (archived at https://perma.cc/9NCR-LL7D) (Accessed: 8 August 2022)

Zevenbergen, C, Fu, D & Pathirana, A (2018) Transitioning to sponge cities: Challenges and opportunities to address urban water problems in China. *Water*, 10(9), 1230

10

Creating the new urban order

The issue of future urban development is not simply one of housing policies, planning laws and the need to manage basic functions and infrastructures. If significant change and meaningful impact are to be achieved, it needs a much more holistic approach, seeing the urban centres as part of a wider ecosphere in which they play a part but equally have a high level of dependency.[1] Urban centres need to become a dynamic component contributing to the health of the biosphere, rather than draining and destroying it.[2] Internally, they also need to reflect the needs of all their citizens, as well as respecting the needs and challenges of the dynamic interplay between the myriad stakeholders involved with every aspect of urban life.

In order to create a sustainable level of management and functionality, the UN Habitat 2020 Report highlights four areas that need to be addressed.[3] The first is social sustainability, which requires the whole population to be taken into account rather than being limited to the needs and demands of those living within structured and managed settlements. This 'all of society' approach would ensure that all voices are heard and that all sections of the population would feel ownership and engagement in the development of their own living environments.

Economic sustainability covers the needs for the urban population to be economically active, which in turn will lessen the burden on the city or state to support them but will contribute to increased health and prosperity across multiple social sectors. Without a viable economy that can support the population in productive employment, there is always the danger of both economic collapse and social unrest, both of which lead to increasing cycles of decay and potential destruction.

The third strand is environmental sustainability, in that the city has often been seen as draining the environment of its resources rather than contributing to its long-term health and sustainability. Cities, in fact, offer an opportunity for urban planning that can have a significant impact not just on the eco-footprint of their activities but on the health and wellbeing, both physical and psychological, of their inhabitants. The sudden shock of the cessation of much of the world's human activities in the immediate aftermath of the global lock-down at the start of Covid-19 in March 2020 gave a dramatic indication of how quickly the urban landscape can change – for the better – if the human part of the equation stops its production of pollution. Within days, air quality had increased, pollution had largely disappeared, water quality in the rivers had improved, and wildlife was returning in terms of both insects and mammals. It was a clear, if unexpected, lesson that actually there are things that we can do which would have a significant impact on many of the issues that we consider as critical but are thought to be without practical solutions.

The development of a sustainable urban framework that recognizes the viability of eco-friendly and non-destructive activity and integrates that into its own planning and development models is perhaps one of the most impactful approaches that can be taken in terms of creating urban environments that are healthy, progressive and supportive, and which in turn have an impact on the health of the planet as a whole.

The fourth strand of the new urban order is spatial sustainability, which refers to the physical attributes of the city that either encourage and support or act as a barrier and disincentive to social inclusivity. For a city to be viable in the long term, it needs to ensure that nobody is left behind. It is the ability to build a societal infrastructure that offers opportunity to everyone and sees all of its activities through the prism of the overarching eco-sphere rather than minority-enabled and empowered sections of the community that live outlier lives, often on the back of as well as in the face of wider suffering. Access to water, transport and jobs is all part of the wider city space. To limit access to those to one part of the population is to have a deleterious effect on the whole population.

Medellin: a model of urban renewal

One city that has exemplified the 'all of society' approach to its development, and at the same time has become a living example of what the impacts of a long-term, sustainable integrated urban development and management policy could look like, is Medellin, in Colombia. It is a living case study of how a comprehensive policy of urban development and social integration has transformed what was by any measure a failing city – as well as one that was infamous as the centre of the narco empire run by Pablo Escobar – and turned it into something that was considered an outstanding example of a global success, one that both instructed and inspired city planners across the world.

In the 1980s the rise of the cocaine economy, personified by Pablo Escobar, meant that Medellin had developed a social, political and economic model that was fully dependent on cocaine production, which created a level of violence that destroyed any semblance of national governance in the city. However, this was not taking place in an environment isolated from historical antecedents. There had been political violence in Colombia from the 1950s, with armed peasant groups formed to protect the rural population from violent land grabs by the ruling classes, which then led to the formation of political guerrilla groups, which continue to play a central role in Colombia's political landscape today. Rapid population growth saw the movement of large numbers of the population from rural to urban centres and a corresponding growth in the unmanaged urban sprawls of the favelas, where running battles between violent paramilitary groups and community self-defence groups led to more than 55,000 deaths between 1990 and 2002[4] and *TIME* magazine calling it 'the most dangerous city in the world'.[5]

The death of Escobar in 1993 created an opportunity for a semblance of normalcy to be returned. Although the cocaine economy was deeply entrenched in every aspect of Medellin life, and with it the competing gangs and militias who used extreme violence to protect their territory and attack others, there was a gradual realization that there were other avenues to social integration and economic progress. The single most significant step was to give the inhabitants of the favelas living on the side of isolated hills, with little access to the jobs being created by the economic success story taking place in the central valley, a way to get from the favelas to the city and thereby become part of the wider economic development that was rapidly taking place.

The introduction of a series of Metrocable ski lift-style transport systems that were then connected to the city's subway system meant that the favelas became part of the urban economic hub and for the first time there was the realistic possibility of participating in the economic life of the city. This of course had to take place in a wider context of political and economic support, as well as the development of the social support and facilities that underpin any successful suburb, but the fact that this was achieved in Medellin, over a period of decades and with the support of multiple successive administrations, is a shining example of what is possible.[6]

The impact of these policies can be seen by the fact that Medellin was awarded the Lee Kuan Yew World City prize in 2016,[7] the Netexplo Smart City Award 2020 (sponsored by UNESCO),[8] and was nominated in multiple sectors for the 2020 World Travel Awards, considered the 'Oscars' of the global tourism industry.[9]

We are increasingly seeing cities as the destination of last resort for those that have been displaced from their homes, whether because of climate change and the associated impacts of flooding and drought, war, political instability or other pressures that have made them make the decision to uproot themselves from the place where they are known and have an identity within their communities, with personal and social networks, to move to places that are foreign, unknown and often actively hostile. Given the pressure on every aspect of human society across the globe it is likely that these pressures will only increase over the coming years, and the need to manage large influxes of outsiders, often without the necessary skills to integrate smoothly into the local population, will create pressures and stresses that will test the ability of social, political, religious and other leaders to set a framework that would be appropriate, sustainable and humane.

Covid-19 brought a dramatic re-evaluation of what cities are, how they function and how we interact with them. By mid-2022, it was clear that cities were returning to their pre-Covid state and that we would need to continue to engage with the challenges that had been part of the urban landscape prior to Covid and which hadn't gone away. However, the UN Habitat World Cities Report 2022 was defiantly upbeat, noting that 'a sense of optimism is returning that the pandemic is providing us with the opportunity to build back differently'.[10]

While we often see our engagement with urban challenges as being defensive – trying to deal with situations that are already sub-optimal and then trying to prevent them from getting worse – the report also paints a more positive vision: 'An optimistic scenario of urban futures that relies on collaborative and effective interventions to tackle multidimensional poverty and inequalities; promote vibrant, resilient, diversified urban economies and productive urban futures; build healthy and thriving cities; strengthen the drive towards green urban futures; promote well-planned and managed urbanization processes; and ensure inclusive digital economies for the future.'[11]

Social sustainability is the necessary ingredient that needs to be included in order to bind all of the other pieces of the puzzle together.[12] If social resilience is not considered, then urban planning is reduced to a mechanistic modelling of planning challenges, without taking into account the chaos and messiness that are characteristic of cities once the issue of human lives is factored in. As with any aspect of complex systems modelling, the issue of social resilience cannot in itself be considered an isolated component but must be seen in the wider context of the social/city interface. At the end of the day, it is the lived experience of the individuals and communities in the city that defines its success.

From 'slums' to 'informal settlements': recognizing the marginalized

For anyone following the discourse concerning the future of cities it is easy to believe that it is one of glass and towers, connectivity, leisure quarters and the ability to intermingle with other residents in well-laid-out river-side walkways and elevated boulevards. The reality for many millions of people of course is very different. In fact, the case could be made that it is the experience of the disempowered urban poor that is the true story of the city as we move into the second quarter of the 21st century.

Whether it is the slums and favelas of the great cities of the south or the social housing projects of the US urban landscape, in parallel with (or at least, hidden behind) the success stories of the cities that have pushed developments in so many ways since the middle of the last century it is the story of poverty, ignorance and despair that characterizes the true soul of the city experience. This is reflected in the figures, where it has been estimated that slums are home to between one quarter and one third of the global urban population, with between 1 and 1.5 billion people living in slum conditions.[13]

The fundamental weakness of much of urban management theory is the fact that the definition of what is a city – and specifically what are the differentiating characteristics between a 'successful' city and a 'failing' city – is something that is almost always seen though the judgemental eyes of the Western observer, which seems to presume that a high-rise urban landscape of steel and glass is modern and successful, while one characterized by informality in all of its activities is failing. This binary differentiation can be classed as modern/primitive, developed/undeveloped, global/non-global.[14]

The categorization of 'good cities' (steel and glass modernism) and 'bad cities' (unmanaged urban sprawls) often extends to a judgement on their citizens, who are seen as lacking the skills or discipline to live in an appropriate way. This attitude, which is extremely judgemental in both its fundamental referencing and its outcomes, sees those unmanaged sprawls as outside of the scope of urban planning and is instead noted merely as a blot, a distraction or an aberration. The ability to recognize the value of both the lived experience and the academic study and theoretical modelling of what can be considered as a 'Southern perspective' is a fundamental requisite if we are to move away from what have traditionally been neo-colonial approaches.[15] This perspective sees the removal of the vision of the slum as something exceptional, outside and separate from the main urban issues, but in fact recognizes the fact that the poverty and environmental degradation associated with such areas are actually fundamental to the understanding of the city in its wider context.[16]

Decline and fall

The rise of the emerging world's megacities has been well documented; it is only relatively recently that the 'third world' experience, and particularly that based on the mega-slums and favelas of the emerging south, has been seen as anything other than 'exceptional'.[17] Under this reading, the accepted model of a major city has implied the integrated management and planned development associated with Europe and North America (and to a lesser degree Asia). The vast unmanaged slums of the third world were therefore considered outliers with no particular significance from an urban theory perspective. In fact, so deeply entrenched is the conceptualization of the global south megacity that '[t]he slum has become the most common itinerary through which the Third World city (i.e. the megacity) is recognized'.[18]

Many of today's dysfunctional megacities had previous lives as well-run – and even model – urban centres, mixing Western-style planned development with a local flavour. But sudden, unmanageable growth rates soon outstripped the capabilities of the governance frameworks. Until the mid-1970s, for example, Lagos was a functioning mid-range city, with a relatively simple management system and few complex challenges.[19] Increased urbanization then led to an expanded demand on its services and infrastructure, triggering a self-perpetuating cycle of failure and institutionalized disenfranchisement. While the growth of the developed world megacities was wealth- and opportunity-driven, in the developing world megacities, those that were attracted to the urban centres were often unskilled and without the support networks that would allow them to achieve even the lowest level of self-sustaining lifestyles. This inevitably led to the emergence of shanties and slums which, together with a culture of endemic urban planning violations, rapidly created a monster that grew beyond the powers of its handlers to control.

The descent of Lagos from a fully functioning (and even thriving) urban African centre to a dysfunctional megacity is an issue of political (non-) governance rather than purely one of urban growth. While it might be difficult to differentiate between the causes and the effects of the descent into 'failing city' status in what is undoubtedly a complex series of closed feedback loops, 'to represent the city as it is today as an inherently "African" condition is to ignore the dysfunctional political and social systems that have arrested the growth of the infrastructure of the city and left it in dire need of help'.[20]

If Lagos were a child she would definitely be described, even by the parents that love her, as having 'challenging behavioural traits'. As the foreword to a 2012 government report put it, 'By the turn of the last century, Lagos had become an international poster child for the doomsayers of the coming urban challenge – with a reputation for overcrowded and squalid living conditions, high rates of crime, poor governance, urban and environmental degradation and transport chaos.'[21] If Dubai or Tokyo can claim to be the vision of the future of the hyper-connected 21st-century city, then Lagos could equally claim to be their darker twin sister, projecting its reflection through a distorting mirror of dysfunctionality and chaos.

Informal settlements: urban hell or vibrant community?

Dharavi settlement in Mumbai is often called the biggest slum in Asia. *Smithsonian* magazine called it 'a vision of urban hell'.[22] There is no management of garbage or sewage, businesses are unmanaged, unplanned and in most cases illegal, and the very air is poisonous. However, later in the article, the point was made that actually, to the people who live there, it was a thriving community, both functional and welcoming to its own citizens, providing them all of the services that they need.[23] Even Prince Charles, visiting one year after the *Smithsonian*, called it 'a model of green development'.[24]

There is the belief that the reason that informal communities are failing to manage themselves in an appropriate manner is because of a lack of personal or political awareness. In fact, it is likely that there is an extremely high degree of organization, collaboration and discipline associated with informal living, but in a way that is neither recognized nor valued by those operating in a more structured environment. Even within slums, there is likely to be a high level of social mobility, with the aspiration to move up through the social strata through one's own efforts.[25]

Once this fact is recognized and accepted, then the nature of the discourse concerning the management of informal settlements is not so much a problem that needs to be either ignored or disappeared (as in urban slum clearances), but rather one of empowerment and enablement, ensuring that those local communities are given the support that would allow them to develop the frameworks that would support their already existing community activities.

However, the danger is that these programmes are designed, imposed and managed from the usual 'high tower' management perspective, where the owner and directors of the programme are often located in the city centre planning office, or just as likely are foreign donors who descend on the communities as part of a formal (and formally managed) delegation to the communities during a flying visit. They either admire the fact that a clinic has been built or bemoan the fact that there is no one with whom they can talk within those communities. It is not surprising that the outcome of such programmes is often that the proposals prepared by external consultants are unworkable and bear little relation to the social and economic realities on the ground.[26]

From slums to urban settlements

Slum is, in every sense of the word, a pejorative term. There is nothing positive about a slum, either as a physical reality or in terms of the lived experience of the millions of inhabitants for whom it is the centre of their home, work, family and every other aspect of their individual and communal lives. It was recognized as early as the 1970s that slum-dwellers were a significant part of the urban environment and that by recognizing both their existence and their rights, particularly in terms of the right to a dignified life and the right to have their voices heard, there would be benefit to every aspect of the urban stakeholders.[27]

The 1976 Conference on Human Settlement established the principle that the residents of global informal settlements had the right to the life aspirations of everyone else – health, safety, access to services and the right to a decent and dignified life.[28] This led directly to the Report of Habitat: United Nations Conference on Human Settlements, which recognized these issues as United Nations principles of basic human rights, including aspects such as employment and access to housing, health services, education and recreation.[29] In the dry language of the reports, UN Habitat defined a slum household in operational terms as lacking one or more of the following indicators: a durable housing structure, access to clean water, access to improved sanitation, sufficient living space and secure tenure.[30] It was often the final condition, meaning that the residents of slums had no legal status, no ownership of their property and no inherent right to be here, that created both the insecurity that impacted their daily lives and the conditions that meant there were neither legal frameworks nor political will from the various responsible authorities to either intervene or to actively support the progressive development of such settlements.[31]

The development of a rights-based approach, recognizing the applicability of those rights to all citizens, whatever their specific living condition, was a move away from the mechanistic approach (characterized by 'the reigning authorities in urban planning, the technocrats and bureaucrats, the statisticians and mathematical modellers who turned their backs upon the ecological and cultural realities of the city in the hope of transferring all its essential activities to the computer'[32]) or a client-based approach, where empowered and enabled agencies (usually from the developed north) would suggest and apply solutions based on their own pre-developed theories or non-engaged observations, rather than on engagement and consultancy with the slum-dwellers themselves.[33]

Almost 40 years after the United Nations report, it was recognized that despite the availability of the experience, knowledge, skills and know-how to create an environment where urban slums could be upgraded and integrated into the wider urban landscape in a positive and progressive way, the growth of slums and other informal settlements was getting worse, particularly in parts of Asia, Sub-Saharan Africa and Latin America.[34] Although cities make up only around 24 per cent of Africa's population, around 72 per cent of urban dwellers are estimated to live in informal slums, and in cities such as Addis Ababa, that rises to 80 per cent of their 3 million citizens.[35] In Cairo, the informal settlements known as *ashwaeyat* are thought to accommodate between 12 million and 17 million inhabitants or about 40–50 per cent of Egypt's urban population and over 20 per cent of the total population.[36]

The role of the urban community

The approaches to slum management can be seen from two perspectives. The first involves upgrading the facilities, infrastructure and overall living experience within the slums, and in parallel to that integrating slums into the wider urban network. The alternative approach sees slums as signs of urban failure that need to be knocked down and their inhabitants rehoused, either in replacement housing in the same area or, in many cases, being moved away from the place where they have roots and connections – communities that in many cases had been built up over generations – and rehoused in some new-build community, often involving soulless high-rise tower blocks where the buildings themselves are often badly built and create social and health hazards even as they are offered as a vision of a shining new future.

It's often the fact that slums are geographically and infrastructurally isolated from the surrounding urban experience that both creates and reinforces their isolation, which in turn creates a feedback loop that continually exacerbates already existing conditions and militates against any positive interventions. The mere fact of opening up streets within the slum environment and creating the streets that connect the slum with the adjacent neighbourhoods would itself create the conditions that would allow greater interaction and ongoing urban development and regeneration.[37] Given the natural tendency of cities to expand, putting a continuous pressure to both develop new areas and to utilize existing resources, what were once marginalized informal settlements can quickly come to be seen as prime locations for urban development or regeneration.

One aspect of slum regeneration that is often overlooked is the fact that rather than being unstructured dystopias based on dysfunctionality, desperation and mere survival, they are in fact thriving communities, with multiple mutually supporting networks that cross lines of class (even within slums, there is a class structure based on comparative wealth, power and influence), race and religion, and have often been developed on a multi-generational basis. This is not confined to the developing world. The seminal work by Michael Young and Peter Willmott on the impact of housing resettlement on a previously marginalized working-class east London community identified many of the same issues concerning support networks and social cohesion – as well as the central role played by women in their role in raising children, holding families and communities together.[38] On the 50th anniversary of its publication, it was called 'arguably the most influential piece of sociology in Britain in the 20th century'.[39]

The desire to destroy slums and start again has been a central theme of the 'slum clearance' school of approach since the issue of urban planning first arose, but it is also clear that this destroys the communal networks that underpin the social fabric at the centre of slum life. There is the paradox that it is exactly those policies that are supposed to be improving the lives of those who are most marginalized that are destroying the underlying social fabric that supports them, their families and their communities in a way that allows them to create a semblance of normalcy and stability in what are otherwise uncaring and potentially chaotic environments.[40]

Given that the model used for slum clearance usually involves some form of high-rise replacement, it has been shown that such transference does in fact create greater economic opportunities, as the residents of those tower blocks have access to the job markets that previously would have been unavailable to them, but there is a significant impact in terms of social cohesion, isolation, alienation and mental health.[41]

Grass roots democracy and empowerment

In the discussion of the problem of informal settlements, the voices of those actually living in them are often ignored or completely overlooked as having anything of significance to say. Over and above that, the fact that they are informal settlements is often seen as a code for implying lawlessness, criminality and either a disinterestedness or inability to integrate into the wider city activities.[42]

However, there is also the issue of the political environment within which social resilience is developed. Power is politics and politics is power, and the issues of ownership and engagement are always political as well as social. There is no point in discussing the advantages or otherwise of social and community inclusion if the political frameworks around which power negotiations are handled mitigate, or even actively deter, such involvement by what might traditionally be considered marginalized communities.[43]

Inclusivity is a multi-perspective issue that features in almost every aspect of urban resilience. It is the function that allows individuals and communities to feel ownership and empowerment in terms of community development and integration on a daily basis, but is also the fundamental quality that is seen in the event that an adverse event were to occur, and the city infrastructure and the services that they provide are themselves stressed into failure. It is at these times that the resilience of the community and the network of communities, as well the relationship with the city management and governance infrastructures, become critical.[44]

It is precisely because slums are informal, have a high level of social integration and are in many cases used to responding to adverse events on a regular basis that makes them resilient.[45] There is a repository of community wisdom that knows how to get through the hard times based on lived experience and group memory. It is precisely these softer aspects of community resilience that are missing in the urban centres that are currently under threat. With no lived memory of similar events, little social cohesion and the lack of a family or tribal community that can act both as a safety net and a source of wisdom and information, the individual is precisely that – alone, isolated and unsupported.

Slum Dwellers International has become globally recognized both as a movement and as a model for the empowerment of informal settlements. Its fundamental principle is that any viable process for supporting and integrating those communities into the wider urban management system – something that would have significant benefits for those wider networks as well as for those living in the informal settlements themselves – needs to have a high level of empowerment, engagement and ownership at the community level.

The growth of the global slum movement

The community empowerment approach sees inclusiveness as a fundamental issue, both for the community as a whole and for the sub-sections within. Market women, landlords, representatives from community development areas and community development councils, religious and social leaders, women and youth groups are part of the discussions prior to decisions being made, the implementation once those decision have been made, and the management of the new processes and structures once the changes have been embedded in the community.[46]

This is in direct contrast to the traditional distant management technocratic approach whereby 'the urban population are regarded as an undisciplined impediment to the rationalization of the city, and planning discourse is pre-occupied with how the city can be controlled or shaped according to a pre-conceived set of technical specifications provided by an array of experts'.[47]

One function of this 'grassroots globalization'[48] has been the development of global networks of informal settlements that match the similar networks of support and mutual empowerment of global cities at political, economic and technological levels. Slum Dwellers International has become a global network of community-based organizations across Africa, Asia and Latin America. It is recognized as creating both a voice and a methodology that enables and empowers local communities to engage with their local authorities but also to be part of a global community of like-minded activists. The fact that there is a recognized model for community engagement and empowerment in and of itself creates the environment whereby informal settlement inhabitants can see themselves as having a say in and ownership of their own issues, rather than being passive, marginalized or completely excluded victims of external policies over which they have neither influence nor control.

The growth of grass roots democracy movements sees the development of internal governance structures, supporting frameworks, individual and community engagement and participation and the development of a cohesive awareness and identity among the participants as a slow, emergent process rather than one focused on fast-return projects that have neither relevance nor roots within the communities that they are targeting. This is often at odds with the desire from both politicians and donors to see quick results, and there is no doubt that 'patience as a long-term political strategy is especially hard to maintain'.[49]

Covid and lessons from the informal urban settlements

Although the impacts of Covid-19 have hit informal settlements around the world to an extent that has been largely ignored in terms of understanding the significance of healthcare, pandemics, social security and similarly related issues, it could paradoxically be the opportunity for a radical revision of what the role of informal settlements is and how they need to be integrated into the wider urban context.[50]

The ability of global urban centres to maintain their functionality – and ensure, as much as possible, their safety and security on both a personal and a corporate level – is indicative of many issues that will be facing cities in the future, including increasingly high-impact adverse weather events, resource squeeze (including access to drinkable water), pollution and the impacts of infrastructural failures that can at any time bring cities to a complete stop. At such times, the differentiation between the privileged and empowered and the marginalized and disenfranchised becomes blurred and in many cases meaningless.

In fact, it may well be that the model of Lagos as discussed earlier in this chapter could set an example of what a city that lives by unstructured micro-negotiations rather than being dependent on state-supplied functions and services could look like. The truth for the vast majority of informal settlement inhabitants is that they are, as a material course, living without amenities, access to services, formal working practices, savings or the wider support networks that those living in more formal settlements expect as a matter of course. Within the informal settlements there is a vast collective memory of dealing with what might be considered crisis conditions for those used to a more structured existence, but which for them are the realities of daily life.[51] In Covid-19, as an example, the directives from central government agencies concerning social distancing and isolation would have little meaning, but there is nevertheless an understanding of how to maintain social activity when disease and pandemics are part of the background environment.[52]

Within such an environment of chaos, infrastructural breakdown and the inability to have a clear understanding of what exactly are the issues, the possible response options or the desired outcomes, it is the attempts to impose centralized directive-based policies (that are then often backed up by increasingly authoritarian policing and control) that create a breakdown in social networks and community-based actions that would have been much more effective in monitoring and responding to such outbreaks. It's the ability to recognize and embrace the informality of such settlements and to act in such a way as to support the local communities rather than bypassing or actively disempowering them that lies at the heart of effective interventions.[53]

'Failing cities' and a template for the future

The modern megacity is widely viewed as in a failing state. However, an alternative view based on his study of Lagos is espoused by R. Koolhaas, who sees Lagos as a self-managing organism within which constant negotiations between micro-communities take place outside of any formal city management framework. For Koolhaas, these daily personal negotiations are not a sign of failed management, but rather 'a developed, extreme paradigmatic case-study of a city at the forefront of globalizing modernity'.[54] In this view, the cutting-edge 'modernity' of developing world megacities should be recognized rather than being judgementally labelled as 'primitive' when measured against the template of 'developed' Western cities.[55]

Lagos and its brethren megacities across the developing global south are not second-rate, primitive recreations of 'real' cities but models of a future post-modern urban reality. The problems that these megacities have been wrestling with for decades are increasingly taking centre stage in even the most advanced cities of the Western world. The issue is no longer how to manage better but rather how to create a more appropriate management system. An adherence to a mechanistic, directive-based polity no longer reflects the hyper-complexity of the modern urban experience. Given the chaotic and free-forming nature of much of megacity life, there is a clear parallel between some of the issues being faced in developing an effective crisis management decision-making framework and the same issues being confronted in megacity management circles. If the megacities of the present are to maintain relevance for the future, Lagos may well be the pathfinder for the journey ahead. If, as the saying goes, within chaos there is opportunity, Lagos undoubtedly has no shortage of the former. From this perspective, 'Lagos is not catching up with us. Rather, we may be catching up with Lagos'.[56]

Into the future

The planning of major cities has been throughout history a mark of the desire to create a new world order that would have benefits for both current populations and future generations. The fact that we can see in the cities of Rome, Athens, Cairo, Alexandra, Baghdad and Beijing a continuous line of urban development and renewal that has lasted for thousands of years is living proof of the durability of the city as both vision and reality.[57]

Canberra (Australia, 1930s), Brasilia (Brazil, 1950s), Abuja (Nigeria, 1970s), the cities of the United Arab Emirates (1970s until today), Nur-Sultan (Kazakhstan, 1990s) are all examples of modern cities that have been developed from the drawing board, building on what at the time were best practices and cutting-edge technology to create what was not just a geographical area or a collection of citizens but a confident statement of national aspirations.

The 'garden cities' of the first half of the 20th century in England were designed to create urban oases of order and tranquillity that would support both the lives and the livelihoods of their populations. Almost a century later they are being used as a model that encompasses both sustainability and localization, concepts that are at the heart of 21st-century urban planning.[58] New Delhi in the 1920s and Nevei Bombay (New Bombay) 50 years later were efforts to create urban centres that were not just offshoots of the mother city but children that would grow and finally usurp them, replacing what was old and chaotic with that which was new, ordered and future-looking.[59] The latest manifestation of that is Gurgaon, a satellite city outside Delhi built entirely by private capital, focusing on IT and technology, high-end commercial, educational infrastructure and high-quality residential areas, designed to attract global institutions that would see them as their natural home.[60] The hyper-futuristic vision of NEOM The Line and the 1 km high Jeddah Tower, both in Saudi Arabia, can be seen as merely the continuation of the human desire to build urban centres that are not just places where people live and work but make a statement about the future of humanity and the abilities of urban planners to create transformational progress in everything that they do.

There is no shortage of dystopian visions of the future, but *New Scientist* magazine ran a series of articles in 2016 predicting life in 2076, identifying a series of positive interventions that could have taken place by then.[61] If we had gone backwards 60 years rather than forwards and looked at life as it was in 1955, and the predictions that people would have made about the distant future world of 2016, it would have had much the same impression. In comparing the worlds 60 years apart from a 1950s' perspective, there were clearly significant differences, but the fundamental underlying truths of human existence were surprisingly little changed. People lived in houses with their families, went to work by car, bus or train, bought food and other things in shops, went to cinemas, sporting events or music concerts for entertainment – in fact, it was pretty much the same life in 2016 as in 1955, with a modern sheen over it. There would have been a worry about population, pollution and inflation, and the fact that the younger generation had lost respect for their elders and their sense of moral responsibility, as there is in every generation, but the surprising thing would be how much things had stayed the same rather than how different they had become.

In the *New Scientist* article, much the same could be said about their vision of the future for 2076. The problem of climate change and the impacts of fossil fuels are still at the top of the list of worries, but technology has been harnessed to find solutions. Clean cities that take carbon dioxide out of the atmosphere have been built in tandem with vast arrays of wind turbines. The sky looks white due to the particles that have been seeded into the sky to protect us from the heat of the sun.

However, it is equally true that the changes that will undoubtedly be produced may not have the level of transformational impact expected, and what appears in headlines may not be reflected in the reality. It is possible that fusion could create cost-free energy – but it is likely that it wouldn't, and even if the possibility existed, then the control by major corporations would still create a profit-making business model around it. Superconductivity, the other source of theoretically free energy, could still be in the future. Artificial intelligence might have superseded human capacities (which is already the case in 2022), but pure computing power doesn't challenge humankind's position at the top of the evolutionary tree. It is possible that there might be thousands of people who have colonized Mars (although even if they did, 'there is nothing to do there except try not to die'[62]), but it is equally likely that the logistical issues that challenge such possibilities today will still be in place.

However, to see a vision of the city of the future, it is not necessary to make a leap of faith based on guesswork and simple optimism. The realities of the next generation of theoretical urban development are all around us. Two of the most extreme examples are showing once again what the power of almost limitless wealth, combined with a desire to be at the cutting edge of human development, can achieve.

NEOM The Line: the new future?

Just as Dubai and Abu Dhabi demonstrated that in their development since the 1970s from simple fishing economies to the ultimate vision of the hyper-futuristic city, so Saudi Arabia has taken on that baton for their next great leap forwards. Students of history will recognize this phrase from the attempts by Mao Zedong to turn China from a simple peasant-based agricultural economy to a centralized Communist one from 1958–62, based on collectivism and increased use of technology. The impact this had on the Chinese economy was catastrophic, within an estimated 15–55 million people dying of starvation, making the Great Chinese Famine the single largest cause of human death in history.[63]

NEOM The Line, the city of the future due to be built in the Rub' al Khali, the Empty Quarter desert of Saudi Arabia, is a 175 km long 200 m wide vision of what humanity can create if money is no object and the limitations of current reality are ignored. Designed to be the antithesis of the traditional city that has meant that 'humanity has existed within dysfunctional and polluted cities that ignored nature', it is (apparently without irony) claiming to be a city that will not only protect nature but enhance it.[64] Although there are those that have not accepted these claims without comment (the 'megalomaniac fantasy of an authoritarian ruler'[65]), the gleaming towers that are present in every oil-based capital city across the world suggest that where there is money and leadership support (particularly in a system where autocratic control means that the limitations of democratic decision-making are not present), there is no shortage of experts who would make themselves available to help make the dream a reality – or at least attempt to do so, on someone else's budget.[66]

If the NEOM vision is one of horizontal grandeur then, staying in Saudi Arabia, the Jeddah Tower is its equivalent on a vertical plane. Designed to be the first 1 km high tower, it will be the tallest building in human history. Although its construction was halted in 2018, it was by then a viable construction project estimated to be one third completed.[67]

Such visionary (and some would say hubristic) aspirations are not new. Frank Lloyd Wright proposed a mile-high building in 1957, the Illinois Tower, that he claimed was technically possible even using technology available at the time. The scale of it can be understood by the fact that it was four times the height of what was then the tallest building in the world, the Empire State Building, and twice as high as the current record holder, the Burj Khalifa in Dubai.[68] It is interesting to note in Botham's paper how similar the design of the proposed Illinois Tower was in 1957 to the actual Burj Khalifa built 50 years later. Going even further back in human history, the Tower of Babel was a similar attempt to use the metaphor and the construction of a supertower to redefine, or perhaps deny, the limitations of humanity's physical constrictions as creatures that walk the earth.

Whether or not such cities will be built (and ignoring the question of whether they should be built, even if we have the technological capabilities to do so), the reality of the next 50 years for the vast majority of urban citizens is likely to be much more mundane. It will be an issue of access to resources (dependent on increasingly fragile global supply chains), access to water, the ability to move though overcrowded transport systems, and the ability to maintain basic functions in an environment characterized by increasing numbers of urban dwellers and increasingly fragile, and often failing, infrastructures.

The holistic city

In the current global risk climate, the ability to model a future vision of the city is something that will have a critical impact both on the lives of billions of urban inhabitants and in the way that humankind organizes and manages its interactions within an environment that is gradually becoming challenging and potentially catastrophic. Global supply chains are increasingly fragile and susceptible to disruptions through human error (the blocking of the Suez Canal in March 2021 that led to the immediate disruption of one third of the global supply chain), natural disasters (the 2011 tsunami in Fukushima, Japan, led to the disruption of global distribution of Japanese car parts that in turn led to the closure of car plants around the world) or political interference (Russia's use of gas as a geo-political weapon following its invasion of Ukraine in February 2022, or the Chinese government's disruption of microchip supplies that has impacted multiple industries and sectors that were dependent on a single source of a critical component). The return to localization is a movement that had been predicted previously but is gaining relevance.

The city as a model of a hyper-concentrated group of people that is able to build efficiency into every aspect of their individual and collective action is not just a utopian aspiration but has been offered as a very real alternative to untrammelled globalization. Although it might seem that a Californian house-boat community would have little if anything in common with the great cities of the world, it was in fact the inspiration for an alternative vision of urban living as espoused by one of the most significant thought-leaders of the 1970s' counterculture, Stewart Brand.

Although slums might be seen as chaotic, Brand saw them rather as hyper-effective, self-balancing ecosystems that relied on multiple micro-negotiations that created opportunities for entrepreneurship, collaboration and highly efficient cooperative interaction.[69] In the increasingly stressful environments that we find ourselves living and operating in, whether at the individual, community city or global level, it is likely that the pressures on informal settlements will continue to grow. Whatever the aspirations might be, the reality is that urban informal settlement populations are growing year on year and there is little if any likelihood of that trend reversing. Informal settlements have traditionally been seen as aberrations, symbols of urban planning failures and human weaknesses that have meant that the success story of the modern city has bypassed or forgotten a significant part of their population. They have simply been written out of the story. If we are to find ways of creating socially secure and stable frameworks that can recognize the realities of the existence of the urban poor and to integrate them into wider urban experience on every level, that can only have benefits for all strata of society.

Vision and reality

If there has been one lesson learned from our attempts to develop a sustainable framework for urban living, one that acknowledges the challenges that we are facing – and that are growing at an exponential rate in terms of frequency, impact and disruption – then it is that we are basically incapable of learning lessons. To misquote a phrase from a different context, 'We never miss an opportunity to miss an opportunity' (used by Abba Eban in the context of 1960s' Middle East peace talks). There have been warnings for the last 50 years about the impact of climate change on our cities and the need to adjust the way we live and work in urban settings that have become increasingly dysfunctional even as their populations have grown. And yet, we seem incapable of facing the reality.

Houston, Texas announced in April 2022 that its newly developed Ion District Urban Community would join the Global Network of innovation Districts, part of collaborative network of global hotspots of innovation. Nowhere in the prospectus is it mentioned that Houston has seen catastrophic flooding on an almost annual basis since 2015. Between 2015 and 2017 there were three 'once-in-500-year floods' back to back.[70]

In 2021, Houston suffered a catastrophic breakdown in its city infrastructure in the face of what was described as an 'unprecedented snowstorm'. It caused billions of dollars of damage and hundreds of deaths.[71] For anyone used to the regular metre-high winter snows of Scandinavia, Eastern Europe or northern Japan, it was hard to know what the fuss was about. Pictures show a few inches of snow and people walking down the streets quite normally. The issue was not with the snowstorm but with the fact that it shouldn't have been happening in Houston.

In 2019, there was a major conference in Paris, hosted by HSBC. Entitled 'Cities of the Future 2019 – Smarter Connections' it had sessions on The New Mega Regions, Digital Transformations and New Industries, Demographics and Global Urbanization, Leading the Future Cities, and others. What no one thought to mention was that exactly one year earlier, Paris has been under water.[72] Adelaide, the city of the future as described in its own literature, makes no mention of the catastrophic flooding that has been happening on a repeated basis since 2022.[73]

The truth is that all of our cities are under major stress. Whether it is climate change, resource depletion, global supply chains, aging infrastructure or the inability to manage either the pressures created by the current population or the additional stress caused by the ever-growing informal settlements that make up increasing proportions of their inhabitants, urban life as we know it is at the edge of a cliff of potential risks, threats, impacts and consequences.[74] Covid-19 has been an indication of how fragile our global networks are, and there is no doubt that we are increasingly vulnerable to similar local, national and global failures that will have catastrophic impacts and long-term legacies.

Conclusion

The future has always been with us. The ability to project forwards is, perhaps, one of the things that defines us as humans. The problem, as the physicist Niels Bohr is reputed to have stated (though it is possible that the originator was Mark Twain), is that 'prediction is difficult, particularly about the future'.

The fundamental question associated with urban development over the next 100 years is whether urban development and regeneration are going to transform the way we interact with the world around us and find a solution to the sustainability challenges that we are already facing, or whether the future of the city is a dystopian nightmare of degeneration, degradation and despair.

The optimistic scenario is one where there is systemic implementation of the New Urban Agenda in order to benchmark against and achieve the Sustainable Development Goals as set out in UN action plans. While the language may seem overly optimistic (and, in the face of recent history, even delusional), the report paints a picture where 'with appropriately implemented measures, the response to the current urban crisis can lead to a collective reprioritization of cities across the world towards shared prosperity and inclusion'.[75]

On the other hand, business as usual, the continuation of the policies and trends that we are currently operating under, would lead to a much less optimistic scenario: increasing polarization between haves and have-nots, the introduction of legislation that would embed those social trends in national policy, the over-dependence on high-polluting fossil fuels and the lack of investment in infrastructure, both new and legacy systems, all of which, both individually and collectively, would lead to the failure to offer even the most basic services to the most vulnerable and marginalized.[76]

While there is little that we have seen in terms of a global preparedness to take the hard decisions that would allow such visions to be realized, it is important that we have an understanding of what positive interventions could look like and the range of outcomes they could produce. 'Think Global, Act Local' is a phrase that has been associated with the Friends of the Earth movement since the early 1970s. In our increasingly globalized yet simultaneously fragmented world, it seems that the phrase has regained significance and power.

If these challenges are to be met and the objectives realized, then it will be through the development of a structured understanding of the threats, the establishment of a range of realistic interventions that are both achievable and sustainable, and a clearly stated desire at every level from the global structures through national government and down to local community levels to act with a sense of urgency, commitment and shared purpose.

Endnotes

1 Barles, S (2010) Society, energy and materials: The contribution of urban metabolism studies to sustainable urban development issues. *Journal of Environmental Planning and Management*, 53(4), 439–455

2 Baccini, P (1997) A city's metabolism: Towards the sustainable development of urban systems. *Journal of Urban Technology*, 4(2), 27–39

3 UN Habitat (2020) The New Urban Agenda Illustrated, United Nations Human Settlements Programme. Available at: https://unhabitat.org/sites/default/files/2020/12/nua_handbook_14dec2020_2.pdf (archived at https://perma.cc/AYD7-A8WP)

4 Cardona, M, García, H I, Giraldo, C A, López, M V, Suárez, C M, Corcho, D C, Posada, C H & Flórez, M N (2005) Homicidios en Medellín, Colombia, entre 1990 y 2002: actores, móviles y circunstancias. Cadernos de saude publica, 21, 840–851

5 Time (1988) Colombia the most dangerous city: Welcome to Medellin, coke capital of the world. *Time Magazine*, 23 March. Available at: https://content.time.com/time/subscriber/article/0,33009,967029,00.html (archived at https://perma.cc/7U6Y-F5S8) (Accessed: 8 August 2022)

6 Drummond, H, Dizgun, J & Keeling, D J (2012) Medellin: A city reborn? *FOCUS on Geography*, 55(4), 146–154

7 Lee Kuan Yew World City Prize (2016) 2016 Prize Laureate – Medellin. Available at: https://www.leekuanyewworldcityprize.gov.sg/medellin/#:~:text=Medell%C3%ADn%20is%20awarded%20the%202016,violence%20due%20to%20social%20inequalities (archived at https://perma.cc/C23P-MMLL) (Accessed: 8 August 2022)

8 Netexplo (2020) Medellín receives an international smart city award for its social, urban and cultural transformation. Available at: https://www.acimedellin.org/medellin-receives-an-international-smart-city-award-for-its-social-urban-and-cultural-transformation/?lang=en (archived at https://perma.cc/6W6F-RLN7) (Accessed: 8 August 2022)

9 Rios, S (2020) Medellín nominated in six categories for the 'Oscars' of tourism. Available at: https://www.bureaumedellin.com/medellin-nominated-in-six-categories-for-the-oscars-of-tourism/ (archived at https://perma.cc/FU33-KU6D) (Accessed: 8 August 2022)

10 UN Habitat (2022) Envisaging the future of cities, 2022. United Nations Human Settlements Programme. Available at: https://unhabitat.org/sites/default/files/2022/06/wcr_2022.pdf (archived at https://perma.cc/DQV2-4KYQ)

11 UN Habitat (2022) Envisaging the future of cities, 2022. United Nations Human Settlements Programme. Available at: https://unhabitat.org/sites/default/files/2022/06/wcr_2022.pdf (archived at https://perma.cc/DQV2-4KYQ)

12 Keck, M & Etzold, B (2013) Risk and resilience in Asian megacities. *Erdkunde*, 1–3

13 UN-Habitat (2012) Streets as tools for urban transformation in slums: A street-led approach to citywide slum upgrading. Available at: https://www.ohchr.org/sites/default/files/Documents/Issues/Housing/InformalSettlements/UNHABITAT_StreetsasToolsforUrbanTransformationinSlums.pdf (archived at https://perma.cc/S6T2-43P5) (Accessed: 8 August 2022); UN Stats (2021) Make cities and human settlements inclusive, safe, resilient and sustainable. Available at: https://unstats.un.org/sdgs/report/2021/goal-11/ (archived at https://perma.cc/5XT7-Z8Q4) (Accessed: 8 August 2022)

14 Fraser, J C (2006) Globalization, development and ordinary cities: A review essay. *Journal of World-Systems Research*, 189–197

15 Bhan, G (2019) Notes on a Southern urban practice. *Environment and Urbanization*, 31(2), 639–654. Available at: https://journals.sagepub.com/doi/full/10.1177/0956247818815792 (archived at https://perma.cc/B7L2-TJBV) (Accessed: 8 August 2022)

16 Gandy, M (2006) Planning, anti-planning, and the infrastructure crisis facing metropolitan Lagos. *Cities in contemporary Africa*, 247–264. New York: Palgrave Macmillan

17 Patel, S (2004) Tools and methods for empowerment developed by slum and pavement dwellers' federations in India. *Participatory Learning and Action*, 50, 117–130

18 Roy, A (2011) Slumdog cities: Rethinking subaltern urbanism. *International Journal of Urban and Regional Research*, 35(2), 223–238

19 Onwuanyi, O (2019) Lagos's chequered history: How it came to be the megacity it is today. The Conversation, 1 October. https://theconversation.com/lagoss-chequered-history-how-it-came-to-be-the-megacity-it-is-today-124306 (archived at https://perma.cc/SL4X-UGXP)

20 Isichei, U (2002) From and for Lagos, Nigeria. *Archis*, 1, 12–15, 2

21 Filani, M O (2012) The changing face of Lagos: From vision to reform and transformation. Cities Alliance, page 4

22 Lancaster, J (2007) Next stop, squalor: is poverty tourism 'poorism,' they call it exploration or exploitation? *Smithsonian Magazine*, March. Available at: https://www.smithsonianmag.com/travel/next-stop-squalor-148390665/ (archived at https://perma.cc/Z8EM-6V32) (Accessed: 8 August 2022)

23 Pearce, F (2018) Is the way we think about overpopulation racist? *The Guardian*, 19 March. Available at: https://www.theguardian.com/cities/2018/mar/19/overpopulation-cities-environment-developing-world-racist-paul-ehrlich (archived at https://perma.cc/86SY-3WN7) (Accessed: 8 August 2022)

24 Booth, R (2009) Charles declares Mumbai shanty town model for the world. Robert Booth, *The Guardian*, 6 February. Available at: https://www.theguardian.com/artanddesign/2009/feb/06/prince-charles-slum-comments (archived at https://perma.cc/HA3S-E6K8) (Accessed: 8 August 2022)

25 Gupta, M K (2015) The future of slums hinges on sustainability. Dialogues of sustainable urbanisation: Social science research and transitions to urban contexts. https://pressbooks.pub/isscbookofblogs/chapter/the-future-of-slums-on-the-line-between-hope-despair/ (archived at https://perma.cc/3CBH-EQH5)

26 Gandy, M (2006) Planning, anti-planning, and the infrastructure crisis facing metropolitan Lagos. *Cities in contemporary Africa*, 247–264. New York: Palgrave Macmillan

27 Habitat for Humanity (nd) Urbanisation and the rise of slum housing: The birth and growth of informal settlements. Available at: https://www.habitatforhumanity.org.uk/blog/2018/09/urbanisation-slum-housing/ (archived at https://perma.cc/93J9-L4Y4) (Accessed: 8 August 2022)

28 United Nations Habitat (1976) United Nations Conference on Human Settlements – Habitat I Vancouver, Canada, 31 May–11 June. Available at: https://www.un.org/en/conferences/habitat/vancouver1976 (archived at https://perma.cc/GVE8-CHUK) (Accessed: 8 August 2022)

29 UN Habitat (1976) United Nations Conference on Human Settlements – Habitat I Vancouver, Canada, 31 May–11 June. Available at: https://www.un.org/en/conferences/habitat/vancouver1976 (archived at https://perma.cc/GVE8-CHUK) (Accessed: 8 August 2022)

30 UN-Habitat (2018) SDG indicator 11.1.1 training module: Adequate housing and slum upgrading. United Nations Human Settlement Programme (UN-Habitat), Nairobi. Available at: https://unhabitat.org/sites/default/files/2020/06/indicator_11.1.1_training_module_adequate_housing_and_slum_upgrading.pdf (archived at https://perma.cc/J7LS-GFY5) (Accessed: 8 August 2022)

31 Patel, S, Baptist, C & d'Cruz, C (2012) Knowledge is power – informal communities assert their right to the city through SDI and community-led enumerations. *Environment and Urbanization*, 24(1), 13–26

32 Mumford, L (2016) The culture of cities. Open Road Media. Available at: https://monoskop.org/images/5/5a/Mumford_Lewis_The_Culture_of_Cities.pdf (archived at https://perma.cc/YML7-MMWS) (Accessed: 8 August 2022)

33 Mitlin, D & Patel, S (2014) The urban poor and strategies for a pro-poor politics: Reflections on Shack/Slum Dwellers International. In *The Routledge handbook on cities of the global south* (pp. 318–330). Routledge

34 UN-Habitat (2012) Streets as tools for urban transformation in slums: A street-led approach to citywide slum upgrading. Available at: https://www.ohchr.org/sites/default/files/Documents/Issues/Housing/InformalSettlements/UNHABITAT_StreetsasToolsforUrbanTransformationinSlums.pdf (archived at https://perma.cc/S6T2-43P5) (Accessed: 8August 2022)

35 Teferi, Z A & Newman, P (2017) Slum regeneration and sustainability: Applying the extended metabolism model and the SDGs. *Sustainability*, 9(12), 2273. Available at: https://www.researchgate.net/publication/321687709_Slum_Regeneration_and_Sustainability_Applying_the_Extended_Metabolism_Model_and_the_SDGs/link/5a2ce63945851552ae7cb7ae/download (archived at https://perma.cc/P7F6-VBXB) (Accessed: 8 August 2022)

36 Hassan, G F (2012) Regeneration as an approach for the development of informal settlements in Cairo metropolitan. *Alexandria Engineering Journal*, 51(3), 229–239. Available at: https://www.sciencedirect.com/science/article/pii/S1110016812000166 (archived at https://perma.cc/2SKX-3DLT) (Accessed: 8 August 2022)

37 Filani, M O (2012) The changing face of Lagos: From vision to reform and transformation. Cities Alliance, Brussels. Available at: https://www.citiesalliance.org/sites/default/files/Lagos-reform-report-lowres.pdf (archived at https://perma.cc/JH4Q-3ZXP); UN-Habitat (2012) Streets as tools for urban transformation in slums: A Street-Led Approach to Citywide Slum Upgrading. Available at: https:// www.ohchr.org/sites/default/files/Documents/Issues/Housing/InformalSettlements/UNHABITAT_StreetsasToolsforUrbanTransformationinSlums.pdf (archived at https://perma.cc/S6T2-43P5) (Accessed: 8 August 2022); Vinnitskaya, I (2011) Regeneration of the Favela de Rocinha Slum/Jan Kudlicka. ArchDaily, 1 July. Available at: https://www.archdaily.com/146314/regeneration-of-the-favela-de-rocinha-slum-jan-kudlicka (archived at https://perma.cc/7GQQ-CN9C) (Accessed: 8 August 2022)

38 Young, M & Willmott, P (2013) *Family and kinship in East London*. Routledge

39 Bunting, M (2007) Kin outrage. *The Guardian*, 25 April. Available at: https://www.theguardian.com/society/2007/apr/25/communities.britishidentityandsociety (archived at https://perma.cc/6Z8S-52SD) (Accessed: 8 August 2022)

40 Mitlin, D and Patel, S (2014) The urban poor and strategies for a pro-poor politics: Reflections on Shack/Slum Dwellers International. In *The Routledge handbook on cities of the Global South* (pp. 318–330). Routledge

41 Teferi, Z A & Newman, P (2017) Slum regeneration and sustainability: Applying the extended metabolism model and the SDGs. *Sustainability*, 9(12), 2273. Available at: https://www.researchgate.net/publication/321687709_Slum_Regeneration_and_Sustainability_Applying_the_Extended_Metabolism_Model_and_the_SDGs/link/5a2ce63945851552ae7cb7ae/download (archived at https://perma.cc/P7F6-VBXB) (Accessed: 8 August 2022)

42 Gandy, M (2006) Planning, anti-planning, and the infrastructure crisis facing metropolitan Lagos. *Cities in contemporary Africa*, 247–264. New York: Palgrave Macmillan; Mitlin, D & Patel, S (2014) The urban poor and strategies for a pro-poor politics: Reflections on Shack/Slum Dwellers International. *The Routledge handbook on cities of the global south*, 318–330. Routledge

43 Keck, M & Sakdapolrak, P (2013) What is social resilience? Lessons learned and ways forward. *Erdkunde*, 5–19

44 Braun, B & Aßheuer, T (2011) Floods in megacity environments: Vulnerability and coping strategies of slum dwellers in Dhaka/Bangladesh. *Natural Hazards*, 58(2), 771–787

45 Braun, B & Aßheuer, T (2011) Floods in megacity environments: Vulnerability and coping strategies of slum dwellers in Dhaka/Bangladesh. *Natural Hazards*, 58(2), 771–787

46 Filani, M O (2012) The changing face of Lagos: From vision to reform and transformation. Cities Alliance, Brussels. Available at: https://www.citiesalliance.org/sites/default/files/Lagos-reform-report-lowres.pdf (archived at https://perma.cc/JH4Q-3ZXP)

47 Gandy, M (2006) Planning, anti-planning, and the infrastructure crisis facing metropolitan Lagos. *Cities in contemporary Africa*, 247–264. New York: Palgrave Macmillan

48 Appadurai, A (2001) Deep democracy: Urban governmentality and the horizon of politics. *Environment and Urbanization*, 13(2), 23–43

49 Appadurai, A (2001) Deep democracy: Urban governmentality and the horizon of politics. *Environment and Urbanization*, 13(2), 23–43

50 Patel, A & Shah, P (2021) Rethinking slums, cities, and urban planning: Lessons from the Covid-19 pandemic. *Cities & Health*, 5(sup1), 145–147

51 Corburn, J, Vlahov, D, Mberu, B, Riley, L, Caiaffa, W T, Rashid, S F, Ko, A, Patel, S, Jukur, S, Martínez-Herrera, E & Jayasinghe, S (2020) Slum health: Arresting Covid-19 and improving well-being in urban informal settlements. *Journal of Urban Health*, 97(3), 348–357

52 Wilkinson, A, Ali, H, Bedford, J, Boonyabancha, S, Connolly, C, Conteh, A, Dean, L, Decorte, F, Dercon, B, Dias, S & Dodman, D (2020) Local response in health emergencies: Key considerations for addressing the Covid-19 pandemic in informal urban settlements. *Environment and Urbanization*, 095624782092284

53 Duque Franco, I, Ortiz, C, Samper, J & Millan, G (2020) Mapping repertoires of collective action facing the Covid-19 pandemic in informal settlements in Latin American cities. *Environment and Urbanization*, 32(2), 523–546

54 Koolhaas, R, Belanger, P, Chung, C J, Comaroff, J, Cosmas, M, Gandhi, S, Hamilton, D A, Ip, L Y, Kim, J, Shepard, G, Singh, R, Slayton, N, Stone, J and Wahba, S (2000) Lagos, Harvard Project on the City. In Koolhaas, R, Kwinter, S, Boeri, S, Tazi, N & Obrist, H U (eds.), Mutations, événement culturel sur la ville contemporaine, Arc en Rêve, Centre d'architecture, Bordeaux, page 653

55 Robinson, J (2004) In the tracks of comparative urbanism: Difference, urban modernity and the primitive. *Urban Geography*, 25(8), 709–723

56 Roy, A (2011) Slumdog cities: Rethinking subaltern urbanism. *International Journal of Urban and Regional Research*, 35(2), 223–238, 225

57 Riffat, S, Powell, R & Aydin, D (2016) Future cities and environmental sustainability. *Future Cities and Environment*, 2(1), 1–23. Available at: https://web.archive.org/web/20171114182400id_/http://publisher-connector.core.ac.uk/resourcesync/data/Springer-OA/pdf/edf/aHR0cDovL2xpbmsuc3ByaW5nZXIuY29tLzEwLjExODYvczQwOTg0LTAxNi0wMDE0LTIucGRm.pdf (archived at https://perma.cc/6S2M-RPJR) (Accessed: 11 August 2022)

58 Vernet, N & Coste, A (2017) Garden cities of the 21st century: A sustainable path to suburban reform. *Urban Planning*, 2(4), 45–60

59 Vedula, A (2007) Blueprint and reality: Navi Mumbai, the city of the 21st century. *Habitat International*, 31(1), 12–23

60 Doshi, V (2016, July 4) Gurgaon: What life is like in the Indian city built by private companies. *The Guardian*. Available at: https://www.theguardian.com/sustainable-business/2016/jul/04/gurgaon-life-city-built-private-companies-india-intel-google (archived at https://perma.cc/Q9W6-35ZM) (Accessed 11 August 2022); Rajagopalan, S & Tabarrok, A (2014) Lessons from Gurgaon, India's private city. *Cities and private planning*. Edward Elgar Publishing

61 Grossman, L (2016) The world in 2076: Thousands of people have settled on Mars. *New Scientist*. Available at: https://www.newscientist.com/article/mg23231001-000-the-world-in-2076-thousands-of-people-have-settled-on-mars/ (archived at https://perma.cc/9DX9-VAAC) (Accessed: 11 August 2022)

62 Grossman, L (2016). The world in 2076: Thousands of people have settled on Mars. *New Scientist*. Available at: https://www.newscientist.com/article/mg23231001-000-the-world-in-2076-thousands-of-people-have-settled-on-mars/ (archived at https://perma.cc/9DX9-VAAC) (Accessed: 11 August 2022)

63 Dikötter, F (nd) Mao's great famine: Ways of living, ways of dying. Dartmouth University. Available at: https://web.archive.org/web/*/http://www.dartmouth.edu/~crossley/HIST5.03/FILES/OHMC_DIkotter.pdf (archived at https://perma.cc/P4KQ-AK8A) (Accessed: 11 August 2022)

64 NEOM (2022) The Line: NEOM – Saudi Arabia smart city. Available at: https://www.neom.com/theline-neom/smart-city-ksa

65 Keller, E (2022, August 5) The visions for NEOM, Saudi Arabia's linear megacity in the desert, reveal contemporary shortcomings more than a future utopia. The Architect's Newspaper. Available at: https://www.archpaper.com/2022/08/visions-neom-saudi-arabia-contemporary-shortcomings-future-utopia/ (archived at https://perma.cc/L487-5ZPR) (Accessed: 11 August 2022)

66 Nerreim, V (2022, July 14) MBS's $500 billion desert dream just keeps getting weirder. Bloomberg. Available at: https://www.bloomberg.com/features/2022-mbs-neom-saudi-arabia/ (archived at https://perma.cc/RXT3-J8PF) (Accessed: 11 August 2022)

67 Andrea, L (2018, January 17) CNN Jeddah Tower: What does the world's next tallest skyscraper look like now? CNN. Available at: https://edition.cnn.com/style/article/jeddah-tower-saudi-arabia-new/index.html (archived at https://perma.cc/9M55-P6PJ) (Accessed: 11 August 2022)

68 Botham, J (2021, February 16) Frank Lloyd Wright's mile high skyscraper proposal. On Verticality. Available at: https://www.onverticality.com/blog/frank-lloyd-wright-mile-high-skyscraper (archived at https://perma.cc/6HA3-MA6H) (Accessed: 11 August 2022)

69 Brand, S (2010) *Whole earth discipline*. Atlantic Books Ltd

70 Lind, D (2017, August 28) The '500-year' flood, explained: Why Houston was so underprepared for Hurricane Harvey. Vox. Available at: https://www.vox.com/science-and-health/2017/8/28/16211392/100-500-year-flood-meaning (archived at https://perma.cc/WKH5-GVSY) (Accessed: 11 August 2022)

71 Ohara, J, Miznazi, A & Wisemann, T (2022) 'It looked like the end of the world': Listen to the stories of Texans who lived through 2021's historic winter storm. (February 17). *The Texas Tribune*

72 Brueck, H. (2018, January 2018) The heart of Paris is underwater — and the images are a shocking reminder that the city is unprepared. Business Insider. Available at: https://www.businessinsider.com/see-paris-underwater-as-the-seine-floods-the-streets-hundred-year-flood-2018-1?r=US&IR=T (archived at https://perma.cc/9ZHS-M3EQ) (Accessed: 11 August 2022)

73 ABC News (2022) Heavy rain turns Adelaide streets into rivers, as late summer storm also hits Barossa. (2022, February 28). Available at: https://www.abc.net.au/news/2022-02-28/rain-and-storms-lash-adelaide-and-barossa/100868852 (archived at https://perma.cc/9E77-9NL4) (Accessed 11 August 2022); Hams, S (2022) Wild wet weather smashes Adelaide as emergency services work to clean up damage while bracing for more rain. ABC News (June 5). Available at: https://www.abc.net.au/news/2022-06-05/wild-weather-hit-adelaide-emergency-services-cleaning-up/101127078 (archived at https://perma.cc/Q9N3-Q5MR) (Accessed: 11 August 2022)

74 Dickson, E, Judy L B, Daniel H & Asmita, T (2012) Urban risk assessments: Understanding disaster and climate risk in cities. Urban Development Series. Washington DC: World Bank

75 UN Habitat (2022) Envisaging the future of cities, 2022. United Nations Human Settlements Programme. Available at: https://unhabitat.org/sites/default/files/2022/06/wcr_2022.pdf (archived at https://perma.cc/DQV2-4KYQ)

76 ASLCG (2021) Missing in action: responding to Australia's climate and security failure. Available at: www.aslcg.org/wp-content/uploads/2021/09/ASLCG_MIA_Report.pdf (archived at https://perma.cc/N6AH-4FEJ) (Accessed: 8 August 2022)

Further reading

ABC News (2022) Heavy rain turns Adelaide streets into rivers, as late summer storm also hits Barossa (February 28). Available at: https://www.abc.net.au/news/2022-02-28/rain-and-storms-lash-adelaide-and-barossa/100868852 (archived at https://perma.cc/9E77-9NL4) (Accessed: 11 August 2022)

Andrea, L (2018, January 17) CNN Jeddah Tower: What does the world's next tallest skyscraper look like now? CNN. Available at: https://edition.cnn.com/style/article/jeddah-tower-saudi-arabia-new/index.html (archived at https://perma.cc/9M55-P6PJ) (Accessed: 11 August 2022)

Appadurai, A (2001) Deep democracy: Urban governmentality and the horizon of politics. *Environment and Urbanization*, 13(2), 23–43

ASLCG (2021) Missing in action: Responding to Australia's climate and security failure. Available at: www.aslcg.org/wp-content/uploads/2021/09/ASLCG_MIA_Report.pdf (archived at https://perma.cc/N6AH-4FEJ) (Accessed: 8 August 2022)

Australian Government (2021) Australia's long-term emissions reduction plan: A whole-of-economy plan to achieve net zero emissions by 2050. Australian Government.

Baccini, P (1997) A city's metabolism: Towards the sustainable development of urban systems. *Journal of Urban Technology*, 4(2), 27–39

Barles, S (2010) Society, energy and materials: The contribution of urban metabolism studies to sustainable urban development issues. *Journal of Environmental Planning and Management*, 53(4), 439–455

Bhan, G (2019) Notes on a southern urban practice. *Environment and Urbanization*, 31(2), 639–654. Available at: https://journals.sagepub.com/doi/full/10.1177/0956247818815792 (archived at https://perma.cc/B7L2-TJBV) (Accessed: 8 August 2022)

Booth, R (2009) Charles declares Mumbai shanty town model for the world. *The Guardian*, 6 February. Available at: https://www.theguardian.com/artanddesign/2009/feb/06/prince-charles-slum-comments (archived at https://perma.cc/HA3S-E6K8). (Accessed: 8 August 2022)

Botham, J (2021, February 16) Frank Lloyd Wright's mile high skyscraper proposal. On Verticality. Available at: https://www.onverticality.com/blog/frank-lloyd-wright-mile-high-skyscraper (archived at https://perma.cc/6HA3-MA6H) (Accessed: 11 August 2022)

Brand, S (2010) *Whole earth discipline*. Atlantic Books Ltd

Braun, B & Aßheuer, T (2011) Floods in megacity environments: Vulnerability and coping strategies of slum dwellers in Dhaka/Bangladesh. *Natural Hazards*, 58(2), 771–787

Brueck, H (2018, January). The heart of Paris is underwater – and the images are a shocking reminder that the city is unprepared. *Business Insider*. Available at: https://www.businessinsider.com/see-paris-underwater-as-the-seine-floods-the-streets-hundred-year-flood-2018-1?r=US&IR=T (archived at https://perma.cc/9ZHS-M3EQ) (Accessed: 11 August 2022)

Bunting, M (2007) Kin outrage. *The Guardian*, 25 April. Available at: https://www.theguardian.com/society/2007/apr/25/communities.britishidentityandsociety (archived at https://perma.cc/6Z8S-52SD) (Accessed: 8 August 2022)

Cardona, M, García, H I, Giraldo, C A, López, M V, Suárez, C M, Corcho, D C, Posada, C H & Flórez, M N (2005) Homicidios en Medellín, Colombia, entre 1990 y 2002: actores, móviles y circunstancias. *Cadernos de saude publica*, 21, 840–851

City of Adelaide (2022) Our sustainable city. Adelaide. Available at: https://www.cityofadelaide.com.au/about-adelaide/our-sustainable-city/ (archived at https://perma.cc/CDU6-5MY9) (Accessed: 11 August 2022)

Corburn, J, Vlahov, D, Mberu, B, Riley, L, Caiaffa, W T, Rashid, S F, Ko, A, Patel, S, Jukur, S, Martínez-Herrera, E & Jayasinghe, S (2020) Slum health: Arresting Covid-19 and improving well-being in urban informal settlements. *Journal of Urban Health*, 97(3), 348–357

Dickson, E, Judy L B, Daniel H & Asmita T (2012) Urban risk Assessments: Understanding disaster and climate risk in cities. Urban Development Series. Washington DC: World Bank

Dikötter, F (nd) Mao's great famine: Ways of living, ways of dying. Dartmouth University. Available at: https://web.archive.org/web/20200716231543/ (archived at https://perma.cc/MYR3-WWS9) http://www.dartmouth.edu/~crossley/HIST5.03/FILES/OHMC_DIkotter.pdf (Accessed: 11 August 2022)

Doshi, V (2016, July 4) Gurgaon: What life is like in the Indian city built by private companies. *The Guardian*. Available at: https://www.theguardian.com/sustainable-business/2016/jul/04/gurgaon-life-city-built-private-companies-india-intel-google (archived at https://perma.cc/Q9W6-35ZM) (Accessed: 11 August 2022)

Downer Group (2022) Reconophalt. Available at: https://www.downergroup.com/reconophalt (archived at https://perma.cc/5TVF-DMXB) (Accessed: 11 August 2022)

Drummond, H, Dizgun, J & Keeling, D J (2012) Medellin: A city reborn? *FOCUS on Geography*, 55(4), 146–154

Duque Franco, I, Ortiz, C, Samper, J & Millan, G (2020) Mapping repertoires of collective action facing the Covid-19 pandemic in informal settlements in Latin American cities. *Environment and Urbanization*, 32(2), 523–546

EIT Climate-KIC (2022) Available at: https://www.climate-kic.org/ (archived at https://perma.cc/P8RY-BQNY) (Accessed: 11 August 2022)

European Commission (2017) Essen becomes the European Green Capital for 2017. European Commission Environment. Available at: https://ec.europa.eu/environment/europeangreencapital/essen-ecc-2017/ (archived at https://perma.cc/UGL4-SQ9U) (Accessed: 11 August 2022)

European Union (nd) A European green deal. European Union. Available at: https://ec.europa.eu/info/strategy/priorities-2019-2024/european-green-deal_en (archived at https://perma.cc/DFK9-PH43) (Accessed: 11 August 2022)

Filani, M O (2012) The changing face of Lagos: From vision to reform and transformation. Cities Alliance, Brussels. Available at: https://www.citiesalliance.org/sites/default/files/Lagos-reform-report-lowres.pdf (archived at https://perma.cc/JH4Q-3ZXP)

Fraser, J C (2006) Globalization, development and ordinary cities: A review essay. *Journal of World-Systems Research*, 189–197

Friends of The Earth (2017) Available at: https://friendsoftheearth.uk/ (archived at https://perma.cc/ML2K-SQFY) (Accessed: 11 August 2022)

Gandy, M (2006) Planning, anti-planning, and the infrastructure crisis facing metropolitan Lagos. *Cities in contemporary Africa*, 247–264. New York: Palgrave Macmillan.

Grossman, L (2016) The world in 2076: Thousands of people have settled on Mars. *New Scientist*. Available at: https://www.newscientist.com/article/mg23231001-000-the-world-in-2076-thousands-of-people-have-settled-on-mars/ (archived at https://perma.cc/9DX9-VAAC) (Accessed: 11 August 2022)

Gupta, M K (2015) The future of slums hinges on sustainability. *Dialogues of sustainable urbanisation: Social science research and transitions to urban contexts.*

Habitat for Humanity (n.d.) Urbanisation and the rise of slum housing: The birth and growth of informal settlements. Available at: https://www.habitatforhumanity.org.uk/blog/2018/09/urbanisation-slum-housing/ (archived at https://perma.cc/93J9-L4Y4) (Accessed: 8 August 2022)

Hams, S (2022, June 5). Wild wet weather smashes Adelaide as emergency services work to clean up damage while bracing for more rain. ABC News. Available at: https://www.abc.net.au/news/2022-06-05/wild-weather-hit-adelaide-emergency-services-cleaning-up/101127078 (archived at https://perma.cc/Q9N3-Q5MR) (Accessed: 11 August 2022)

Hassan, G F (2012) Regeneration as an approach for the development of informal settlements in Cairo metropolitan. *Alexandria Engineering Journal*, 51(3), 229–239. Available at: https://www.sciencedirect.com/science/article/pii/S1110016812000166 (archived at https://perma.cc/2SKX-3DLT) (Accessed: 8 August 2022)

Keck, M & Etzold, B (2013) Risk and resilience in Asian megacities. *Erdkunde*, 1–3

Keck, M & Sakdapolrak, P (2013) What is social resilience? Lessons learned and ways forward. *Erdkunde*, 5–19

Keller, E (2022, August 5) The visions for NEOM, Saudi Arabia's linear megacity in the desert, reveal contemporary shortcomings more than a future utopia. The Architect's Newspaper. Available at: https://www.archpaper.com/2022/08/visions-neom-saudi-arabia-contemporary-shortcomings-future-utopia/ (archived at https://perma.cc/L487-5ZPR) (Accessed: 11 August 2022)

Lancaster, J (2007) Next stop, squalor is poverty tourism 'poorism,' they call it exploration or exploitation? *Smithsonian Magazine*, March. Available at: https://www.smithsonianmag.com/travel/next-stop-squalor-148390665/ (archived at https://perma.cc/Z8EM-6V32) (Accessed: 8 August 2022)

Lee Kuan Yew World City Prize (2016) 2016 Prize Laureate – Medellin. Available at: https://www.leekuanyewworldcityprize.gov.sg/medellin/#:~:text=Medell%C3%ADn%20is%20awarded%20the%202016,violence%20due%20to%20social%20inequalities (archived at https://perma.cc/C23P-MMLL) (Accessed: 8 August 2022)

Lind, D (2017, August 28) The '500-year' flood, explained: Why Houston was so underprepared for Hurricane Harvey. Vox. Available at: https://www.vox.com/science-and-health/2017/8/28/16211392/100-500-year-flood-meaning (archived at https://perma.cc/WKH5-GVSY) (Accessed: 11 August 2022)

Meng, X, Qian, N & Yared, P (2015) The institutional causes of China's Great Famine, 1959–1961. *The Review of Economic Studies*, 82(4), 1568–1611. Available at: https://www.nber.org/system/files/working_papers/w16361/w16361.pdf (archived at https://perma.cc/X7AW-ZZSR) (Accessed: 11 August 2022)

Miller, N (2022, June 13) Three pioneering cities, one sustainable future: This is how our lives will change if cities realize their climate goals. UPM.com. Available at: https://www.upm.com/articles/beyond-fossils/22/three-pioneering-cities-one-sustainable-future/ (archived at https://perma.cc/3WST-FSFC) (Accessed: 11 August 2022)

Mitlin, D & Patel, S (2014) The urban poor and strategies for a pro-poor politics: Reflections on Shack/Slum Dwellers International. *The Routledge handbook on cities of the global south*, 318–330. Routledge

Mumford, L (2016) The culture of cities. Open Road Media. Available at: https://monoskop.org/images/5/5a/Mumford_Lewis_The_Culture_of_Cities.pdf (archived at https://perma.cc/YML7-MMWS) (Accessed: 8 August 2022)

NEOM (2022) The Line: NEOM – Saudi Arabia smart city. Available at: www.neom.com/en-us/regions/theline (archived at https://perma.cc/NS4M-3T6T)

Nerreim, V (2022, July 14) MBS's $500 billion desert dream just keeps getting weirder. Bloomberg. Available at: https://www.bloomberg.com/features/2022-mbs-neom-saudi-arabia/ (archived at https://perma.cc/RXT3-J8PF) (Accessed: 11 August 2022)

Netexplo (2020) Medellín Receives an international smart city award for its social, urban and cultural transformation. Available at: https://www.acimedellin.org/medellin-receives-an-international-smart-city-award-for-its-social-urban-and-cultural-transformation/?lang=en (archived at https://perma.cc/6W6F-RLN7) (Accessed: 8 August 2022)

Nottingham City Council (2020) Carbon neutral Nottingham 2020–2028 action plan. Available at: www.nottinghamcity.gov.uk/media/2619917/2028-carbon-neutral-action-plan-v2-160620.pdf (archived at https://perma.cc/QP24-6ZJW) (Accessed: 11 August 2022)

Ohara, J, Miznazi, A & Wisemann, T (2022) 'It looked like the end of the world': Listen to the stories of Texans who lived through 2021's historic winter storm. (February 17). *The Texas Tribune*

Patel, A & Shah, P (2021) Rethinking slums, cities, and urban planning: Lessons from the Covid-19 pandemic. *Cities & Health*, 5(sup1), 145–147

Patel, S, Baptist, C & d'Cruz, C (2012) Knowledge is power – informal communities assert their right to the city through SDI and community-led enumerations. *Environment and Urbanization*, 24(1), 13–26

Pearce, F (2018) Is the way we think about overpopulation racist? *The Guardian*, 19 March. Available at: https://www.theguardian.com/cities/2018/mar/19/overpopulation-cities-environment-developing-world-racist-paul-ehrlich (archived at https://perma.cc/86SY-3WN7) (Accessed: 8 August 2022)

Rajagopalan, S & Tabarrok, A (2014) Lessons from Gurgaon, India's private city. *Cities and private planning*. Edward Elgar Publishing

Riffat, S, Powell, R & Aydin, D (2016) Future cities and environmental sustainability.*Future Cities and Environment*, 2(1), 1–23. Available at: https://web.archive.org/web/20171114182400id_/http://publisher-connector.core.ac.uk/resourcesync/data/Springer-OA/pdf/edf/aHR0cDovL2xpbmsuc3ByaW5nZXIuY29tLzEwLjExODYvczQwOTg0LTAxNi0wMDE0LTIucGRm.pdf (archived at https://perma.cc/6S2M-RPJR) (Accessed: 11 August 2022)

Rios, S (2020) Medellín nominated in six categories for the 'Oscars' of tourism. Available at: https://www.bureaumedellin.com/medellin-nominated-in-six-categories-for-the-oscars-of-tourism/ (archived at https://perma.cc/FU33-KU6D) (Accessed: 8 August 2022)

Saini, L, Meena, C S, Raj, B P, Agarwal, N & Kumar, A (2022) Net zero energy consumption building in India: An overview and initiative toward sustainable future. *International Journal of Green Energy*, 19(5), 544–561.

Teferi, Z A & Newman, P (2017) Slum regeneration and sustainability: Applying the extended metabolism model and the SDGs. *Sustainability*, 9(12), 2273. Available at: https://www.researchgate.net/publication/321687709_Slum_Regeneration_and_Sustainability_Applying_the_Extended_Metabolism_Model_and_the_SDGs/link/5a2ce63945851552ae7cb7ae/download (archived at https://perma.cc/P7F6-VBXB) (Accessed: 8 August 2022)

Time (1988) Colombia the most dangerous city: Welcome to Medellin, coke capital of the world. *Time Magazine*, 23 March. Available at: https://content.time.com/time/subscriber/article/0,33009,967029,00.html (archived at https://perma.cc/7U6Y-F5S8) (Accessed: 8 August 2022)

UN Habitat (1976) United Nations Conference on Human Settlements – Habitat I Vancouver, Canada, 31 May–11 June. Available at: https://www.un.org/en/conferences/habitat/vancouver1976 (archived at https://perma.cc/GVE8-CHUK) (Accessed: 8 August 2022)

UN Habitat (2012) Streets as tools for urban transformation in slums: A street-led approach to citywide slum upgrading. Available at: https://www.ohchr.org/sites/default/files/Documents/Issues/Housing/InformalSettlements/UNHABITAT_StreetsasToolsforUrbanTransformationinSlums.pdf (archived at https://perma.cc/S6T2-43P5) (Accessed: 8 August 2022)

UN Habitat (2018) SDG indicator 11.1.1 training module: Adequate housing and slum upgrading. United Nations Human Settlement Programme (UN-Habitat), Nairobi. Available at: https://unhabitat.org/sites/default/files/2020/06/indicator_11.1.1_training_module_adequate_housing_and_slum_upgrading.pdf (archived at https://perma.cc/J7LS-GFY5) (Accessed: 8 August 2022)

UN Habitat (2020) The new urban agenda illustrated, United Nations Human Settlements Programme. Available at: https://unhabitat.org/sites/default/files/2020/12/nua_handbook_14dec2020_2.pdf (archived at https://perma.cc/AYD7-A8WP)

UN Habitat (2022) Envisaging the future of cities, 2022. United Nations Human Settlements Programme. Available at: https://unhabitat.org/sites/default/files/2022/06/wcr_2022.pdf (archived at https://perma.cc/DQV2-4KYQ)

UN Stats (2021) Make cities and human settlements inclusive, safe, resilient and sustainable. Available at: https://unstats.un.org/sdgs/report/2021/goal-11/ (archived at https://perma.cc/5XT7-Z8Q4) (Accessed: 8 August 2022)

Urban Nature Atlas (2021) Restoration of the Emscher River. Available at: (https://una.city/nbs/essen/restoration-emscher-river (archived at https://perma.cc/QFY3-CCMR) (Accessed: 11 August 2022)

Vedula, A., 2007. Blueprint and reality: Navi Mumbai, the city of the 21st century. *Habitat International*, 31(1), 12–23

Vernet, N & Coste, A (2017) Garden cities of the 21st century: A sustainable path to suburban reform. *Urban Planning*, 2(4), 45–60

Vinnitskaya, I (2011) Regeneration of the Favela de Rocinha Slum/Jan Kudlicka. ArchDaily, 1 July. Available at: https://www.archdaily.com/146314/regeneration-of-the-favela-de-rocinha-slum-jan-kudlicka (archived at https://perma.cc/7GQQ-CN9C) (Accessed: 8 August 2022)

Wilkinson, A, Ali, H, Bedford, J, Boonyabancha, S, Connolly, C, Conteh, A, Dean, L, Decorte, F, Dercon, B, Dias, S & Dodman, D (2020) Local response in health emergencies: Key considerations for addressing the Covid-19 pandemic in informal urban settlements. *Environment and Urbanization*, 095624782092284

Willis, K (2018) Whose right to the smart city? Kitchen, R, Cardullo, P & di Feliciantonio, (eds). *The right to the smart city*. Emerald Publishing

Young, M & Wilmott, P (2013) *Family and kinship in East London*. Routledge

11

In the stranglehold of a pandemic: learning from Covid-19

When news started circulating in November 2019 that something bad was happening in Wuhan, China, it soon became clear to those involved in monitoring and engaging with global health issues that this was, potentially, something that could have significant implications. The scale of the event and the potential impacts it could have started to emerge as Chinese authorities made moves to impose lockdown on their cities.

This was unprecedented in modern times and it seemed to be an indication of the seriousness with which the authorities were taking the issue, but also the level of impact such interventionist policies might have. Little did we know that little more than three months later, the world would be in the grip of a global pandemic and the word *lockdown* would have entered our global lexicon.

The possibility of a global pandemic was certainly nothing that should have taken anyone by surprise. It was a scenario that had been discussed both theoretically as an event that should be modelled and prepared for and technically in that it had appeared on national risk registers, in national exercising programmes and at the heart of national strategic risk modelling.[1] The United Nations General Assembly had issued a report following the Ebola outbreak in West Africa that had identified that the world's preparedness was 'woefully insufficient' and that the likelihood of a devastating event that would cause major social, political and economic disruption was 'a not unlikely scenario'.[2]

The fact that when both global and national governance systems were faced with the challenges of engaging with an actual pandemic event all of their crisis planning and preparation seemed to disappear like mist in the morning sun is yet another indication. So is the indictment as to the weakness of large-scale strategic risk and crisis management capabilities in the face of what were described as unprecedented events, but actually should have been front and centre in national and global pandemic planning.

It can be said that the greatest gift that a risk manager can have is a near-miss. That is something that goes beyond models, simulations or exercises and gives a powerful indication of how systems and processes respond in the face of an actual event. It is an opportunity to reality-test systems under pressure – and to identify exactly how well they are able to deliver precisely those services that they are tasked with, once those services are called upon.

As with almost all major crises, and as discussed in detail across this book, it is necessary to differentiate the external event from the crisis. Hurricane Katrina was an event, the Fukushima tsunami was an event and Covid-19 was an event. The crisis in each of these cases was an inability of exactly those agencies that were tasked with modelling, preparing for and then taking ownership and leadership of the response programmes once such an event was actually occurring, to deliver those services when required. And further than that, once reviews were conducted as to why those responses had failed, it became clear that the weaknesses and vulnerabilities that led to those failures were widely known and discussed. They were exactly the same issues that had led to similar failures in previous events and had been identified as structural vulnerabilities in their own post-incident reviews.

In this chapter we look at the lessons learned from Covid-19 from a strategic risk and crisis management perspective and what can be done in future to ensure that such lessons are not simply identified and then forgotten but are embedded into every aspect of our national and global crisis management capabilities. This will help us to be better prepared when the next critical challenge arises, as it will surely do.

Who knew what, and when?

One of the features of the coronavirus/Covid-19 development is that it was highly documented from the very first moments. Although the issue of a potential pandemic had been identified in theory, governments were on the whole unwilling to invest time, capital, resources or political capital in either discussing it or preparing for it. However, the major global organizations tasked with monitoring and preparing for a potential global pandemic were extremely sensitive to the possibilities of a viral outbreak spreading beyond its initial place of origin and given the realities of the modern world's connectivity, escalating rapidly to a global event.[3]

By 31 December 2019, the fact that something was happening in Wuhan was known, as was the concern that this was something that was not fitting in with normal patterns. The Wuhan Municipal Health Commission had published a media statement on its website talking of 'viral pneumonia' in Wuhan. ProMED (a programme of the International Society for Infectious Diseases) had also noted the clusters, listing them as 'pneumonia of unknown cause', and information had been uploaded to WHO's Epidemic Intelligence from Open Sources platform (ISID; WHO EIOS).[4]

All information in the section below (unless otherwise referenced) is from the WHO's 'Timeline: WHO's COVID-19 Response'.

By 1 January 2020, WHO had activated its Incident Management Support Team, which coordinated activities across the headquarters, regional and country levels for public health emergencies.

On 5 January, WHO shared information with all of its member states and issued its first Disease Outbreak Report.

On 10 January, the WHO director-general spoke with head of the National Health Commission of the People's Republic of China, as well as with the director of the Chinese Center for Disease Control and Prevention.

By 10 January WHO had issued a series of directives outlining the concerns for the spreading of what had been identified as a new disease and guidance for the management of the disease. This included infection prevention and control, laboratory testing, national capacities review tool, risk communication and community engagement, travel advice and clinical management.

On 11 January, the first reports of a death from novel coronavirus appeared in Chinese media.

On 15 January, there was a report from Japan of an infection in someone who had travelled to Wuhan. WHO responded by stating that given global travel patterns, it was likely that similar patterns of infections would be seen in other countries.

By 21 January WHO could state that it seemed clear that coronavirus spread was due at least in part to human-to-human transmission and that infections among healthcare workers had strengthened the evidence for such modelling.

On that same day, there was also the first case in the US.

On 22 January, the WHO director-general convened an emergency committee of 15 global experts to determine whether coronavirus met the threshold for being declared a public health emergency of international concern (PHEIC). It was decided at the time that there was not enough information available to make a definitive statement, but it was a weakness of the system that there was only a binary choice available – PHEIC/Not PHEIC. The decision to not declare a PHEIC was used both at the time and retrospectively to justify the fact that governments did not take decisive action at that stage.

On 24 January, the first European cases were reported in France, all from people who had travelled from Wuhan. By 24 January, WHO was confident enough in both the severity of the outbreaks and the significance of their spreading patterns that it issued a series of statements outlining the importance of being ready at the local and national levels for detecting, testing and managing outbreaks.

The significance of the Wuhan-based emergent disease can be seen by the fact that WHO director-general flew to Beijing to meet with local public health officials to learn more about their activities and to offer support and technical assistance. As part of his trip, he met with Chinese president Xi Jinping.

The first Middle Eastern case was reported in the United Arab Emirates on 29 January and on the same day WHO established the Pandemic Supply Chain Network (PSCN) in collaboration with the World Economic Forum, with the mission to 'create and manage a market network allowing for WHO and private sector partners to access any supply chain functionality and asset from end-to-end anywhere in the world at any scale'.

On 30 January, WHO officially declared that novel coronavirus had reached the threshold to be classified as a PHEIC. At that stage there were 98 cases and no deaths in 18 countries outside China.

By the start of February 2020, it had become clear that novel coronavirus had the potential to become the global pandemic that had been the nightmare scenario for global health planners over the previous generation. By this stage, the broad range of activities was no longer confined to trying to establish whether this new virus was or was not a global threat but had transitioned to a crisis response process that tried to generate a sense of urgency across all stakeholders, and particularly national government that had the power to deploy local assets in the amount and at the speed required.

On 4 February, in a briefing to the executive board, WHO director-general stated, 'We have a window of opportunity. While 99 per cent of cases are in China, in the rest of the world we only have 176 cases.'

On 11 February, novel coronavirus was given the official designation Covid-19. The naming protocols are specifically designed to not include the names of regions, animals or people in order to avoid the stigma that could be created by labels such as Spanish Flu, Hong Kong Flu, Avian Flu or Swine Flu, as had been used in previous cases.

From 11–12 February WHO convened a Global Research and Innovation Forum on the novel coronavirus, attended in person by more than 300 experts and funders from 48 countries, with a further 150 joining online.

On 12 February, WHO published Operational Planning Guidelines to Support Country Preparedness and Response, structured around the eight pillars of country level:

- coordination, planning and monitoring;
- risk communication and community engagement;
- surveillance, rapid response teams and case investigation;
- points of entry;
- national laboratories;
- infection prevention and control;
- case management; and
- operational support and logistics.

These guidelines were designed to give practical guidance to support the implementation of technical guidance that had been issued previously.

On 15 February, the director-general spoke at the Munich Security Conference, a global forum dedicated to issues of international security. In his speech the director-general made three requests of the international community: use the window of opportunity to intensify preparedness, adopt a whole-of-government approach and be guided by solidarity, not stigma. He also expressed concern at the global lack of urgency in funding the response.

By 24 February the leaders of the WHO–China Joint Mission on Coronavirus held a press conference to report on the main findings of their collaboration. The overarching message was both stark and simple: the world was not yet taking Covid-19 with the necessary level of seriousness and the failure to act decisively at this stage would have consequences.

The Mission warned that 'much of the global community is not yet ready, in mindset and materially, to implement the measures that have been employed to contain Covid-19 in China'.

Issues identified included the need to implement large-scale public health measures, and for those countries with actual cases the activation of 'the highest level of national response management protocols to ensure the all-of-government and all-of-society approach needed to contain Covid-19'.

The Mission stressed that 'to reduce Covid-19 illness and death, near-term readiness planning must embrace the large-scale implementation of high-quality, non-pharmaceutical public health measures', such as case detection and isolation, contact tracing and monitoring/quarantining and community engagement.

Major recommendations were developed for the People's Republic of China, countries with imported cases and/or outbreaks of Covid-19, uninfected countries, the public and the international community. For example, in addition to the above, countries with imported cases and/or outbreaks were recommended to 'immediately activate the highest level of national response management protocols to ensure the all-of-government and all-of-society approach needed to contain Covid-19'.

On 25 February, there were the first confirmed cases in Africa (one each in Egypt and Algeria).

On 27 February, WHO published guidance on the use of personal protective equipment (PPE).

On 29 February, WHO published guidelines on quarantines, including who should be quarantined and the minimum conditions that would be required to avoid further transmission.

On 3 March, WHO issued a call for industry and governments to increase manufacturing of PPE by 40 per cent in response to the existing global shortage that was already affecting health workers worldwide.

On 7 March confirmed global Covid-19 cases passed the 100,000 mark. WHO issued a package of guidelines covering the preparedness, readiness and response actions for four different transmission scenarios: no cases, sporadic cases, clusters of cases and community transmission.

On 11 March, WHO made the assessment that Covid-19 could be characterized as a pandemic. This was based not only on an assumed severity of the spread but on the lack of action from governments to prepare themselves for the impact of the pandemic.

Recognizing that Covid-19 was not just a public health crisis but one that would touch every sector, WHO's call – made from the beginning – was restated for countries to take a whole-of-government, whole-of-society approach, built around a comprehensive strategy to prevent infections, save lives and minimize impact, emphasizing that 'we cannot say this loudly enough, or clearly enough, or often enough' and stressing that 'all countries can still change the course of this pandemic' if they 'detect, test, treat, isolate, trace, and mobilize their people in the response'.

The director-general further underlined that 'the challenge for many countries who are now dealing with large clusters or community transmission is not whether they can do the same – it's whether they will'.

Why did the world not pay attention?

It was not just the WHO that had been calling for the world to pay attention. The fear of a possible pandemic – in fact the certainty that at some stage a pandemic would become a major global issue – had been highlighted by global leaders for years.

President Barack Obama gave a presentation in 2014 in which he outlined in detail the threats of a global pandemic. He stated, 'We have to put in place an infrastructure not just here at home but globally, that allows us to see it quickly, isolate it quickly and respond to it quickly.'[5]

This was not the first time that Obama had raised this issue. As a freshman US senator in 2005, he had written an Op-Ed column in *The New York Times* highlighting the fact that as well as major threats to national security such as nuclear proliferation and weapons of mass destruction, a pandemic 'could cause millions of deaths, destabilize Southeast Asia (its likely place of origin), and threaten the security of governments around the world'.[6]

He went on to identify the need for global cooperation that would allow early identification and intervention before such incidents became full-blown pandemics. There followed a recognition that there was the need to pay forward, to prepare then for what would happen 'five or ten years down the road', especially in a globalized world where the potential for almost instantaneous spread beyond its initial triggering area was a factor that had not been as significant in previous events.

On 3 April 2015, Bill Gates gave a TED talk entitled 'The next outbreak? We're not ready'.[7] In it, he identified the greatest risk of a global crisis catastrophe not as nuclear war but as the impacts of a highly infectious virus – 'not missiles, but microbes'. He identified the issue of detection and surveillance – and in places that did not have the benefits of advanced technology such as existed in many of the places where global policymakers are working from. There were not enough people with the appropriate range of expertise, given that the response to an epidemic outbreak would require hundreds of thousands of workers. There was no understanding of what the diagnostic and treatment methodologies should look like to allow a level of scalability appropriate to a challenge of this nature, and there was no existing global framework that would support this sort of integrated multi-disciplinary approach, including the ability to create fast-surge capacities that could respond to what would be an unexpected, high-impact and fast-moving event.

Gates identified the fact that advances in biotechnologies meant that we would have vastly reduced turn-around time for the development of new drugs and vaccines that could be developed in order to counter specific pathogens. He also used the analogy of a war, where there are both full-time professionals and a cadre of reservists who can be used to respond in the event that they need to reinforce existing capabilities at short notice. Militaries, both at country level and at multinational levels (NATO or the African Union, for example), have fast-reaction forces that are trained and maintained to fulfil exactly that role.

He identified the need to strengthen local-level healthcare facilities and capabilities, as that sets the foundation of whatever responses are required in the event that a pandemic was to occur. That is in parallel to a well-trained, equipped and funded medical corps that can act as a fast-reaction team, responding to events before they escalate to full-blown epidemic status.[8] There is then the need to pair the medical and the military facilities and capabilities in order to be able to deliver the greatest impact in the fastest way across the greatest area. The military are of course trained to respond to a wide range of potential scenarios in exactly this manner and it is no surprise that when standard facilities are overwhelmed, it is the military that are called in as a back-up.[9]

Gates quoted the World Bank estimation that a global pandemic would cause a shrinkage of total global wealth at about $3 trillion, so an investment in preventative and responsive capabilities would be a meaningful and cost-effective investment. Such efforts would also have benefits beyond the simple ability to respond to a pandemic. He concluded by saying that there was no need to panic, but we did need to get going, because time was not on our side. He identified the Ebola outbreak as a wake-up call and his final words were, 'If we start now, we can be ready for the next epidemic.' Those words were not paid attention to then and we have seen the outcomes when a global pandemic does hit. If we replace 'Ebola' with 'Covid-19', it stands as a warning and an opportunity for this generation, just as it did for the previous one.

Exercise Cygnus (UK, 2016)

Exercise Cygnus was a national-level pandemic exercise held in 2016.[10] Despite the fact that pandemic had been identified in the UK's national risk register, the scale and scope of the exercise had been 'massively scaled down from what was originally planned' because of the focus on terrorist and other issues that were considered to be more threatening to the national security. This in turn was impacted by the need to take government planning resources to prepare for a post-Brexit transition, which took both focus and support away from other aspects of national risk planning.[11]

Exercise Cygnus was a command post exercise that was designed to assess the UK's preparedness for a pandemic influenza outbreak, with the scenario presuming that the peak of the pandemic would affect up to 50 per cent of the UK population, with 200,000–400,000 deaths.

The headline lessons from the report on the exercise identified some structural issues that would be recognizable to any complex organization facing a major disruptive event. They included:

- The development of a pandemic concept of operations would increase the understanding of the response mechanisms among all stakeholders and support the development of an integrated response capability.
- Many organizations had little awareness of current guidelines, or were using outdated documents, or had not integrated those guidelines into their own frameworks. Even those that had formal guidelines had often not carried out the training that would ensure that their own people were familiar with their own protocols and would have an understanding of both their personal and team responsibilities, as well as the overall corporate response.

- Many organizations had few if any formal pandemic response procedures in place and were dependent on the corporate memory that had been developed in response to the previous major pandemic scare, the H1N1 pandemic of 2011. However, the lessons learned and the capabilities developed as part of that response were already fading and many of the people who had been involved in those incidents were no longer available to give support.
- There is the need to have the legislative capabilities to introduce legislation that would support the necessary level of healthcare surge arrangements and the need to keep essential services running. Given that these were two of the critical issues at the heart of the Covid-19 response, the parallels between the challenges of the flu pandemic of the exercise and the Covid-19 pandemic that actually hit the country (and the world) are clear.
- There was little understanding of how the public would respond to a national pandemic of this scale, but it was recognized that there was a weakness in the ability to formulate and share public messaging in an adequate manner. It was specifically identified that the moral and ethical issues around mass burials and the need for public health triage (prioritizing the needs of one section of society over others) was an area where such understanding was lacking. It was identified that communication strategies are an integral part of emergency management planning, particularly in areas where there were decisions to be made that would be unprecedented in their nature and which would have significant impact in terms of the technical responses but also in public perception.

This was an issue that was reflected in the fact that the UK government delayed imposing a national lockdown at the start of the Covid-19 pandemic because of the fear that the public would simply not accept one, even though it had already been introduced in other European countries and was widely recognized as being one of the major response protocols that could help dampen the spread of infections.

The report also recognized the need to create delegated ownership of the response, moving from a centralized national management system to one that was more localized. This was aligned with the likely requirement that there would be the need for expert support for various aspects of the impacts and consequences of a major pandemic (such as excess deaths). Local agencies and frameworks would have neither the resources nor the knowledge to manage such situations, especially given that they would be taking place in an environment suffering under the other issues associated with the pandemic, and the likelihood that they would be overwhelmed at some stage when a limited number of available experts would be required to support multiple different agencies and jurisdictions.

While Exercise Cygnus was undoubtedly a useful tool in identifying lessons learned, and for the 900 participants from multiple agencies it had value both in the learning they undertook and the opportunity to work with and build relationships between different agencies, there was one significant issue that prevented the exercise and the lessons learned (or more correctly identified) from having the maximum impact: the government's refusal to release the report of the exercise and the fact that it was not shared even among other agencies.

By October 2020, the government was still appealing repeated judgments that it should release the report, based on the fact that it was unclear whether there was public interest in doing so.

Exercise Crimson Contagion (US, 2019)

Exercise crimson Contagion was an eight-month exercise run by the US Department of Health and Human Services (HSS) that included numerous national, state and local, private and public organizations.[12] The scenario was frighteningly similar to the actual development of Covid-19, in that it originated in a group of 30 tourists returning from China, bringing with them a novel influenza, a respiratory virus, into the US. The final scenario involved 110 million Americans being infected,[13] 7.7 million hospitalizations and 586,000 fatalities.

The subsequent *Key Findings Report* issued by the HSS found that:

- federal government lacked sufficient funding to respond to a severe influenza pandemic;
- exercise participants lacked clarity on the roles of different federal agencies and what information was important to pass on to federal partners;
- HHS had issues providing accurate and relevant information to hospitals and other public health organizations;
- there was confusion between HHS, FEMA and the Department of Homeland Security on which federal agency would take the lead in the crisis;

- the United States lacked the production capacity to meet the demands for protective equipment and medical devices such as masks and ventilators imposed by a pandemic;[14]
- states were unable to efficiently request resources due to the lack of a standardized request process.

Johns Hopkins University had run a similar crisis management scenario (in partnership with the Bill and Melinda Gates Foundation and the World Economic Forum) as part of its ongoing programme to model and explore issues around biological threats, pandemics and similar disaster scenarios. In Autumn 2019, it ran a one-day event (Event 201) around the issues of a SARS-like virus spreading from a pig farm in Brazil[15] and eventually becoming a global pandemic. It included the fact that there was a lack of vaccines and an inability to produce the level required in the time demanded, as well as an impact on trade and travel, sending the global economy into free fall.

Mistakes made...

It is the responsibility of governments to protect the safety, security and well-being of their citizens, and a failure to do so can be considered a dereliction of duty. There is no doubt that the possibility of a pandemic hitting the UK was a risk that had been identified, discussed and, in theory at least, prepared for.

The 2017 UK National Risk Register had identified pandemic influenza as its highest risk, with a likelihood of four out of five of occurring over the next five years and an impact of five out of five. The impact figure was largely based on the recognition that the additional stresses triggered by a major flu outbreak would cause unsustainable pressure on the already over-burdened National Health Service.

In the same register, emergent infectious diseases (i.e. global pandemics) was given the same likelihood value, which given that it was being compared to pandemic influenza meant there was an almost certainty that it would take place in the next five years, but an impact level of three out of five. As in all risk registers, the two significant questions that need to be asked are:

1. Is the range of risks that have been identified and listed a reasonable reflection of the risk environment that you are operating in?
2. For the risks that you have identified – do you understand what that means?

It is the ability to understand the significance of potential impacts and consequences, and the ability to use the risk register as the foundation for the development of appropriate pre-event preparations and post-event response capabilities, that add value to the risk management programme. The fact that there was the possibility of a global pandemic occurring was recognized in the report: it cites more than 30 new (or newly recognized) emerging infectious diseases that had been identified around the world, such as Ebola, Zika and Middle East Respiratory Syndrome (MERS).

The UK government's claims that it was ready and prepared was challenged by those people who were working on the ground and engaging with both the impacts and the consequences of the new disease. The *British Medical Journal* editorial in May 2020 was headlined 'The UK's public health response to Covid-19: too little, too late, too flawed'.[16] A national programme designed to contain, delay, research and mitigate Covid-19 was published on 3 March 2020 and yet by 12 May there had been 30,000 hospital and community deaths.

The consequences of pandemic flu were estimated at up to 50 per cent of the UK population experiencing symptoms and 20,000–750,000 fatalities. The case study of Ebola in West Africa in 2013–14 was used by the UK authorities to model potential fatalities from a similar event in the UK and came to the conclusion that it would be limited to 100 deaths. Ebola had a number of specific conditions that meant it would not spread as fast or as widely as an influenza-style pandemic would. First, its contamination and infection were spread by touch rather than as an air-borne virus. Second, by the time people became infectious they were already likely to be severely ill, so that they were bed-ridden and had limited opportunities to infect others through casual contact, And third, it had been largely limited to rural areas in three west African countries and had not spread to the urban centres. If it had become a city-based epidemic rather village-based, then the spread patterns would have been radically different.

On 11 March, speaking at the Covid-19 media briefing, the WHO director-general highlighted how WHO had been in full response mode since being notified of the first cases and 'called every day for countries to take urgent and aggressive action'. The three pillars that were considered critical to develop an effective all-of-society response were fast decision-making by top leaders, operational thoroughness by public health systems and societal engagement.

The first Covid-19 lockdown was imposed in Italy by 11 March, followed by France and Spain. The UK took another approach, with the Scientific Advisory Group for Emergencies (SAGE) deciding that the population would not accept such unprecedented measures. The pressure for political considerations to supersede what was even at the time and on the basis of available evidence considered best practice meant there was the lack of a clear strategic framework that would set the foundation for further decisions to be based on. Despite the fact that the WHO standard approach of find, test, trace and isolate had been adopted by those countries that had managed to contain the spread of the virus, the UK government downplayed the importance of containment and testing and decided that rather than regional testing across the country (which would have allowed the early identification of spreads and clusters), all testing capacity would be focused on hospital patients.

Entry through airports and ports remained unrestricted, despite the fact that the UK's position as an island would have allowed relatively simple measures to be put in place to take advantage of this geographic feature as there was control of all points of entry, as opposed to countries facing similar challenges in mainland Europe where the borders were conceptual rather than involving actual control mechanisms. Although global trends were clearly indicating that a major pandemic was potentially on the cards, the UK government downgraded the status of Covid-19 on 19 March from Level 4 (the highest) to Level 3. This impacted the level of personal protective equipment that staff in hospitals and other healthcare environments were required to use. Combined with a policy of discharging elderly people from hospitals to care homes without having tests, this meant that rather than containing the spread of Covid-19, government decisions seemed to actively create the perfect environment in which the virus could be spread as widely as possible and to the most vulnerable of communities. Boin and Lodge identified this as the principle approach,[17] based on a pre-set understanding of what the correct mode should be rather than the pragmatic, which is much more events-orientated and accepts that policy-setting in such circumstances is always based on the realities of the changes in the operating environment and the challenges that creates.

The desire to believe that the pandemic could be controlled and that the world could return to its previous condition with minimal disruption or the need for radical measures was captured in the UK government's report, issued in May 2020 (two months after the initial Covid-19 lockdown was introduced), which stated:

> On 11 May the government published 'Our plan to rebuild: the UK Government's Covid-19 recovery strategy'. The government's aim at the centre of that plan was to return to life as close to normal as possible, for as many people across the UK as possible, as fast and fairly as possible; in a way that avoids a new epidemic, minimises lives lost and maximises health, economic and social outcomes. We have followed our plan and the virus is in retreat.[18]

The question that needs to be asked is why a country that is the sixth largest economy in the world, that has a world-leading academic and scientific community, and that prides itself on its public health system could get it so wrong. While it is recognized that situations such as the spread of Covid-19 require fast decision-making, and almost always on the basis of incomplete, fast-changing and often contradictory information, it is also clear that the design of the decision-making process in itself creates in-built biases. Those biases are then embedded into both the processes and the final outcomes, even though such biases may not be either conscious for those within the decision-making process or identifiable to those outside it. The members of SAGE are scientific modellers and epidemiologists, and there was no one with any experience in developing or implementing a public health response, just as there was no one with a background in emergency or crisis planning, logistical management or any of the other areas which would have a critical impact on the ability to model, develop and deliver a programme that would have the required impacts across local and national levels in the face of an unprecedented and highly disruptive event. It was also identified that women and ethnic minorities were under-represented, even though many of the steps that were implemented had a disproportionate impact on those sections of the community in particular.[19]

... And lessons learned

At times of national emergency, there is the temptation for what became known as 'boosterism' in the political terminology of the day, following the habits of the UK's prime minister Boris Johnson to give what was considered to be morale-boosting slogans rather than an accurate description of the situation at hand, the challenges ahead and the likely steps that would need to be taken.

However, in parallel to the legitimate need to maintain national confidence and morale, there needs to be the development of society-wide frameworks that can support the local initiatives that would be at the heart of efforts to respond to any disruptive event, not only a pandemic.[20] At the heart of such developments is trust, whether between the government and the public or between the different ministries, agencies and organizations that would be an integral part of the multi-stranded efforts to create effective and appropriate responses in the face of such complex challenges.[21]

It has been debated to what extent the failure of the WHO to declare a PHEIC was contributory to the failure of governments around the world to implement appropriate monitoring and control processes. However, the significant issue according to those involved at the time is not whether the warning was given but whether governments would pay attention. The president of Médecins Sans Frontières, a person who works on the frontline of public health in multiple countries across the world, made it clear that it was the governments' failures rather than the speed of the WHO warning that was the critical issue. 'The biggest issue for me is that for six to eight weeks after the PHEIC declaration, countries, except in Asia, sat on their hands.'[22]

To a large extent, the ability to respond to a public health warning such as Covid is as much to do with whether it attracts people's attention (including politicians) in the midst of multiple competing stories. Although PHEIC is a globally recognized term with specific significance, it was only when the word *pandemic* started to be used that there was global attention, despite the fact that there are no agreed criteria for the use of the word as a technical term.[23]

The WHO is, at heart, a political body. This means that it requires the support of its funders and their willingness to share information, which in turn means that there always are the political considerations as to how WHO should respond to and engage with issues that have potential global impact but are also subject to political sensitivities. From the outset, WHO leadership had to be extremely sensitive in their dealing with the Chinese government in order to gain access to Wuhan for their teams of scientists, and the response from the US when it had political interest in blaming China for the pandemic and attacking WHO for its own political objectives. These considerations meant that decisions that should have been taken purely on public health grounds were instead subject to multiple pressures, both internally and externally, from multiple sources trying to manipulate the situation for their own benefit.

It's true that pandemics, though unique in themselves, nevertheless follow a pattern that can be recognized across multiple examples. This is something that can be seen in the aftermath of Ebola, which affected West Africa in

2013–15. Although there were multiple reviews into the outbreak from multiple perspectives, lessons were not learned. Médecins Sans Frontières former president Joanne Liu said, 'Less than 10 per cent of the recommendations were followed up on. We have an amazing talent to outrage ourselves about a situation, but when it comes time to deliver any change, there is very little traction, and people go back to doing whatever they had done before.'[24]

Although the initial response to Covid-19 was to see it purely in terms of a medical and public health perspective, it soon became clear that in reality it was a whole-of-society issue. It was one that needed to be responded to in a holistic manner, though this was often not acted upon, and had seemingly little if any impact on government policies and approaches. The circumstance that those people responding on the front line were put under unprecedented pressure and were themselves suffering both from the risk of infection and the mental strain that working on the front line of a pandemic would create in anyone, together with the fact that every aspect of their work experience was both unrelenting and overwhelming, was not taken into consideration. It was estimated that up to one third of people working on the front line in the UK health system suffered from mental health issues as a result of their work, and two thirds reported suffering some form of mental distress.[25]

The consequences of dealing with a long-lasting, high-impact event such as a pandemic do not last just for the length of the incident but have long-term consequences. Our systems are overloaded and overstressed even before being faced with the challenges of a global event, which means that there is no surge capacity. It also means that morale, mental wellbeing and the ability to adapt to change and absorb additional stress, both systemic and personal, are at a minimum.[26]

Although high-impact events such as pandemics are disruptive in their very nature, they also offer the opportunity for fast learning in ways that are not possible under normal operating conditions. Just as Covid-19 proved to be a turbocharger for the development of new skills and technologies, whether it was the development of new vaccines, the ability to adapt to the needs of work from home, or the speed with which we all became familiar with online meetings and video calls, it was also a fast learning environment for organizational skills and capabilities. The ability to create cross-sector partnerships, to share skills in developing innovative solutions to fast-moving and often fast-escalating challenges, meant that normal decision-making and policy-development processes fell by the wayside, and personal and inter- and intra-organizational relationships became key.[27]

As is often the case in high-stress environments, the issue is not so much a lack of information. It is rather the overwhelming amount of information that is being generated from multiple sources, but without the ability to filter and evaluate the information so that the useful nuggets can be extracted from the background sludge. Pandemics and similar fast-moving events give little or no time for the more strategic overviews that would allow optimal decisions to be made and actions to be taken. The ability to have a trusted source of information, and to establish a framework that could gather and collate such information from multiple sources, including the learning that had taken place in other countries undergoing the same challenges, would offer a significant benefit. This would allow a level of coordination and alignment that would ensure that the maximum possible value could be extracted from limited resources, in terms of both personnel and equipment but also learning time.

The failure to either identify the critical issues associated with national-level emergencies or to learn lessons from previous ones is of course not just a UK problem. In the US, the CSIS (Center for Strategic and International Studies) Commission Report on US national pandemic readiness identified a *boom and bust* cycle where national attention was raised during actual pandemics (SARS, MERS, Zika, Ebola) but then swiftly disappeared from the national consciousness once the initial panic had passed.[28]

As with all such reports, although the specific details relating to the particular national management structures might change, the overarching lessons did not. In fact, the executive summary of any of the reports could be cut and pasted in their entirety to every other report – and they would fully maintain their validity:

- There should be sustained and focused support at the highest levels of political leadership.
- Ongoing and long-term funding for both research and response agencies.
- Create a national pandemic task force that could bring together the broad range of expertise that is required and to ensure that such a body had both a voice and influence at the top table.
- Create a rapid response capability with the sensitivity to emerging pandemic threats and which could have the necessary level of surge capacity to allow them to move to full response capability in the time frames required.

- Have the ability to deliver the necessary services even when there was the scale of disruption associated with a pandemic event.
- Have the ability to engage with the general population throughout the event, to ensure their ongoing understanding and support.

Nightingale hospitals: fast response to unprecedented challenges

The Nightingale hospitals in the UK are an example of this. Created in response to the surge in cases in Italy that had overwhelmed the local health services, five fully equipped emergency hospitals, with a capacity of 10,000 patients, were built using military planning and support. In the event, the expected surge did not happen, and in fact 51 patients were treated at the London ExCel Centre, a 4,000-bed facility. Other Nightingale hospitals reported either zero patients or only a handful treated.[29] Questioning whether this was a wasteful exercise is of course always possible in hindsight, and the case was made that there had either been a misunderstanding of the data or that political decisions had been made in a knee-jerk response to alarmist headlines.[30]

Lessons learned concerning the building of large-scale centralized facilities rather than smaller-scale local facilities were reflected in the initiatives in December 2021 in response to fears that the Omicron variant could cause a new surge in infections. Plans were announced to create 8 Nightingale hospitals with a capacity of 100 patients each. These would be sited in existing hospital grounds to ensure the ability to maximize limited resources in responding to the surge in demand the use of such facilities would create. There was the option to create an additional capability of up to 4,000 beds in the event of a *super surge*.[31] This is an example of the benefit that experience brings and that it is only through such experience that effective capabilities are developed. It is why it is critical that focused learning takes place as fast and as early as possible, in the recognition that early attempts to respond to what are unprecedented events are likely to be at best sub-optimal and at worst completely inappropriate or ineffective. As experience is gathered and learning takes place, later iterations would have a much greater understanding both of the challenges created and of the range of possible options available.

The decision to use military capabilities and capacities to support ongoing national response had a precedent. The ability to develop a joint management/

command and control structure in response to the pandemic in 2020 was directly based on the experiences gained during coordination of the military response during the London 2012 Olympic Games. This was both for planned engagements as part of the Games preparations and also when the contracted security company, G4S, failed to deliver the tens of thousands of front-line security personnel as promised and the military was used to provide fast surge back-up and support. Although this was clearly different from the pandemic, it was the fact that the personnel who had been involved in the Olympics response had both the personal connections and the organizational memory of how to integrate civilian and military resources that had significant impact in supporting a response that was short notice, fast moving and required a high level of flexibility on both sides.

In the military, there is the concept of the 7Ps of Planning: Proper Prior Planning Prevents Pretty Poor Performance. There is the need to run simulations – what Gates called 'germ games, not war games', but there is also the need to ensure that the exercises that are run are appropriate to the scenarios and challenges being planned for and, even more importantly, that lessons identified are then used as the basis for further development and implementation. Prior to the Covid pandemic, there had been multiple exercises run by multiple organizations, all of which identified similar gaps and vulnerabilities in national structures, capabilities and preparedness. The reality showed: almost all findings had been routinely ignored – and in some cases actively suppressed.

Female leadership: a significant issue?

The use of language and metaphor is critical in establishing the nature of the crisis and the way in which we engage with it. From the start of the coronavirus pandemic, the metaphor that was the natural hook on which all other developments were based was one of war. It was of defeating the enemy. In setting out the relationship with Covid-19 in these terms, it also became necessary to create a feeling of national unity and one in which it would be seen as treasonous to take a contrary view or to challenge the legitimacy of the leaders. Despite this, in many countries, rather than taking the example of war-time to mean that there should be, for example, a government of national unity, it was used as an excuse to concentrate power even more than usual in the hands of a small number of people at the centre of an increasingly autocratic decision-making framework.

The relationship between the government and the general population became a critical issue and one that both set the foundation for future dialogue but also reflected the existing internal tensions. Most countries recognized the importance of establishing an inclusive, collaborative approach, where it was the responsibility of the government to explain to the populace the nature of the decisions being made and to ensure that there was a feeling of 'we are all in this together'. However, there was a clear distinction between those that managed to do so in a way that reflected a genuine desire to create national unity and those where such pronouncements were in themselves divisive and helped to increase alienation and polarization.

It is no surprise that the nature of the approaches taken reflected the personalities of the leaders themselves. Angela Merkel (Germany), Jacinda Ardern (New Zealand) and the leaders of the Scandinavian states, Sanna Marin (Finland), Mette Frederiksen (Denmark), Magdalena Andersson (Sweden) and Katrín Jakobsdóttir (Iceland), are all considered to have created a national dialogue that bypassed the confrontational approach taken by other leaders. However, they were also all leaders that took hard decisions (to lock down their countries in the face of persuasive but hardly definitive evidence) at an earlier stage than their male counterparts. These can be considered as interventions that had a significant impact on the wellbeing of their citizens, with multiple papers reporting that countries with female leaders have fared significantly better than those led by men on a wide range of dimensions concerning the global health crisis.[32]

It was in fact the outstanding feature of both the US and the UK (both countries headed by leaders that prided themselves on being unorthodox in their leadership and decision-making approaches) that those leaders (US president Donald Trump and UK prime minister Boris Johnson) either ignored the seriousness of the Covid-19 threat or actively downplayed it.[33] This matches a well-known study by Finucane et al from 2000[34] in which it was identified that those who were more privileged and felt more secure tended to underestimate risks, while those who were considered more vulnerable – women, people from minorities and those from lower socio-economic groups – tended to overestimate risks.

The fact that they are all female may in itself be a significant factor in the approach that they took. The characteristics associated with female leadership, such as good listening skills, the tendency to seek input and counsel for major decisions, the ability to provide a big-picture overview of a situation and proficiency in risk management,[35] are certainly those that would follow or initiate a more inclusive approach to the challenges that any crisis event would create. The role taken by the male leader is often the one of the exclusive protector, pushing aside others in order that they can stand at the front – the leader as heroic figure. For the female leader, it is often the case that the approach to protectiveness is more inclusive and empathetic.[36] However, it is also possible that these women had been elected because the social, cultural and political environment that they were operating in already recognized the value of those characteristics. As always, we come back to the issue of culture, whether it is on an organizational or a national scale, and the impact that has on all aspects of power, leadership and the associated decision-making structures and approaches.

It is interesting that the correlation between female leadership style and the effectiveness of Covid-19 policies was recreated internally within the US political system. A review of the actions of female state governors found that states with women governors went into lockdown earlier and had fewer deaths.[37]

Empathetic rather than policy-driven approaches are more likely to be collaborative, discursive and pragmatic rather than didactic and based on pre-set political differentiation. At a time when there was the need to offer reassurance to the country, at a time when there was genuine concern as to the impacts of the pandemic, but also on a very personal level, as to how that would impact families and communities, and particularly those that were already vulnerable and under-resourced, the male approach to reassurance tends to be projected in terms of knowledge and control, while the female approach tends to be more of health and security.[38]

Developing crisis situations, when there is little information about an unprecedented event that is highly unstable, the ability to make decisions that are both decisive and inclusive (rather than divisive and exclusive, where a significant part of the population feels that their wellbeing or interests are not being acknowledged or safeguarded)[39] is a critical issue.

The importance of creating a response that engenders the feeling of unity during a time of acute national stress is something that was highlighted in the UK's House of Commons report 'Coronavirus: Lessons learned to date'.[40] In it, it was made clear that the trust associated with public messaging was a critical issue in creating a unified response and that consistent messaging was a critical component of that.

Emergency response or crisis management?

There remains a basic lack of understanding of the difference between an emergency and a crisis, and the inability to do so means that there is a lack of clarity in the use of terminology that naturally leads to a lack of clarity in conceptualizing and modelling a genuine crisis event as opposed to routine emergency situations. In the UK's National Audit Office (NAO) report from November 2021 (18 months into Covid-19),[41] 'The government's preparedness for the COVID-19 pandemic: Lessons for government on risk management', this lack of discrimination is clear. 'Emergencies can take many forms, such as natural disasters, terrorist attacks, industrial accidents, critical supply chain disruptions or disease outbreaks. In the UK, recent emergencies include the London and Manchester terrorist attacks, the "Beast from the East" winter storm, serious flooding incidents and the Covid-19 pandemic.' A 2020 paper stated that Covid-19 was 'quite different from many other crises, such as those caused by floods or earthquakes, where the causes are clear, the central problem obvious, and the solutions and emergency responses, from a policy standpoint, clear'.[42]

The failure to differentiate between emergency response and crisis management in both a government and academic context suggests that it is this failure that is a critical issue in understanding the capability gaps that are uncovered when crisis management challenges are triggered, as well as the actual physical and organizational failures.

The NAO report's executive summary highlights the fact that planners have created a risk management framework that would suit their own requirements, being simple, scenario-focused and allowing for the development of detailed plans based on clearly understood events. Rather than horizon-scanning for emergent risks, national emergency preparedness planning and modelling is limited to a two-year horizon. It is focused on a single scenario for each risk. As the report itself states, despite the fact that the UK is considered to be world leader in national-level risk management, the programmes themselves were simplistic, focused on triggering events rather than subsequent consequences, and did not appear to engage in the development of an understanding of overlapping and interconnected challenges that would require an all-of-government response rather than a single programme led by the ministry.

The UK National Risk Register had emergent infectious diseases as one of its highest risks since 2008. The projections for the impacts of pandemic influenza, something that happens on a regular basis (in fact, an annual basis, without necessarily reaching the levels of a full-blown pandemic), are up to half of the UK population experiencing symptoms and 20,000–750,000 fatalities. It was identified (not unreasonably) that this would have an impact on high levels of absence for work. It has been used as an excuse across government that the UK was prepared for an influenza pandemic, not a coronavirus pandemic, and therefore there was not the level of preparedness in terms of PPE, hospital space, surge capacity and the like. However, it is exactly at this stage that the ability to differentiate between the emergency (the medical response to the pandemic) and the crisis (the impact on the country) becomes critical.

If it is a truism of crisis management that the triggering event is relatively unimportant, and it is the issue of consequence management that is at the heart of crisis management, then it should be clear that while the issues in dealing with the medical implications of a coronavirus outbreak rather than an influenza outbreak might be significant at the response level, in terms of maintaining critical national capabilities, the issue of whether it is the impacts from 750,000 influenza deaths or 150,000 coronavirus deaths is not a significant variable.

The central question was, how do we maintain critical capabilities when there are such high-level impacts across the system? There has been little if no discussion of what the plans for national management were in the event that a level of fatalities as had been identified in repeated national risk registers had actually occurred, but if there had been such plans available, then it is clear that they would have been highly relevant in modelling and responding to the challenges that Covid-19 threw at the country in March 2020.

The famous saying by former heavyweight boxing champion Mike Tyson that 'everyone has a plan, until they get punched in the face' is equally applicable to crisis management. Every organization has a plan until something actually happens. It then becomes clear that what the organization had been doing in its preparations was little more than fantasy planning[43] based on fantasy documents[44] that had little or no connection with the realities of an actual event that it might be facing. The NAO report identified exactly these findings, saying that 'a review of pandemic planning arrangements, carried out by a cross-government working group in February and March 2020, rated 82 per cent of plans as being unable to meet the demands of any actual incident'.[45]

The challenges associated with these scenarios are not unknown issues. The reports following Exercise Winter Willow, another national-level exercise modelling the response to an influenza pandemic, warned that there was a need for greater cross-department and multi-partner collaboration and coordination. The conclusions to the report come under what can only be described as the blindingly obvious. Although influenza pandemic had been repeatedly identified as the leading potential risk at a national level, there were few or no plans to maintain functionality on issues such as the impact of 50 per cent loss of work attendance or the ability to maintain education; there was little if any cross-government end-to-end planning that would allow the full impacts of a major pandemic to be understood and prepared for; there was a lack of learning from exercises that had been run and issues that had been identified; and there was a lack of understanding of the need for developing resilience based on effective partnerships across government departments, with the private sector and also with international partners.

Like so many reports of this nature, it is hard to identify what has been learned from this specific review and what could considered generic lessons that could have been learned from any of the hundreds of other reports written about hundreds of other events, both large and small, from multiple sectors and impacting both local and national capabilities in multiple ways.

Lessons learned for the future

Although it would be encouraging to believe that the lessons learned from the global pandemic we have experienced since the end of 2019, as well as the shock of recognition that these issues are not going to go away, would create both the awareness and the urgency associated with developing an effective governance model for the future, the sad truth is that much as in all other previous shocks, the window of opportunity for creating meaningful change is both narrow and fragile.

The Independent Panel for Pandemic Preparedness and Response, established by the World Health Agency, a division of the WHO, pretty well summed it up in its report in November 2021, following up on its initial report in May 2021:

> The manifest failures of the Covid-19 response to date should motivate all stakeholders to make serious reforms and minimise the impact of future disease threats.... Much of the groundwork to identify the steps to reform has been done – what is needed now is for countries to make a final push so that the

> opportunity to create a safer world does not slip through our fingers.
> **We ask: if this pandemic cannot catalyse real change, what will?**
> (IPPPR Report, 2021:b). Bold in the original)[46]

The initial report had noted both the unprecedented levels of impact and the disruption caused by Covid-19 across the world, and also the need to use that as a wake-up call to create the multinational, multi-jurisdictional and multi-disciplinary frameworks required to model and engage with an event on this scale. It also set out a vision of a world that would take these issues so seriously that they could act in a substantive and sustained manner to prevent such incidents, or at least their tragic consequences, from happening in future.

The fact that by the middle of 2022, Covid-19 related infections were once again climbing to unprecedented levels, meant that not only had those warnings not been heeded but basic measures to monitor and control infection rates had been put aside under the more immediate pressures of other issues. This especially shows in the data collected throughout the pandemic. In Germany, a report issued by a commission of experts reviewing the Covid-19 restrictions introduced by the government concluded that the responses not only cut off any discussions about alternate prevention approaches and with this blighted a holistic discussion about how to successfully deal with this pandemic, but also had no research concept to collect the right data that would allow better decision-making. Even the offer from health insurers to get access to their enormous amount of data has been ignored. Parts of the important data are not readable by machines or would be usable only with a massive additional effort. In a world that is as connected and full of technology as ours, this is a harsh conclusion for a country as developed as Germany. Still, it makes clear: if we don't invest in proper data (from gathering to maintenance and evaluation), we don't have or can't make them available in times when we need them the most, be it only to reduce otherwise unforeseeable collateral damage.

Among the many lessons learned is the fact that there are no simple or clear responses, and in fact there are unlikely to be any responses that offer a complete solution to the wide array of secondary and tertiary impacts and consequences that are triggered by the main event. Although there may be a desire to offer big-package solutions, the likelihood is that there is a much higher chance to require a large number of smaller, locally owned responses rather than one all-encompassing solution, that can be clearly defined and centrally managed. In this sense, we are moving from the vision of the crisis leader as being heroic to something that is more administrative minded. Boin and Lodge labelled this 'pragmatic crisis management'[47] and positioned it firmly in the context of the lessons learned from Covid-19. It embodies the lessons learned from other large-scale events, all of which have had a high level of disruption and uncertainty, and a need to move forward in incremental stages rather than creating a fully developed response plan from the start.

There is also the issue of the post-crisis recovery. The number of virus mutations and its capabilities to escape vaccines will continue to present significant challenges, especially for countries with a poor infrastructure or response, or for businesses to answer complex ethical, security and duty-of-care questions, for example policies concerning staff travelling to high-risk areas. Covid-19 was a global socioeconomic shock, driving unemployment, food insecurity, urban poverty and mental health issues. Children were suffering (not only education wise but also socially) and women were under additional pressure (heading households, providing home schooling, working in sectors that were more impacted such as hospitality). Pre-existing vulnerabilities have been enforced or covered up ruthlessly. With this, it is clear that the impacts and consequences of Covid-19 will be long-lasting – in many cases, generational and potentially even multi-generational. The outstanding lesson of the first half of 2022 has been how quickly the world moves on and how little time there is for making genuinely significant and substantive changes. Although crises are often seen as the opportunity for radical reform, the truth is that we are much more likely to return to the pre-crisis situation than use that as the opportunity to develop radical new operating systems.[48] Although President Barack Obama's chief of staff Rahm Emanuel famously said 'you should never let a good crisis go to waste', the way that is manifested is more likely to be in terms of short-term advantages rather than long-term change.

Boin and 't Hart addressed these issues in their widely referenced 2003 paper, 'Public leadership in times of crisis: Mission impossible?'.[49] In it, they identified six fallacies that led to false expectations from crisis leaders:

1. **Popular expectation: Leaders should put public safety first.**
   Research finding: Leaders consider the economic and political costs of regulating and enforcing maximum safety too expensive. They settle for, and pay for, sub-optimal levels of safety.
2. **Popular expectation: Leaders should prepare for worst-case scenarios.**
   Research finding: Most government and business leaders are reluctant to prepare themselves for their crisis-response roles.

3 **Popular expectation: Leaders should heed warnings about future crises.** Research finding: Most man-made disasters and violent conflicts are preceded by incubation periods during which policy makers misinterpret, are ignorant of or flat-out ignore repeated indications of impending danger.

4 **Popular expectation: During a crisis, leaders take charge and provide clear direction to crisis-management operations.** Research finding: Crisis operations are multi-organizational, trans-jurisdictional, polycentric response networks. They demand lateral coordination, not top-down command and control.

5 **Popular expectation: Leaders should be compassionate toward victims of crises. This empathy should play out in both word and deed.** Research finding: Leaders want to provide victims with care, but they often fall prey to their own unrealistic promises.

6 **Popular expectation: Leaders strive to learn lessons after a crisis.** Research finding: Leaders get caught in the politics of blaming that dominates the aftermath of modern contemporary crises. Learning is encumbered in this atmosphere.

It is an indication of the universality of the underlying truths of crisis management that these points are as relevant in 2022 as they were in 2003, and as they were undoubtedly true throughout history. While the identification of these points does not in itself offer a solution to these problems, it does suggest a framework through which such issues can be legitimately engaged with and which can (perhaps) offer a foundation on which subsequent discussions and policy-making can take place.

Conclusion

Covid-19 was perhaps a forewarning of what future crises might look like. To say that they are unprecedented and overwhelming is both simplistic and unacceptable. The truth is that Covid-19 is something that had been predicted for decades and for which there had been multiple precursor events that should have allowed those in authority, whether in science, public health, national administration or political leadership, to develop protocols and frameworks that could have supported effective decision-making as well as national, transnational and global collaboration in order to offer effective responses to what was, in many ways, a planetary-level existential threat.

Although Covid-19 could have been described as a creeping crisis, it was in fact one for which there was a clear timeframe during which protective and pre-emptive steps could have been taken that undoubtedly would have had a significant impact both on the initial spread of the virus and on the subsequent impacts and consequences.[50] These steps were well recognized, widely shared and clearly signposted. Despite that, there was a disinclination to recognize the potential, and then the actual, impacts of the pandemic even as it was escalating during its incubating period.[51] The question is not 'How did this happen?' but 'Why did people not pay attention?'.

Covid-19 was not a particularly serious pandemic, it should have been managed under the emergency management frameworks which had been put in place to respond to exactly this sort of national event. The fact that the responses failed so miserably, and with such catastrophic consequences, is due to the failure of risk, emergency and crisis management skills rather than to the intrinsic nature of the pandemic.

Covid-19 has given strategic task and crisis management planners the greatest gift they can have: a near-miss. It is a clear warning sign that what they thought of as effective planning measures were in fact not so (and that was something that should have been known to them long before those plans and capabilities were tested by the reality of an actual pandemic event). The likelihood is that the next existential crisis will not be a pandemic and may be something that is not even on our current risk registers. While the details of the individual event may be different, the pressures and challenges created for our local, national and transnational systems are likely to be similar to those identified during Covid-19. We were not ready for Covid-19. We have the responsibility to make sure that we are ready for future shocks. If the lessons identified from Covid-19 are not taken on board, then next time we may not be so lucky in avoiding what could be a truly catastrophic event, and not one from which we escape so lightly.

There is of course the constant dynamic tension between those that hold expert knowledge and those that need to make judgement-based decisions. It is not just that there is no single correct answer, but it is often the case that it is not clear as to what the correct question might be. Although there was the oft-stated commitment to 'follow the science', the science itself is often unclear, emergent, contextual and sometimes just plain ignorant. In fact, it is in the nature of scientific enquiry that information is based on best available evidence with a clear acknowledgement that the overarching sense-making that would allow it to act as the foundation for definitive decision-making is missing.

However, while there may not be the ability to make a definitive decision, there is nevertheless the ability – the responsibility – to create an atmosphere in which the seriousness of the situation can be acknowledged. The tendency of some leaders (high-profile examples include US president Donald Trump, Brazil's president Jair Bolsonaro and UK prime minister Boris Johnson) to 'deny and trivialize' the significance of Covid-19 meant that there were internal tensions that would significantly impact the ability to create a unified national response.[52]

The inability of the UK government to recognize the seriousness of the pending pandemic and to realize the scale of the possible impacts can be gauged by the fact that the first meeting of the UK's national crisis management framework (COBR) was only held on 24 January, chaired by the Minister of Health, and only four meetings were held over the following six weeks. The first COBR meeting chaired by the prime minister was not until 2 March.[53] This showed that this was not high on the government's agenda even when warnings from the WHO and the numbers and trends identified across the world clearly indicated that this could have a significant impact.

The desire to have clear and simple solutions that not only did not necessitate deep analysis of the problems and challenges being faced but required little if any additional effort on the part of the decision-makers and those charged with implementing their policies meant that there was a tendency not only to over-simplify the issues but to trivialize the responses. The fact that the UK government spent significant time and effort trying to work out what exactly a meal in a pub consisted of, or announced that all children should be forced to return to school on 48 hours' notice, even though there was little or no opportunity for schools to create effective Covid-19 management protocols, or even to discuss what those might be, meant that there was a consistent failure to communicate an effective and widely shared long-term policy that could help all sectors of society plan for and engage with those issues. There was a consistent pattern of policies being created and announced with little if any warning, and certainly no explanation as to their reasoning or their implications in the context of the wider response to the pandemic, and those policies were themselves often changed, abandoned or quietly ignored within days of their release.

Covid-19 has undoubtedly been the highest-impact event that the world has faced in modern times. It is not, however, the highest-impact event that it could face and based on the increasingly unstable risk environment that we are operating in on a planetary scale, it is quite possible that it is not the highest-impact event that we will face in our lives. The fundamental truth of Covid-19 is that although the pandemic itself was a significant triggering event, the way that the narrative played out across the world was not an inevitable occurrence but the result of a generation of chances missed, bad decisions made and a refusal to either face up to the truth of the challenges that we are facing or to accept the responsibility to act in a way that would minimize the likelihood of those events happening and to maximize our abilities to engage with them effectively if and when they did occur.

Our ancestors may have believed that such events were the acts of capricious gods, and that the only response was to make sacrifices to appease them. We now know differently. They are part of the ecosphere in which we exist and often a result of the mistakes that we have made. Our ability to use risk management principles to understand and engage with those issues, and to prepare ourselves at every level from the global to the community, is the foundation on which the future wellbeing of this planet and everyone on it rests.

Endnotes

1 Cabinet Office (2017) National risk register of civil emergencies, 2017 edition. Available at: https://assets.publishing.service.gov.uk/government/uploads/system/uploads/attachment_data/file/644968/UK_National_Risk_Register_2017.pdf (archived at https://perma.cc/ZWW3-KHYM) (Accessed: 20 April, 2022)

2 United Nations (2016) Protecting humanity from future health crises. Available at: https://digitallibrary.un.org/record/822489?ln=en (archived at https://perma.cc/8S6V-2687) (Accessed: 5 April 2022)

3 The pandemic-scenario exercise held in the US in October 2019 was titled Event 201 because there were around 200 epidemic events every year that did not escalate to full-blown global status (Nature, 2020).

4 WHO EIOS. World Health Organization epidemic intelligence from open sources. Available at: https://www.who.int/initiatives/eios (archived at https://perma.cc/9QCV-DXUB) (Accessed: 5 April 2022)

5 Obama, B (2014) Obama warned the U.S. to prepare for a pandemic back in 2014. Available at: https://www.youtube.com/watch?v=pBVAnaHxHbM (archived at https://perma.cc/S4XQ-5V7K) (Accessed: 5 April 2022)

6 Obama, B & Lugar R (2005) Grounding a pandemic. *The New York Times*, 6 June. Available at: https://www.nytimes.com/2005/06/06/opinion/grounding-a-pandemic.html (archived at https://perma.cc/PJ66-XDZP) (Accessed: 5 April 2022)

7 Gates, B (2015) The next outbreak? we're not ready. TED Talk, March. Available at: https://www.ted.com/talks/bill_gates_the_next_outbreak_we_re_not_ready?language=dz (archived at https://perma.cc/U3B4-8EKV) (Accessed: 5 April 2022)

8 Nature (2020) Two decades of pandemic war games failed to account for Donald Trump. Available at: https://www.nature.com/articles/d41586-020-02277-6 (archived at https://perma.cc/5K7J-HPN2) (Accessed: 5 April 2022)

9 Sabbagh, D (2020) Army likely to embed medics in NHS hospitals to help fight coronavirus. *The Guardian* (16 March). Available at: https://www.theguardian.com/world/2020/mar/16/army-likely-to-embed-medics-in-nhs-hospitals-to-help-fight-coronavirus-operation-broadshare (archived at https://perma.cc/4372-PQT8) (Accessed: 5 April 2022)

10 Public Health England (2017) Exercise Cygnus Report. Tier one command post exercise, pandemic influenza, 18 to 20 October 2016. Available at: https://assets.publishing.service.gov.uk/government/uploads/system/uploads/attachment_data/file/927770/exercise-cygnus-report.pdf (archived at https://perma.cc/UND4-TESU) (Accessed: 5 April 2022)

11 UK Parliament (2020) Manpower or mindset: Defence's contribution to the UK's pandemic response. Available at: https://publications.parliament.uk/pa/cm5801/cmselect/cmdfence/357/full-report.html (archived at https://perma.cc/9W5L-EK37) (Accessed: 5 April 2022)

12 HHS (2019) Crimson Contagion. https://archive.org/details/crimson-contagion-2019/page/13/mode/2up (archived at https://perma.cc/3JGQ-HWQU) (Accessed: 5 April 2022)

13 Wikipedia (2019) Crimson Contagion. https://en.wikipedia.org/wiki/Crimson_Contagion (archived at https://perma.cc/NPJ2-X9B4) (Accessed: 5 April 2022)

14 The New York Times (2019) Crimson Contagion 2019 functional exercise key findings. Available at: https://int.nyt.com/data/documenthelper/6824-2019-10-key-findings-and-after/05bd797500ea55be0724/optimized/full.pdf (archived at https://perma.cc/QAM5-DUNP) (Accessed: 5 April 2022)

15 Centre for Health Security (2019) Event 201. Available at: https://www.centerforhealthsecurity.org/our-work/exercises/event201/191017-press-release.html (archived at https://perma.cc/892V-EJUE) (Accessed 05 April 2022); Pearce, K (2019) Pandemic simulation exercise spotlights massive preparedness gap. John Hopkins University. Available at: https://hub.jhu.edu/2019/11/06/event-201-health-security/ (archived at https://perma.cc/A28L-AULK) (Accessed: 5 April 2022)

16 BMJ (2020) Pandemic preparedness: Government must release 2016 report, says Information Commissioner. http://dx.doi.org/10.1136/bmj.m3953 (archived at https://perma.cc/KR8W-6BA6) (Accessed: 5 April 2022); Cabinet Office (2017) National Risk Register Of Civil Emergencies, 2017 Edition. Available at: https://assets.publishing.service.gov.uk/government/uploads/system/uploads/attachment_data/file/644968/UK_National_Risk_Register_2017.pdf (archived at https://perma.cc/ZWW3-KHYM). (Accessed: 20 April 2022)

17 Boin, A & Lodge, M (2021) The attractions and limitations of pragmatist crisis management: A discussion in light of Covid-19 experiences. LSE Public Policy Review, 1(4), 9, 1–8. Available at: https://doi.org/10.31389/lseppr.22 (archived at https://perma.cc/73HA-RTDW) (Accessed: 20 April 2022)

18 HM Government, July 2020. Available at: https://assets.publishing.service.gov.uk/government/uploads/system/uploads/attachment_data/file/901521/6.6783_CO_Our_Plan_to_Rebuild_FINAL_170720_WEB.pdf (archived at https://perma.cc/37XT-F49L) (Accessed: 20 April 2022)

19 HM Government, July 2020. Available at: https://assets.publishing.service.gov.uk/government/uploads/system/uploads/attachment_data/file/901521/6.6783_CO_Our_Plan_to_Rebuild_FINAL_170720_WEB.pdf (archived at https://perma.cc/37XT-F49L) (Accessed: 20 April 2022)

20 HM Government, July 2020. Available at: https://assets.publishing.service.gov.uk/government/uploads/system/uploads/attachment_data/file/901521/6.6783_CO_Our_Plan_to_Rebuild_FINAL_170720_WEB.pdf (archived at https://perma.cc/37XT-F49L) (Accessed: 20 April 2022)

21 HM Government, July 2020. Available at: https://assets.publishing.service.gov.uk/government/uploads/system/uploads/attachment_data/file/901521/6.6783_CO_Our_Plan_to_Rebuild_FINAL_170720_WEB.pdf (archived at https://perma.cc/37XT-F49L) (Accessed: 20 April 2022)

22 Maxmen, A (2021) Why did the world's pandemic warning system fail for Covid?' *Nature*, 289

23 Maxmen, A (2021) Why did the world's pandemic warning system fail for Covid? *Nature*, 289

24 Maxmen, A (2021) Why did the world's pandemic warning system fail for Covid? *Nature*, 289

25 RCoA (Royal College of Anaesthetists) (2020) View from the frontline of anaesthesia during Covid-19. Available at: https://rcoa.ac.uk/sites/default/files/documents/2020-07/View-from-the-frontline-anaesthesia-during-COVID-19-July2020.pdf (archived at https://perma.cc/3F2F-ADAH) (Accessed: 20 April 2022)

26 RCoA (Royal College of Anaesthetists) (2017) A report on the welfare, morale and experiences of anaesthetists in training: The need to listen. Available at: https://rcoa.ac.uk/sites/default/files/documents/2020-09/Welfare-Morale2017.pdf (archived at https://perma.cc/9U6A-GTY3) (Accessed: 20 April 2022)

27 RCoA (Royal College of Anaesthetists) (2021) 10 lessons learnt from Covid-19; Professional Standards Authority (2021) Learning from Covid-19: A case-study review of the initial crisis response of 10 UK health and social care professional regulators in 2020. Available at: https://www.professionalstandards.org.uk/publications/detail/learning-from-covid-19-a-case-study-review (archived at https://perma.cc/UZ2U-WKBR) (Accessed: 20 April 2022)

28 CSIS (2019) Ending the cycle of crisis and complacency in U.S. global health security: A report of the CSIS Commission on strengthening America's health security. Available at: https://csis-website-prod.s3.amazonaws.com/s3fs-public/publication/191122_EndingTheCycle_GHSC_WEB_FULL_11.22.pdf (archived at https://perma.cc/K3Q2-7QLN) (Accessed: 20 April 2022)

29 NHS (2021) NHS plans new Nightingale facilities in response to Omicron (30 December). Available at: https://www.england.nhs.uk/2021/12/nhs-plans-new-nightingale-facilities-in-response-to-omicron/ (archived at https://perma.cc/K5BU-AGAE) (Accessed: 20 April 2022)

Further reading

BMJ (2020) UK's response to covid-19 'too little, too late, too flawed'. Available at: https://www.bmj.com/company/newsroom/uks-response-to-covid-19-too-little-too-late-too-flawed/ (archived at https://perma.cc/GXL3-TL8M) (Accessed: 20 April 2022)

BMJ (2020) Pandemic preparedness: Government must release 2016 report, says information commissioner. http://dx.doi.org/10.1136/bmj.m3953 (archived at https://perma.cc/KR8W-6BA6) (Accessed: 20 April 2022).

Boin, A & Lodge, M (2021a) The attractions and limitations of pragmatist crisis management: A discussion in light of Covid-19 experiences. *LSE Public Policy Review*, 1(4), 1–8

Boin, A & Lodge, M (2021b) Responding to the Covid-19 crisis: A principled or pragmatist approach? *Journal of European Public Policy*, 28(8), 1131–1152

Boin, A & 't Hart, P (2022) From crisis to reform? Exploring three post-Covid pathways. *Policy and Society*, 41(1), 13–24

Boin, A & 't Hart, P (2003) Public leadership in times of crisis: mission impossible? *Public Administration Review*, 63(5), 544–553

Cabinet Office (2017) National Risk Register Of Civil Emergencies, 2017 Edition. Available at: https://assets.publishing.service.gov.uk/government/uploads/system/uploads/attachment_data/file/644968/UK_National_Risk_Register_2017.pdf (archived at https://perma.cc/ZWW3-KHYM). (Accessed: 20 April 2022)

Capano, G, Howlett, M, Jarvis, D S, Ramesh, M and Goyal, N (2020) Mobilizing policy (in) capacity to fight Covid-19: Understanding variations in state responses. *Policy and Society*, 39(3), 285–308

Centre for Health Security (2019) Event 201. Available at: https://www.centerforhealthsecurity.org/our-work/exercises/event201/191017-press-release.html (archived at https://perma.cc/892V-EJUE) (Accessed: 20 April 2022)

Clarke, L (1999) *Mission improbable: Using fantasy documents to tame disaster*. University of Chicago Press

Clarke, L & Perrow, C (1996) Prosaic organizational failure. *American Behavioral Scientist*, 39(8), 1040–1056

Coscieme, L, Fioramonti, L, Mortensen, L F, Pickett, K E, Kubiszewski, I, Lovins, H, Mcglade, J, Ragnarsdottir, K V, Roberts, D, Costanza, R & De Vogli, R (2020) Women in power: Female leadership and public health outcomes during the Covid-19 pandemic. *MedRxiv*

CSIS (2019) Ending the cycle of crisis and complacency in U.S. global health security: A report of the CSIS Commission on strengthening America's health security. Available at: https://csis-website-prod.s3.amazonaws.com/s3fs-public/publication/191122_EndingTheCycle_GHSC_WEB_FULL_11.22.pdf (archived at https://perma.cc/K3Q2-7QLN) (Accessed: 20 April 2022)

Day, M (2020) Covid-19: Nightingale hospitals set to shut down after seeing few patients. *British Medical Journal*. Available at: https://www.bmj.com/content/bmj/369/bmj.m1860.full.pdf (archived at https://perma.cc/9T3B-4M4A) (Accessed: 20 April 2022)

Engström, A, Luesink, M & Boin, A (2021) From creeping to full-blown crisis: Lessons from the Dutch and Swedish response to Covid-19, in A Boin et al (eds.), *Understanding the creeping crisis*

Exercise Winter Willow: Lesson identified (2007). UK Department of Health. Available at: http://data.parliament.uk/DepositedPapers/Files/DEP2007-0334/DEP2007-0334.pdf (archived at https://perma.cc/3FTW-DW5U) (Accessed: 20 April 2022)

Gates, B (2015) The next outbreak? We're not ready. TED Talk, March 2015. Available at: https://www.ted.com/talks/bill_gates_the_next_outbreak_we_re_not_ready?language=dz (archived at https://perma.cc/U3B4-8EKV) (Accessed: 20 April 2022)

Gonzales, C F (2021) Let her lead: Acknowledging women leadership in the time of pandemic. *Sapienza: International Journal of Interdisciplinary Studies*, 2(4), 252–260

HHS (2019) Crimson Contagion. Available at: https://archive.org/details/crimson-contagion-2019/page/13/mode/2up (archived at https://perma.cc/3JGQ-HWQU) (Accessed: 20 April 2022)

HM Government, July 2020. Available at: https://assets.publishing.service.gov.uk/government/uploads/system/uploads/attachment_data/file/901521/6.6783_CO_Our_Plan_to_Rebuild_FINAL_170720_WEB.pdf (archived at https://perma.cc/37XT-F49L) (Accessed: 20 April 2022)

IPPPR Report (2021a) Covid-19: Make it the last pandemic. Independent Panel for Pandemic Preparedness and Response. Available at: https://theindependentpanel.org/wp-content/uploads/2021/05/COVID-19-Make-it-the-Last-Pandemic_final.pdf (archived at https://perma.cc/3VM3-9FEY) (Accessed: 20 April 2022)

IPPPR Report (2021b) Losing time: End this pandemic and secure the future. Independent Panel for Pandemic Preparedness and Response. Available at: https://theindependentpanel.org/wp-content/uploads/2021/11/COVID-19-Losing-Time_Final.pdf (archived at https://perma.cc/4FN5-WKEK) (Accessed: 20 April 2022)

ISID ProMed. International Society for Infectious Diseases. Available at: https://promedmail.org/ (archived at https://perma.cc/X5NF-FN8N) (Accessed: 20 April 2022)

Kawata, Y (2001) Disaster mitigation due to next Nankai earthquake tsunamis occurring in around 2035. Research Centre for Disaster Reduction Systems, Kyoto. University, Japan. Available at: http://nthmp-history.pmel.noaa.gov/its2001/Separate_Papers/1-08_Kawata.pdf (Accessed: 20 April 2022)

Kharlamenkova, N E (2015) Sex and gender differences in representations of psychological safety. *Social Psychology and Society*, 6(2), 51–60

Kuenssberg, L (2021) Covid: The inside story of the government's battle against the virus (15 March). Available at: https://www.bbc.com/news/uk-politics-56361599 (archived at https://perma.cc/PZ67-STQL) (Accessed: 20 April 2022)

Maxmen, A (2021) Why did the world's pandemic warning system fail for Covid? *Nature*, 289

National Audit Office (2021) The government's preparedness for the Covid-19 pandemic: lessons for government on risk management. Available at: https://www.nao.org.uk/wp-content/uploads/2021/11/The-governments-preparedness-for-the-COVID-19-pandemic-lessons-for-government-on-risk-management.pdf (archived at https://perma.cc/HWE2-NKD4) (Accessed: 20 April 2022)

Nature (2020) Two decades of pandemic war games failed to account for Donald Trump. Available at: https://www.nature.com/articles/d41586-020-02277-6 (archived at https://perma.cc/5K7J-HPN2) (Accessed: 20 April 2022)

New York Times (2019) Crimson Contagion 2019 functional exercise key findings. Available at: https://int.nyt.com/data/documenthelper/6824-2019-10-key-findings-and-after/05bd797500ea55be0724/optimized/full.pdf (archived at https://perma.cc/QAM5-DUNP) (Accessed: 20 April 2022)

NHS (2021) NHS plans new Nightingale facilities in response to Omicron (30 December). Available at: https://www.england.nhs.uk/2021/12/nhs-plans-new-nightingale-facilities-in-response-to-omicron/ (archived at https://perma.cc/K5BU-AGAE) (Accessed: 20 April 2022)

Obama, B (2014) Obama warned the U.S. to prepare for a pandemic back in 2014. Available at: https://www.youtube.com/watch?v=pBVAnaHxHbM (archived at https://perma.cc/S4XQ-5V7K) (Accessed: 20 April 2022)

Obama, B & Lugar R (2005) Grounding a pandemic. *The New York Times*, 6 June. Available at: https://www.nytimes.com/2005/06/06/opinion/grounding-a-pandemic.html (archived at https://perma.cc/PJ66-XDZP) (Accessed: 20 April 2022)

Pearce, K (2019) Pandemic simulation exercise spotlights massive preparedness gap. Johns Hopkins University. Available at: https://hub.jhu.edu/2019/11/06/event-201-health-security/ (archived at https://perma.cc/V56E-M3TR) (Accessed: 20 April 2022)

Policy and Society, Volume 41, Issue 1, January 2022, 13–24

Professional Standards Authority (2021) Learning from Covid-19: A case-study review of the initial crisis response of 10 UK health and social care professional regulators in 2020. Available at: https://www.professionalstandards.org.uk/publications/detail/learning-from-covid-19-a-case-study-review (archived at https://perma.cc/UZ2U-WKBR) (Accessed: 20 April 2022)

Public Health England (2017) Exercise Cygnus report. Tier one command post exercise, pandemic influenza, 18 to 20 October 2016. Available at: https://assets.publishing.service.gov.uk/government/uploads/system/uploads/attachment_data/file/927770/exercise-cygnus-report.pdf (archived at https://perma.cc/UND4-TESU) (Accessed: 20 April 2022)

RCoA (2017) A report on the welfare, morale and experiences of anaesthetists in training: The need to listen. Available at: https://rcoa.ac.uk/sites/default/files/documents/2020-09/Welfare-Morale2017.pdf (archived at https://perma.cc/9U6A-GTY3) (Accessed: 20 April 2022)

RCoA (Royal College of Anaesthetists) (2020) View from the frontline of anaesthesia during Covid-19. Available at: https://rcoa.ac.uk/sites/default/files/documents/2020-07/View-from-the-frontline-anaesthesia-during-COVID-19-July2020.pdf (archived at https://perma.cc/3F2F-ADAH) (Accessed: 20 April 2022)

RCoA (2021) 10 lessons learnt from Covid-19

Rutledge, P E (2020) Trump, Covid-19, and the war on expertise. *The American Review of Public Administration*, 50(6–7), 505–511

Sabbagh, D (2020) Army likely to embed medics in NHS hospitals to help fight coronavirus. *The Guardian* (16 March). Available at: https://www.theguardian.com/world/2020/mar/16/army-likely-to-embed-medics-in-nhs-hospitals-to-help-fight-coronavirus-operation-broadshare (archived at https://perma.cc/4372-PQT8) (Accessed: 20 April 2022)

Sergent, K & Stajkovic, A D (2020) Women's leadership is associated with fewer deaths during the Covid-19 crisis: Quantitative and qualitative analyses of United States governors. *Journal of Applied Psychology*, 105(8), 771

Taub, A (2020) Why are women-led nations doing better with Covid-19? *The New York Times* (15 May). Available at: https://www.nytimes.com/2020/05/15/world/coronavirus-women-leaders.html (archived at https://perma.cc/H7DD-RCCT) (Accessed: 20 April 2022)

UK Parliament (2020) Manpower or mindset: Defence's contribution to the UK's pandemic response. Available at: https://publications.parliament.uk/pa/cm5801/cmselect/cmdfence/357/full-report.html (archived at https://perma.cc/9W5L-EK37) (Accessed: 20 April 2022)

United Nations (2016) Protecting humanity from future health crises. Available at: https://digitallibrary.un.org/record/822489?ln=en (archived at https://perma.cc/8S6V-2687) (Accessed: 20 April 2022)

WHO EIOS. World Health Organization epidemic intelligence from open source. Available at: https://www.who.int/initiatives/eios (archived at https://perma.cc/9QCV-DXUB) (Accessed: 20 April 2022)

Wikipedia (2019) Crimson Contagion. https://en.wikipedia.org/wiki/Crimson_Contagion (archived at https://perma.cc/NPJ2-X9B4) (Accessed: 20 April 2022)

Windsor, L C, Yannitell, R G, Windsor, A J, Ostergard, R, Allen, S & Burns, C (2020) Gender in the time of Covid-19: Evaluating national leadership and Covid-19 fatalities. Available at: https://journals.plos.org/plosone/article?id=10.1371/journal.pone.0244531 (archived at https://perma.cc/Q4QP-BMKV) (Accessed: 20 April 2022)

Wodak, R (2021) Crisis communication and crisis management during Covid-19, *Global Discourse*, 11(3), 329–353. Available at: https://bristoluniversitypressdigital.com/view/journals/gd/11/3/article-p329.xml (archived at https://perma.cc/T46R-YVU2)

12

Wicked problems

Part 1: an introduction

Risk management and rational problems

Our understanding of risk management, whatever the historical period, cultural setting or threat environment, is based on a simple, fundamental principle. It is that we can observe the past, model the present and use that to project into the future. There is a belief that our present condition and situation are part of an ongoing continuum, where what was leads to what is and what is will create what will be. Although there have been changes throughout history, and in fact change is part of the environment that we operate in, there is nonetheless a belief in a single unchanging aspect of the world, and that is its rationality.

Without that belief, we would not be able to see the patterns that allow us to understand risk and to create models of engaging with it. If things happened randomly – if horses appeared out of mid-air, or apples fell upwards from a tree rather than downwards, or a fork we were holding could disappear without cause – then the world would be fundamentally irrational, at least as seen from our current perspective, and we would not be able to make any plans in order to engage with it in a meaningful way.

However, the world is not like that and we are able to presume that what was will continue to be and what is gives us an understanding of what will be in the future. Unfortunately, as I write this chapter, it is questionable as to how much these preceding statements still hold true. There has been a new word introduced into our lexicon that means that we must question the rationality of the world that we live in, or at least our ability to perceive the rationality beneath the seeming chaos that we observe and are caught up in. That word is 'unprecedented'. If something is unprecedented, then by definition it falls outside of the framework of cause-and-effect rationality on which we have built our model of the universe.

It can be argued that in many cases, rather than describing a genuinely unique situation that could not have been predicted, the use of the word unprecedented can be seen as an excuse to avoid blame and responsibility. In fact, rather than being unprecedented, the situations being described more accurately fall under the description of someone not paying attention or actively ignoring the signs that were in front of them.

Coronavirus and Covid-19 were not unprecedented. We have been having minor pandemics on a regular basis throughout this century, with SARS, MERS, swine flu, avian flu, Zika and Ebola, and that is not counting the regular outbreaks of pandemic influenza that have impacted health systems around the world. While the impacts of Covid-19 were undoubtedly unprecedented – a global lockdown that deeply affected every aspect of our lives – the medical aspects of the pandemic were not only known but had been widely predicted and in many cases exercised and practised.

However, it is also true that on a global scale, the challenges that we are facing from changing global conditions, whether it is climate change and adverse weather patterns, global supply chains, impacts on food production and distribution, or the increasingly common high-impact failures of global infrastructures such as power, water and information, are creating conditions that go beyond anything we have faced before. The question that we need to ask, as people studying and engaging with strategic risk, and who are perhaps being tasked with developing tools and models that will allow us to engage with those issues on an ongoing basis, and on which the safety, security and wellbeing of our organizations and societies depend, is how do we engage with risks that are genuinely irrational, that do not conform to any pattern and that transcend our ability to understand or model them?

For a problem or challenge to be 'rational', it needs to satisfy four criteria. First, you need to be able to define it. This may seem a simplistic statement, but for many problems we face it is impossible to define what the actual problem is. Climate change, the war on terror or the war on drugs are all issues that affect us deeply on many levels but for which it is in fact almost impossible to define what exactly the problem is, even though we recognize them in multiple aspects of our daily lives. The act of defining something is also an act of limitation – it creates a differentiation between that which is included inside the scope of the problem and everything else that is outside. It may be an arbitrary decision, but at least it is one that then allows for rational actions to be taken in terms of what is considered to be relevant to the discussion.

Second, there needs to be a limited list of potential options that can be used to engage with or solve those problems. In classical management speak, any option can be either fast, cheap or effective. You can have two out of three, but you can't have all three. The choice of which option you take is an act of judgement, based on inclusion of some desired outcomes and excluding others. In the case of Covid-19, as an example, the choice was between locking down and minimizing the infection rate, and maintaining a functioning economy. In issues of climate change the choice could be between impacting people's lifestyles by making decisions that reduce carbon emissions or continuing to use fuels that are polluting the planet in ways that are ultimately unsustainable.

Third, in order to decide which of those listed options you will choose, you then need to have a list of objectives that you want to achieve. What is your desired outcome? In buying a car, do you want one that is new or used? Is it important that it is hi-tech, has high status or can achieve high speeds, or is it more important that it is economical, cheaper to maintain and unlikely to cost you additional money each year? It is only by identifying the criteria that you can start to make the judgements that will allow you to exclude certain options and then leave you with a final short list that you can then decide on, often in ways that might appear irrational to someone judging the issue from a purely objective basis. For the car it might be that it is the colour, or the way an advertisement affected you, or a childhood memory that might trigger that impacts your final choice. These are no longer purely rational decisions – they are personal and emotional, but they nevertheless allow you to make a decision that you are happy to live with.

The final criterion for a rational problem is that you are then able to predict what the outcomes of the choice that you make will be. You have chosen a path that suits you – that maximizes your personal or corporate benefit – and you will then live with the consequences of that choice or those choices. If it then turns out that actually it didn't work out as expected, then the presumption is that you either did not understand the nature of the problem fully (based on the first criterion), you didn't understand the nature of the options you were choosing (based on the second criterion), which might mean that either you did not have enough information about the possible options, you were given false information, or you did not sufficiently understand that information, or your expectation as to the outcomes of the choice you made was unrealistic (third criterion).

Whatever it might be, there is the expectation that there is a cause–effect relationship between the choices made and the outcomes achieved. But what happens when there is no way of knowing what the outcome of a decision might be, either because there is simply not enough information or because the nature of the problem is so complex that it is impossible to predict outcomes with any degree of accuracy? These then become non-rational problems and the traditional ways of dealing with them will no longer work.

Dilemmas in a general theory of planning (1973)

This is the issue that was first discussed in one of the seminal risk management papers, 'Dilemmas in a general theory of planning', written by Horst Rittel and Melvin Webber in 1973.[1] This is the most highly cited paper published in *Policy Sciences*. It had achieved over 3,137 citations and 13,000 downloads by 2017. Google Scholar, based on a wider set of sources, recorded more than 21,000 citations at the start of September 2022.

Rittel and Webber were not originally thinking about crisis management when they came up with their theory of 'wicked problems' but were actually looking at issues of urban planning in California in the 1970s. This was a time of an economic boom, with the first post-Second World War baby-boomers entering the labour and housing market (and having babies of their own). There was a rapid expansion of all aspects of urban living in America – the cities were getting bigger, there was a massive increase in the growth of what could be considered the professional middle classes, which in turn was accompanied by an unprecedented growth in consumerism. In particular this was seen in the growth in urban and suburban housing, which in turn resulted in the significant expansion of car ownership.

Rittel and Webber at the time were university professors, looking at issues around urban growth and planning. The brilliant insight that they came up with was that as the problems got bigger and more complex, they were going beyond what it was possible to map and model in terms of 'rational planning'. That is, there was no way that they could know enough about the problems they were facing, and in particular the consequences of any solution that they might offer, that would allow them to suggest something that could be considered as a definitively 'correct' option.

Rittel and Webber's 1973 analysis of what they described as 'non-rational' problems, and for which they coined the title 'wicked problems', is undoubtedly one of the most influential academic papers on risk and crisis management ever written. It single-handedly created an approach to risk management that has since been widely (and often incorrectly) attached to challenging planning and management issues in a wide range of fields.

Despite the fact that we are divided by 50 years of history and political, social and economic development, the language that they use to describe the intellectual, political and social changes that they were living through in the 1970s clearly reflects the challenges we are facing today. That is both in the existential doubts they express about the political and social upheavals that the US was going through on the one hand as well as the seemingly unprecedented (and unprecedentedly disruptive) technological innovations on the other.

At the heart of their paper is the question as to whether what had been accepted previously as the unquestioned foundation of planning and management, namely the ability to model the problem, develop a range of potential solutions and then choose which of those could be considered the optimal option, could be considered appropriate, or even relevant, in the new class of problems that was emerging from developments in technology and increased urbanization. The revolutionary developments in technical capabilities were accompanied by a loss of faith in public leaders that they described using language that could be taken from the editorial section of any newspaper anywhere in the world today.

Risk management and professional interventions[2]

> Few of the modern professionals seem to be immune from the popular attack – whether they be social workers, educators, housers, public health officials, policemen, city planners, highway engineers or physicians. Our restive clients have been telling us that they don't like the educational programs that schoolmen have been offering, the redevelopment projects urban renewal agencies have been proposing, the law enforcement styles of the police, the administrative behavior of the welfare agencies, the locations of the highways, and so on. In the courts, the streets, and the political campaigns, we've been hearing ever-louder public protests against the professions' diagnoses of the clients' problems, against professionally designed governmental programs, against professionally certified standards for the public services.'

Rittel and Webber described the professional's role as that of the technocrat, responsible for solving problems 'that appeared to be definable, understandable and consensual'. In terms of solving problems of the mid-section of the 20th century, '[their] record has been quite spectacular, of course; the contemporary city and contemporary urban society stand as clear evidence of professional prowess. The streets have been paved, and roads now connect all places; houses shelter virtually everyone; the dread diseases are virtually gone; clean water is piped into nearly every building; sanitary sewers carry wastes from them; schools and hospitals serve virtually every district; and so on. The accomplishments of the past century in these respects have been truly phenomenal'.

However, there was also the recognition that these problems were relatively simple in their conception and conducive to engineering/management solutions that could be developed, imposed and managed with a general acceptance that they were good for society. The paper goes on to highlight the growing concerns as to whether those same processes and principles would be able to meaningfully engage with the emerging social problems and issues that were becoming both increasingly critical and increasingly divisive as changing social arrangements and expectations coincided with fast-developing sophisticated technical capabilities:

> The professionalized cognitive and occupational styles that were refined in the first half of this century, based in Newtonian mechanistic physics, are not readily adapted to contemporary conceptions of interacting open systems and to contemporary concerns with equity.

It seems that issues associated with 'contemporary conceptions of interacting open systems and to contemporary concerns with equity' are not confined to Facebook, Google and billion-user data sources.

HOW MUCH SHOULD WE DO?

One of the defining characteristics of this changing concept of 'management for the public good' was the transition of what might seem to be a simplistic question from the technical enquiry 'What do systems do?' to the social/political question 'What should these systems do?' (which Rittel and Webber defined as 'the most difficult question of all').

The social background to all of this would also be familiar to contemporary commentators, with an anti-authoritarian public movement that saw challenges to the very fabric of American society in terms of race and class upheavals, anti-government demonstrations over the Vietnam war, student radicalization and a President (Nixon) who saw a significant part of the American population as an enemy to be feared and controlled (and lied to). At the same time, there was a growing consumerist class that was benefiting from the post-Second World War economic boom combined with the emergence of a nascent ecological/conservationist movement that saw the mixture of exponentially growing global population, rapid rise in urbanization and the increase in manufacturing to support the growth of an emergent global middle class as structurally unsustainable and which would lead to many of the global problems that we are facing today.

The belief in history as a generally progressive process was being challenged by internal (and perhaps unavoidable) dynamic tension between two forces. On the one hand there was the belief in the 'makeability' of history through effective planning and management, tied in with the inherent innovativeness of human intellect and creativity, and on the other hand there was the desire for a more 'feeling approach', based on passionate engagement and dramatic action, 'even of a revival of mysticism, aiming at overcoming The System which is seen as the evil source of misery and suffering'.

The words written by Rittel and Webber almost 50 years ago, and in the days when the computer itself was in its infancy and the possibilities inherent in a globally connected world were unthought of, are so prescient that they are worth repeating in their entirety.

> The Enlightenment may be coming to full maturity in the late 20th century, or it may be on its deathbed. Many Americans seem to believe both that we can perfect future history – that we can deliberately shape future outcomes to accord with our wishes – and that there will be no future history. Some have arrived at deep pessimism and some at resignation. To them, planning for large social systems has proved to be impossible without loss of liberty and equity. Hence, for them the ultimate goal of planning should be anarchy because it should aim at the elimination of government over others. Still another group has arrived at the conclusion that liberty and equity are luxuries which cannot be afforded by a modern society, and that they should be substituted by cybernetically feasible values.

HOW DO YOU SOLVE A PROBLEM YOU CAN'T DESCRIBE?

The critical issue that lay at the heart of this problem, according to Rittel and Webber, was the inability to accurately articulate what exactly the problem was that they were trying to find a solution for. Or rather, that in articulating a problem in one way, we are by its very nature excluding other aspects and issues from consideration. Given that this articulation/definition would always be arbitrary and there is no way of reaching a decisive conclusion as to what the limits or boundaries of that definition could/should be, it is unavoidable that any solution proposed would also be arbitrary, partial and incomplete.

This becomes increasingly clear as the systems that we are dealing with become increasingly complex. Once they reach the societal level, the conceptualization of the problem we are trying to deal with reaches a stage where it is functionally impossible to identify all the issues involved or model the consequences and outcomes of all of the myriad possible interactions, both internal and external, that could cascade from any 'solution' that we tried to impose. The conclusion that Rittel and Webber drew from these musings was not that what was required was a better understanding of planning and management but rather that the paradigm being used was false. From this perspective, the category error lies in the belief that the intrinsically Newtonian approach to engineering – the development of a single 'correct ' solution – could be transposed to the arena of social science, where such lineal and binary (true/false, right/wrong) frameworks were simply not applicable.

Once this is accepted, the underlying issue is not one of language but of metaphor. To describe this new class of problem, Rittel and Webber coined the phrase 'wicked problems'. This does not mean that they are bad or evil but rather that they are ill-defined, they are 'elusive'. Engineering problems are open to 'solutions' but wicked problems don't have solutions, only resolutions. That is, there is no stopping point, no final stage at which the planner can step back and say, 'It is done.' These are not technical/engineering issues but social/political ones.

THE TEN PRINCIPLES OF WICKED PROBLEMS

1. There is no definitive formulation of a wicked problem.
2. Wicked problems have no stopping rule.
3. Solutions to wicked problems are not true or false but good or bad.
4. There is no immediate and no ultimate test of a solution to a wicked problem.
5. Every solution to a wicked problem is a 'one-shot operation'; because there is no opportunity to learn by trial-and-error, every attempt counts significantly.

6. Wicked problems do not have an enumerable (or an exhaustively describable) set of potential solutions, nor is there a well-described set of permissible operations that may be incorporated into the plan.
7. Every wicked problem is essentially unique.
8. Every wicked problem can be considered to be a symptom of another problem.
9. The existence of a discrepancy representing a wicked problem can be explained in numerous ways. The choice of explanation determines the nature of the problem's resolution.
10. The planner has no right to be wrong.

Rittel and Webber listed 10 properties associated with wicked problems, which have been widely quoted in a multitude of contexts. They are listed above, but it is worth identifying two seemingly contradictory issues that they highlight.

The first is that any 'solution' offered is not a final solution but only the creation of a new generation of problems. Building a bridge may be a solution to one problem – but it is the harbinger of others. A policy on drug management, education, use of resources in the National Health Service or an approach to immigration are all issues that are often approached as though they can be defined in isolation, and that there is a 'right' solution, which if only it were managed more effectively then the desired outcomes would be realized. From a wicked problem perspective, this is an approach that is doomed to failure, not because of weaknesses in the design or management of the solutions but because of a failure to understand the basic nature of the problem.

The second point is the final, tenth principle of wicked problems. It is simply, 'The planner has no right to be wrong'. A Newtonian, engineering approach to problem management on a social level misunderstands the nature of scientific enquiry as much as it does social problems. Scientific enquiry is built upon the hypothesis–trial–solution process. Within this, it is an inherent part of the process to fail, amend the hypothesis, fail again better and then through a series of trial and error ('refutation/corroboration') to approach a final understanding of what the 'correct' solution might be.

As Rittel and Webber put it, 'In the world of planning and wicked problems no such immunity is tolerated. Here the aim is not to find the truth, but to improve some characteristics of the world where people live. Planners are liable for the consequences of the actions they generate; the effects can matter a great deal to those people that are touched by those actions.'

Although one hesitates to correct a paper as iconic as Rittel and Webber's, I believe that Principle 3 could be improved by being stated as 'Solutions to wicked problems are neither true or false nor good or bad, but can only be useful or not useful'. That is, they allow us to understand the environment and context we are operating in and to offer solutions that can help us move towards our desired outcome, fully aware that those decisions are made based on incomplete information and in the possibility (and often likelihood) that conditions might change or new information will be provided that would make those approaches outdated or even obsolete.

At a time when the problems that the world is facing are becoming increasingly challenging, disruptive and destructive, it seems that one of the fundamental demands we should make of those responsible for developing and managing potential responses is that they have a true understanding of the nature of those problems and of the range of holistic and multi-tiered approaches that they will need to develop to engage with them in a meaningful way. A rereading of this classic from 1973 could be a good start.

Part 2: wicked problems and policy setting in a modern context

Although we like to believe that the answer to complex problems is 'more integration', the truth is that the environment we are operating in, whether it is legal, corporate or social, mitigates against that. In fact, it is more likely that both the problems we are facing and the range of potential solutions that we can offer come under the heading of 'fragmentation' rather than integration.[3] This is in terms of both the problem itself – we each see a different aspect of it or consider a different facet to be of greater or lesser importance – and our ability to create integrated teams across multi-disciplinary, trans-boundary and trans-jurisdictional frameworks.

Given the tendency that the larger a problem becomes, the more complex it is, and the more complex it is, the harder it is to agree common terms of reference that all stakeholders can use as a basic touchstone when discussing the problem,[4] it is hardly surprising that in facing the planetary-level challenges that we are experiencing today we are failing to even agree on the nature of the problem, never mind a common understanding of the response approaches that would be necessary in order to be effective and timely.

Management approaches to wicked problems

Although the discussion of wicked problems has become mainstream and it has entered the lexicon of strategic planners and managers,[5] there is often a fundamental misunderstanding of the nature of wicked problems and the range of challenges that they bring. The belief that adjusting the management structure of an organization one way or another makes it more competent to manage wicked problems is one such error.

Management solutions tend to fall into three classes: authoritative, competitive and collaborative.[6] The authoritative approach can be seen when someone in power decides what the problem is and that then becomes the accepted orthodoxy. The fact that that is only one out of almost limitless ways of describing or defining a problem is neither recognized nor acknowledged, as is the fact that other stakeholders may well have a different view of the problem and may see the approach taken by the authoritative decision-maker as unhelpful, inappropriate or even antagonistic.

The 'management' approach to wicked problems is typified in the quote below:

> Authoritative strategies are 'taming strategies'. They diminish the level of conflict inherent in wicked problems by putting problem solving into the hands of a few stakeholders who have the authority to define a problem and come up with a solution... Reliance on experts also can make problem solving more 'professional' and 'objective', especially when specialization provides them with knowledge and sophisticated problem solving tools that laymen do not possess.[7]

The idea that there are 'experts' who know how to solve a wicked problem and who can bring together solutions that merely need to be implemented effectively in order to deliver the desired outcomes is a fundamental misunderstanding of the nature of wicked problems. It ignores Rittel and Webber's ninth principle of wicked problems, which is that they can be described in many ways and that the choice of the description in itself creates a conceptualization of the potential resolutions – but at the cost of all other alternative options, many of which might have been equally as valid based on available evidence and assessments of the wider risk and social contexts, offering a 'multiplicity of legitimate perspectives'.[8]

A third level of differentiation, lying between the expert and the policy maker, is that of the analyst.[9] This is the stage where differing opinions, often involving highly technical material that would have little if any meaning to the lay person, are brought together in a single syncretic (and often simplistic) package and offered to the corporate decision-maker or political policy maker, often with a highly geared recommendation towards one option or another. If you think about the issues associated with nuclear energy, climate change, global micro-chip supply chains, differing educational systems or the impact of fishing on coastal communities, it is unlikely that the people making those decisions will have detailed understanding of all the nuances of those issues and the multiple potential competing agendas. In the case of the fishing policy question, stakeholders with differing, and often competing, agendas would include regulatory authorities, commercial industries, global corporations, fishing communities, logistical management companies, competing countries and potentially environmental and ecological pressure groups.

Given the nature of the complexity of wicked problems, there is often a 'democracy gap' in both the defining of the problem and the development of possible approaches, in that the impossibility of establishing an all-inclusive definition means that there will always be those who are excluded or marginalized. The fact that attempts to find 'solutions' to wicked problems tend to focus on specific aspects of the problem (which can be considered as tame problems, in that there are specific strategies that can be used to solve specific aspects of the problems they cause) means that actually they are not engaging with underlying issues. In 2000, it was claimed that what had appeared to be an unsolvable problem (environmental degradation that results from using oil and gasoline) had seen a potential resolution through the development of a new hydrogen fuel cell that offered a cleaner, less polluting option than other forms of energy.[10] Another approach was that of biofuel, which would replace carbon-based fuels. However, the rapid expansion of transference of traditional food-producing land to biofuel crops led to a significant shift in global food production.[11] The belief in a 'magic bullet' that can solve problems that are deeply systemic is a sign that there is a misunderstanding of both the nature of the problem and the nature of any potential engagement with it. It also ignores another of Rittel and Webber's principles, that every intervention, rather than producing a solution merely creates a new generation of problems.

One of the problems associated with engaging with wicked problems is that the options proposed are often seen to be reverting to standard management issues that have little or any connection with wicked problems themselves. In describing the third options for management approaches to wicked problems, following on from authoritative and competitive was described as collaboration. 'Even competitors of the same product line find virtue in working together to deliver better products and services to their customers. Redundancies are eliminated and organizational efficiencies achieved when organizations outsource tasks and functions that enable both the organization and its supplier to add value by concentrating on what they do best'.[12]

Beyond 'normal science'

One of the fundamental errors underlying the misclassification of wicked problems is the belief that they can be engaged with using 'normal science'.[13] From this perspective, if only there is enough information, a model of reality can be created, various hypotheses can be developed and then tried, and final possible or optimal solutions can be proposed.[14] Of course there are other issues associated with turning science into policy or even allowing science to influence policy, but nevertheless the normal science approach follows a model of linear rationality that has been the underpinning model of scientific truth since the Age of the Enlightenment at the end of the 17th century. It correlates the ability to gather information and to decrease uncertainty with the ability to find the 'correct' solution. It is in fact the failure to recognize the inapplicability of linear 'puzzle solving' to wicked problems that is one of the reasons that we fail to engage with them effectively.[15]

It has been a feature of the latter part of the 20th century, and certainly the 21st century so far, that science was no longer seen as a necessary function of human improvement. While the development of the train, car and aeroplane, the telegraph, electricity and light bulb in one era, and the availability of computers, instant communications and data sharing in another, had been seen (in the most part) as signs of the continued progress of civilization, more recent times have seen science considered either as part of the polluting of the atmosphere and the destruction of the biosphere, the development of genetically mutated crops and energy-draining crypto-currencies on the one hand, or on the other at best unable to engage with the problems we are facing in any meaningful ways. The tendency noted by Rittel and Webber in 1973 concerning the loss of faith in experts was captured in the World Conference on Science, 'Science for the Twenty-first Century', held in Budapest in 1999, with over 1,800 delegates from 150 countries. That recognized the need for a new relationship between science, policy and society, one that ensured that the benefits of science were shared across the population and that it was used in ways appropriate to the needs of the global community:

> There is a growing feeling from many quarters that science is not responding adequately to the challenges of our times, and particularly those posed by the quest for sustainable development. We are not including in our consideration the attacks to science coming from antiscientific sectors, but only the criticism and complaints generated by those who are supportive of the role of science for the understanding of the world and for solving practical problems.[16]

The language of an academic paper exploring the changing role of science as we moved into the 21st century is almost completely matched by the language of one of the foremost observers and commentators of global change, Klaus Schwab, executive chairman of the World Economic Forum, writing almost 20 years later:

> The world now is moving through a period of extraordinary turbulence reflecting the genesis and intensification of deep economic, social, political, and cultural changes associated with the current techno-economic revolution. In addition, the speed and magnitude of global change, the increasing connectedness of the social and natural systems at the planetary level, and the growing complexity of societies and of their impacts upon the biosphere result in a high level of uncertainty and unpredictability, presenting new threats (and also new opportunities) for humankind. We stand on the brink of a technological revolution that will fundamentally alter the way we live, work, and relate to one another. In its scale, scope, and complexity, the transformation will be unlike anything humankind has experienced before. We do not yet know just how it will unfold, but one thing is clear: the response to it must be integrated and comprehensive, involving all stakeholders of the global polity, from the public and private sectors to academia and civil society.[17]

Just as the challenges that the world is facing are transcendental and transformational, so must be the nature of the scientific enquiry we bring to it. The messiness of the problems we are facing does not fit neatly into government ministries or university departmental sub-divisions.[18] In dealing with complexity and uncertainty what is required is not a set of rigid rules or procedures but rather a guiding question and an enquiring mind, that allows one to explore various options that look like they might have value or utility, in the full awareness that many times it may ultimately turn out that they may not – but the exploration of them will in itself add value to the overall enquiry. Post-normal science can be highly abstruse and understandable by only few higher-level academics (complexity economics, for example, which is highly mathematical and statistical), or it can be more intuitively understandable to the general population, as in ecological economics, which mixes physical, biological and social aspects that would be, in its simpler terms, both recognizable and comprehensible to the general observer.[19]

If we accept the need for the general population to be both aware of and engaged with these issues, then the question of risk communication becomes paramount.

Describing wicked problems

Although the term 'wicked problem' has entered into both general and specialist lexicons, and in fact has often been used as shorthand for 'there is nothing that we can do about it', it is in fact only one of a number of terms that have been used to describe the same sort of unstructured problem. Other terms include 'intractable controversies',[20] 'unstructured' or 'incorrigible' problems',[21] 'tangled problems'[22] and 'complex problems'.[23]

Although it might be true that from an overall strategic perspective there is no starting point in engaging with a wicked problem in what may be considered a meaningful way (one need only think of poverty or climate change as examples), that does not mean that there are no frameworks that could allow the problem to be moved from the intractable to the actionable.[24] Simplifying complexity to reasonable levels, identifying core issues and creating a framework and methodology that would allow an engagement to be developed that was both impactful (even if only on a local level) and sustainable, is a fair starting point. The belief that even issues of national context need to be engaged with at the local level – and in fact it is imperative that they are done so – is neither new nor radical.[25] It does, however, allow for the development of impactful actions that can create change in a meaningful way.

The acceptance of responsibility is the hallmark of a high-reliability organization,[26] but it is also the hallmark of a society that recognizes the need to engage with wicked problems in ways that have meaning and significance rather than being used as empty phrases. Actions have consequences and if decisions are taken that create consequences that are actively detrimental to the cause being adhered to, then there is little to be done that would reverse those impacts. The decisions to increase the use of polluting fuels despite the apocalyptic warnings[27] coming from the 2021 COP 26 climate change summit, or to continue to deforest the Amazon,[28] or to open up Arctic territories to oil exploration[29] are actions that are in direct conflict with the objectives that have been identified.

Along with acceptance of responsibility (which is notional and aspirational) is the parallel path of active engagement by corporations and other entities in the political debate around the wicked problems that we are facing. The fact that we are living in an interconnected world means that the actions that we take cannot be arbitrarily limited, isolated or excluded from the wider context. An action that leads to the deforestation of the Amazon or the melting of the glaciers is something that has an impact on all of us and therefore bestows a duty of care and obligation.[30]

From wickedness to super wickedness

There is no doubt that the use of the term 'wicked problem' has been used to cover a multitude of sins, or at least incompetence, ignorance or mendacity.[31] There is the tendency to see an inflationary trend in the use of wicked problems to describe those that in previous generation would have been considered to be simply complex or challenging, but there is at least the recognition that as a concept, if nothing else, wickedness is useful in describing a class of complex strategy-setting or decision-making that is not conducive to management though traditional problem-solving means. In fact, there is a school of thought that describes super-wickedness as the true mark of what we have come to think of a wicked problem, in order to differentiate them for those that are routinely described as wicked but in fact do not reach the criteria to be accurately labelled as such.[32] Such instances include the problem of climate change,[33] AI (artificial intelligence),[34] pandemics[35] and oceanic sustainability.[36]

Super-wicked problems were described as adding four criteria to the classical wicked problem categorization.[37] They were that:

- time is running out;
- there is no one that has ownership of or authority over the problem;
- the people who claim they are seeking to solve the problems are exactly the same people who are causing them (oil companies claiming to work to prevent pollution, or food companies who claim to be working to reduce obesity); and
- they critically discount future impacts, believing that 'It will be okay and we will work something out'.

While there are those who believe that not only do wicked problems exist but there is a new level of wickedness that requires a completely new categorization ('We believe that the complexities and entanglement associated with multiple super wicked problems constitutes an increased degree of wickedness inherent in the problem, meriting consideration as a new class of wicked problem, e.g. a super, super wicked problem'[38]), there are also those who would claim that there is in fact no such thing as wicked problems as a distinct class of problems ('Contrary to many "wicked problem" scholars, we conclude that there is no special ontological class of "wicked" problems, and therefore these require no special research program, nor special approaches to problem solving'[39]).

Wickedness as a spectrum

From this contrarian perspective, wicked problems are merely at the higher end of a spectrum or continuum that includes all matters of policy, which have the common challenge of 'problematicity', that is they are trying to find solutions to problems for which there is always the need to make subjective decisions in the face of uncertainty and confusion. While that claim may seem to go against the accepted value and utility of the wicked problem concept, it does introduce the question of whether all problems have some level of wickedness in them and therefore there is no longer the binary option of wicked/tame problems but only more/less wicked or more/less tame.[40] A more structured approach to developing a taxonomy of wickedness suggested that there could be three potential options: Type 1 situations where both the problem and the solution are understood; Type 2 situations where the problem is understood but the response is not; and Type 3 situations where neither the problem nor the solution is understood.[41]

The path towards meaningful engagement with a wicked problem is not characterized by elegance, with neatly defined boxes, flow charts and predetermined outcomes, but rather by clumsy solutions based on a 'what it is that we can agree on now' basis. From this perspective, rather than being an intrinsic property of a particular problem, it is rather an indication of two factors. The first is that it is unstructured, or in the language of other researchers, fuzzy,[42] messy[43] or it takes place on the 'edge of chaos',[44] in a constant state of innovation and dynamic equilibrium which involves 'the science of muddling through'[45] and the need to be both scientist and poet.[46] The second factor is the inability to create a shared understanding of the problem because of ideological, cultural or other social differences that prevent the emergence of a shared conceptualization, language and model of the problem.[47]

The approaches that are suggested by researchers in an attempt to find ways that would allow meaningful engagement with wicked problems are, unsurprisingly, relatively traditional in their basic principles. The first is more, and more open, communication. In what has been described as meta-dialogues,[48] there is the necessity for an understanding that we are all facing the same problems and that fragmentation on the basis the basis of geographical, political or jurisdictional differentiation is simply meaningless.[49]

The need to accept that there are problems for which no solution is available and for which resolution (finding a way to live with it) is a more realistic option than solving (in which a definitive pathway to conclusion is identified, implemented and managed over sustained periods of time) leads to the concept of *satisficing*.[50] The attempt to reconcile global human activity with the need to reduce global warming, and specifically to reduce the polluting actions that are leading to it, is a clear example of where the challenges of super wickedness (and the lack of a meta-dialogue that could have led to the sort of long-term and strategic initiatives that could have had an impact much earlier in the crisis development cycle), is confining the ambition to limiting the level of damage rather than producing the ultimately desirable outcome of a safer, more stable world.

Super wickedness and Covid-19

The Covid-19 pandemic, and the attempts to create a global response to what was in a different way from global warming but nevertheless a planetary-level event, offered a different perspective on policy making in response to super wicked problems. In a similar way to climate change, there was a need for an agreed set of policy choices that could set the foundation for all future action, even though the continuously mutating nature of the problems, and the specific impacts and consequences that they were creating on both a global and a local level, was a toxic mixture of being unknown, complex and ever-changing. In contrast to the policy choices associated with global warming, however, there was an acknowledgement from the beginning that the policy decisions made in relation to Covid-19 and the impacts those were having would need to adapt quickly in the face of either emerging threats (e.g. new variants or increased spread) or alternative solutions (the development of vaccines or an increased understanding of social interaction management initiatives).[51] The third component of the response to Covid-19 was the concentrated efforts to use science and technology to create solutions in ways that would not have been considered possible prior to the pandemic. The speed of the development, testing, production and delivery of vaccines was something that literally rewrote the concepts of what was possible in those contexts.[52]

Although there is the desire to have policy goals and objectives that can be identified well in advance,[53] for an event such as Covid-19, which had been predicted and modelled but never directly experienced, the idea that policies put together around a ministerial or executive boardroom would be seen to be realistic or realizable in the cauldron of an actual event was fanciful. The need to respond to high-impact events in ways that create the optimal outcome (however that may be defined) is a complex mixture of triage and zero-sum gaming. The first challenge is to identify which is the most pressing need, with the awareness that that can change as the overall picture becomes clearer. As an example, it is perhaps understandable that in the first stages of Covid-19 it was not clear what was the best approach in terms of keeping schools open or not, in that there was an awareness that there were many issues associated with the accessibility of schools to their pupils that went beyond merely attending lessons. That could include socialization skills that could be lost, especially in very young children; the access to a daily meal for those living in relative poverty; the ability of parents to continue to work if the child was no longer in school (an issue that particularly impacted working mothers); or the higher likelihood that the child would be subject to physical, sexual or other abuse through extended periods of isolation in a house with other adults.[54]

However, the inability to either identify the threats (or in true wicked problem terminology, even to define the problem) or to develop appropriate policies should be a feature of the initial confusion, not part of the long-term event management. After the first 12-month cycle of Covid-19, by year two of the pandemic there should have been a clearly articulated set of policies that could identify desired outcomes ('The priority is…') and an agreed set of procedures to allow that to happen. At that stage, that is no longer crisis management or indeed a wicked problem but rather effective management of challenging issues – something which should be a central part of an organization's ability to maintain delivery of its core services.

Fragmentation as a barrier to wicked problem engagement

It is not just the nature of wicked problems that creates barriers to engagement and resolution but also the management structures of the government organizations that are tasked with dealing with them. The 1980s saw the growth of 'managerialism' in government service, where the highly differentiated divisions of a corporate management structure were seen as offering a solution to the increasingly complex problems being faced by government ministries that lacked the required level of technical or professional capabilities to wrestle with them.[55] Among Margaret Thatcher's first actions, just four days after taking office as UK prime minister in 1979, was to establish an Efficiency Unit. Although the ultimate objective was to adhere to the economic theories of Friedrich Hayek and Milton Friedman, both of whom believed that it was not the role of the government to support the poor or vulnerable, the methods involved splitting ministries that traditionally had held ownership and oversight of both policy and delivery into service delivery units, under the title of executive agencies. The fact that they were modelled on corporate rather than political lines could be seen in the fact that they were headed up by chief executives rather than government ministers.

Although the purpose of such 'agencification'[56] was to separate policy from management ('separate the steering from the rowing'[57]), it also meant that rather than having an overarching view of strategic objectives, such agencies and their leaders became risk averse, in that they gained nothing from being innovative or creative and would be marked on their success purely in terms of delivering tightly defined outcomes – which usually involved either saving money or cutting services. This led to a culture of 'threat rigidity', whereby the presence of something unexpected or outside of the normal routine would in itself induce a self-limiting flinch response from the organization.[58]

Wicked problems and collaborative governance

A fundamental aspect of effective wicked problem management is the development of collaborative governance structures that can take the necessary level of strategic overview and create the required frameworks as part of an ongoing capability- and readiness-development programme. This is in contrast to the more usual reality, which is a panicked response to a situation that should have been acknowledged and engaged with but was in fact repeatedly ignored despite continuous and increasingly urgent warnings about both the impending likelihood and the possible dangers of such events happening.[59]

The analysis of what were the critical failure points in responding to Covid-19, including its mapping against similar super-wicked problems, brought about three policy recommendations that can be captured in three simple terms: have someone in charge, get ready for future challenges rather than responding to immediate threats, and don't simply do the opposite of what happened last time but failed.[60]

The need to create frameworks that can be sustained over the extended time frames associated with wicked and super-wicked problems means that they are not simply policy problems but political ones.[61] The need to 'stay ahead' to create sustainable programmes, either by investing money and resources or forgoing potential benefits such as the ability to have cheap fuel, have exotic fruits year-round in the local supermarket or be allowed to travel by air as much as one would like, means that there is continuous pressure to roll back policy decisions that had been made in the context of creating long-term benefits. The processes associated with climate change, for example, have seen attempts to minimize the use of coal, to roll back the use of nuclear power and the desire to introduce mandatory targets for the limiting of polluting activity. None of these has been respected in either letter or spirit and in fact they have been breached regularly either through ignoring the written law and continuing to engage in illegal and often what could be considered immoral activity or in changing the laws so that what is seen as repressive, regressive or simply limiting restrictions are removed and commercial and other actors are simply allowed to continue with their previous activities.[62]

Incrementalism as a wicked problem policy

The desire to look for a single, all-encompassing policy that will 'solve the problem' has been labelled 'faux paradigmatic',[63] in that major policy decisions are announced but are then either left to slowly rot due to lack of attention or may be reversed by an equally high-profile policy change when a new administration comes to power. The alternative to this is 'classic incrementalism', which is where small and relatively low-level changes are introduced which may or may not have an effect but which over time have little if any impact on the overarching problem.

A further option for policy development has been labelled 'progressive incrementalism', which is used to create a long-term and sustainable commitment to change but takes place on a step-by-step and progressive basis. While there may not be the dramatic impact of a paradigm-shifting announcement, it is the incremental nature of the change that creates its own longevity, in that what is introduced soon becomes accepted as normal and there is little opportunity to roll back something that has become part of the accepted way of doing things. In terms of public health, the restriction on smoking is an example of what had once been universally accepted but is now almost universally seen as non-desirable, even by those who are still addicted to their daily nicotine hits.[64]

The acceptance of the normalcy of a particular intervention is described in terms of *stickability* – the ability to hang around long enough to become the norm; *entrenchment*, in that it becomes deeply rooted and not liable to reversal; and *expansionist* in that it impacts and is accepted by increasingly large parts of the population. Just as Martin Luther King famously claimed that 'the arc of the moral universe is long, but it bends toward justice', so the arc of wicked problem engagement and the development of solutions that are appropriate to the scale and scope of those challenges must be seen in the same context of both longevity (sustainability) and righteousness (social justice).[65]

Covid-19 as a wicked problem: a success story

The paradox of crisis management studies is that they are, almost by definition, the study of failure. We do not know about the oil spills that did not happen, the data breaches that were successfully prevented or the flood management programmes that fulfilled their task. It can sometimes feel that there is little if any demonstration of how the theories, models, academic insights and practitioner experiences covered in this book can have a significant impact in turning what could have been an unmitigated disaster into a relatively benign major event.

And yet in Covid-19 we have a clear demonstration of the value that a correct understanding of the nature of high-impact events, and an ability to take on board all the lessons concerning pre-emptive planning, leadership, resilience, agility, social inclusion and a general 'all-of-society' approach, can bring.

In Singapore, which was ranked by Bloomberg as number one in the world for Covid resilience in April 2001,[66] the public health system is both universal and respected and state agencies were able to impose aggressive initiatives that were widely accepted and adhered to. The presence of a well-established and trusted healthcare service means that people are more likely to report for testing and that, paradoxically, there may be a high rate of infection reporting than in those countries where there is either no existing public health infrastructure that can respond to the demands of a mass public health outbreak or the authorities are generally so mistrusted that the local population is suspicious of any need to engage with them.

This was combined with government payments to those who were quarantined, which took away the disincentive to be tested that was seen in other countries where a positive test would mean an inability to work or earn. In Hong Kong, as a contrast, mistrust of state agencies meant there was a low take-up of testing (70 per cent of Hong Kong's population had taken two doses of the vaccine against 91 per cent in Singapore[67]), with the inevitable subsequent impact on infection spread.[68]

However, perhaps the single most significant aspect of Singapore's response to Covid-19 was the fact that it had experienced previous outbreaks of SARS (2002–03) and avian flu (2009). This allowed it to have a process in place to trigger government and social responses that had already been both practised in theory and implemented in reality and which meant that there was a familiarity with those processes and frameworks at all levels of society, from government to policy makers through health sector technocrats and managers and across the general population Thus, following the WHO announcement of the Covid-19 outbreak on 31 December 2019, Singapore was able to introduce a raft of management processes by 2 January 2020, including border controls, contact tracing and testing and mandatory 14-day quarantines for all returning residents. When it became clear that the source of much of the infections was among 'dormitory' populations – largely immigrant communities that came to Singapore for work and were housed in high-density dormitory housing – specific programmes were put in place to monitor and manage those populations.[69]

Lessons learned from the previous public health scares meant that the government was able to create a shared consensus as to what was needed, and the fact that it held national elections in July 2020, a month after national lockdown had been introduced as a pandemic circuit-breaker, allowed it to claim a genuine popular mandate for its actions and leadership. The SARS legacy meant that there were both facilities available and a willingness by senior leadership to make decisive decisions. The ability to have 'sense-making' meant that there was a framework in place to discuss the outbreak and its potential implications in ways that had common meaning to all stakeholders. The Disease Outbreak Response System Condition framework[70] had been well established and there was the availability of the National Centre for Infectious Diseases, a 330-bed purpose-built facility designed to bring together the specialist support that could integrate prevention and response management programmes. This meant that even from the start of the Covid-19 outbreak, there was a well-managed and coordinated programme that allowed for a structured and progressive response.

At the other end of the process, in terms of creating a management system that allowed some level of normalcy to return to the country, Singapore has again shown the way, offering a clear alternative to the more authoritarian regime imposed in its regional neighbour, Hong Kong. Although both had relatively low death rates (Hong Kong had 3 deaths per 100,000 versus Singapore's 15;[71] by comparison, in January 2022 England was still suffering from over 70 deaths per 100,000 of population[72]), what was different was that Singapore had balanced restrictive conditions in terms of lockdowns and isolation, both internally and from the outside world, with efforts to allow incoming traffic into the country and internal movement for work and leisure.[73]

The overarching lessons from Singapore's experience of Covid-19 are neither surprising nor unknown. Although resources matter, it is confident leadership, a clearly articulated policy, effective provision of support and an all-of-society approach that underpins all other aspects of the response. There is also the matter of learning from previous experiences. As in almost any disruptive high-impact event, whether it is personal, corporate or national, the feeling of being ready, of having learned the lessons from previous experiences in order to prepare for the next one, is a fundamental quality that underpins all other aspects of the operation.

Conclusion

It may seem that in the 2020s we are truly living in an 'age of wicked problems'. The range of events that we are facing and the challenges that they are causing seem to be without cause, reason or pattern. And yet it is precisely the ability to see patterns, to recognize that the fundamental underlying principles of strategic risk and crisis management are still functional and valid even in the face of wicked problems – or even super-wicked problems – that offers a pathway to sense-making, engagement and, potentially, resolution.

The lessons learned from the study of wicked problems is not that they are intractable or unsolvable but rather that if we are to engage with them in meaningful ways, we have to accept the responsibility of recognizing that it may need to involve some level of change in our own behaviours, and that without those changes we cannot expect some magic process to happen whereby those problems will suddenly go away.

Whether it is pandemics, flood management, snowstorms, drought or satellite failures, the ability to recognize the changing environments that create the conditions in which those incidents can occur, and to prepare ourselves in meaningful and sustainable ways, is the underlying bedrock on which all other actions must take place.

Whether or not these events are truly wicked is open to debate, but the fact that they are part of our global reality is not. They will happen whether we are ready or not. We might not be able to influence the events themselves, but we can mitigate the impact and potentially manage the consequences. However, what we absolutely have the power to control is our ability to respond, whether in terms of technical readiness or the leadership that demands. In the event that we do not create that readiness, then we, all of us, whether on a global, national or community level, will have to live with the consequences.

Endnotes

1 Rittel, H W & Webber, M M (1973) Dilemmas in a general theory of planning. *Policy Sciences*, 4(2), 155–169

2 All direct quotes in this section are from Rittel, H W & Webber, M M (1973) Dilemmas in a general theory of planning. *Policy Sciences*, 4(2), 155–169.

3 Conklin, J (2006) *Wicked Problems & Social Complexity* (Vol 11). Napa, US: CogNexus Institute

4 Conklin, J (2006) *Wicked Problems & Social Complexity* (Vol 11). Napa, US: CogNexus Institute

5 Alford, J & Head, B W (2017) Wicked and less wicked problems: A typology and a contingency framework. *Policy and Society*, 36(3), 397–413

6 Roberts, N (2000) Wicked problems and network approaches to resolution. *International Public Management Review*, 1(1), 1–19

7 Roberts, N (2000) Wicked problems and network approaches to resolution. *International Public Management Review*, 1(1), 1–19

8 Gallopín, G C, Funtowicz, S, O'Connor, M & Ravetz, J (2001) Science for the twenty-first century: From social contract to the scientific core. *International Social Science Journal*, 53(168), 219–229

9 Stephenson, K (2003) Environmental goal setting. In M R Tool and P D Bush (eds.) *Institutional analysis and economic policy*. Boston, MA: Kluwer, pp. 443–460

10 Roberts, N (2000) Wicked problems and network approaches to resolution. *International Public Management Review*, 1(1), 1–19

11 Grint, K (2010) Wicked problems and clumsy solutions: The role of leadership. In *The New Public Leadership Challenge* (pp. 169–186) London: Palgrave Macmillan

12 Roberts, N (2000) Wicked problems and network approaches to resolution. *International Public Management Review*, 1(1), 1–19

13 Batie, S S (2008) Fellows address: Wicked problems and applied economics. *American Journal of Agricultural Economics*, 90(5), 1176–1191

14 Peters, B G (2017) What is so wicked about wicked problems? A conceptual analysis and a research program. *Policy and Society*, 36(3), 385–396

15 Grint, K (2010) Wicked problems and clumsy solutions: The role of leadership. In *The new Public Leadership Challenge* (pp. 169–186) London: Palgrave Macmillan

16 Gallopín, G C, Funtowicz, S, O'Connor, M & Ravetz, J (2001) Science for the twenty-first century: From social contract to the scientific core. *International Social Science Journal*, 53(168), 219–229

17 Schwab, K (2016) The Fourth Industrial Revolution: What it means, how to respond. https://www.weforum.org/agenda/2016/01/the-fourth-industrial-revolution-what-it-means-and-how-to-respond/ (archived at https://perma.cc/22S8-JAEC)

18 Batie, S S (2008) Fellows address: Wicked problems and applied economics. *American Journal of Agricultural Economics*, 90(5), 1176–1191

19 Gallopín, G C, Funtowicz, S, O'Connor, M & Ravetz, J (2001) Science for the twenty-first century: From social contract to the scientific core. *International Social Science Journal*, 53(168), 219–229

20 Schön, D & Rein, M (1994) *Frame Reflection: Toward the resolution of intractable policy controversies*. Basic Books

21 Hoppe, R (2010) A problem-processing perspective on governance. In *The governance of Problems* (pp. 1–22) Policy Press

22 Dawes, S S, Creswell, A & Pardo, T (2009) From 'need to know' to 'need to share': Tangled problems, information boundaries, and the building of public sector knowledge networks. *Public Administration Review*, 69(3), 392–402

23 May, P J, Jochim, A E & Pump, B (2013) Political limits to the processing of policy problems. *Politics and Governance*, 1(2)

24 Reinecke, J & Ansari, S (2016) Taming wicked problems: The role of framing in the construction of corporate social responsibility. *Journal of Management Studies*, 53(3), 299–329

25 House of Lords (2022) Preparing for extreme risks: Building a resilient society. House of Lords Select Committee on Risk Assessment and Risk Planning: Report of Session 2021–22. https://publications.parliament.uk/pa/ld5802/ldselect/ldrisk/110/110.pdf (archived at https://perma.cc/23S4-AZKB)

26 Weick, K E (1987) Organizational culture as a source of high reliability. *California Management Review*, 29(2), 112–127

27 COP 2016. COP26 Summary Report. https://www.ieta.org/resources/Resources/COP/COP26-Summary-Report.pdf (archived at https://perma.cc/GZ54-QAXU)

28 Cursino, M (2022) Amazon rainforest: Highest deforestation rate in six years. 9 July. https://www.bbc.co.uk/news/world-latin-america-62103336 (archived at https://perma.cc/C9ZN-SVAT)

29 Ainger, J (2021) Arctic oil, gas production is booming despite climate fears. Greenpeace. Arctic oil drilling. https://www.greenpeace.org/usa/arctic/issues/oil-drilling/ (archived at https://perma.cc/X2PM-GKLH)

30 Young, I (2006) Responsibility and global justice: A social connection model. *Social Philosophy and Policy*, 23(1), 102–130. doi:10.1017/S0265052506060043

31 Alford, J & Head B W (2017) Wicked and less wicked problems: A typology and a contingency framework. Policy and Society 36, no. 3, 397–413

32 Peters, B G (2017) What is so wicked about wicked problems? A conceptual analysis and a research program. *Policy and Society*, 36(3), 385–396

33 Lazarus, R J (2008) Super wicked problems and climate change: Restraining the present to liberate the future. *Cornell L. Rev*, 94, 1153
Levin, K, Cashore, B, Bernstein, S & Auld, G (2012) Overcoming the tragedy of super wicked problems: Constraining our future selves to ameliorate global climate change. *Policy Sciences*, 45(2), 123–152

34 Gruetzemacher, R (2018) Rethinking AI strategy and policy as entangled super wicked problems. In Proceedings of the 2018 AAAI/ACM Conference on AI, Ethics, and Society, December, p. 122

35 Auld, G, Bernstein, S, Cashore, B & Levin, K (2021) Managing pandemics as super wicked problems: Lessons from, and for, Covid-19 and the climate crisis. *Policy Sciences*, 1–22

36 de Salas, K, Scott, J L, Schüz, B & Norris, K (2022) The super wicked problem of ocean health: A socio-ecological and behavioural perspective. *Philosophical Transactions of the Royal Society B*, 377: 20210271

37 Levin, K, Cashore, B, Bernstein, S & Auld, G (2009) Playing it forward: Path dependency, progressive incrementalism, and the 'super wicked' problem of global climate change. In IOP Conference Series. Earth and Environmental Science (Vol 6, No 50), February. IOP Publishing

38 Gruetzemacher, R (2018:124) Rethinking AI strategy and policy as entangled super wicked problems. In Proceedings of the 2018 AAAI/ACM Conference on AI, Ethics, and Society, December p. 122

39 Turnbull, N & Hoppe, R (2019:316) Problematizing 'wickedness': A critique of the wicked problems concept, from philosophy to practice. *Policy and Society*, 38(2), 315–337

40 Coyne, R (2005) Wicked problems revisited. *Design Studies*, 26(1), 5–17

41 Head, B W & Alford, J (2015) Wicked problems: Implications for public policy and management. *Administration & Society*, 47(6), 711–739

42 Dror, Y (1999) Beyond uncertainty: Facing the inconceivable. *Technological Forecasting and Social Change*, 62(1), 151–153

43 Flood, R L & Carson, E R (1993) *Dealing with complexity: An introduction to the theory and applications of the systems science*. Plenum Press
Ackoff, R L (1979) The future of operational research is past. *Journal of the Operational Research Society*, 30(2), 93–104

44 Waddock, S, Meszoely, G M, Waddell, S & Dentoni, D (2015:996) The complexity of wicked problems in large scale change. *Journal of Organizational Change Management*, 28(6)

45 Lindblom, C E (1959) The science of 'muddling through'. *Public Administration Review*, 79–88

46 Coyne, R (2005) Wicked problems revisited. *Design Studies*, 26(1), 5–17

47 Head, B W & Alford, J (2015) Wicked problems: Implications for public policy and management. *Administration & Society*, 47(6), 711–739; Turnbull, N & Hoppe, R (2019) Problematizing 'wickedness': A critique of the wicked problems concept, from philosophy to practice. *Policy and Society*, 38(2), 315–337

48 Gruetzemacher, R (2018) Rethinking AI strategy and policy as entangled super wicked problems. In Proceedings of the 2018 AAAI/ACM Conference on AI, Ethics, and Society, December, p. 122

49 Conklin, J (2006) *Wicked Problems & Social Complexity* (Vol 11). Napa, US: CogNexus Institute

50 Gruetzemacher, R (2018) Rethinking AI strategy and policy as entangled super wicked problems. In Proceedings of the 2018 AAAI/ACM Conference on AI, Ethics, and Society, December, p. 122

51 Nembhard, I M, Burns, L R & Shortell, S M (2020) Responding to Covid-19: Lessons from management research. *NEJM Catalyst Innovations in Care Delivery*, 1(2)

52 Auld, G, Bernstein, S, Cashore, B & Levin, K (2021) Managing pandemics as super wicked problems: Lessons from, and for, Covid-19 and the climate crisis. *Policy Sciences*, pp. 1–22

53 Cashore, B & Bernstein, S (2020) Why experts disagree on how to manage Covid-19: Four problem conceptions, not one. https://www.globalpolicyjournal.com/blog/07/04/2020/why-experts-disagree-how-manage-covid-19-four-problem-conceptions-not-one (archived at https://perma.cc/CU86-STTW)

54 Fantini, M P, Reno, C, Biserni, G B, Savoia, E & Lanari, M (2020) Covid-19 and the re-opening of schools: A policy maker's dilemma. *Italian Journal of Pediatrics*, 46(1), 1–3; Gurdasani, D, Pagel, C, McKee, M, Michie, S, Greenhalgh, T, Yates, C, Scally, G & Ziauddeen, H (2022) Covid-19 in the UK: Policy on children and schools. *BMJ*, 378

55 Head, B W & Alford, J (2015) Wicked problems: Implications for public policy and management. *Administration & Society*, 47(6), 711–739

56 Cooper, C, Tweedie, J, Andrew, J & Baker, M (2021) 15 April. https://blogs.lse.ac.uk/politicsandpolicy/thatcher-agencification-of-government/ (archived at https://perma.cc/BP6N-C585)

57 Cooper, C, Tweedie, J, Andrew, J & Baker, M (2022:194) From 'business-like' to businesses: Agencification, corporatization, and civil service reform under the Thatcher administration. *Public Administration*, 100(2), 193–215

58 Wynen, J, Kleizen, B, Verhoest, K, Lægreid, P & Rolland, V (2020) Keeping a watchful eye in times of turmoil? How repeated structural reform leads to more attention to political signals. *Public Administration*, 98(3), 570–590

59 Auld, G, Bernstein, S, Cashore, B & Levin, K (2021) Managing pandemics as super wicked problems: Lessons from, and for, Covid-19 and the climate crisis. *Policy Sciences*, 1–22

60 Auld, G, Bernstein, S, Cashore, B & Levin, K (2021) Managing pandemics as super wicked problems: Lessons from, and for, Covid-19 and the climate crisis. *Policy Sciences*, 1–22

61 Levin, K, Cashore, B, Bernstein, S & Auld, G (2009) Playing it forward: Path dependency, progressive incrementalism, and the 'super wicked' problem of global climate change. In IOP Conference Series. Earth and Environmental Science (Vol 6, No 50), February. IOP Publishing

62 Lazarus, R J (2008) Super wicked problems and climate change: Restraining the present to liberate the future. *Cornell L. Rev*, 94, 1153

63 Levin, K, Cashore, B, Bernstein, S & Auld, G (2009) Playing it forward: Path dependency, progressive incrementalism, and the 'super wicked' problem of global climate change. In IOP Conference Series. Earth and Environmental Science (Vol 6, No 50), February. IOP Publishing

64 Lemstra, M, Neudorf, C & Opondo, J (2008) Implications of a public smoking ban. *Canadian Journal of Public Health* (*Revue Canadienne de Sante Publique*), 99(1), 62–65; Levin, K, Cashore, B, Bernstein, S & Auld, G (2009) Playing it forward: Path dependency, progressive incrementalism, and the 'super wicked' problem of global climate change. In IOP Conference Series. Earth and Environmental Science (Vol 6, No 50). IOP Publishing

65 Waddock, S, Meszoely, G M, Waddell, S & Dentoni, D (2015) The complexity of wicked problems in large scale change. *Journal of Organizational Change Management*, 28(6)

66 Hong, J (2021) Singapore Is now the world's best place to be during Covid. *Bloomberg Newsletter*, 27 April. https://www.bloomberg.com/news/newsletters/2021-04-27/singapore-is-now-the-world-s-best-place-to-be-during-covid (archived at https://perma.cc/5GVH-VYEG)

67 Lew, L (2022) Singapore vs. Hong Kong: Covid strategies push rivals further apart. https://www.bloomberg.com/news/articles/2022-02-22/singapore-is-winning-in-hong-kong-s-all-out-fight-against-covid (archived at https://perma.cc/H9G6-U6AD)

68 Khor, S K (2020) Why is Southeast Asia responding differently to Covid-19? https://www.thinkglobalhealth.org/article/why-southeast-asia-responding-differently-covid-19#:~:text=Singapore's%20sophisticated%20health%20care%20system,public%20trust%20in%20these%20institutions (archived at https://perma.cc/H43W-KYHN)

69 Amul, G G, Ang, M, Kraybill, D, Ong, S E & Yoong, J (2022) Responses to Covid-19 in Southeast Asia: Diverse paths and ongoing challenges. *Asian Economic Policy Review*, 17(1), 90–110

70 Ministry of Health, Singapore. Being prepared for a pandemic. https://www.moh.gov.sg/diseases-updates/being-prepared-for-a-pandemic (archived at https://perma.cc/9L4E-TJJU)

71 Lew, L (2022) Singapore vs. Hong Kong: Covid strategies push rivals further apart. https://www.bloomberg.com/news/articles/2022-02-22/singapore-is-winning-in-hong-kong-s-all-out-fight-against-covid (archived at https://perma.cc/H9G6-U6AD)

72 ONS UK (2022) Coronavirus (Covid-19) latest insights: Deaths. https://www.ons.gov.uk/peoplepopulationandcommunity/healthandsocialcare/conditionsanddiseases/articles/coronaviruscovid19latestinsights/deaths (archived at https://perma.cc/M22H-CRHR)

73 Lew, L (2022) Singapore vs. Hong Kong: Covid strategies push rivals further apart. https://www.bloomberg.com/news/articles/2022-02-22/singapore-is-winning-in-hong-kong-s-all-out-fight-against-covid (archived at https://perma.cc/H9G6-U6AD)

Further reading

Ackoff, R L (1979) The future of operational research is past. *Journal of the Operational Research Society*, 30(2), 93–104

Ainger, J (2021) Arctic oil, gas production is booming despite climate fears. 23 September. https://www.bloomberg.com/news/articles/2021-09-23/arctic-oil-and-gas-exploration-is-booming-despite-climate-fears (archived at https://perma.cc/9624-53M5)

Alford, J & Head, B W (2017) Wicked and less wicked problems: A typology and a contingency framework. *Policy and Society*, 36(3), 397–413

Amazon Conservation. https://www.amazonconservation.org/the-challenge/threats/ (archived at https://perma.cc/4N6T-6QZE)

Amul, G G, Ang, M, Kraybill, D, Ong, S E & Yoong, J (2022) Responses to Covid-19 in Southeast Asia: Diverse paths and ongoing challenges. *Asian Economic Policy Review*, 17(1), 90–110

Arbuthnot, J (2022) ISRM strategic leadership breakfast briefing with Lord James Arbuthnot, 17 February. https://theisrm.org/en/isrm-strategic-leadership-breakfast-briefing-with-lord-james-arbuthnot (archived at https://perma.cc/52ND-JEP4)

Auld, G, Bernstein, S, Cashore, B & Levin, K (2021) Managing pandemics as super wicked problems: Lessons from, and for, Covid-19 and the climate crisis. *Policy Sciences*, 1–22

Batie, S S (2008) Fellows address: Wicked problems and applied economics. *American Journal of Agricultural Economics*, 90(5), 1176–1191

BBC (2022) Experts had too much power over Covid lockdowns, says Rishi Sunak. 25 August. https://www.bbc.co.uk/news/uk-politics-62664537 (archived at https://perma.cc/9K8K-Z3NA)

Cashore, B & Bernstein, S (2020) Why experts disagree on how to manage Covid-19: Four problem conceptions, not one. https://www.globalpolicyjournal.com/blog/07/04/2020/why-experts-disagree-how-manage-covid-19-four-problem-conceptions-not-one (archived at https://perma.cc/CU86-STTW)

Conklin, J (2005) *Dialogue mapping: Building shared understanding of wicked problems*. John Wiley & Sons, Inc

Conklin, J (2006) *Wicked Problems & Social Complexity* (Vol 11). Napa, US: CogNexus Institute

Cooper, C, Tweedie, J, Andrew, J & Baker, M (2021) The agencification of government under Thatcher continues to have profound repercussions for UK democracy. 15 April. https://blogs.lse.ac.uk/politicsandpolicy/thatcher-agencification-of-government/ (archived at https://perma.cc/BP6N-C585)

Cooper, C, Tweedie, J, Andrew, J & Baker, M (2022) From 'business-like' to businesses: Agencification, corporatization, and civil service reform under the Thatcher administration. *Public Administration*, 100(2), 193–215

COP 2016. COP26 summary report. https://www.ieta.org/resources/Resources/COP/COP26-Summary-Report.pdf (archived at https://perma.cc/GZ54-QAXU)

Coyne, R (2005) Wicked problems revisited. *Design Studies*, 26(1), 5–17

Crowley, K & Head, B W (2017) The enduring challenge of 'wicked problems': Revisiting Rittel and Webber. *Policy Sciences*, 50(4), 539–547

Cursino, M (2022) Amazon rainforest: Highest deforestation rate in six years. 9 July. https://www.bbc.co.uk/news/world-latin-america-62103336 (archived at https://perma.cc/C9ZN-SVAT)

Dawes, S S, Creswell, A & Pardo, T (2009) From 'need to know' to 'need to share': Tangled problems, information boundaries, and the building of public sector knowledge networks. *Public Administration Review*, 69(3), 392–402

de Salas, K, Scott, J L, Schüz, B & Norris, K (2022) The super wicked problem of ocean health: A socio-ecological and behavioural perspective. *Philosophical Transactions of the Royal Society B*, 377: 20210271

Dror, Y (1999) Beyond uncertainty: Facing the inconceivable. *Technological Forecasting and Social Change*, 62(1), 151–153

Fantini, M P, Reno, C, Biserni, G B, Savoia, E & Lanari, M (2020) Covid-19 and the re-opening of schools: A policy maker's dilemma. *Italian Journal of Pediatrics*, 46(1), 1–3

Flood, R L & Carson, E R (1993) *Dealing with complexity: An introduction to the theory and applications of the systems science*. Plenum Press

Gallopín, G C, Funtowicz, S, O'Connor, M & Ravetz, J (2001) Science for the twenty-first century: From social contract to the scientific core. *International Social Science Journal*, 53(168), 219–229

Greenpeace. Arctic oil drilling. https://www.greenpeace.org/usa/arctic/issues/oil-drilling/ (archived at https://perma.cc/X2PM-GKLH)

Grint, K (2010) Wicked problems and clumsy solutions: The role of leadership. In *The New Public Leadership Challenge* (pp. 169–186), London: Palgrave Macmillan

Gruetzemacher, R (2018) Rethinking AI strategy and policy as entangled super wicked problems. In Proceedings of the 2018 AAAI/ACM Conference on AI, Ethics, and Society, December, p. 122

Gurdasani, D, Pagel, C, McKee, M, Michie, S, Greenhalgh, T, Yates, C, Scally, G & Ziauddeen, H (2022) Covid-19 in the UK: Policy on children and schools. *BMJ*, 378

Head, B W and Alford, J (2015) Wicked problems: Implications for public policy and management. *Administration & Society*, 47(6), 711–739

Hong, Jinshan (2021) Singapore is now the world's best place to be during Covid. *Bloomberg Newsletter*, 27 April. https://www.bloomberg.com/news/newsletters/2021-04-27/singapore-is-now-the-world-s-best-place-to-be-during-covid (archived at https://perma.cc/5GVH-VYEG)

Hoppe, R (2010) A problem-processing perspective on governance. In *The Governance of Problems* (pp. 1–22), Policy Press

House of Lords (2022) Preparing for extreme risks: Building a resilient society, House of Lords Select Committee on Risk Assessment and Risk Planning: Report of Session 2021–22. https://publications.parliament.uk/pa/ld5802/ldselect/ldrisk/110/110.pdf (archived at https://perma.cc/23S4-AZKB)

IPCC (2018) The evidence is clear: The time for action is now. We can halve emissions by 2030. https://www.ipcc.ch/2022/04/04/ipcc-ar6-wgiii-pressrelease/ (archived at https://perma.cc/937P-BJ8H)

IPCC (2022) Summary for policymakers. https://www.ipcc.ch/report/ar6/wg2/downloads/report/IPCC_AR6_WGII_SummaryForPolicymakers.pdf (archived at https://perma.cc/5CVQ-SZ3K)

Khor, S K (2020) Why is Southeast Asia responding differently to Covid-19? https://www.thinkglobalhealth.org/article/why-southeast-asia-responding-differently-covid-19#:~:text=Singapore's%20sophisticated%20health%20care%20system,public%20trust%20in%20these%20institutions (archived at https://perma.cc/VRT7-V9BE)

Lazarus, R J (2008) Super wicked problems and climate change: Restraining the present to liberate the future. *Cornell L. Rev, 94*, 1153

Lemstra, M, Neudorf, C & Opondo, J (2008) Implications of a public smoking ban. *Canadian Journal of Public Health (Revue Canadienne de Sante Publique)*, 99(1), 62–65

Levin, K, Cashore, B, Bernstein, S & Auld, G (2009) Playing it forward: Path dependency, progressive incrementalism, and the 'super wicked' problem of global climate change. In IOP Conference Series. Earth and Environmental Science (Vol 6, No 50), February. IOP Publishing

Levin, K, Cashore, B, Bernstein, S & Auld, G (2012) Overcoming the tragedy of super wicked problems: Constraining our future selves to ameliorate global climate change. *Policy Sciences*, 45(2), 123–152

Lew, L (2022) Singapore vs. Hong Kong: Covid strategies push rivals further apart. https://www.bloomberg.com/news/articles/2022-02-22/singapore-is-winning-in-hong-kong-s-all-out-fight-against-covid/

Lindblom, C E (1959) The science of 'muddling through'. *Public Administration Review*, 79–88

Ministry of Health, Singapore. Being prepared for a pandemic. https://www.moh.gov.sg/diseases-updates/being-prepared-for-a-pandemic (archived at https://perma.cc/9L4E-TJJU)

Nembhard, I M, Burns, L R & Shortell, S M (2020) Responding to Covid-19: Lessons from management research. *NEJM Catalyst Innovations in Care Delivery*, 1(2)

Oh, J, Lee, J K, Schwarz, D, Ratcliffe, H L, Markuns, J F & Hirschhorn, L R (2020) National Response to Covid-19 in the Republic of Korea and lessons learned for other countries

ONS UK (2022) Coronavirus (Covid-19) latest insights: Deaths. https://www.ons.gov.uk/peoplepopulationandcommunity/healthandsocialcare/conditionsanddiseases/articles/coronaviruscovid19latestinsights/deaths (archived at https://perma.cc/M22H-CRHR)

Peters, B G (2017) What is so wicked about wicked problems? A conceptual analysis and a research program. *Policy and Society*, 36(3), 385–396

Reinecke, J & Ansari, S (2016) Taming wicked problems: The role of framing in the construction of corporate social responsibility. *Journal of Management Studies*, 53(3), 299–329

Roberts, N (2000) Wicked problems and network approaches to resolution. *International Public Management Review*, 1(1), 1–19

Schön, D & Rein, M (1994) *Frame reflection: Toward the resolution of intractable policy controversies*. Basic Books

Schwab, Klaus (2016) The fourth industrial revolution: What it means, how to respond. https://www.weforum.org/agenda/2016/01/the-fourth-industrial-revolution-what-it-means-and-how-to-respond/ (archived at https://perma.cc/22S8-JAEC)

Stephenson, K (2003) Environmental goal setting. In M R Tool & P D Bush (eds.) *Institutional Analysis and Economic Policy*. Boston, MA: Kluwer, pp. 443–460

Tan, J B, Cook, M J, Logan, P, Rozanova, L & Wilder-Smith, A (2021) Singapore's pandemic preparedness: An overview of the first wave of Covid-19. *International Journal of Environmental Research and Public Health*, 18(1), 252

Turnbull, N & Hoppe, R (2019) Problematizing 'wickedness': A critique of the wicked problems concept, from philosophy to practice. *Policy and Society*, 38(2), 315–337

Waddock, S, Meszoely, G M, Waddell, S & Dentoni, D (2015) The complexity of wicked problems in large scale change. *Journal of Organizational Change Management*, 28(6)

Weick, K E (1987) Organizational culture as a source of high reliability. *California Management Review*, 29(2), 112–127

Wynen, J, Kleizen, B, Verhoest, K, Lægreid, P & Rolland, V (2020) Keeping a watchful eye in times of turmoil? How repeated structural reform leads to more attention to political signals. *Public Administration*, 98(3), 570–590

Young, I (2006) Responsibility and global justice: A social connection model. *Social Philosophy and Policy*, 23(1), 102–130. doi:10.1017/S0265052506060043

13

Case studies

Cyber attack: UK National Health Service WannaCry attack (2017)

An example of a crisis event that was almost instantaneous, and that demanded immediate action from the people who happened to be in the room at the time rather than anyone who was designated as a crisis management decision-maker, was the WannaCry cyber-attack on 12 May 2017. The whole event lasted just over seven hours (it worked by locking organizations out of their own computer systems) and yet within that time it was estimated to have affected more than 200,000 computers across 150 countries, with total damages ranging from hundreds of millions to billions of dollars.

The impact of such attacks on organizations, and their ability to learn and adapt (though admittedly after the event has happened), even those as complex as the NHS, can be seen in the fact that in the three years after WannaCry, the NHS had been hit by only six successful ransomware attacks – compared with 203 in the three years prior to that.

The WannaCry attack on the NHS is a classic example of where the nature, scale and scope of the attack are so severe that it can be considered to be unprecedented. As is almost always the case with such claims, a closer investigation shows that there were repeated warnings of the possibility of such attacks, and repeated calls for the vulnerabilities inherent in the system that would allow such attacks to happen to be closed.

Similar cyber-attacks on the NHS had occurred the previous year, leading to much the same impacts that were seen in the WannaCry attack. The government department responsible for data management and security published a report that identified cyber-attack as a real threat, highlighted the use of old and unpatched systems as a vulnerable attack point, and recommended that all health and care organizations needed to provide evidence that they were taking action to improve cyber-security, including moving away from old operating systems. However, there was no mechanism in place to ensure that the healthcare organizations were actually taking action and no way of monitoring whether they did. When NHS Digital had conducted an on-site cyber-security assessment for 88 out of 236 trusts in the year prior to the attack, none had passed.

The Department of Health had developed a plan, which included roles and responsibilities of national and local organizations for responding to an attack, but had not tested the plan at a local level. This meant the NHS was not clear what actions it should take when it was affected by WannaCry. Although the NHS as an organization was used to dealing with critical incidents and had a well-developed process as well as the individual and institutional connections that could allow adaptive responses to be put in place, WannaCry was a different sort of event, and did not fit in with the processes that had been developed for planned scenarios such as major traffic accidents or responding to terrorist attacks. Because of this, the initial question that is always at the heart of any crisis response – 'What has just happened and what does that mean?' – couldn't be answered in any meaningful way.

There had not been any exercises around a major cyber-attack previously and it was not clear who had responsibility for managing the response. Although the attacks were initiated at 7.45am, it was not until 4.00pm that the NHS declared it a major incident and at 6.45pm initiated its existing emergency, preparedness, resilience and response plans, which formally empowered the organization to act as the single point of coordination for incident management. However, given that there had been little if any focus on cyber-attacks, it was not clear to local organizations who the official point of contact was and so they spoke to whoever was available, including their own local councils and the local police. Besides that, they had either been locked out of their own IT systems and so could not access email, or had closed down their systems as a precautionary measure, which had the same effect. This of course impacted their ability both to communicate with other parts of the organization and to access what would have been the crisis management plans.

Many people were limited to using their personal mobile phones, which of course had a significant impact at the start of the crisis to build an overall picture of what had happened and to develop the necessary communication channels that would have allowed a structured response based on existing protocols.

Once the event was over, an enquiry was held and the lessons listed in the official enquiry report are hardly earth-shattering:

- develop a response plan setting out what the NHS should do in the event of a cyber-attack and establish the roles and responsibilities of local and national NHS bodies and the department;
- ensure organizations implement the critical steps identified in email alerts from NHS Digital, including applying software patches and keeping anti-virus software up to date;
- ensure essential communications are getting through during an attack when systems are down;
- ensure that organizations, boards and their staff are taking the cyber-threat seriously, understand the direct risks to front-line services and are working proactively to maximize their resilience and minimize impacts on patient care.

Drone incidence: Gatwick Airport (2018)

The response to a drone incident at Gatwick Airport in December 2018 gives a clear example of how difficult the restart process can be – especially when it can be definitely agreed that the initial triggering event is over. The incident started when a drone was reported to have been seen flying in the vicinity of the outer fence at Gatwick Airport. As it was classified as a potential threat to aircraft (and at that stage it was not known if there was a terrorist aspect to the sighting), it was decided to close the runway to both incoming and departing flights. This naturally had an immediate impact both on the passengers in the airport and on those flights in the air expecting to arrive at Gatwick.

What was not expected, however, was the length of the runway closure: three days. In the aftermath of the event, during which there was confusion over what exactly were the measures that could neutralize the drone threat and what role the police and military would be taking, almost all of the discussions around the incident have concentrated on the technical/preventative/reactive side of the picture. That is, what can be done to identify drone threats and to prevent them from negatively impacting on airports' operations. What has been missing has been a review of the situation from a risk management perspective.

One of the rules of crisis management is that we must differentiate the external event from the crisis. Hurricane Katrina was an event. It was the failure of the response agencies to fulfil their role in responding to the damage and disruption caused in New Orleans, in exactly the sort of situation that they should have prepared for, that caused the crisis. In much the same way, it was not the drone that caused the closure of a major global hub airport for three days but the failure of the airport management in general, and risk managers in particular, to prepare for a situation that was not only predictable but, in the present risk climate, almost inevitable.

As far as the airport managers are concerned, it is to be hoped that the possibility of a drone in the vicinity of their airport was high on their risk register and had been extensively modelled in order to identify both the challenges associated with such an incident and a full range of response options in the event that such an incident was to occur. In fact, this was not the first time that a drone sighting had caused disruption to Gatwick's operations. There had been two much smaller incidents in 2017, both of which should have been red lights that flagged up the necessity of having a fully developed response capability given the high likelihood that such an event would occur again.

One of the basic differences between security management and risk management is that security management is preventative (how do we stop a drone from disrupting our airport?) while risk management is about consequence management (what do we do in the event that the airport is disrupted?). From this perspective, in terms of risk management, the drone itself was relatively unimportant. The significant issue from the airport management perspective was 'loss of airport functionality'. Under this heading, it is not substantively significant whether the loss of functionality was due to a technical failure (global check-in IT crash, September 2017), volcanic ash (May 2011) or terrorism (9/11 2001, 2006 liquid bomb plots).

One of the issues that differentiates a major incident from a crisis event is that the former is recognized and understood and there is a range of response options that can be put in place by responding managers and operation commanders who have had both training and personal experience of such incidents previously, whereas the latter involves a situation that has been unknown previously and for which there are no set response plans or frameworks. It seems from various written and verbal reports that there was no clear understanding of what the correct procedures should be or even of assessing what the level of threat was. As is often the case when a situation is experienced for the first time, rather than making a nuanced analysis of the level of threat and the ranges of possible response that were available, the knee-jerk reaction was to go for the binary solution: on/off.

It is always easy to second guess risk management decisions after the fact, and it may well have been that in that specific situation and under those particular circumstances, shutting down airport operations was the best thing to do. However, the critical component missing in that decision was the fact that there was no clear way to trigger the re-opening of the airport. Under a risk-averse decision-making environment (which was almost certainly the situation within the airport senior management at the time) it would always have been the prudent decision, in terms of career protection if not operations management, to say, 'We are not certain that it is safe to re-open the airport, therefore we will put off making that decision until we have more information.'

This is a classic example of crisis management as a 'loss of sense-making'. The first question in crisis management is rarely 'What do we need to do?'. It is much more likely that the first questions will be 'What the hell has just happened? What does that mean? What impact is that going to have on us?'. These are all questions that were clearly not sufficiently well answered as part of the Gatwick risk management/crisis management process.

It is clear that the decision to close an airport is never one that is taken lightly. However, given the experience of such situations over the last few years, it is reasonable to expect that there would be a well-rehearsed process not only for making that decision but for managing the consequences of it. As in any crisis situation, that would come down to communication. It is communicating with the service users, and particularly the passengers affected. As in all cases that involve national facilities and a critical suspension of operations, the story quickly turns from one of safety and security to the competence or otherwise of management. It seems almost unbelievable that there is not a programme in place that can be triggered as part of the airport operations suspension to ensure that passengers are informed, those that need to be are given an appropriate level of support, and that the impression given both within the UK and to the wider global audience is a management team responsibility that is responding to a critical incident in a strong and effective manner.

We are still waiting for the authoritative post-incident report to be issued, but it is clear that there are a number of lessons from this incident that will be of value to any risk manager, whatever environment they are operating in.

The first, and perhaps most obvious, is that if your risk register is not regularly reviewed and updated, and the lessons learned from that review are not integrated into your overall risk management process, then you are likely to be victim to a critical incident that will escalate beyond what would have been necessary had your risk management processes been in place. There was nothing about the presence of an actual/suspected drone in the vicinity of the airport that should not have been planned for and there were no consequences of the decision to close the airport that could not have been predicted.

The second point is that risk management is always about judgement. It is rare, especially in an unstable and potentially escalating situation, that there is a clear sign that the event is over. The ability to understand both the external risk and the need to monitor the organization's own risk appetite, and the ability to adapt that to the needs of the specific situation, are a critical part of the responsibility associated with risk management. It is also one of the areas where the executive committee/C-Suite will be held responsible both for the making of the decisions and for the impact of the consequences in the event that they (in hindsight) are seen to get it wrong. This is a critical area where the effective training of C-Suite decision-makers can have a critical impact in the overall success or otherwise of a crisis management situation.

The third lesson is that the first time an event happens is always chaotic, with an inability to get a true sense of either the nature and scale of the threat or the nature and scale of the appropriate response. This is an almost inescapable rule of crisis management. The way that you learn to deal with a crisis is to live through one and then the second time that the situation arises the learning taken from the first one will have a significant, and often dramatic, impact on the nature and effectiveness of the consequent response. Whether it is the difference between the first and second foot and mouth disease scare in the UK, the first and second evacuation of New York in the face of severe flooding or the response to the first and second eruption of the Icelandic volcano, the fact that the response management teams had actually experienced a live event previously gave them an understanding of both the event and the associated decision-making environment that could not have been replicated by any amount of training, preparation or exercising.

While we can never recreate the pressures of a true live event, we can take advantage of 'near misses' to practise our response options in as near a live context as possible. It would be interesting to know how often the Gatwick management team had modelled and practised the response to a drone event, and particularly one that had such a significant impact on the overall operations of their airport.

Of course, this is not something that should have been limited to Gatwick. To a certain extent they got unlucky that it happened to be them. In truth, this is something that should have been on the radar (excuse the expression) of every airport management and risk management team in the country. The possibility of a drone being seen near an airport, even if its purpose was unknown, should not have taken airport managers by surprise. However, being lucky is an integral part of risk management and as the Gatwick management team have learned, while we cannot affect the external event, we can certainly – and we must – take responsibility for our own preparation and the ability to respond effectively in the event that the crisis situation occurs.

The ability to prepare for an event that is in fact recognized, and that 'makes sense' within the confines of the existing risk management frameworks, can be evidenced by the fact that when a similar event happened at Heathrow Airport one month later, the managers there were able to respond to it with a known process (the temporary suspension of flights) and then to give it a risk rating that allowed them to reopen the airport within an hour.

Natural disaster: Texas snowstorm (2021)

It is relatively easy to identify the qualities associated with resilience and the desired outcomes that are achieved if resilient frameworks are put in place. However, these still tend to focus on resilience as a reactive aspect of risk management – it is what happens when something has gone wrong.

However, in order to have true significance and impact, the concept of reliance needs to be moved from the right of bang reactive side of the equation to the left of bang proactive and pre-emptive side. To put it in its simplest terms, the way you cross the road safely is to develop a methodology that allows you to identify potential threats and to act in such a way as to avoid them and in fact to reduce them to zero if all aspects of that process are adhered to. It is not about either wearing enough protective clothing so that if you are hit by a vehicle there is little damage or teaching someone how to survive multiple impacts.

For those organizations that do develop an intrinsic resilience, there seems to be a pattern of repeated interactions and the development of community capital that is separate to, or at least parallel to, the strictly skill-based issues that might traditionally be considered as the prerequisites for developing an effective crisis management or response capability.

In terms of general resilience, we can see how a failure to develop resilience capabilities that either support systems and communities when put under increasing pressure or fail to deliver the services expected when they were supposed to step forward and take responsibility for protecting the safety, security and wellbeing of their communities at exactly the time that they needed it most cannot be explained through blaming 'unprecedented' events, but should be seen in terms of long-term and systemic neglect, often in the face of warnings that have highlighted those dangers on a repeated basis.

The Texas snowstorm of February 2021 was unprecedented in both the severity and scale of the event itself and the level of impact that it had across Houston and the wider region. The power outage that followed the storm led to almost 4.5 million people being left without power, heat and running water for days. As the US's largest energy producer, 90 per cent of its entire power supply is self-generated and self-owned, allowing it to have total control over the critical resource that underpins every other aspect of its activities.

Given the weather patterns that have been seen across the United States over the last decade, the likelihood of a severe winter weather event was certainly not unpredictable. It actually could be considered to be inevitable. The main cause of the blackout (the worst in the US since the power outages in the north-east region in 2003) was failure of the main supply systems – natural gas, coal and nuclear facilities – to have prepared themselves to operate in such conditions. Given Texas's propensity for warm winters, there had not been the necessary level of forethought or preparation to ensure that there was capacity and capabilities that would maintain the necessary level of service provision in the event that a cold spell was to occur. It was unclear, even according to official government announcements, as to what the correct course of action should be to prevent pipes from bursting. Although the official advice was to keep water trickling from the taps, so as to prevent freezing, this meant that water levels were soon dangerously low and the opposite guidance was then issued. It was admitted that the move to close off taps in order to preserve water facilities for hospitals and other emergency services could then create the situation that they would freeze and burst, which would only cause greater problems down the line, but at that stage that was a secondary problem in the greater scheme of things. These are not unexpected issues, and the expectation to create a critical infrastructure framework can maintain functionality and service provision in such conditions is not an impossible demand. Those countries that experience sub-zero temperatures on a regular basis (such as Canada and Sweden) have systems that are not only weather-resistant but dependable. Their ability to maintain functionality in such conditions is built into their operating frameworks. The question is not if it is possible but rather whether those people that control strategic planning, budgets and resource deployment are prepared to make the decisions ahead of time that will allow those frameworks to be in place when they are finally needed.

The interconnectedness of issues such as vulnerability, resilience and capability development can be seen by the fact that Texas legislators in Washington had previously (in 2015 and 2018) written to the Texas governor demanding that an all-hazards capability be developed across the state power system. Although the threats identified in those demands were primarily electromagnetic pulses (EMPs), which could have been triggered either by solar activity or hostile attack, the ability to maintain functionality and service delivery within the context of an EMP event undoubtedly would have had value in a severe weather event as well.

Although the immediate crisis was the storm, the fundamental vulnerabilities that led to that storm (which was a natural and predictable event), creating significant and in some cases catastrophic consequences, were the result of political decisions that had been made over decades. As seen in every event that we have explored, it is the failure to plan ahead and pay ahead, to put in place the frameworks and capabilities that would be of critical value when an event strikes, that creates the crisis that impacts so many people and triggers additional costs, consequences and losses for every level of society, from national-level legislators to families trying to work out how to flush their toilet or where they can find drinking water.

Suicide attack: Manchester Arena bombing (2017)

For any emergency service, however much planning and training goes into preparing to face a major incident, whether it is a natural disaster, critical infrastructure failure or a major terrorist attack, the likelihood is that there are going to be procedural failures that lead to a significant degradation of service delivery. This can be either because of the impact of the external event or failures in internal management controls. The event at the Manchester Arena on 22 May 2017, when a suicide bomber detonated a bomb just outside the arena, killing 22 people, many of them children who had been attending an Ariana Grande concert, was undoubtedly high-impact and put all of the emergency management networks, including emergency services, hospitals, transport managers, city managers and civic leaders, under immense pressure.

However, it is also exactly the sort of high-impact terrorist attack that must be considered as a core strategic capability for any organization operating in the present-day threat environment. The Kerslake Report[1] into the response of the emergency services to the incident (released on 27 March 2018) makes it clear that much of what was achieved across all aspects of the emergency response was effective and appropriate. More than that, many members of the emergency services went over and above the call of duty in ensuring that they were able to respond to the incident, care for the casualties and ensure the safety and wellbeing of all those caught up in the immediate event and also affected by it in secondary ways (either by their relationships with actual and potential victims or by being caught up in the natural disruption that follows any large-scale urban attack).

As the Kerslake Report points out, although the Greater Manchester Resilience Forum had carried out many multi-agency planning and emergency response exercises, the events of 22 May were something none of those involved had ever encountered before. This was a real-world test of the plans and assumptions in a way that can never be replicated in training exercises, however realistic they might try to be.

Overall, the fact that there had been multiple multi-agency exercises, and in fact a major exercise had been carried out at the Trafford Centre in Manchester only a few months before the attack, meant that most of the emergency response agencies at the scene were able to work together with the confidence that repeated joint exercising brings. This was especially clear in the way that decisions were made at the time that did not fit into 'accepted procedures' but were felt to be the most appropriate course of action in the specific (and often chaotic) circumstances. One example was the decision to establish the casualty clearing station on the station concourse and to allow emergency staff and members of the public to remain in the foyer notwithstanding its designation at the time as a 'hot' zone. These were vital judgements that significantly influenced the course of events over the evening.

However, and without wishing to give the impression of being judgemental, the root causes of the major critical failures in the response operation were not issues that were unexpected or could not have been prepared for, but were exactly those failures that could have been predicted as part of the basic principles of multi-agency major event response. They are in fact the same issues that are highlighted in the executive summary of every post-event review and report, whatever the specific details of those incidents might be.

In the simplest terms these are the challenges associated with communication and integration – information exchange, joint decision-making and the ability to create a common operating picture between all the responding agencies, both horizontally on a multi-agency framework and hierarchically through the various command levels: Gold, Silver, Bronze.

As an example, we would like to offer excerpts from a number of reports. It should be clear that they could probably be cut and pasted in their entirety and dropped into any emergency response post-action review and be as equally relevant whatever situation they were referring to:

> I heard this refrain again and again from [...] emergency planners: excellent work within individual agencies, but still a lack of government-wide disaster response planning. Interagency coordination is still weak, and in most cases the government's disaster response plans are woefully short of detail. Most agencies are unfamiliar with the disaster response plans and capabilities of other agencies, impeding efforts to develop well-coordinated plans. Underlying all of this is the [...] government system, which does not appear to encourage rapid decision-making or interagency coordination. (Bosner, 2002)

> In essence, there is concern that the regional disaster prevention plans that have been created to satisfy those involved in local government will be useless when put into action. [Specific programmes] are just that, over-produced systems that cannot be easily operated or revised. Ironically, these deficiencies are obvious to the governments that paid for them. (Kawata, 2001)

> The preparation and response to [...] shows that we are still an analogue government in a digital age. We must recognize that we are woefully incapable of storing, moving and accessing information, especially in times of crisis. Many of the problems we have identified can be categorized as "information gaps" – or at least problems with information-related implications, or failure to act decisively because information was sketchy at best. One would think that we could share information by now. But [...] again proved that we can't. (Executive Summary of Findings, Congressional Report)

The two major failures in the Manchester bombing response both involved communications. The first was that, in the words of the report, 'the Greater Manchester Fire and Rescue Service (GMFRS) did not arrive at the scene and therefore played no meaningful role in the response to the attack for nearly two hours. This compares to the average response time for the service of less than six minutes'.

The other communication failure involved the Casualty Bureau, which should have been set up as a point of contact and centralized information-sharing for anyone wanting information on the missing, injured or dead. This was meant to be managed by Vodafone under the National Mutual Aid Telephony system, and in the words of the Kerslake Report it was 'a complete failure'. This involved both the ability of local families to contact the help line and the inability to integrate the Manchester system into the wider national framework, which was supposed to give the option of increased capacity in exactly this sort of situation.

One additional point that was highlighted in the executive summary involved the fundamental issue of multi-agency response and collaboration. Given the growth of locally radicalized home-grown terrorists, creating high-impact attacks using either weapons (marauding firearms attacks) or vehicles as their method of attack, it is to be expected that the planning for the response to such incident would be at the heart of modern policing and major city management. In the case of Manchester this was the case and there was a well-practised multi-agency response framework in place: Operation PLATO, which is the multi-agency response to a marauding firearm attack. However, as the report states, '[T]here was not a shared communication across the agencies of the declaration of Operation PLATO..., nor was there a shared understanding of its implications.'

Although the circumstances were different, the use of Operation Kratos that underpinned the killing of Charles de Menezes in 2005 shows remarkably similar issues in terms of confusion at the highest level of leadership, lack of understanding of the implications of the operation in question and, as always, breakdown in communication. The 168-page report issued by the Independent Police Complaints Commission, which reviewed the incident, clearly stated, 'The main and central issue in this tragedy is whether the level of identification was properly communicated from the surveillance team to Room 1600 and CO19.'

It is a sign of the significance of the seriousness of decision-taking under the extreme pressure of command that the report also states:

> Commander Dick has endorsed that she was the person in command.
> **Prosecution Service may wish to consider whether the manner in which this**

> **operation was commanded, the failures to have resources properly deployed and the absence of any other tactical options could be considered to be grossly negligent.** (Independent Police Complaints Commission, para 20.87, page 135, bold in the original)

Discussion

By their very nature, events such as the need to respond to what was, at the time, perceived to be a credible threat in terms of a suicide bomber approaching his target in London during a period of highest national alert, or to respond to a major terrorist attack in a crowded concert venue, puts every aspect of the system under pressure. However, this cannot be used as an excuse for failure, especially when the causes of failure are recognized as being exactly those points that are most likely to fail and which would have the greatest impact on the ability of all responding agencies to act quickly and effectively, in collaboration with all of the other myriad teams operating around them at the same time. While there is no desire to apportion blame, there is the need to recognize responsibility (as I am sure responders at every level of those agencies would acknowledge).

We all recognize that communications and information transfer are at the heart of any multi-agency response, and it is the failure to manage those issues, under the intense stress of an actual response environment, that is almost always the root cause of operational failures. It is not enough to expect that things will go well, or as planned. In fact, the significant point at the heart of the responses to both the Manchester bombing and the Charles de Menezes shooting was how well the relevant agencies were able to adapt and respond to highly unstable situations that were evolving and mutating on a minute-by-minute basis, and for which they often had only partial information – and even that information was unclear or unverified.

It is the ability to manage the transfer of complex information, under pressure, between multiple stakeholders, within the confusion of an actual crisis event that is the foundation of effective crisis response. If that is not achieved, it is impossible to then deliver a cohesive, integrated multi-agency response, whatever else might be achieved.

The need to do so is not unknown. The tragedy is that the lessons that need to be learned are written in blood...

> Minutes after the south tower collapsed at the World Trade Center, police helicopters hovered near the remaining tower to check its condition. 'About

> 15 floors down from the top, it looks like it's glowing red,' the pilot of one helicopter, Aviation 14, radioed at 10:07 a.m. 'It's inevitable.'
>
> Seconds later, another pilot reported: 'I don't think this has too much longer to go. I would evacuate all people within the area of that second building.'
>
> Those clear warnings, captured on police radio tapes, were transmitted 21 minutes before the building fell, and officials say they were relayed to police officers, most of whom managed to escape. Yet most firefighters never heard those warnings, or earlier orders to get out. Their radio system failed frequently that morning. Even if the radio network had been reliable, it was not linked to the police system. And the police and fire commanders guiding the rescue efforts did not talk to one another during the crisis' (*The New York Times*, 2002).

343 fire fighters died in the Twin Towers. Thanks to the warning given over the police radio system, 'only' 60 police officers died, from the Port Authority of New York, New Jersey Police Department and New York City Police Department.

It is a truth of crisis response that responders cannot affect the incident itself, but what they can do is take responsibility for preparing themselves to manage the response in the best manner available and in light of the responsibility that their communities entrust to them. As Rittel and Webber say in their Tenth Law of Wicked Problems, 'The planner has no right to be wrong'.[2]

Complexity and fragility: the case of the Ever Given

On the morning of 23 March 2021, strong winds in the Suez Canal battered the containership *Ever Given* with waves, complicating navigation in the narrow canal and causing the ship to become wedged between the canal banks, effectively cutting off a large portion of the trade between Europe, Asia and the Middle East for six days. In what seemed to be a bemusing and localized event in public perception flared up by an online community that poked fun at the failures of the local Egyptian authority, the whole situation and resulting consequences were a nightmare scenario for anyone involved in logistics and supply chain management. The *Ever Given* incident insistently highlighted the complexity and fragility of the global supply chain.

When the Suez Canal opened in 1869, the idea of connecting the Mediterranean Sea to the Red Sea already had a long history and historic predecessors, dating back as far as the Egyptian pharaohs around 1850 BCE. The first modern plans in the 18th century to build a canal were part of the power struggle in Europe, with France trying to weaken British dominance on global trade. After several unsuccessful attempts by the French, the Egyptians finally gave them construction rights which started in 1859. After completion and amidst political unrest in Egypt in the late 19th century, Britain took over the Suez Canal and later the whole of Egypt. The Suez Canal allowed them not only to significantly reduce the time to sail to India but also to effectively control the trade routes between Europe and the Arabian Sea. In 1956, Egypt nationalized the Canal, prompting a crisis and an invasion by British, French and Israeli forces that was only stopped after US intervention. After the start of the Six-Day War in 1967, the Suez Canal was closed for eight years, significantly impacting global trade.

Since its reopening in 1975, the Suez Canal has become a major artery for global trade, connecting Europe, the Middle East and Asia. 12 per cent of the global trade, 30 per cent of all global container traffic, as well as 8–10 per cent of the world's oil and liquid gas pass through the almost 200 km long canal, allowing more than 50 ships daily to bypass the much longer route through the Cape of Africa, significantly cutting transportation cost by hundreds of thousands of dollars and time by weeks. Today's container ships are behemoths of the sea, often reaching 400 m in length and capable of loading up to 24,000 containers, which would be equivalent to a 70 km train. The *Ever Given* is one of those behemoths with almost 400m in length and a capacity of 20,000 containers. Simply looking at the incident in isolation, it comes as no surprise that it was no easy feat to free the ship after it banked in the canal. The struggle to free the ship was perfectly symbolized by the photo of a single badger removing small bits of sand from the bow of the massive ship, turning it into a modern-day equivalent of Sisyphus pushing his boulder up the hill. Although Zeus's punishment was intended for all eternity, the *Ever Given* could be freed after 6 days with the help of 14 tugboats. If the *Ever Given* could indeed be treated as an isolated incident, the story would end here, probably with the ship floating off into the sunset. Unfortunately, it is part of a complex and fragile system and the incident had a significant impact on it: the global supply chain.

As with many concepts that look great on paper, the global supply chain was heralded as one of the systems that would increase global prosperity, moving resources and products quickly, cheaply and on a global scale. Modern supply chain management is built on *just-in-time*, which was pioneered in Japan by Toyota in the 1950s and 1960s as part of its lean management process. In essence, just-in-time is a process of inventory management where supplies for production or sale are ordered only as needed, allowing constantly low inventory and companies to reduce cost and increase production efficiency. One of the downsides of the just-in-time system is that it relies on a fast and reliable network of suppliers. However, that was no issue in the early 2000s when the system worked as intended and was celebrated by authors such as Thomas Friedman who cited the global supply chain as one of 10 forces that helped to flatten the earth, removing distance, borders and allowing equal competition in the wake of growing globalization. One of the issues with many concepts coming out of the 1990s and early 2000s is that they were envisioned in a euphoric period of rapid technological and political change. History did not end as Francis Fukuyama predicted, and globalization did not flatten the earth. While logistics providers continue to deliver impressive work in an increasingly difficult environment, the global supply chain in itself is fragile and different crises will continue to affect it if the network as a whole will not become more resilient.

As Perrow stated, complexity makes failure inevitable and the supply chain in itself is so highly intertwined and complex that it is unsurprising that there is not a single point of failure but an array of interactions at various points in the chain that cause shortages, delays and an increase in prices. It is also undeniable that the Covid-19 pandemic has played a significant role in exacerbating many of the existing issues. During the first six months of the pandemic and at the height of uncertainty, global shipping plummeted. After people settled into their home offices and realized that most of their free time and social activities were off the table for the foreseeable future, they started to spend their money on things that they could easily order online. The global supply chain had been operating with seasonal surges in demand, especially in preparation for the holiday season, but suddenly every month had been peak season. It is a little-known fact that passenger planes have been carrying one third of all cargo. After commercial flights had been reduced to an absolute minimum, that cargo was now hastily transferred to container shipping.

Container shipping had been the backbone of international logistics for decades and a driver for globalization. When the first container ship left port in 1956, it started a revolution. The metal boxes these ships carried allowed them to transport more cargo, massively increased the efficiency of shipping and arguably stitched the global economy together even more than the internet. With the sudden surge in consumer demand, containers themselves became a hot commodity. The issue was not the number of circulating containers but the fact that great numbers were either stuck in the wrong places or were used as temporary storage. Logistics is global. With fewer empty containers making their way back to Asia, fewer containers and ships were available for exports. This caused shipping prices to skyrocket, from around $4,000 to up to $20,000 for a single container. Additionally, even if a container was available, there was no guarantee of an immediate spot on a container ship, causing further delays.

When a container ship would finally reach port, it would face yet another hurdle. The majority of ports suffer from congestion and ships have to wait days or even weeks for a chance to dock and unload their cargo. Much of the congestion is caused by Covid-19 precautions. Many ports have mandatory quarantine periods and PCR tests and cargo operations are not allowed to proceed until there are negative test results. Mandatory quarantine can last between 14–28 days in Chinese ports. After a Covid-19 outbreak in one of the busiest container terminals in China, the Chinese government mandated ships to anchor and wait as part of its measures to control the outbreak. The general scale of the operation is another cause for congestion. During the last 10–15 years, ships have doubled or even tripled in size, take much longer to unload and need more infrastructure, especially trains and trucks. This has been aggravated by a continuing labour shortage, especially after many workers were either laid off or left the profession during the first few months of the pandemic. The truck driver shortage has become a critical issue in the UK after Brexit, but the situation is only slightly better in the rest of the world.

The problems for the global supply chain do not end there. Extreme weather events have caused massive damage to infrastructure in the past years, but there has been little progress in resilience planning. Out of 300 ports in the United States, only 10 have gone through such a process. While ports are generally more resilient against sea level rise, port operations and connected infrastructure such as railway networks, roadways and the electrical grid are still vulnerable to hurricanes or coastal flooding as previous cases have shown. In case of such an extreme weather event, the impact on an affected port would put additional stress on an already stressed system as ships would need to be rerouted, causing further delays and congestion.

Finally, the reliance on a functioning supply chain, spreading product assembly across various markets and maintaining low cost through minimal inventory, has created a precarious system. For consumers this has been evident in the drop in available computer hardware, monitors or furniture. The shortages can be traced back to miscalculations, factory closings due to Covid-19 outbreaks and climate change. Many industries are not receiving supplies, which caused a pipette shortage in the United States in early 2021, for example. When demand for pipettes soared because of Covid-19 tests, the Texas

Freeze in February 2021 broke a critical link in the pipette supply chain. Due to power outages, several plants that produced polypropylene resin, the raw material for pipette tips, had to shut down, affecting 85 per cent of the US production capacity and causing shortages in hospitals all over the country. The worldwide semiconductor shortage is another example. Semiconductors are a critical component in automobile production but are reliant on the availability of water for production. Some of the largest producers have already announced that they will produce 80,000–100,000 fewer cars per year than expected. Among those affected are also producers of heavy-duty trucks, which have ironically been ordered to mitigate some of the negative effects of the global supply chain crisis only to fall victim to them.

Coming back to the *Ever Given* stuck in the Suez Canal, none of those issues was caused by the ship being stuck itself. However, these pre-existing problems were exacerbated and put more stress on a system that was already strained and fragile. The ripple effects of those six days would be felt for months. Not only were more than 300 other cargo ships also stuck and unsure whether or not to take the trip around the Cape of Africa as every day that these ships were waiting significant amounts of money were lost, but the wait further increased the existing shortage of ships and containers as hundreds of ships and thousands of containers were taken out of the cycle. Production cycles that were overly relying on timely supply were disrupted and much-needed consumer goods faced further delays.

Despite the many challenges the logistics sector faces, the current state of the global supply chain is still relatively stable. It has not come to a standstill. Despite delays, products keep moving across the world and since the start of the pandemic, carriers, logistics providers and supply chain managers have been excelling at keeping the system running and continue to find solutions in a chaotic environment. The bad news is that the system remains highly complex and fragile. Even if the ripples even out eventually, there will be new challenges and further disruptions ahead. In the risk and crisis landscape of the 2020s, the question needs to be asked as to whether the current model of minimal inventory and spread-out production sites will be sustainable. With climate change and events such as the war in Ukraine, the stress on the system will continue to grow and congestion will turn into crisis whenever an incident such as the *Ever Given* occurs.

Endnotes

1 Kerslake Report: An independent review into the preparedness for, and emergency response to, the Manchester Arena attack on 22 May 2017. https://www.kerslakearenareview.co.uk/media/1022/kerslake_arena_review_printed_final.pdf (archived at https://perma.cc/9KUK-J3LN)

2 Rittel, H W & Webber, M M (1973) Dilemmas in a general theory of planning. *Policy Sciences*, 4(2), 155–169

Further reading

UK National Health Service

BBC (2017) Cyber-attack: Europol says it was unprecedented in scale (13 May). Available at: https://www.bbc.com/news/world-europe-39907965 (archived at https://perma.cc/CN97-VJYS). (Accessed: 28 April 2022)

Morse, A (2018) Report by the comptroller and auditor general: *Investigation: WannaCry cyber attack and the NHS*. Printed by the House of Commons

Smart, W (2018) Lessons learned review of the WannaCry ransomware cyber attack. Department of Health and Social Care. Available at: https://www.england.nhs.uk/wp-content/uploads/2018/02/lessons-learned-review-wannacry-ransomware-cyber-attack-cio-review.pdf (archived at https://perma.cc/9VJG-6ZKS). (Accessed: 28 April 2022)

Gatwick Airport

BBC News (2018) Gatwick runway reopens after drone chaos. 21 December. Available at: https://www.bbc.co.uk/news/uk-england-sussex-46643173 (archived at https://perma.cc/7XPY-TPML) (Accessed: 23 June 2022)

BBC News (2019) Gatwick drone chaos was 'foreseeable' experts says (17 January). Available at: https://www.bbc.co.uk/news/uk-england-sussex-46906796 (archived at https://perma.cc/GZ7A-6YAT) (Accessed: 23 June 2022)

BBC News (2019) Heathrow airport: Drone sighting halts departures (8 January). Available at: https://www.bbc.co.uk/news/uk-46803713 (archived at https://perma.cc/UK7Y-ZLGU) (Accessed: 23 June 2022)

Texas snowstorm

Cohen, A (2021) Texas energy crisis is an epic resilience and leadership failure. *Forbes* (19 February). Available at: https://www.forbes.com/sites/arielcohen/2021/02/19/texas-energy-crisis-is-an-epic-resilience-and-leadership-failure/?sh=7c2e6aa46eee (archived at https://perma.cc/H6ZS-SVDF) (Accessed: 23 June 2022)

Congress of the United States (2015) Delegation letter to Governor Abbott regarding electric grid. Available at: https://securethegrid.com/wp-content/uploads/2021/02/7-2015-Congressional-Letter-to-Gov.-Abbott.pdf (archived at https://perma.cc/YNN7-FCHN) (Accessed: 23 June 2022)

Congress of the United States (2018) Congressional letter to Gov. Abbott. Available at: https://securethegrid.com/wp-content/uploads/2021/02/9-2018-Congressional-Letter-to-Gov.-Abbott.pdf (archived at https://perma.cc/NP5M-6RN7) (Accessed: 23 June 2022)

National Infrastructure Advisory Council (2010) A framework for establishing critical infrastructure resilience goals. Final report and recommendations by the Council. Available at: https://www.dhs.gov/xlibrary/assets/niac/niac-a-framework-for-establishing-critical-infrastructure-resilience-goals-2010-10-19.pdf (archived at https://perma.cc/F2FG-CMBS) (Accessed: 23 June 2022)

Samuels, A (2021) Nearly 12 million Texans now face water disruptions. The state needs residents to stop dripping taps. *The Texas Tribune*, 17 February. Available at: https://www.texastribune.org/2021/02/17/texas-water-boil-notices/ (archived at https://perma.cc/49GK-W6TM) (Accessed: 23 June 2022)

Waller, T (2021) Will Texas fail to lead on grid resilience? Centre for Security Policy, 30 June. Available at: https://centerforsecuritypolicy.org/will-texas-fail-to-lead-on-grid-resilience/ (archived at https://perma.cc/CYT6-68VW) (Accessed: 23 June 2022)

Manchester Arena bombing

Bosner, L (2002) Disaster preparedness: How Japan and the United States compare. *Asia Perspectives*, 4(2), 17–20

Executive summary of findings, Congressional Report. The federal response to Katrina: Lessons learned

Independent Police Complaints Commission. 'Stockwell One. Investigation into the shooting of Jean Charles de Menezes at Stockwell underground station on 22nd July 2005. http://policeauthority.org/Metropolitan/downloads/scrutinites/stockwell/ipcc-one.pdf (archived at https://perma.cc/WH67-4HTX)

Kawata, Y (2001) Disaster mitigation due to next Nankai earthquake tsunamis occurring in around 2035. Research Centre for Disaster Reduction Systems, Kyoto. University, Japan. In Proc. International Tsunami Symposium (pp. 315–329)

Kerslake Report: An independent review into the preparedness for, and emergency response to, the Manchester Arena attack on 22 May 2017. https://www.kerslakearenareview.co.uk/media/1022/kerslake_arena_review_printed_final.pdf (archived at https://perma.cc/9KUK-J3LN)

New York Times (2002) Fatal confusion: A troubled emergency response; 9/11 exposed deadly flaws in rescue plan, 7 July. Available at: https://www.nytimes.com/2002/07/07/nyregion/fatal-confusion-troubled-emergency-response-9-11-exposed-deadly-flaws-rescue.html (archived at https://perma.cc/G4LZ-7CNX) (Accessed: 23 June 2022)

The Ever Given

Embassy of New Zealand in Cairo (2021) The importance of the Suez Canal to global trade (18 April). Available at: https://www.mfat.govt.nz/en/trade/mfat-market-reports/market-reports-middle-east/the-importance-of-the-suez-canal-to-global-trade-18-april-2021/ (archived at https://perma.cc/8B7R-HQ38) (Accessed: 23 June 2022)

Friedman, T (2006) *The world is flat*. London: Penguin Books

George-Parkin, H (2021) The fallout from the Suez Canal ship is coming to a store near you (2 April), Vox. Available at: https://www.vox.com/the-goods/2021/4/2/22364278/suez-canal-ship-effects-ever-given-supply-chain (archived at https://perma.cc/H3ER-7DKD) (Accessed: 23 June 2022)

Leach, A, Probyn, M & Gutiérrez, P (2021) One toy's journey through the supply chain crisis: From Chinese factory to UK child's stocking (8 December), *The Guardian*. Available at: https://www.theguardian.com/business/ng-interactive/2021/dec/08/one-toys-journey-through-the-supply-chain-crisis-from-chinese-factory-to-uk-childs-stocking (archived at https://perma.cc/8X2U-B8A3) (Accessed: 23 June 2022)

Sheridan, K (2021) How blackouts, fires, and a pandemic are driving shortages of pipette tips — and hobbling science (28 April), Statnews. Available at: https://www.statnews.com/2021/04/28/pipette-tips-shortage/ (archived at https://perma.cc/93FX-JHCL) (Accessed: 23 June 2022)

Tharoor, I (2021) The Suez Canal, a chokepoint of history. *The Washington Post* (26 March). Available at: https://www.washingtonpost.com/world/2021/03/26/suez-canal-history/ (archived at https://perma.cc/263V-WT8H) (Accessed: 23 June 2022)

Youd, F (2021) Global shipping container shortage: The story so far. (29 April), *Ship Technology*. Available at: https://www.ship-technology.com/analysis/global-shipping-container-shortage-the-story-so-far/ (archived at https://perma.cc/9QDX-W3SP) (Accessed: 23 June 2022)

INDEX